S0-AEL-251

Modern Compiler Implementation in Java
Second Edition

This textbook describes all phases of a compiler: lexical analysis, parsing, abstract syntax, semantic actions, intermediate representations, instruction selection via tree matching, dataflow analysis, graph-coloring register allocation, and runtime systems. It includes good coverage of current techniques in code generation and register allocation, as well as the compilation of functional and object-oriented languages, which is missing from most books. The most accepted and successful techniques are described concisely, rather than as an exhaustive catalog of every possible variant. Detailed descriptions of the interfaces between modules of a compiler are illustrated with actual Java classes.

The first part of the book, Fundamentals of Compilation, is suitable for a one-semester first course in compiler design. The second part, Advanced Topics, which includes the compilation of object-oriented and functional languages, garbage collection, loop optimization, SSA form, instruction scheduling, and optimization for cache-memory hierarchies, can be used for a second-semester or graduate course.

This new edition has been rewritten extensively to include more discussion of Java and object-oriented programming concepts, such as visitor patterns. A unique feature is the newly redesigned compiler project in Java for a subset of Java itself. The project includes both front-end and back-end phases, so that students can build a complete working compiler in one semester.

Andrew W. Appel is Professor of Computer Science at Princeton University. He has done research and published papers on compilers, functional programming languages, runtime systems and garbage collection, type systems, and computer security; he is also author of the book *Compiling with Continuations*. He is a designer and founder of the Standard ML of New Jersey project. In 1998, Appel was elected a Fellow of the Association for Computing Machinery for "significant research contributions in the area of programming languages and compilers" and for his work as editor-in-chief (1993–97) of the *ACM Transactions on Programming Languages and Systems,* the leading journal in the field of compilers and programming languages.

Jens Palsberg is Associate Professor of Computer Science at Purdue University. His research interests are programming languages, compilers, software engineering, and information security. He has authored more than 50 technical papers in these areas and a book with Michael Schwartzbach, *Object-oriented Type Systems*. In 1998, he received the National Science Foundation Faculty Early Career Development Award, and in 1999, the Purdue University Faculty Scholar award.

Modern Compiler Implementation in Java

Second Edition

ANDREW W. APPEL
Princeton University

with JENS PALSBERG
Purdue University

CAMBRIDGE
UNIVERSITY PRESS

PUBLISHED BY THE PRESS SYNDICATE OF THE UNIVERSITY OF CAMBRIDGE
The Pitt Building, Trumpington Street, Cambridge, United Kingdom

CAMBRIDGE UNIVERSITY PRESS
The Edinburgh Building, Cambridge CB2 2RU, UK
40 West 20th Street, New York, NY 10011-4211, USA
477 Williamstown Road, Port Melbourne, VIC 3207, Australia
Ruiz de Alarcón 13, 28014 Madrid, Spain
Dock House, The Waterfront, Cape Town 8001, South Africa

http://www.cambridge.org

© Cambridge University Press 2002

This book is in copyright. Subject to statutory exception
and to the provisions of relevant collective licensing agreements,
no reproduction of any part may take place without
the written permission of Cambridge University Press.

First edition published 1998
Second edition published 2002

Printed in the United States of America

Typefaces Times, Courier, and Optima   *System* LATEX [AU]

A catalog record for this book is available from the British Library.

Library of Congress Cataloging in Publication data

Appel, Andrew W., 1960–
    Modern compiler implementation in Java / Andrew W. Appel with Jens Palsberg. —
[2nd ed.]
        p.   cm.
    Includes bibliographical references and index.
    ISBN 0-521-82060-X
    1. Java (Computer program language) 2. Compilers (Computer programs) I. Palsberg,
    Jens. II. Title.
    QA76.73.J38 A65 2002
    005.4′53—dc21

                                                    2002073453

ISBN 0 521 58274 1   Modern Compiler Implementation in ML (first edition, hardback)
ISBN 0 521 82060 X   Modern Compiler Implementation in Java (hardback)

Contents

Preface

This book is intended as a textbook for a one- or two-semester course in compilers. Students will see the theory behind different components of a compiler, the programming techniques used to put the theory into practice, and the interfaces used to modularize the compiler. To make the interfaces and programming examples clear and concrete, we have written them in Java. Another edition of this book is available that uses the ML language.

Implementation project. The "student project compiler" that we have outlined is reasonably simple, but is organized to demonstrate some important techniques that are now in common use: abstract syntax trees to avoid tangling syntax and semantics, separation of instruction selection from register allocation, copy propagation to give flexibility to earlier phases of the compiler, and containment of target-machine dependencies. Unlike many "student compilers" found in other textbooks, this one has a simple but sophisticated back end, allowing good register allocation to be done after instruction selection.

This second edition of the book has a redesigned project compiler: It uses a subset of Java, called MiniJava, as the source language for the compiler project, it explains the use of the parser generators JavaCC and SableCC, and it promotes programming with the Visitor pattern. Students using this edition can implement a compiler for a language they're familiar with, using standard tools, in a more object-oriented style.

Each chapter in Part I has a programming exercise corresponding to one module of a compiler. Software useful for the exercises can be found at
http://uk.cambridge.org/resources/052182060X   (outside North America);
http://us.cambridge.org/titles/052182060X.html (within North America).

Exercises. Each chapter has pencil-and-paper exercises; those marked with a star are more challenging, two-star problems are difficult but solvable, and the occasional three-star exercises are not known to have a solution.

Course sequence. The figure shows how the chapters depend on each other.

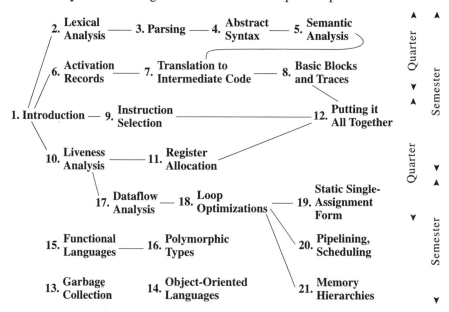

- A one-semester course could cover all of Part I (Chapters 1–12), with students implementing the project compiler (perhaps working in groups); in addition, lectures could cover selected topics from Part II.
- An advanced or graduate course could cover Part II, as well as additional topics from the current literature. Many of the Part II chapters can stand independently from Part I, so that an advanced course could be taught to students who have used a different book for their first course.
- In a two-quarter sequence, the first quarter could cover Chapters 1–8, and the second quarter could cover Chapters 9–12 and some chapters from Part II.

Acknowledgments. Many people have provided constructive criticism or helped us in other ways on this book. Vidyut Samanta helped tremendously with both the text and the software for the new edition of the book. We would also like to thank Leonor Abraido-Fandino, Scott Ananian, Nils Andersen, Stephen Bailey, Joao Cangussu, Maia Ginsburg, Max Hailperin, David Hanson, Jeffrey Hsu, David MacQueen, Torben Mogensen, Doug Morgan, Robert Netzer, Elma Lee Noah, Mikael Petterson, Benjamin Pierce, Todd Proebsting, Anne Rogers, Barbara Ryder, Amr Sabry, Mooly Sagiv, Zhong Shao, Mary Lou Soffa, Andrew Tolmach, Kwangkeun Yi, and Kenneth Zadeck.

PART ONE

Fundamentals of Compilation

1

Introduction

> A **compiler** was originally a program that "compiled" subroutines [a link-loader]. When in 1954 the combination "algebraic compiler" came into use, or rather into misuse, the meaning of the term had already shifted into the present one.
>
> Bauer and Eickel [1975]

This book describes techniques, data structures, and algorithms for translating programming languages into executable code. A modern compiler is often organized into many phases, each operating on a different abstract "language." The chapters of this book follow the organization of a compiler, each covering a successive phase.

To illustrate the issues in compiling real programming languages, we show how to compile MiniJava, a simple but nontrivial subset of Java. Programming exercises in each chapter call for the implementation of the corresponding phase; a student who implements all the phases described in Part I of the book will have a working compiler. MiniJava is easily extended to support class extension or higher-order functions, and exercises in Part II show how to do this. Other chapters in Part II cover advanced techniques in program optimization. Appendix A describes the MiniJava language.

The interfaces between modules of the compiler are almost as important as the algorithms inside the modules. To describe the interfaces concretely, it is useful to write them down in a real programming language. This book uses Java – a simple object-oriented language. Java is *safe*, in that programs cannot circumvent the type system to violate abstractions; and it has garbage collection, which greatly simplifies the management of dynamic storage al-

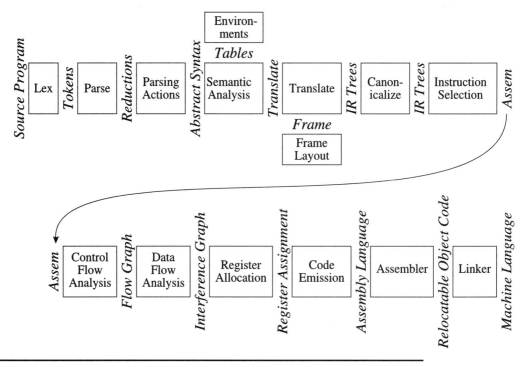

FIGURE 1.1.   Phases of a compiler, and interfaces between them.

location. Both of these properties are useful in writing compilers (and almost any kind of software).

This is not a textbook on Java programming. Students using this book who do not know Java already should pick it up as they go along, using a Java programming book as a reference. Java is a small enough language, with simple enough concepts, that this should not be difficult for students with good programming skills in other languages.

1.1   MODULES AND INTERFACES

Any large software system is much easier to understand and implement if the designer takes care with the fundamental abstractions and interfaces. Figure 1.1 shows the phases in a typical compiler. Each phase is implemented as one or more software modules.

Breaking the compiler into this many pieces allows for reuse of the components. For example, to change the target machine for which the compiler produces machine language, it suffices to replace just the Frame Layout and Instruction Selection modules. To change the source language being compiled, only the modules up through Translate need to be changed. The compiler can be attached to a language-oriented syntax editor at the *Abstract Syntax* interface.

The learning experience of coming to the right abstraction by several iterations of *think–implement–redesign* is one that should not be missed. However, the student trying to finish a compiler project in one semester does not have this luxury. Therefore, we present in this book the outline of a project where the abstractions and interfaces are carefully thought out, and are as elegant and general as we are able to make them.

Some of the interfaces, such as *Abstract Syntax, IR Trees,* and *Assem,* take the form of data structures: For example, the Parsing Actions phase builds an *Abstract Syntax* data structure and passes it to the Semantic Analysis phase. Other interfaces are abstract data types; the *Translate* interface is a set of functions that the Semantic Analysis phase can call, and the *Tokens* interface takes the form of a function that the Parser calls to get the next token of the input program.

DESCRIPTION OF THE PHASES

Each chapter of Part I of this book describes one compiler phase, as shown in Table 1.2

This modularization is typical of many real compilers. But some compilers combine Parse, Semantic Analysis, Translate, and Canonicalize into one phase; others put Instruction Selection much later than we have done, and combine it with Code Emission. Simple compilers omit the Control Flow Analysis, Data Flow Analysis, and Register Allocation phases.

We have designed the compiler in this book to be as simple as possible, but no simpler. In particular, in those places where corners are cut to simplify the implementation, the structure of the compiler allows for the addition of more optimization or fancier semantics without violence to the existing interfaces.

1.2   TOOLS AND SOFTWARE

Two of the most useful abstractions used in modern compilers are *context-free grammars*, for parsing, and *regular expressions*, for lexical analysis. To make the best use of these abstractions it is helpful to have special tools,

Chapter	Phase	Description
2	Lex	Break the source file into individual words, or *tokens*.
3	Parse	Analyze the phrase structure of the program.
4	Semantic Actions	Build a piece of *abstract syntax tree* corresponding to each phrase.
5	Semantic Analysis	Determine what each phrase means, relate uses of variables to their definitions, check types of expressions, request translation of each phrase.
6	Frame Layout	Place variables, function-parameters, etc. into activation records (stack frames) in a machine-dependent way.
7	Translate	Produce *intermediate representation trees* (IR trees), a notation that is not tied to any particular source language or target-machine architecture.
8	Canonicalize	Hoist side effects out of expressions, and clean up conditional branches, for the convenience of the next phases.
9	Instruction Selection	Group the IR-tree nodes into clumps that correspond to the actions of target-machine instructions.
10	Control Flow Analysis	Analyze the sequence of instructions into a *control flow graph* that shows all the possible flows of control the program might follow when it executes.
10	Dataflow Analysis	Gather information about the flow of information through variables of the program; for example, *liveness analysis* calculates the places where each program variable holds a still-needed value (is *live*).
11	Register Allocation	Choose a register to hold each of the variables and temporary values used by the program; variables not live at the same time can share the same register.
12	Code Emission	Replace the temporary names in each machine instruction with machine registers.

TABLE 1.2.   Description of compiler phases.

such as *Yacc* (which converts a grammar into a parsing program) and *Lex* (which converts a declarative specification into a lexical-analysis program). Fortunately, such tools are available for Java, and the project described in this book makes use of them.

The programming projects in this book can be compiled using any Java

$Stm \rightarrow Stm$; Stm (CompoundStm)
$Stm \rightarrow$ id := Exp (AssignStm)
$Stm \rightarrow$ print ($ExpList$)   (PrintStm)
$Exp \rightarrow$ id   (IdExp)
$Exp \rightarrow$ num   (NumExp)
$Exp \rightarrow Exp$ $Binop$ Exp (OpExp)
$Exp \rightarrow$ (Stm , Exp)   (EseqExp)

$ExpList \rightarrow Exp$, $ExpList$ (PairExpList)
$ExpList \rightarrow Exp$ (LastExpList)
$Binop \rightarrow +$ (Plus)
$Binop \rightarrow -$ (Minus)
$Binop \rightarrow \times$ (Times)
$Binop \rightarrow /$ (Div)

GRAMMAR 1.3. A straight-line programming language.

---

compiler. The parser generators *JavaCC* and *SableCC* are freely available on the Internet; for information see the World Wide Web page

    http://uk.cambridge.org/resources/052182060X (outside North America);
    http://us.cambridge.org/titles/052182060X.html (within North America).

Source code for some modules of the MiniJava compiler, skeleton source code and support code for some of the programming exercises, example Mini-Java programs, and other useful files are also available from the same Web address. The programming exercises in this book refer to this directory as $MINIJAVA/ when referring to specific subdirectories and files contained therein.

1.3   DATA STRUCTURES FOR TREE LANGUAGES

Many of the important data structures used in a compiler are *intermediate representations* of the program being compiled. Often these representations take the form of trees, with several node types, each of which has different attributes. Such trees can occur at many of the phase-interfaces shown in Figure 1.1.

Tree representations can be described with grammars, just like programming languages. To introduce the concepts, we will show a simple programming language with statements and expressions, but no loops or if-statements (this is called a language of *straight-line programs*).

The syntax for this language is given in Grammar 1.3.

The informal semantics of the language is as follows. Each *Stm* is a statement, each *Exp* is an expression. s_1; s_2 executes statement s_1, then statement s_2. i:=e evaluates the expression e, then "stores" the result in variable i.

$\text{print}(e_1, e_2, \ldots, e_n)$ displays the values of all the expressions, evaluated left to right, separated by spaces, terminated by a newline.

An *identifier expression*, such as i, yields the current contents of the variable i. A *number* evaluates to the named integer. An *operator expression* e_1 op e_2 evaluates e_1, then e_2, then applies the given binary operator. And an *expression sequence* (s, e) behaves like the C-language "comma" operator, evaluating the statement s for side effects before evaluating (and returning the result of) the expression e.

For example, executing this program

```
a := 5+3; b := (print(a, a-1), 10*a); print(b)
```

prints

```
8 7
80
```

How should this program be represented inside a compiler? One representation is *source code*, the characters that the programmer writes. But that is not so easy to manipulate. More convenient is a tree data structure, with one node for each statement (Stm) and expression (Exp). Figure 1.4 shows a tree representation of the program; the nodes are labeled by the production labels of Grammar 1.3, and each node has as many children as the corresponding grammar production has right-hand-side symbols.

We can translate the grammar directly into data structure definitions, as shown in Program 1.5. Each grammar symbol corresponds to an `abstract class` in the data structures:

Grammar	class
Stm	Stm
Exp	Exp
ExpList	ExpList
id	String
num	int

For each grammar rule, there is one *constructor* that belongs to the class for its left-hand-side symbol. We simply *extend* the abstract class with a "concrete" class for each grammar rule. The constructor (class) names are indicated on the right-hand side of Grammar 1.3.

Each grammar rule has right-hand-side components that must be represented in the data structures. The CompoundStm has two Stm's on the right-hand side; the AssignStm has an identifier and an expression; and so on.

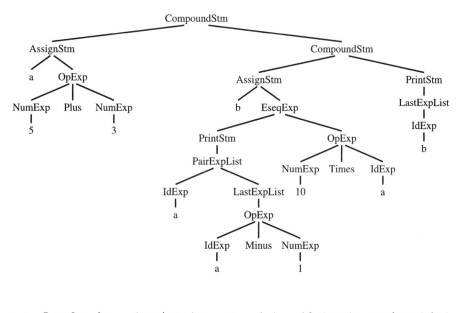

```
a := 5 + 3 ; b := ( print ( a , a - 1 ) , 10 * a ) ; print ( b )
```

FIGURE 1.4.   Tree representation of a straight-line program.

These become *fields* of the subclasses in the Java data structure. Thus, CompoundStm has two fields (also called *instance variables*) called `stm1` and `stm2`; AssignStm has fields `id` and `exp`.

For Binop we do something simpler. Although we could make a Binop class – with subclasses for Plus, Minus, Times, Div – this is overkill because none of the subclasses would need any fields. Instead we make an "enumeration" type (in Java, actually an integer) of constants (`final int` variables) local to the OpExp class.

Programming style. We will follow several conventions for representing tree data structures in Java:

1. Trees are described by a grammar.
2. A tree is described by one or more abstract classes, each corresponding to a symbol in the grammar.
3. Each abstract class is *extended* by one or more subclasses, one for each grammar rule.

```
public abstract class Stm {}

public class CompoundStm extends Stm {
   public Stm stm1, stm2;
   public CompoundStm(Stm s1, Stm s2) {stm1=s1; stm2=s2;}}

public class AssignStm extends Stm {
   public String id; public Exp exp;
   public AssignStm(String i, Exp e) {id=i; exp=e;}}

public class PrintStm extends Stm {
   public ExpList exps;
   public PrintStm(ExpList e) {exps=e;}}

public abstract class Exp {}

public class IdExp extends Exp {
   public String id;
   public IdExp(String i) {id=i;}}

public class NumExp extends Exp {
   public int num;
   public NumExp(int n) {num=n;}}

public class OpExp extends Exp {
   public Exp left, right; public int oper;
   final public static int Plus=1,Minus=2,Times=3,Div=4;
   public OpExp(Exp l, int o, Exp r) {left=l; oper=o; right=r;}}

public class EseqExp extends Exp {
   public Stm stm; public Exp exp;
   public EseqExp(Stm s, Exp e) {stm=s; exp=e;}}

public abstract class ExpList {}

public class PairExpList extends ExpList {
   public Exp head; public ExpList tail;
   public PairExpList(Exp h, ExpList t) {head=h; tail=t;}}

public class LastExpList extends ExpList {
   public Exp head;
   public LastExpList(Exp h) {head=h;}}
```

PROGRAM 1.5.   Representation of straight-line programs.

4. For each nontrivial symbol in the right-hand side of a rule, there will be one field in the corresponding class. (A trivial symbol is a punctuation symbol such as the semicolon in CompoundStm.)

5. Every class will have a constructor function that initializes all the fields.

6. Data structures are initialized when they are created (by the constructor functions), and are never modified after that (until they are eventually discarded).

Modularity principles for Java programs. A compiler can be a big program; careful attention to modules and interfaces prevents chaos. We will use these principles in writing a compiler in Java:

1. Each phase or module of the compiler belongs in its own package.

2. "Import on demand" declarations will not be used. If a Java file begins with

```
import A.F.*; import A.G.*; import B.*; import C.*;
```

then the human reader *will have to look outside this file* to tell which package defines the X that is used in the expression X.put().

3. "Single-type import" declarations are a better solution. If the module begins

```
import A.F.W; import A.G.X; import B.Y; import C.Z;
```

then you can tell *without looking outside this file* that X comes from A.G.

4. Java is naturally a multithreaded system. We would like to support multiple simultaneous compiler threads and compile two different programs simultaneously, one in each compiler thread. Therefore, static variables must be avoided unless they are final (constant). We never want two compiler threads to be updating the same (static) instance of a variable.

PROGRAM STRAIGHT-LINE PROGRAM INTERPRETER

Implement a simple program analyzer and interpreter for the straight-line programming language. This exercise serves as an introduction to *environments* (symbol tables mapping variable names to information about the variables); to *abstract syntax* (data structures representing the phrase structure of programs); to *recursion over tree data structures*, useful in many parts of a compiler; and to a *functional style* of programming without assignment statements.

It also serves as a "warm-up" exercise in Java programming. Programmers experienced in other languages but new to Java should be able to do this exercise, but will need supplementary material (such as textbooks) on Java.

Programs to be interpreted are already parsed into abstract syntax, as described by the data types in Program 1.5.

However, we do not wish to worry about parsing the language, so we write this program by applying data constructors:

```
Stm prog =
new CompoundStm(new AssignStm("a",
                    new OpExp(new NumExp(5),
                              OpExp.Plus, new NumExp(3))),
 new CompoundStm(new AssignStm("b",
    new EseqExp(new PrintStm(new PairExpList(new IdExp("a"),
            new LastExpList(new OpExp(new IdExp("a"),
                            OpExp.Minus,new NumExp(1))))),

            new OpExp(new NumExp(10), OpExp.Times,
                    new IdExp("a")))),
    new PrintStm(new LastExpList(new IdExp("b")))));
```

Files with the data type declarations for the trees, and this sample program, are available in the directory $MINIJAVA/chap1.

Writing interpreters without side effects (that is, assignment statements that update variables and data structures) is a good introduction to *denotational semantics* and *attribute grammars*, which are methods for describing what programming languages do. It's often a useful technique in writing compilers, too; compilers are also in the business of saying what programming languages do.

Therefore, in implementing these programs, never assign a new value to any variable or object field except when it is initialized. For local variables, use the initializing form of declaration (for example, int i=j+3;) and for each class, make a constructor function (like the CompoundStm constructor in Program 1.5).

1. Write a Java function int maxargs(Stm s) that tells the maximum number of arguments of any print statement within any subexpression of a given statement. For example, maxargs(prog) is 2.

2. Write a Java function void interp(Stm s) that "interprets" a program in this language. To write in a "functional programming" style – in which you never use an assignment statement – initialize each local variable as you declare it.

Your functions that examine each Exp will have to use instanceof to determine which subclass the expression belongs to and then cast to the proper subclass. Or you can add methods to the Exp and Stm classes to avoid the use of instanceof.

For part 1, remember that print statements can contain expressions that contain other print statements.

For part 2, make two mutually recursive functions `interpStm` and `interpExp`. Represent a "table," mapping identifiers to the integer values assigned to them, as a list of id × int pairs.

```
class Table {
   String id; int value; Table tail;
   Table(String i, int v, Table t) {id=i; value=v; tail=t;}
}
```

Then `interpStm` is declared as

```
Table interpStm(Stm s, Table t)
```

taking a table t_1 as argument and producing the new table t_2 that's just like t_1 except that some identifiers map to different integers as a result of the statement.

For example, the table t_1 that maps a to 3 and maps c to 4, which we write $\{a \mapsto 3, c \mapsto 4\}$ in mathematical notation, could be represented as the linked list ⟨a|3| →|c|4|⟩ .

Now, let the table t_2 be just like t_1, except that it maps c to 7 instead of 4. Mathematically, we could write,

$$t_2 = \text{update}(t_1, c, 7),$$

where the update function returns a new table $\{a \mapsto 3, c \mapsto 7\}$.

On the computer, we could implement t_2 by putting a new cell at the head of the linked list: ⟨c|7| →|a|3| →|c|4|⟩ , as long as we assume that the *first* occurrence of c in the list takes precedence over any later occurrence.

Therefore, the update function is easy to implement; and the corresponding `lookup` function

```
int lookup(Table t, String key)
```

just searches down the linked list. Of course, in an object-oriented style, `int lookup(String key)` should be a method of the `Table` class.

Interpreting expressions is more complicated than interpreting statements, because expressions return integer values *and* have side effects. We wish to simulate the straight-line programming language's assignment statements without doing any side effects in the interpreter itself. (The `print` statements will be accomplished by interpreter side effects, however.) The solution is to declare `interpExp` as

```
class IntAndTable {int i; Table t;
    IntAndTable(int ii, Table tt) {i=ii; t=tt;}
  }
IntAndTable interpExp(Exp e, Table t) ···
```

The result of interpreting an expression e_1 with table t_1 is an integer value i and a new table t_2. When interpreting an expression with two subexpressions (such as an OpExp), the table t_2 resulting from the first subexpression can be used in processing the second subexpression.

EXERCISES

1.1 This simple program implements *persistent* functional binary search trees, so that if tree2=insert(x,tree1), then tree1 is still available for lookups even while tree2 can be used.

```
class Tree {Tree left; String key; Tree right;
    Tree(Tree l, String k, Tree r) {left=l; key=k; right=r;}

Tree insert(String key, Tree t) {
  if (t==null) return new Tree(null, key, null)
  else if (key.compareTo(t.key) < 0)
        return new Tree(insert(key,t.left),t.key,t.right);
  else if (key.compareTo(t.key) > 0)
        return new Tree(t.left,t.key,insert(key,t.right));
  else return new Tree(t.left,key,t.right);
}
```

a. Implement a member function that returns true if the item is found, else false.

b. Extend the program to include not just membership, but the mapping of keys to bindings:
```
Tree insert(String key, Object binding, Tree t);
Object lookup(String key, Tree t);
```

c. These trees are not balanced; demonstrate the behavior on the following two sequences of insertions:
(a) t s p i p f b s t
(b) a b c d e f g h i

*d. Research balanced search trees in Sedgewick [1997] and recommend a balanced-tree data structure for functional symbol tables. **Hint:** To preserve a functional style, the algorithm should be one that rebalances on insertion but not on lookup, so a data structure such as *splay trees* is not appropriate.

e. Rewrite in an object-oriented (but still "functional") style, so that insertion is now `t.insert(key)` instead of `insert(key,t)`. **Hint:** You'll need an `EmptyTree` subclass.

2

Lexical Analysis

lex-i-cal: of or relating to words or the vocabulary of a language as distinguished from its grammar and construction

Webster's Dictionary

To translate a program from one language into another, a compiler must first pull it apart and understand its structure and meaning, then put it together in a different way. The front end of the compiler performs analysis; the back end does synthesis.

The analysis is usually broken up into

Lexical analysis: breaking the input into individual words or "tokens";
Syntax analysis: parsing the phrase structure of the program; and
Semantic analysis: calculating the program's meaning.

The lexical analyzer takes a stream of characters and produces a stream of names, keywords, and punctuation marks; it discards white space and comments between the tokens. It would unduly complicate the parser to have to account for possible white space and comments at every possible point; this is the main reason for separating lexical analysis from parsing.

Lexical analysis is not very complicated, but we will attack it with high-powered formalisms and tools, because similar formalisms will be useful in the study of parsing and similar tools have many applications in areas other than compilation.

2.1   LEXICAL TOKENS

A lexical token is a sequence of characters that can be treated as a unit in the grammar of a programming language. A programming language classifies lexical tokens into a finite set of token types. For example, some of the token types of a typical programming language are

Type	Examples
ID	`foo  n14  last`
NUM	`73  0 00  515  082`
REAL	`66.1  .5  10.  1e67  5.5e-10`
IF	`if`
COMMA	`,`
NOTEQ	`!=`
LPAREN	`(`
RPAREN	`)`

Punctuation tokens such as IF, VOID, RETURN constructed from alphabetic characters are called *reserved words* and, in most languages, cannot be used as identifiers.

Examples of nontokens are

comment	`/* try again */`
preprocessor directive	`#include<stdio.h>`
preprocessor directive	`#define NUMS 5 , 6`
macro	`NUMS`
blanks, tabs, and newlines	

In languages weak enough to require a macro preprocessor, the preprocessor operates on the source character stream, producing another character stream that is then fed to the lexical analyzer. It is also possible to integrate macro processing with lexical analysis.

Given a program such as

```
float match0(char *s) /* find a zero */
{if (!strncmp(s, "0.0", 3))
  return 0.;
}
```

the lexical analyzer will return the stream

FLOAT	ID(match0)	LPAREN	CHAR	STAR	ID(s)	RPAREN
LBRACE	IF	LPAREN	BANG	ID(strncmp)	LPAREN	ID(s)

COMMA   STRING(0.0)   COMMA   NUM(3)   RPAREN   RPAREN
RETURN   REAL(0.0)   SEMI   RBRACE   EOF

where the token-type of each token is reported; some of the tokens, such as identifiers and literals, have *semantic values* attached to them, giving auxiliary information in addition to the token-type.

How should the lexical rules of a programming language be described? In what language should a lexical analyzer be written?

We can describe the lexical tokens of a language in English; here is a description of identifiers in C or Java:

> An identifier is a sequence of letters and digits; the first character must be a letter. The underscore _ counts as a letter. Upper- and lowercase letters are different. If the input stream has been parsed into tokens up to a given character, the next token is taken to include the longest string of characters that could possibly constitute a token. Blanks, tabs, newlines, and comments are ignored except as they serve to separate tokens. Some white space is required to separate otherwise adjacent identifiers, keywords, and constants.

And any reasonable programming language serves to implement an ad hoc lexer. But we will specify lexical tokens using the formal language of *regular expressions*, implement lexers using *deterministic finite automata*, and use mathematics to connect the two. This will lead to simpler and more readable lexical analyzers.

2.2   REGULAR EXPRESSIONS

Let us say that a *language* is a set of *strings*; a string is a finite sequence of *symbols*. The symbols themselves are taken from a finite *alphabet*.

The Pascal language is the set of all strings that constitute legal Pascal programs; the language of primes is the set of all decimal-digit strings that represent prime numbers; and the language of C reserved words is the set of all alphabetic strings that cannot be used as identifiers in the C programming language. The first two of these languages are infinite sets; the last is a finite set. In all of these cases, the alphabet is the ASCII character set.

When we speak of languages in this way, we will not assign any meaning to the strings; we will just be attempting to classify each string as in the language or not.

To specify some of these (possibly infinite) languages with finite descriptions, we will use the notation of *regular expressions*. Each regular expression stands for a set of strings.

Symbol: For each symbol **a** in the alphabet of the language, the regular expression **a** denotes the language containing just the string a.

Alternation: Given two regular expressions M and N, the alternation operator written as a vertical bar | makes a new regular expression $M \mid N$. A string is in the language of $M \mid N$ if it is in the language of M or in the language of N. Thus, the language of **a** | **b** contains the two strings a and b.

Concatenation: Given two regular expressions M and N, the concatenation operator · makes a new regular expression $M \cdot N$. A string is in the language of $M \cdot N$ if it is the concatenation of any two strings α and β such that α is in the language of M and β is in the language of N. Thus, the regular expression (**a** | **b**) · **a** defines the language containing the two strings aa and ba.

Epsilon: The regular expression ϵ represents a language whose only string is the empty string. Thus, $(a \cdot b) \mid \epsilon$ represents the language {`""`,`"ab"`}.

Repetition: Given a regular expression M, its Kleene closure is M^*. A string is in M^* if it is the concatenation of zero or more strings, all of which are in M. Thus, $((\mathbf{a} \mid \mathbf{b}) \cdot \mathbf{a})^*$ represents the infinite set { `""` , `"aa"`, `"ba"`, `"aaaa"`, `"baaa"`, `"aaba"`, `"baba"`, `"aaaaaa"`,... }.

Using symbols, alternation, concatenation, epsilon, and Kleene closure we can specify the set of ASCII characters corresponding to the lexical tokens of a programming language. First, consider some examples:

$(\mathbf{0} \mid \mathbf{1})^* \cdot \mathbf{0}$	Binary numbers that are multiples of two.
$\mathbf{b}^*(\mathbf{abb}^*)^*(\mathbf{a}\mid\epsilon)$	Strings of a's and b's with no consecutive a's.
$(\mathbf{a}\mid\mathbf{b})^*\mathbf{aa}(\mathbf{a}\mid\mathbf{b})^*$	Strings of a's and b's containing consecutive a's.

In writing regular expressions, we will sometimes omit the concatenation symbol or the epsilon, and we will assume that Kleene closure "binds tighter" than concatenation, and concatenation binds tighter than alternation; so that **ab** | **c** means (**a** · **b**) | **c**, and (**a** |) means (**a** | ϵ).

Let us introduce some more abbreviations: **[abcd]** means (**a** | **b** | **c** | **d**), **[b–g]** means **[bcdefg]**, **[b–gM–Qkr]** means **[bcdefgMNOPQkr]**, $M?$ means $(M \mid \epsilon)$, and M^+ means $(M \cdot M^*)$. These extensions are convenient, but none extend the descriptive power of regular expressions: Any set of strings that can be described with these abbreviations could also be described by just the basic set of operators. All the operators are summarized in Figure 2.1.

Using this language, we can specify the lexical tokens of a programming language (Figure 2.2).

The fifth line of the description recognizes comments or white space but

a	An ordinary character stands for itself.
ϵ	The empty string.
	Another way to write the empty string.
$M \mid N$	Alternation, choosing from M or N.
$M \cdot N$	Concatenation, an M followed by an N.
$M\,N$	Another way to write concatenation.
M^*	Repetition (zero or more times).
M^+	Repetition, one or more times.
$M?$	Optional, zero or one occurrence of M.
[a − zA − Z]	Character set alternation.
.	A period stands for any single character except newline.
`"a.+*"`	Quotation, a string in quotes stands for itself literally.

FIGURE 2.1.   Regular expression notation.

`if`	IF
`[a-z][a-z0-9]*`	ID
`[0-9]+`	NUM
`([0-9]+"."[0-9]*)|([0-9]*"."[0-9]+)`	REAL
`("--"[a-z]*"\n")|(" "|"\n"|"\t")+`	*no token, just white space*
.	*error*

FIGURE 2.2.   Regular expressions for some tokens.

does not report back to the parser. Instead, the white space is discarded and the lexer resumed. The comments for this lexer begin with two dashes, contain only alphabetic characters, and end with newline.

Finally, a lexical specification should be *complete*, always matching some initial substring of the input; we can always achieve this by having a rule that matches any single character (and in this case, prints an "illegal character" error message and continues).

These rules are a bit ambiguous. For example, does `if8` match as a single identifier or as the two tokens `if` and `8`? Does the string `if 89` begin with an identifier or a reserved word? There are two important disambiguation rules used by Lex, JavaCC, SableCC, and other similar lexical-analyzer generators:

Longest match: The longest initial substring of the input that can match any regular expression is taken as the next token.

Rule priority: For a *particular* longest initial substring, the first regular expression that can match determines its token-type. This means that the order of

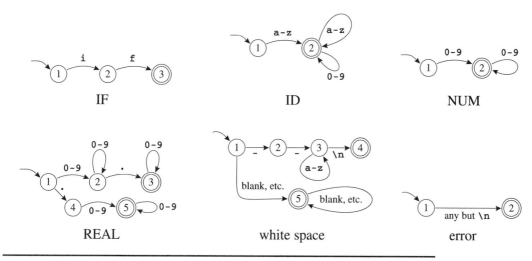

FIGURE 2.3.   Finite automata for lexical tokens. The states are indicated by circles; final states are indicated by double circles. The start state has an arrow coming in from nowhere. An edge labeled with several characters is shorthand for many parallel edges.

writing down the regular-expression rules has significance.

Thus, if8 matches as an identifier by the longest-match rule, and if matches as a reserved word by rule-priority.

2.3   FINITE AUTOMATA

Regular expressions are convenient for specifying lexical tokens, but we need a formalism that can be implemented as a computer program. For this we can use finite automata (N.B. the singular of automata is automaton). A finite automaton has a finite set of *states*; *edges* lead from one state to another, and each edge is labeled with a *symbol*. One state is the *start* state, and certain of the states are distinguished as *final* states.

Figure 2.3 shows some finite automata. We number the states just for convenience in discussion. The start state is numbered 1 in each case. An edge labeled with several characters is shorthand for many parallel edges; so in the ID machine there are really 26 edges each leading from state 1 to 2, each labeled by a different letter.

In a *deterministic* finite automaton (DFA), no two edges leaving from the

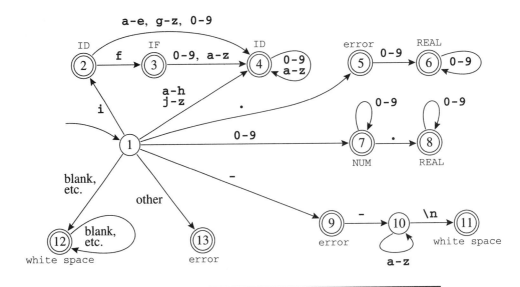

FIGURE 2.4. Combined finite automaton.

same state are labeled with the same symbol. A DFA *accepts* or *rejects* a string as follows. Starting in the start state, for each character in the input string the automaton follows exactly one edge to get to the next state. The edge must be labeled with the input character. After making *n* transitions for an *n*-character string, if the automaton is in a final state, then it accepts the string. If it is not in a final state, or if at some point there was no appropriately labeled edge to follow, it rejects. The *language* recognized by an automaton is the set of strings that it accepts.

For example, it is clear that any string in the language recognized by automaton ID must begin with a letter. Any single letter leads to state 2, which is final; so a single-letter string is accepted. From state 2, any letter or digit leads back to state 2, so a letter followed by any number of letters and digits is also accepted.

In fact, the machines shown in Figure 2.3 accept the same languages as the regular expressions of Figure 2.2.

These are six separate automata; how can they be combined into a single machine that can serve as a lexical analyzer? We will study formal ways of doing this in the next section, but here we will just do it ad hoc: Figure 2.4 shows such a machine. Each final state must be labeled with the token-type that it accepts. State 2 in this machine has aspects of state 2 of the IF machine and state 2 of the ID machine; since the latter is final, then the combined state must be final. State 3 is like state 3 of the IF machine and state 2 of the ID machine; because these are both final we use *rule priority* to disambiguate – we label state 3 with IF because we want this token to be recognized as a reserved word, not an identifier.

We can encode this machine as a transition matrix: a two-dimensional array (a vector of vectors), subscripted by state number and input character. There will be a "dead" state (state 0) that loops to itself on all characters; we use this to encode the absence of an edge.

```
int edges[][] = {  /* ···0 1 2···–···e f g h i j··· */
/* state 0 */     {0,0,···0,0,0···0···0,0,0,0,0,0···},
/* state 1 */     {0,0,···7,7,7···9···4,4,4,4,2,4···},
/* state 2 */     {0,0,···4,4,4···0···4,3,4,4,4,4···},
/* state 3 */     {0,0,···4,4,4···0···4,4,4,4,4,4···},
/* state 4 */     {0,0,···4,4,4···0···4,4,4,4,4,4···},
/* state 5 */     {0,0,···6,6,6···0···0,0,0,0,0,0···},
/* state 6 */     {0,0,···6,6,6···0···0,0,0,0,0,0···},
/* state 7 */     {0,0,···7,7,7···0···0,0,0,0,0,0···},
/* state 8 */     {0,0,···8,8,8···0···0,0,0,0,0,0···},
   et cetera
}
```

There must also be a "finality" array, mapping state numbers to actions – final state 2 maps to action ID, and so on.

RECOGNIZING THE LONGEST MATCH

It is easy to see how to use this table to recognize whether to accept or reject a string, but the job of a lexical analyzer is to find the longest match, the longest initial substring of the input that is a valid token. While interpreting transitions, the lexer must keep track of the longest match seen so far, and the position of that match.

Keeping track of the longest match just means remembering the last time the automaton was in a final state with two variables, Last-Final (the state number of the most recent final state encountered) and Input-Position-at-Last-Final. Every time a final state is entered, the lexer updates these variables; when a *dead* state (a nonfinal state with no output transitions) is reached, the variables tell what token was matched, and where it ended.

Figure 2.5 shows the operation of a lexical analyzer that recognizes longest matches; note that the current input position may be far beyond the most recent position at which the recognizer was in a final state.

Last Final	Current State	Current Input	Accept Action
0	1	⊥if --not-a-com	
2	2	i⊥f --not-a-com	
3	3	if⊥ --not-a-com	
3	0	if⊤⊥--not-a-com	*return* IF
0	1	if⊥ --not-a-com	
12	12	if|⊥-not-a-com	
12	0	if|⊤⊥-not-a-com	*found white space; resume*
0	1	if ⊥-not-a-com	
9	9	if |⊥-not-a-com	
9	10	if |⊤⊥not-a-com	
9	10	if |⊤n⊥ot-a-com	
9	10	if |⊤no⊥t-a-com	
9	10	if |⊤not⊥-a-com	
9	0	if |⊤not-⊥a-com	*error, illegal token '–'; resume*
0	1	if ⊥-not-a-com	
9	9	if -|⊥not-a-com	
9	0	if -|⊤⊥ot-a-com	*error, illegal token '–'; resume*

FIGURE 2.5. The automaton of Figure 2.4 recognizes several tokens. The symbol | indicates the input position at each successive call to the lexical analyzer, the symbol ⊥ indicates the current position of the automaton, and ⊤ indicates the most recent position in which the recognizer was in a final state.

2.4 NONDETERMINISTIC FINITE AUTOMATA

A nondeterministic finite automaton (NFA) is one that has a choice of edges – labeled with the same symbol – to follow out of a state. Or it may have special edges labeled with ϵ (the Greek letter epsilon) that can be followed without eating any symbol from the input.

Here is an example of an NFA:

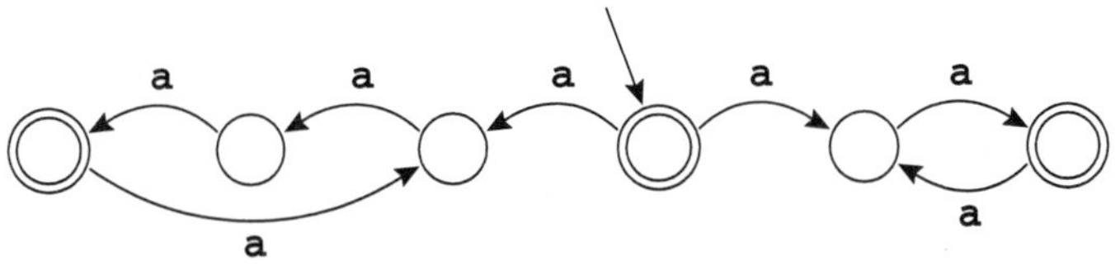

In the start state, on input character a, the automaton can move either right or left. If left is chosen, then strings of a's whose length is a multiple of three will be accepted. If right is chosen, then even-length strings will be accepted. Thus, the language recognized by this NFA is the set of all strings of a's whose length is a multiple of two or three.

On the first transition, this machine must choose which way to go. It is required to accept the string if there is *any* choice of paths that will lead to acceptance. Thus, it must "guess," and must always guess correctly.

Edges labeled with ϵ may be taken without using up a symbol from the input. Here is another NFA that accepts the same language:

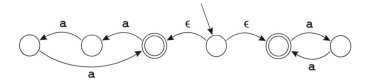

Again, the machine must choose which ϵ-edge to take. If there is a state with some ϵ-edges and some edges labeled by symbols, the machine can choose to eat an input symbol (and follow the corresponding symbol-labeled edge), or to follow an ϵ-edge instead.

CONVERTING A REGULAR EXPRESSION TO AN NFA

Nondeterministic automata are a useful notion because it is easy to convert a (static, declarative) regular expression to a (simulatable, quasi-executable) NFA.

The conversion algorithm turns each regular expression into an NFA with a *tail* (start edge) and a *head* (ending state). For example, the single-symbol regular expression **a** converts to the NFA

The regular expression **ab**, made by combining **a** with **b** using concatenation, is made by combining the two NFAs, hooking the head of **a** to the tail of **b**. The resulting machine has a tail labeled by **a** and a head into which the **b** edge flows.

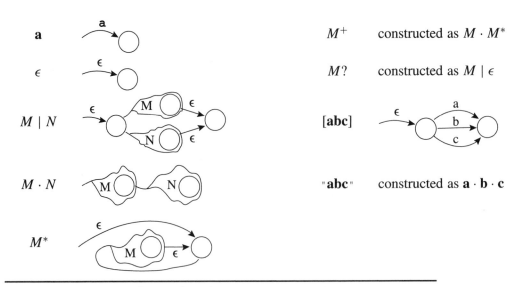

FIGURE 2.6. Translation of regular expressions to NFAs.

In general, any regular expression M will have some NFA with a tail and head:

In general, any regular expression M will have some NFA with a tail and head:

We can define the translation of regular expressions to NFAs by induction. Either an expression is primitive (a single symbol or ϵ) or it is made from smaller expressions. Similarly, the NFA will be primitive or made from smaller NFAs.

Figure 2.6 shows the rules for translating regular expressions to nondeterministic automata. We illustrate the algorithm on some of the expressions in Figure 2.2 – for the tokens IF, ID, NUM, and **error**. Each expression is translated to an NFA, the "head" state of each NFA is marked final with a different token type, and the tails of all the expressions are joined to a new start node. The result – after some merging of equivalent NFA states – is shown in Figure 2.7.

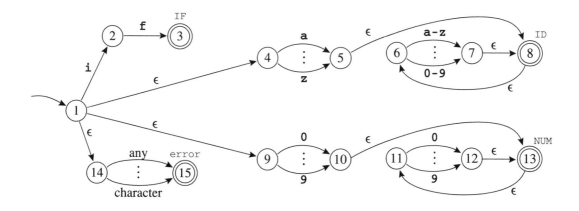

FIGURE 2.7.   Four regular expressions translated to an NFA.

CONVERTING AN NFA TO A DFA

As we saw in Section 2.3, implementing deterministic finite automata (DFAs) as computer programs is easy. But implementing NFAs is a bit harder, since most computers don't have good "guessing" hardware.

We can avoid the need to guess by trying every possibility at once. Let us simulate the NFA of Figure 2.7 on the string in. We start in state 1. Now, instead of guessing which ϵ-transition to take, we just say that at this point the NFA might take any of them, so it is in one of the states $\{1, 4, 9, 14\}$; that is, we compute the ϵ-closure of $\{1\}$. Clearly, there are no other states reachable without eating the first character of the input.

Now, we make the transition on the character i. From state 1 we can reach 2, from 4 we reach 5, from 9 we go nowhere, and from 14 we reach 15. So we have the set $\{2, 5, 15\}$. But again we must compute the ϵ-closure: From 5 there is an ϵ-transition to 8, and from 8 to 6. So the NFA must be in one of the states $\{2, 5, 6, 8, 15\}$.

On the character n, we get from state 6 to 7, from 2 to nowhere, from 5 to nowhere, from 8 to nowhere, and from 15 to nowhere. So we have the set $\{7\}$; its ϵ-closure is $\{6, 7, 8\}$.

Now we are at the end of the string in; is the NFA in a final state? One of the states in our possible-states set is 8, which is final. Thus, in is an ID token.

We formally define ϵ-closure as follows. Let **edge**(s, c) be the set of all NFA states reachable by following a single edge with label c from state s.

For a set of states S, **closure**(S) is the set of states that can be reached from a state in S without consuming any of the input, that is, by going only through ϵ-edges. Mathematically, we can express the idea of going through ϵ-edges by saying that **closure**(S) is the smallest set T such that

$$T = S \cup \left(\bigcup_{s \in T} \mathbf{edge}(s, \epsilon) \right).$$

We can calculate T by iteration:

$T \leftarrow S$
repeat $T' \leftarrow T$
$\qquad T \leftarrow T' \cup (\bigcup_{s \in T'} \mathbf{edge}(s, \epsilon))$
until $T = T'$

Why does this algorithm work? T can only grow in each iteration, so the final T must include S. If $T = T'$ after an iteration step, then T must also include $\bigcup_{s \in T'} \mathbf{edge}(s, \epsilon)$. Finally, the algorithm must terminate, because there are only a finite number of distinct states in the NFA.

Now, when simulating an NFA as described above, suppose we are in a set $d = \{s_i, s_k, s_l\}$ of NFA states s_i, s_k, s_l. By starting in d and eating the input symbol c, we reach a new set of NFA states; we'll call this set **DFAedge**(d, c):

$$\mathbf{DFAedge}(d, c) = \mathbf{closure}(\bigcup_{s \in d} \mathbf{edge}(s, c))$$

Using **DFAedge**, we can write the NFA simulation algorithm more formally. If the start state of the NFA is s_1, and the input string is $c_1, \ldots, c_k$, then the algorithm is

$d \leftarrow \mathbf{closure}(\{s_1\})$
for $i \leftarrow 1$ **to** k
$\quad d \leftarrow \mathbf{DFAedge}(d, c_i)$

Manipulating sets of states is expensive – too costly to want to do on every character in the source program that is being lexically analyzed. But it is possible to do all the sets-of-states calculations in advance. We make a DFA from the NFA, such that each set of NFA states corresponds to one DFA state. Since the NFA has a finite number n of states, the DFA will also have a finite number (at most 2^n) of states.

DFA construction is easy once we have **closure** and **DFAedge** algorithms. The DFA start state d_1 is just **closure**(s_1), as in the NFA simulation algo-

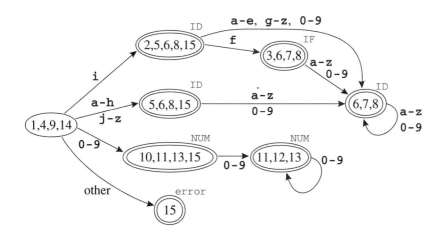

FIGURE 2.8.   NFA converted to DFA.

rithm. Abstractly, there is an edge from d_i to d_j labeled with c if $d_j =$ **DFAedge**(d_i, c). We let Σ be the alphabet.

$$
\begin{aligned}
&\text{states}[0] \leftarrow \{\}; \qquad \text{states}[1] \leftarrow \textbf{closure}(\{s_1\}) \\
&p \leftarrow 1; \quad j \leftarrow 0 \\
&\textbf{while } j \leq p \\
&\quad \textbf{foreach } c \in \Sigma \\
&\qquad e \leftarrow \textbf{DFAedge}(\text{states}[j], c) \\
&\qquad \textbf{if } e = \text{states}[i] \text{ for some } i \leq p \\
&\qquad\quad \textbf{then } \text{trans}[j, c] \leftarrow i \\
&\qquad\quad \textbf{else } p \leftarrow p + 1 \\
&\qquad\qquad \text{states}[p] \leftarrow e \\
&\qquad\qquad \text{trans}[j, c] \leftarrow p \\
&\quad\; j \leftarrow j + 1
\end{aligned}
$$

The algorithm does not visit unreachable states of the DFA. This is extremely important, because in principle the DFA has 2^n states, but in practice we usually find that only about n of them are reachable from the start state. It is important to avoid an exponential blowup in the size of the DFA interpreter's transition tables, which will form part of the working compiler.

A state d is *final* in the DFA if any NFA state in states$[d]$ is final in the NFA. Labeling a state *final* is not enough; we must also say what token is recognized; and perhaps several members of states$[d]$ are final in the NFA. In this case we label d with the token-type that occurred first in the list of regular expressions that constitute the lexical specification. This is how *rule priority* is implemented.

After the DFA is constructed, the "states" array may be discarded, and the "trans" array is used for lexical analysis.

Applying the DFA construction algorithm to the NFA of Figure 2.7 gives the automaton in Figure 2.8.

This automaton is suboptimal. That is, it is not the smallest one that recognizes the same language. In general, we say that two states s_1 and s_2 are equivalent when the machine starting in s_1 accepts a string σ if and only if starting in s_2 it accepts σ. This is certainly true of the states labeled $\boxed{5,6,8,15}$ and $\boxed{6,7,8}$ in Figure 2.8, and of the states labeled $\boxed{10,11,13,15}$ and $\boxed{11,12,13}$. In an automaton with two equivalent states s_1 and s_2, we can make all of s_2's incoming edges point to s_1 instead and delete s_2.

How can we find equivalent states? Certainly, s_1 and s_2 are equivalent if they are both final or both nonfinal and, for any symbol c, trans$[s_1, c] =$ trans$[s_2, c]$; $\boxed{10,11,13,15}$ and $\boxed{11,12,13}$ satisfy this criterion. But this condition is not sufficiently general; consider the automaton

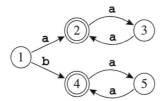

Here, states 2 and 4 are equivalent, but trans$[2, a] \neq$ trans$[4, a]$.

After constructing a DFA it is useful to apply an algorithm to minimize it by finding equivalent states; see Exercise 2.6.

2.5   LEXICAL-ANALYZER GENERATORS

DFA construction is a mechanical task easily performed by computer, so it makes sense to have an automatic *lexical-analyzer generator* to translate regular expressions into a DFA.

JavaCC and SableCC generate lexical analyzers and parsers written in Java. The lexical analyzers are generated from *lexical specifications*; and, as explained in the next chapter, the parsers are generated from grammars.

```
PARSER_BEGIN(MyParser)
   class MyParser {}
PARSER_END(MyParser)
```

/* *For the regular expressions on the right, the token on the left will be returned:* */
```
TOKEN : {
    < IF: "if" >
  | < #DIGIT: ["0"-"9"] >
  | < ID: ["a"-"z"] (["a"-"z"]|<DIGIT>)* >
  | < NUM: (<DIGIT>)+  >
  | < REAL: ( (<DIGIT>)+ "." (<DIGIT>)* ) |
          ( (<DIGIT>)* "." (<DIGIT>)+ )>
}
```

/* *The regular expressions here will be skipped during lexical analysis:* */
```
SKIP : {
    <"--" (["a"-"z"])* ("\n" | "\r" | "\r\n")>
  |  " "
  |  "\t"
  |  "\n"
}
```

/* *If we have a substring that does not match any of the regular expressions in TOKEN or SKIP,*
   JavaCC will automatically throw an error. */
```
void Start() :
{}
{  ( <IF> | <ID> | <NUM> | <REAL> )*  }
```

PROGRAM 2.9.   JavaCC specification of the tokens from Figure 2.2.

For both JavaCC and SableCC, the lexical specification and the grammar are contained in the same file.

JAVACC

The tokens described in Figure 2.2 are specified in JavaCC as shown in Program 2.9. A JavaCC specification starts with an optional list of options followed by a Java compilation unit enclosed between PARSER_BEGIN(name) and PARSER_END(name). The same name must follow PARSER_BEGIN and PARSER_END; it will be the name of the generated parser (MyParser in Program 2.9). The enclosed compilation unit must contain a class declaration of the same name as the generated parser.

Next is a list of grammar productions of the following kinds: a *regular-*

```
Helpers
    digit = ['0'..'9'];
Tokens
    if = 'if';
    id = ['a'..'z'](['a'..'z'] | (digit))*;
    number = digit+;
    real =  ((digit)+ '.' (digit)*) |
            ((digit)* '.' (digit)+);
    whitespace = (' ' | '\t' | '\n')+;
    comments = ('--' ['a'..'z']* '\n');
Ignored Tokens
    whitespace,
    comments;
```

PROGRAM 2.10. SableCC specification of the tokens from Figure 2.2.

---

expression production defines a token, a *token-manager declaration* can be used by the generated lexical analyzer, and two other kinds are used to define the grammar from which the parser is generated.

A lexical specification uses regular-expression productions; there are four kinds: TOKEN, SKIP, MORE, and SPECIAL_TOKEN. We will only need TOKEN and SKIP for the compiler project in this book. The kind TOKEN is used to specify that the matched string should be transformed into a token that should be communicated to the parser. The kind SKIP is used to specify that the matched string should be thrown away.

In Program 2.9, the specifications of ID, NUM, and REAL use the abbreviation DIGIT. The definition of DIGIT is preceded by # to indicate that it can be used only in the definition of other tokens.

The last part of Program 2.9 begins with void Start. It is a *production* which, in this case, allows the generated lexer to recognize any of the four defined tokens in any order. The next chapter will explain productions in detail.

SABLECC

The tokens described in Figure 2.2 are specified in SableCC as shown in Program 2.10. A SableCC specification file has six sections (all optional):

1. Package declaration: specifies the root package for all classes generated by SableCC.
2. Helper declarations: a list of abbreviations.

3. State declarations: support the state feature of, for example, GNU FLEX; when the lexer is in some state, only the tokens associated with that state are recognized. States can be used for many purposes, including the detection of a beginning-of-line state, with the purpose of recognizing tokens only if they appear at the beginning of a line. For the compiler described in this book, states are not needed.

4. Token declarations: each one is used to specify that the matched string should be transformed into a token that should be communicated to the parser.

5. Ignored tokens: each one is used to specify that the matched string should be thrown away.

6. Productions: are used to define the grammar from which the parser is generated.

PROGRAM

LEXICAL ANALYSIS

Write the lexical-analysis part of a JavaCC or SableCC specification for Mini-Java. Appendix A describes the syntax of MiniJava. The directory

$$\texttt{\$MINIJAVA/chap2/javacc}$$

contains a test-scaffolding file `Main.java` that calls the lexer generated by `javacc`. It also contains a `README` file that explains how to invoke `javacc`. Similar files for `sablecc` can be found in `$MINIJAVA/chap2/sablecc`.

FURTHER READING

Lex was the first lexical-analyzer generator based on regular expressions [Lesk 1975]; it is still widely used.

Computing ϵ-closure can be done more efficiently by keeping a queue or stack of states whose edges have not yet been checked for ϵ-transitions [Aho et al. 1986]. Regular expressions can be converted directly to DFAs without going through NFAs [McNaughton and Yamada 1960; Aho et al. 1986].

DFA transition tables can be very large and sparse. If represented as a simple two-dimensional matrix (*states* × *symbols*), they take far too much memory. In practice, tables are compressed; this reduces the amount of memory required, but increases the time required to look up the next state [Aho et al. 1986].

Lexical analyzers, whether automatically generated or handwritten, must manage their input efficiently. Of course, input is buffered, so that a large batch of characters is obtained at once; then the lexer can process one character at a time in the buffer. The lexer must check, for each character, whether the end of the buffer is reached. By putting a *sentinel* – a character that cannot be part of any token – at the end of the buffer, it is possible for the lexer to check for end-of-buffer only once per token, instead of once per character [Aho et al. 1986]. Gray [1988] uses a scheme that requires only one check per line, rather than one per token, but cannot cope with tokens that contain end-of-line characters. Bumbulis and Cowan [1993] check only once around each cycle in the DFA; this reduces the number of checks (from once per character) when there are long paths in the DFA.

Automatically generated lexical analyzers are often criticized for being slow. In principle, the operation of a finite automaton is very simple and should be efficient, but interpreting from transition tables adds overhead. Gray [1988] shows that DFAs translated directly into executable code (implementing states as case statements) can run as fast as hand-coded lexers. The Flex "fast lexical-analyzer generator" [Paxson 1995] is significantly faster than Lex.

EXERCISES

2.1 Write regular expressions for each of the following.

a. Strings over the alphabet $\{a, b, c\}$ where the first a precedes the first b.

b. Strings over the alphabet $\{a, b, c\}$ with an even number of a's.

c. Binary numbers that are multiples of four.

d. Binary numbers that are greater than 101001.

e. Strings over the alphabet $\{a, b, c\}$ that don't contain the contiguous substring baa.

f. The language of nonnegative integer constants in C, where numbers beginning with 0 are *octal* constants and other numbers are *decimal* constants.

g. Binary numbers n such that there exists an integer solution of $a^n + b^n = c^n$.

2.2 For each of the following, explain why you're not surprised that there is no regular expression defining it.

a. Strings of a's and b's where there are more a's than b's.

b. Strings of a's and b's that are palindromes (the same forward as backward).

c. Syntactically correct Java programs.

2.3 Explain in informal English what each of these finite-state automata recognizes.

a.

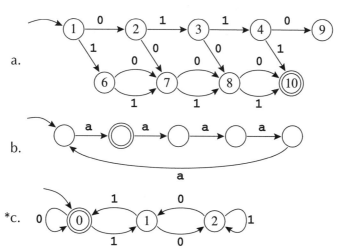

b.

c.

2.4 Convert these regular expressions to nondeterministic finite automata.

a. (**if**|**then**|**else**)

b. **a((b|a*c)x)*|x*a**

2.5 Convert these NFAs to deterministic finite automata.

a.

b.

c.

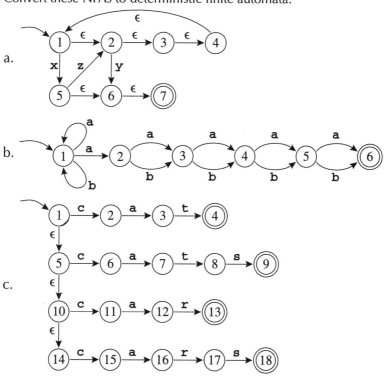

2.6 Find two equivalent states in the following automaton, and merge them to produce a smaller automaton that recognizes the same language. Repeat until there are no longer equivalent states.

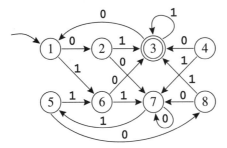

Actually, the general algorithm for minimizing finite automata works in reverse. First, find all pairs of inequivalent states. States X, Y are inequivalent if X is final and Y is not or (by iteration) if $X \overset{a}{\to} X'$ and $Y \overset{a}{\to} Y'$ and X', Y' are inequivalent. After this iteration ceases to find new pairs of inequivalent states, then X, Y are equivalent if they are not inequivalent. See Hopcroft and Ullman [1979], Theorem 3.10.

*2.7 Any DFA that accepts at least one string can be converted to a regular expression. Convert the DFA of Exercise 2.3c to a regular expression. **Hint:** First, pretend state 1 is the start state. Then write a regular expression for excursions to state 2 and back, and a similar one for excursions to state 0 and back. Or look in Hopcroft and Ullman [1979], Theorem 2.4, for the algorithm.

*2.8 Suppose this DFA were used by Lex to find tokens in an input file.

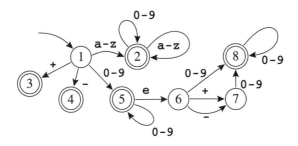

a. How many characters past the end of a token might Lex have to examine before matching the token?

b. Given your answer k to part (a), show an input file containing at least two tokens such that *the first call* to Lex will examine k characters *past the end of the first token* before returning the first token. If the answer to part (a) is zero, then show an input file containing at least two tokens, and indicate the endpoint of each token.

2.9 An interpreted DFA-based lexical analyzer uses two tables,

edges indexed by state and input symbol, yielding a state number, and
final indexed by state, returning 0 or an action-number.

Starting with this lexical specification,

```
(aba)+      (action 1);
(a(b*)a)    (action 2);
(a|b)       (action 3);
```

generate the edges and final tables for a lexical analyzer.

Then show each step of the lexer on the string abaabbaba. Be sure to show the values of the important internal variables of the recognizer. There will be repeated calls to the lexer to get successive tokens.

**2.10 Lex has a *lookahead* operator / so that the regular expression abc/def matches abc only when followed by def (but def is not part of the matched string, and will be part of the next token(s)). Aho et al. [1986] describe, and Lex [Lesk 1975] uses, an incorrect algorithm for implementing lookahead (it fails on (a|ab)/ba with input aba, matching ab where it should match a). Flex [Paxson 1995] uses a better mechanism that works correctly for (a|ab)/ba but fails (with a warning message) on zx*/xy*.

Design a better lookahead mechanism.

3

Parsing

syn-tax: the way in which words are put together to form phrases, clauses, or sentences.

Webster's Dictionary

The abbreviation mechanism discussed in the previous chapter, whereby a symbol stands for some regular expression, is convenient enough that it is tempting to use it in interesting ways:

$digits = [0 − 9]+$
$sum \quad = (digits\ \text{``+''})*\ digits$

These regular expressions define sums of the form `28+301+9`.
But now consider

$digits = [0 − 9]+$
$sum \quad = expr\ \text{``+''}\ expr$
$expr \quad = \text{`` ('' } sum \text{ ``)'' } |\ digits$

This is meant to define expressions of the form:

```
(109+23)
61
(1+(250+3))
```

in which all the parentheses are balanced. But it is impossible for a finite automaton to recognize balanced parentheses (because a machine with N states cannot remember a parenthesis-nesting depth greater than N), so clearly *sum* and *expr* cannot be regular expressions.

So how does a lexical analyzer implement regular-expression abbreviations such as `digits`? The answer is that the right-hand-side (`[0-9]+`) is simply substituted for `digits` wherever it appears in regular expressions, *before* translation to a finite automaton.

This is not possible for the *sum-and-expr* language; we can first substitute *sum* into *expr*, yielding

$$expr = \text{" ("} \; expr \; \text{"+"} \; expr \; \text{")"} \mid digits$$

but now an attempt to substitute *expr* into itself leads to

$$expr = \text{" ("} \; (\; \text{" ("} \; expr \; \text{"+"} \; expr \; \text{")"} \mid digits \;) \; \text{"+"} \; expr \; \text{")"} \mid digits$$

and the right-hand side now has just as many occurrences of *expr* as it did before – in fact, it has more!

Thus, the notion of abbreviation does not add expressive power to the language of regular expressions – there are no additional languages that can be defined – unless the abbreviations are recursive (or mutually recursive, as are *sum* and *expr*).

The additional expressive power gained by recursion is just what we need for parsing. Also, once we have abbreviations with recursion, we do not need alternation except at the top level of expressions, because the definition

$$expr = ab(c \mid d)e$$

can always be rewritten using an auxiliary definition as

$$aux \;\; = c \mid d$$
$$expr = a \; b \; aux \; e$$

In fact, instead of using the alternation mark at all, we can just write several allowable expansions for the same symbol:

$$aux \;\; = c$$
$$aux \;\; = d$$
$$expr = a \; b \; aux \; e$$

The Kleene closure is not necessary, since we can rewrite it so that

$$expr = (a \; b \; c)*$$

becomes

$$expr = (a \; b \; c) \; expr$$
$$expr = \epsilon$$

1. $S \rightarrow S \; ; \; S$
2. $S \rightarrow \text{id} := E$
3. $S \rightarrow \text{print} \; (\; L \;)$

4. $E \rightarrow \text{id}$
5. $E \rightarrow \text{num}$
6. $E \rightarrow E + E$
7. $E \rightarrow (S \, , \, E \,)$

8. $L \rightarrow E$
9. $L \rightarrow L \, , \, E$

GRAMMAR 3.1. A syntax for straight-line programs.

What we have left is a very simple notation, called *context-free grammars*. Just as regular expressions can be used to define lexical structure in a static, declarative way, grammars define syntactic structure declaratively. But we will need something more powerful than finite automata to parse languages described by grammars.

In fact, grammars can also be used to describe the structure of lexical tokens, although regular expressions are adequate – and more concise – for that purpose.

3.1   CONTEXT-FREE GRAMMARS

As before, we say that a *language* is a set of *strings*; each string is a finite sequence of *symbols* taken from a finite *alphabet*. For parsing, the strings are source programs, the symbols are lexical tokens, and the alphabet is the set of token-types returned by the lexical analyzer.

A context-free grammar describes a language. A grammar has a set of *productions* of the form

$$symbol \; \rightarrow \; symbol \; symbol \; \cdots \; symbol$$

where there are zero or more symbols on the right-hand side. Each symbol is either *terminal*, meaning that it is a token from the alphabet of strings in the language, or *nonterminal*, meaning that it appears on the left-hand side of some production. No token can ever appear on the left-hand side of a production. Finally, one of the nonterminals is distinguished as the *start symbol* of the grammar.

Grammar 3.1 is an example of a grammar for straight-line programs. The start symbol is S (when the start symbol is not written explicitly it is conventional to assume that the left-hand nonterminal in the first production is the start symbol). The terminal symbols are

id print num , + ( ) := ;

S
S ; S
S ; id : = E
id : = E ; id : = E
id : = num ; id : = E
id : = num ; id : = E + E
id : = num ; id : = E + (S , E)
id : = num ; id : = id + (S , E)
id : = num ; id : = id + (id : = E , E)
id : = num ; id : = id + (id : = E + E , E)
id : = num ; id : = id + (id : = E + E , id)
id : = num ; id : = id + (id : = num + E , id)
id : = num ; id : = id + (id : = num + num , id)

DERIVATION 3.2.

---

and the nonterminals are S, E, and L. One sentence in the language of this grammar is

```
id := num; id := id + (id := num + num, id)
```

where the source text (before lexical analysis) might have been

```
a := 7;
b := c + (d := 5 + 6, d)
```

The token-types (terminal symbols) are id, num, :=, and so on; the names (a,b,c,d) and numbers (7, 5, 6) are *semantic values* associated with some of the tokens.

DERIVATIONS

To show that this sentence is in the language of the grammar, we can perform a *derivation*: Start with the start symbol, then repeatedly replace any nonterminal by one of its right-hand sides, as shown in Derivation 3.2.

There are many different derivations of the same sentence. A *leftmost* derivation is one in which the leftmost nonterminal symbol is always the one expanded; in a *rightmost* derivation, the rightmost nonterminal is always the next to be expanded.

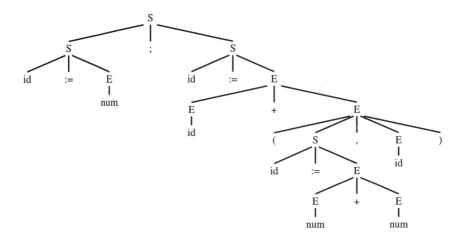

FIGURE 3.3. Parse tree.

Derivation 3.2 is neither leftmost nor rightmost; a leftmost derivation for this sentence would begin,

$$
\begin{aligned}
&\underline{S} \\
&\underline{S}\; ;\; S \\
&\text{id} := \underline{E}\; ;\; S \\
&\text{id} := \text{num}\; ;\; \underline{S} \\
&\text{id} := \text{num}\; ;\; \text{id} := \underline{E} \\
&\text{id} := \text{num}\; ;\; \text{id} := \underline{E} + E \\
&\qquad \vdots
\end{aligned}
$$

PARSE TREES

A *parse tree* is made by connecting each symbol in a derivation to the one from which it was derived, as shown in Figure 3.3. Two different derivations can have the same parse tree.

AMBIGUOUS GRAMMARS

A grammar is *ambiguous* if it can derive a sentence with two different parse trees. Grammar 3.1 is ambiguous, since the sentence `id := id+id+id` has two parse trees (Figure 3.4).

Grammar 3.5 is also ambiguous; Figure 3.6 shows two parse trees for the sentence `1-2-3`, and Figure 3.7 shows two trees for `1+2*3`. Clearly, if we use

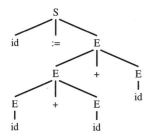 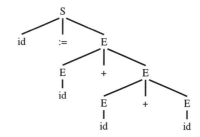

FIGURE 3.4.   Two parse trees for the same sentence using Grammar 3.1.

$$E \rightarrow \text{id}$$
$$E \rightarrow \text{num}$$
$$E \rightarrow E * E$$
$$E \rightarrow E / E$$
$$E \rightarrow E + E$$
$$E \rightarrow E - E$$
$$E \rightarrow (E)$$

GRAMMAR 3.5.

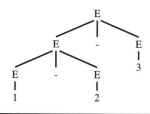 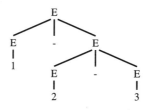

FIGURE 3.6.   Two parse trees for the sentence $1-2-3$ in Grammar 3.5.

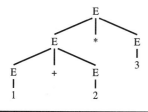 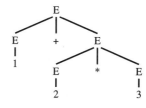

FIGURE 3.7.   Two parse trees for the sentence $1+2*3$ in Grammar 3.5.

$$E \rightarrow E + T \qquad T \rightarrow T * F \qquad F \rightarrow \text{id}$$
$$E \rightarrow E - T \qquad T \rightarrow T / F \qquad F \rightarrow \text{num}$$
$$E \rightarrow T \qquad T \rightarrow F \qquad F \rightarrow (E)$$

GRAMMAR 3.8.

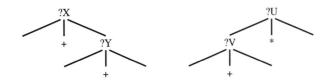

FIGURE 3.9.   Parse trees that Grammar 3.8 will never produce.

parse trees to interpret the meaning of the expressions, the two parse trees for
1-2-3 mean different things: $(1 - 2) - 3 = -4$ versus $1 - (2 - 3) = 2$.
Similarly, $(1 + 2) \times 3$ is not the same as $1 + (2 \times 3)$. And indeed, compilers
do use parse trees to derive meaning.

Therefore, ambiguous grammars are problematic for compiling: In general, we would prefer to have unambiguous grammars. Fortunately, we can
often transform ambiguous grammars to unambiguous grammars.

Let us find an unambiguous grammar that accepts the same language as
Grammar 3.5. First, we would like to say that * *binds tighter* than +, or has
higher precedence. Second, we want to say that each operator *associates to
the left*, so that we get $(1 - 2) - 3$ instead of $1 - (2 - 3)$. We do this by
introducing new nonterminal symbols to get Grammar 3.8.

The symbols E, T, and F stand for *expression*, *term*, and *factor*; conventionally, factors are things you multiply and terms are things you add.

This grammar accepts the same set of sentences as the ambiguous grammar, but now each sentence has exactly one parse tree. Grammar 3.8 can never
produce parse trees of the form shown in Figure 3.9 (see Exercise 3.17).

Had we wanted to make * associate to the right, we could have written its
production as $T \rightarrow F * T$.

We can usually eliminate ambiguity by transforming the grammar. Though
there are some languages (sets of strings) that have ambiguous grammars
but no unambiguous grammar, such languages may be problematic as *programming* languages because the syntactic ambiguity may lead to problems
in writing and understanding programs.

$S \rightarrow E\ \$$

	$T \rightarrow T * F$	$F \rightarrow \text{id}$
$E \rightarrow E + T$	$T \rightarrow T\ /\ F$	$F \rightarrow \text{num}$
$E \rightarrow E - T$	$T \rightarrow F$	$F \rightarrow (\ E\ )$
$E \rightarrow T$		

GRAMMAR 3.10.

$S \rightarrow \text{if } E \text{ then } S \text{ else } S$	$L \rightarrow \text{end}$
$S \rightarrow \text{begin } S\ L$	$L \rightarrow \ ;\ S\ L$
$S \rightarrow \text{print } E$	
	$E \rightarrow \text{num } = \text{ num}$

GRAMMAR 3.11.

END-OF-FILE MARKER

Parsers must read not only terminal symbols such as +, -, num, and so on, but also the end-of-file marker. We will use $ to represent end of file.

Suppose S is the start symbol of a grammar. To indicate that $ must come after a complete S-phrase, we augment the grammar with a new start symbol S' and a new production $S' \rightarrow S\$$.

In Grammar 3.8, E is the start symbol, so an augmented grammar is Grammar 3.10.

3.2 PREDICTIVE PARSING

Some grammars are easy to parse using a simple algorithm known as *recursive descent*. In essence, each grammar production turns into one clause of a recursive function. We illustrate this by writing a recursive-descent parser for Grammar 3.11.

A recursive-descent parser for this language has one function for each non-terminal and one clause for each production.

```
final int IF=1, THEN=2, ELSE=3, BEGIN=4, END=5, PRINT=6,
          SEMI=7, NUM=8, EQ=9;

int tok = getToken();

void advance() {tok=getToken();}
void eat(int t) {if (tok==t) advance(); else error();}

void S() {switch(tok) {
        case IF:    eat(IF); E(); eat(THEN); S();
                    eat(ELSE); S(); break;
        case BEGIN: eat(BEGIN); S(); L(); break;
        case PRINT: eat(PRINT); E(); break;
        default:    error();
        }}
void L() {switch(tok) {
        case END:   eat(END); break;
        case SEMI:  eat(SEMI); S(); L(); break;
        default:    error();
        }}
void E() {  eat(NUM); eat(EQ); eat(NUM); }
```

With suitable definitions of `error` and `getToken`, this program will parse very nicely.

Emboldened by success with this simple method, let us try it with Grammar 3.10:

```
void S() {  E(); eat(EOF); }
void E() {switch (tok) {
        case ?: E(); eat(PLUS); T(); break;
        case ?: E(); eat(MINUS); T(); break;
        case ?: T(); break;
        default: error();
        }}
void T() {switch (tok) {
        case ?: T(); eat(TIMES); F(); break;
        case ?: T(); eat(DIV); F(); break;
        case ?: F(); break;
        default: error();
        }}
```

There is a *conflict* here: The E function has no way to know which clause to use. Consider the strings `(1*2-3)+4` and `(1*2-3)`. In the former case, the initial call to E should use the $E \rightarrow E + T$ production, but the latter case should use $E \rightarrow T$.

$Z \rightarrow d$	$Y \rightarrow$	$X \rightarrow Y$
$Z \rightarrow X\ Y\ Z$	$Y \rightarrow c$	$X \rightarrow a$

GRAMMAR 3.12.

Recursive-descent, or *predictive*, parsing works only on grammars where the *first terminal symbol* of each subexpression provides enough information to choose which production to use. To understand this better, we will formalize the notion of FIRST sets, and then derive conflict-free recursive-descent parsers using a simple algorithm.

Just as lexical analyzers can be constructed from regular expressions, there are parser-generator tools that build predictive parsers. But if we are going to use a tool, then we might as well use one based on the more powerful LR(1) parsing algorithm, which will be described in Section 3.3.

Sometimes it's inconvenient or impossible to use a parser-generator tool. The advantage of predictive parsing is that the algorithm is simple enough that we can use it to construct parsers by hand – we don't need automatic tools.

FIRST AND FOLLOW SETS

Given a string γ of terminal and nonterminal symbols, FIRST(γ) is the set of all terminal symbols that can begin any string derived from γ. For example, let $\gamma = T * F$. Any string of terminal symbols derived from γ must start with id, num, or $($. Thus, FIRST($T * F$) = $\{\text{id}, \text{num}, (\}$.

If two different productions $X \rightarrow \gamma_1$ and $X \rightarrow \gamma_2$ have the same left-hand-side symbol (X) and their right-hand sides have overlapping FIRST sets, then the grammar cannot be parsed using predictive parsing. If some terminal symbol I is in FIRST(γ_1) and also in FIRST(γ_2), then the X function in a recursive-descent parser will not know what to do if the input token is I.

The computation of FIRST sets looks very simple: If $\gamma = X\ Y Z$, it seems as if Y and Z can be ignored, and FIRST(X) is the only thing that matters. But consider Grammar 3.12. Because Y can produce the empty string – and therefore X can produce the empty string – we find that FIRST($X\ Y Z$) must include FIRST(Z). Therefore, in computing FIRST sets, we must keep track of which symbols can produce the empty string; we say such symbols are *nullable*. And we must keep track of what might follow a nullable symbol.

With respect to a particular grammar, given a string γ of terminals and nonterminals,

- nullable(X) is true if X can derive the empty string.
- FIRST(γ) is the set of terminals that can begin strings derived from γ.
- FOLLOW(X) is the set of terminals that can immediately follow X. That is, $t \in$ FOLLOW(X) if there is any derivation containing Xt. This can occur if the derivation contains $X Y Z t$ where Y and Z both derive ϵ.

A precise definition of FIRST, FOLLOW, and nullable is that they are the smallest sets for which these properties hold:

For each terminal symbol Z, FIRST[Z] = $\{Z\}$.

for each production $X \rightarrow Y_1 Y_2 \cdots Y_k$
    if $Y_1 \ldots Y_k$ are all nullable (or if $k = 0$)
        then nullable[X] = true
    for each i from 1 to k, each j from $i + 1$ to k
        if $Y_1 \cdots Y_{i-1}$ are all nullable (or if $i = 1$)
            then FIRST[X] = FIRST[X] $\cup$ FIRST[Y_i]
        if $Y_{i+1} \cdots Y_k$ are all nullable (or if $i = k$)
            then FOLLOW[Y_i] = FOLLOW[Y_i] $\cup$ FOLLOW[X]
        if $Y_{i+1} \cdots Y_{j-1}$ are all nullable (or if $i + 1 = j$)
            then FOLLOW[Y_i] = FOLLOW[Y_i] $\cup$ FIRST[Y_j]

Algorithm 3.13 for computing FIRST, FOLLOW, and nullable just follows from these facts; we simply replace each equation with an assignment statement, and iterate.

Of course, to make this algorithm efficient it helps to examine the productions in the right order; see Section 17.4. Also, the three relations need not be computed simultaneously; nullable can be computed by itself, then FIRST, then FOLLOW.

This is not the first time that a group of equations on sets has become the algorithm for calculating those sets; recall the algorithm on page 28 for computing ϵ-closure. Nor will it be the last time; the technique of iteration to a fixed point is applicable in dataflow analysis for optimization, in the back end of a compiler.

We can apply this algorithm to Grammar 3.12. Initially, we have:

	nullable	FIRST	FOLLOW
X	no		
Y	no		
Z	no		

Algorithm to compute FIRST, FOLLOW, *and* nullable.

Initialize FIRST and FOLLOW to all empty sets, and nullable to all false.

for each terminal symbol Z

    FIRST[Z] ← {Z}

repeat

    for each production $X \rightarrow Y_1 Y_2 \cdots Y_k$

        if $Y_1 \ldots Y_k$ are all nullable (or if $k = 0$)

          then nullable[X] ← true

        for each i from 1 to k, each j from $i + 1$ to k

          if $Y_1 \cdots Y_{i-1}$ are all nullable (or if $i = 1$)

            then FIRST[X] ← FIRST[X] ∪ FIRST[Y_i]

          if $Y_{i+1} \cdots Y_k$ are all nullable (or if $i = k$)

            then FOLLOW[Y_i] ← FOLLOW[Y_i] ∪ FOLLOW[X]

          if $Y_{i+1} \cdots Y_{j-1}$ are all nullable (or if $i + 1 = j$)

            then FOLLOW[Y_i] ← FOLLOW[Y_i] ∪ FIRST[Y_j]

until FIRST, FOLLOW, and nullable did not change in this iteration.

ALGORITHM 3.13. Iterative computation of *FIRST, FOLLOW,* and *nullable*.

In the first iteration, we find that $a \in$ FIRST[X], Y is nullable, $c \in$ FIRST[Y], $d \in$ FIRST[Z], $d \in$ FOLLOW[X], $c \in$ FOLLOW[X], $d \in$ FOLLOW[Y]. Thus:

	nullable	FIRST	FOLLOW
X	no	a	c d
Y	yes	c	d
Z	no	d	

In the second iteration, we find that X is nullable, $c \in$ FIRST[X], $\{a, c\} \subseteq$ FIRST[Z], $\{a, c, d\} \subseteq$ FOLLOW[X], $\{a, c, d\} \subseteq$ FOLLOW[Y]. Thus:

	nullable	FIRST	FOLLOW
X	yes	a c	a c d
Y	yes	c	a c d
Z	no	a c d	

The third iteration finds no new information, and the algorithm terminates.

	a	c	d
X	$X \rightarrow a$ $X \rightarrow Y$	$X \rightarrow Y$	$X \rightarrow Y$
Y	$Y \rightarrow$	$Y \rightarrow$ $Y \rightarrow c$	$Y \rightarrow$
Z	$Z \rightarrow XYZ$	$Z \rightarrow XYZ$	$Z \rightarrow d$ $Z \rightarrow XYZ$

FIGURE 3.14. Predictive parsing table for Grammar 3.12.

It is useful to generalize the FIRST relation to strings of symbols:

$$FIRST(X\gamma) = FIRST[X] \qquad \text{if not nullable}[X]$$
$$FIRST(X\gamma) = FIRST[X] \cup FIRST(\gamma) \qquad \text{if nullable}[X]$$

and similarly, we say that a string γ is nullable if each symbol in γ is nullable.

CONSTRUCTING A PREDICTIVE PARSER

Consider a recursive-descent parser. The parsing function for some nonterminal X has a clause for each X production; it must choose one of these clauses based on the next token T of the input. If we can choose the right production for each (X, T), then we can write the recursive-descent parser. All the information we need can be encoded as a two-dimensional table of productions, indexed by nonterminals X and terminals T. This is called a *predictive parsing* table.

To construct this table, enter production $X \rightarrow \gamma$ in row X, column T of the table for each $T \in FIRST(\gamma)$. Also, if γ is nullable, enter the production in row X, column T for each $T \in FOLLOW[X]$.

Figure 3.14 shows the predictive parser for Grammar 3.12. But some of the entries contain more than one production! The presence of duplicate entries means that predictive parsing will not work on Grammar 3.12.

If we examine the grammar more closely, we find that it is ambiguous. The sentence d has many parse trees, including:

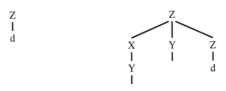

An ambiguous grammar will always lead to duplicate entries in a predictive parsing table. If we need to use the language of Grammar 3.12 as a programming language, we will need to find an unambiguous grammar.

Grammars whose predictive parsing tables contain no duplicate entries are called LL(1). This stands for *left-to-right parse, leftmost-derivation, 1-symbol lookahead.* Clearly a recursive-descent (predictive) parser examines the input left-to-right in one pass (some parsing algorithms do not, but these are generally not useful for compilers). The order in which a predictive parser expands nonterminals into right-hand sides (that is, the recursive-descent parser calls functions corresponding to nonterminals) is just the order in which a leftmost derivation expands nonterminals. And a recursive-descent parser does its job just by looking at the next token of the input, never looking more than one token ahead.

We can generalize the notion of FIRST sets to describe the first k tokens of a string, and to make an LL(k) parsing table whose rows are the nonterminals and columns are every sequence of k terminals. This is rarely done (because the tables are so large), but sometimes when you write a recursive-descent parser by hand you need to look more than one token ahead.

Grammars parsable with LL(2) parsing tables are called LL(2) grammars, and similarly for LL(3), etc. Every LL(1) grammar is an LL(2) grammar, and so on. No ambiguous grammar is LL(k) for any k.

ELIMINATING LEFT RECURSION

Suppose we want to build a predictive parser for Grammar 3.10. The two productions

$$E \rightarrow E + T$$
$$E \rightarrow T$$

are certain to cause duplicate entries in the LL(1) parsing table, since any token in FIRST(T) will also be in FIRST($E + T$). The problem is that E appears as the first right-hand-side symbol in an E-production; this is called *left recursion.* Grammars with left recursion cannot be LL(1).

To eliminate left recursion, we will rewrite using right recursion. We introduce a new nonterminal E', and write

$$E \rightarrow T \ E'$$

$$E' \rightarrow + T \ E'$$
$$E' \rightarrow$$

$$S \rightarrow E \$$$

$$E \rightarrow T E'$$

$$E' \rightarrow + T E'$$
$$E' \rightarrow - T E'$$
$$E' \rightarrow$$

$$T \rightarrow F T'$$

$$T' \rightarrow * F T'$$
$$T' \rightarrow / F T'$$
$$T' \rightarrow$$

$$F \rightarrow id$$
$$F \rightarrow num$$
$$F \rightarrow (E)$$

GRAMMAR 3.15.

	nullable	FIRST	FOLLOW
S	no	(id num	
E	no	(id num	) $
E'	yes	+ -	) $
T	no	(id num	) + - $
T'	yes	* /	) + - $
F	no	(id num	) * / + - $

TABLE 3.16.   Nullable, FIRST, and FOLLOW for Grammar 3.15.

This derives the same set of strings (on T and +) as the original two productions, but now there is no left recursion.

In general, whenever we have productions $X \rightarrow X\gamma$ and $X \rightarrow \alpha$, where α does not start with X, we know that this derives strings of the form $\alpha\gamma*$, an α followed by zero or more γ. So we can rewrite the regular expression using right recursion:

$$
\begin{pmatrix} X \rightarrow X\,\gamma_1 \\ X \rightarrow X\,\gamma_2 \\ X \rightarrow \alpha_1 \\ X \rightarrow \alpha_2 \end{pmatrix} \implies \begin{pmatrix} X \rightarrow \alpha_1\,X' \\ X \rightarrow \alpha_2\,X' \\ X' \rightarrow \gamma_1\,X' \\ X' \rightarrow \gamma_2\,X' \\ X' \rightarrow \end{pmatrix}
$$

Applying this transformation to Grammar 3.10, we obtain Grammar 3.15.

To build a predictive parser, first we compute nullable, FIRST, and FOL-LOW (Table 3.16). The predictive parser for Grammar 3.15 is shown in Table 3.17.

	+	*	id	(	)	$
S			$S \to E\$$	$S \to E\$$		
E			$E \to TE'$	$E \to TE'$		
E'	$E' \to +TE'$				$E' \to$	$E' \to$
T			$T \to FT'$	$T \to FT'$		
T'	$T' \to$	$T' \to *FT'$			$T' \to$	$T' \to$
F			$F \to$ id	$F \to (E)$		

TABLE 3.17. Predictive parsing table for Grammar 3.15. We omit the columns for num, /, and -, as they are similar to others in the table.

LEFT FACTORING

We have seen that left recursion interferes with predictive parsing, and that it can be eliminated. A similar problem occurs when two productions for the same nonterminal start with the same symbols. For example:

$$S \to \text{if } E \text{ then } S \text{ else } S$$
$$S \to \text{if } E \text{ then } S$$

In such a case, we can *left factor* the grammar – that is, take the allowable endings (*else S* and ϵ) and make a new nonterminal X to stand for them:

$$S \to \text{if } E \text{ then } S \ X$$
$$X \to$$
$$X \to \text{else } S$$

The resulting productions will not pose a problem for a predictive parser. Although the grammar is still ambiguous – the parsing table has two entries for the same slot – we can resolve the ambiguity by using the *else S* action.

ERROR RECOVERY

Armed with a predictive parsing table, it is easy to write a recursive-descent parser. Here is a representative fragment of a parser for Grammar 3.15:

```
void T() {switch (tok) {
    case ID:
    case NUM:
    case LPAREN:  F(); Tprime(); break;
    default:  error!
  }}

void Tprime() {switch (tok) {
    case PLUS:    break;
    case TIMES:   eat(TIMES); F(); Tprime(); break;
    case EOF:     break;
    case RPAREN:  break;
    default:  error!
  }}
```

A blank entry in row T, column x of the LL(1) parsing table indicates that the parsing function T() does not expect to see token x – this will be a syntax error. How should *error* be handled? It is safe just to raise an exception and quit parsing, but this is not very friendly to the user. It is better to print an error message and recover from the error, so that other syntax errors can be found in the same compilation.

A syntax error occurs when the string of input tokens is not a sentence in the language. Error recovery is a way of finding some sentence similar to that string of tokens. This can proceed by deleting, replacing, or inserting tokens.

For example, error recovery for T could proceed by inserting a num token. It's not necessary to adjust the actual input; it suffices to pretend that the num was there, print a message, and return normally.

```
void T() {switch (tok) {
    case ID:
    case NUM:
    case LPAREN: F(); Tprime(); break;
    default:  print("expected id, num, or left-paren");
  }}
```

It's a bit dangerous to do error recovery by insertion, because if the error cascades to produce another error, the process might loop infinitely. Error recovery by deletion is safer, because the loop must eventually terminate when end-of-file is reached.

Simple recovery by deletion works by skipping tokens until a token in the FOLLOW set is reached. For example, error recovery for T' could work like this:

```
int Tprime_follow [] = {PLUS, RPAREN, EOF};

void Tprime() { switch (tok) {
        case PLUS:   break;
        case TIMES:  eat(TIMES); F(); Tprime(); break;
        case RPAREN: break;
        case EOF:    break;
        default:   print("expected +, *, right-paren,
                         or end-of-file");
                   skipto(Tprime_follow);
    }}
```

A recursive-descent parser's error-recovery mechanisms must be adjusted (sometimes by trial and error) to avoid a long cascade of error-repair messages resulting from a single token out of place.

3.3 LR PARSING

The weakness of LL(k) parsing techniques is that they must *predict* which production to use, having seen only the first k tokens of the right-hand side. A more powerful technique, LR(k) parsing, is able to postpone the decision until it has seen input tokens corresponding to the entire right-hand side of the production in question (and k more input tokens beyond).

LR(k) stands for *left-to-right parse, rightmost-derivation, k-token lookahead.* The use of a rightmost derivation seems odd; how is that compatible with a left-to-right parse? Figure 3.18 illustrates an LR parse of the program

```
a := 7;
b := c + (d := 5 + 6, d)
```

using Grammar 3.1, augmented with a new start production $S' \rightarrow S\$$.

The parser has a *stack* and an *input*. The first k tokens of the input are the *lookahead*. Based on the contents of the stack and the lookahead, the parser performs two kinds of actions:

Shift: Move the first input token to the top of the stack.
Reduce: Choose a grammar rule $X \rightarrow A\ B\ C$; pop C, B, A from the top of the stack; push X onto the stack.

Initially, the stack is empty and the parser is at the beginning of the input. The action of shifting the end-of-file marker $ is called *accepting* and causes the parser to stop successfully.

Stack	Input	Action
1	a := 7 ; b := c + (d := 5 + 6 , d) \$	shift
1 id_4	:= 7 ; b := c + (d := 5 + 6 , d) \$	shift
1 id_4 $:=_6$	7 ; b := c + (d := 5 + 6 , d) \$	shift
1 id_4 $:=_6$ num_{10}	; b := c + (d := 5 + 6 , d) \$	reduce $E \to num$
1 id_4 $:=_6$ E_{11}	; b := c + (d := 5 + 6 , d) \$	reduce $S \to id := E$
1 S_2	; b := c + (d := 5 + 6 , d) \$	shift
1 S_2 $;_3$	b := c + (d := 5 + 6 , d) \$	shift
1 S_2 $;_3$ id_4	:= c + (d := 5 + 6 , d) \$	shift
1 S_2 $;_3$ id_4 $:=_6$	c + (d := 5 + 6 , d) \$	shift
1 S_2 $;_3$ id_4 $:=_6$ id_{20}	+ (d := 5 + 6 , d) \$	reduce $E \to id$
1 S_2 $;_3$ id_4 $:=_6$ E_{11}	+ (d := 5 + 6 , d) \$	shift
1 S_2 $;_3$ id_4 $:=_6$ E_{11} $+_{16}$	(d := 5 + 6 , d) \$	shift
1 S_2 $;_3$ id_4 $:=_6$ E_{11} $+_{16}$ $(_8$	d := 5 + 6 , d) \$	shift
1 S_2 $;_3$ id_4 $:=_6$ E_{11} $+_{16}$ $(_8$ id_4	:= 5 + 6 , d) \$	shift
1 S_2 $;_3$ id_4 $:=_6$ E_{11} $+_{16}$ $(_8$ id_4 $:=_6$	5 + 6 , d) \$	shift
1 S_2 $;_3$ id_4 $:=_6$ E_{11} $+_{16}$ $(_8$ id_4 $:=_6$ num_{10}	+ 6 , d) \$	reduce $E \to num$
1 S_2 $;_3$ id_4 $:=_6$ E_{11} $+_{16}$ $(_8$ id_4 $:=_6$ E_{11}	+ 6 , d) \$	shift
1 S_2 $;_3$ id_4 $:=_6$ E_{11} $+_{16}$ $(_8$ id_4 $:=_6$ E_{11} $+_{16}$	6 , d) \$	shift
1 S_2 $;_3$ id_4 $:=_6$ E_{11} $+_{16}$ $(_8$ id_4 $:=_6$ E_{11} $+_{16}$ num_{10}	, d) \$	reduce $E \to num$
1 S_2 $;_3$ id_4 $:=_6$ E_{11} $+_{16}$ $(_8$ id_4 $:=_6$ E_{11} $+_{16}$ E_{17}	, d) \$	reduce $E \to E + E$
1 S_2 $;_3$ id_4 $:=_6$ E_{11} $+_{16}$ $(_8$ id_4 $:=_6$ E_{11}	, d) \$	reduce $S \to id := E$
1 S_2 $;_3$ id_4 $:=_6$ E_{11} $+_{16}$ $(_8$ S_{12}	, d) \$	shift
1 S_2 $;_3$ id_4 $:=_6$ E_{11} $+_{16}$ $(_8$ S_{12} $,_{18}$	d) \$	shift
1 S_2 $;_3$ id_4 $:=_6$ E_{11} $+_{16}$ $(_8$ S_{12} $,_{18}$ id_{20}	) \$	reduce $E \to id$
1 S_2 $;_3$ id_4 $:=_6$ E_{11} $+_{16}$ $(_8$ S_{12} $,_{18}$ E_{21}	) \$	shift
1 S_2 $;_3$ id_4 $:=_6$ E_{11} $+_{16}$ $(_8$ S_{12} $,_{18}$ E_{21} $)_{22}$	\$	reduce $E \to (S, E)$
1 S_2 $;_3$ id_4 $:=_6$ E_{11} $+_{16}$ E_{17}	\$	reduce $E \to E + E$
1 S_2 $;_3$ id_4 $:=_6$ E_{11}	\$	reduce $S \to id := E$
1 S_2 $;_3$ S_5	\$	reduce $S \to S; S$
1 S_2	\$	accept

FIGURE 3.18. Shift-reduce parse of a sentence. Numeric subscripts in the *Stack* are DFA state numbers; see Table 3.19.

In Figure 3.18, the stack and input are shown after every step, along with an indication of which action has just been performed. The concatenation of stack and input is always one line of a rightmost derivation; in fact, Figure 3.18 shows the rightmost derivation of the input string, upside-down.

LR PARSING ENGINE

How does the LR parser know when to shift and when to reduce? By using a deterministic finite automaton! The DFA is not applied to the input – finite automata are too weak to parse context-free grammars – but to the stack. The edges of the DFA are labeled by the symbols (terminals and non-

	id	num	print	;	,	+	:=	(	)	$	S	E	L
1	s4		s7								g2		
2				s3						a			
3	s4		s7								g5		
4						s6							
5				r1	r1					r1			
6	s20	s10						s8				g11	
7								s9					
8	s4		s7								g12		
9	s20	s10						s8				g15	g14
10				r5	r5	r5			r5	r5			
11				r2	r2	s16				r2			
12				s3	s18								
13				r3	r3					r3			
14					s19				s13				
15					r8				r8				
16	s20	s10						s8				g17	
17				r6	r6	s16			r6	r6			
18	s20	s10						s8				g21	
19	s20	s10						s8				g23	
20				r4	r4	r4			r4	r4			
21									s22				
22				r7	r7	r7			r7	r7			
23					r9	s16			r9				

TABLE 3.19.   LR parsing table for Grammar 3.1.

terminals) that can appear on the stack. Table 3.19 is the transition table for Grammar 3.1.

The elements in the transition table are labeled with four kinds of actions:

sn Shift into state n;

gn Goto state n;

rk Reduce by rule k;

a   Accept;

Error (denoted by a blank entry in the table).

To use this table in parsing, treat the shift and goto actions as edges of a DFA, and scan the stack. For example, if the stack is id : = E, then the DFA goes from state 1 to 4 to 6 to 11. If the next input token is a semicolon, then the ";" column in state 11 says to reduce by rule 2. The second rule of the grammar is $S \rightarrow$ id : = E, so the top three tokens are popped from the stack and S is pushed.

The action for "+" in state 11 is to shift; so if the next token had been + instead, it would have been eaten from the input and pushed on the stack.

0 $S' \rightarrow S\$$

3 $L \rightarrow S$

1 $S \rightarrow (L)$

4 $L \rightarrow L , S$

2 $S \rightarrow x$

GRAMMAR 3.20.

Rather than rescan the stack for each token, the parser can remember instead the state reached for each stack element. Then the parsing algorithm is

Look up top stack state, and input symbol, to get action;

If action is

Shift(n):   Advance input one token; push n on stack.

Reduce(k): Pop stack as many times as the number of
symbols on the right-hand side of rule k;
Let X be the left-hand-side symbol of rule k;
In the state now on top of stack, look up X to get "goto n";
Push n on top of stack.

Accept: Stop parsing, report success.

Error: Stop parsing, report failure.

LR(0) PARSER GENERATION

An LR(k) parser uses the contents of its stack and the next k tokens of the input to decide which action to take. Table 3.19 shows the use of one symbol of lookahead. For $k = 2$, the table has columns for every two-token sequence and so on; in practice, $k > 1$ is not used for compilation. This is partly because the tables would be huge, but more because most reasonable programming languages can be described by $LR(1)$ grammars.

LR(0) grammars are those that can be parsed looking only at the stack, making shift/reduce decisions without any lookahead. Though this class of grammars is too weak to be very useful, the algorithm for constructing LR(0) parsing tables is a good introduction to the LR(1) parser construction algorithm.

We will use Grammar 3.20 to illustrate LR(0) parser generation. Consider what the parser for this grammar will be doing. Initially, it will have an empty stack, and the input will be a complete S-sentence followed by $; that is, the right-hand side of the S' rule will be on the input. We indicate this as $S' \rightarrow .S\$$ where the dot indicates the current position of the parser.

In this state, where the input begins with S, that means that it begins with any possible right-hand side of an S-production; we indicate that by

$$
\boxed{
\begin{array}{l}
S' \rightarrow .S\$ \\
S \rightarrow .x \\
S \rightarrow .(L)
\end{array}
}^{\,1}
$$

Call this state 1. A grammar rule, combined with the dot that indicates a position in its right-hand side, is called an *item* (specifically, an *LR(0) item*). A state is just a set of items.

Shift actions. In state 1, consider what happens if we shift an x. We then know that the end of the stack has an x; we indicate that by shifting the dot past the x in the $S \rightarrow x$ production. The rules $S' \rightarrow .S\$$ and $S \rightarrow .(L)$ are irrelevant to this action, so we ignore them; we end up in state 2:

$$
\boxed{S \rightarrow x.}^{\,2}
$$

Or in state 1 consider shifting a left parenthesis. Moving the dot past the parenthesis in the third item yields $S \rightarrow (.L)$, where we know that there must be a left parenthesis on top of the stack, and the input begins with some string derived by L, followed by a right parenthesis. What tokens can begin the input now? We find out by including all L-productions in the set of items. But now, in one of those L-items, the dot is just before an S, so we need to include all the S-productions:

$$
\boxed{
\begin{array}{l}
S \rightarrow (.L) \\
L \rightarrow .L, S \\
L \rightarrow .S \\
S \rightarrow .(L) \\
S \rightarrow .x
\end{array}
}^{\,3}
$$

Goto actions. In state 1, consider the effect of parsing past some string of tokens derived by the S nonterminal. This will happen when an x or left parenthesis is shifted, followed (eventually) by a reduction of an S-production. All the right-hand-side symbols of that production will be popped, and the parser will execute the goto action for S in state 1. The effect of this can be simulated by moving the dot past the S in the first item of state 1, yielding state 4:

$$
\boxed{S' \rightarrow S.\$}^{\,4}
$$

Reduce actions. In state 2 we find the dot at the end of an item. This means that on top of the stack there must be a complete right-hand side of the corresponding production $(S \rightarrow x)$, ready to reduce. In such a state the parser could perform a reduce action.

The basic operations we have been performing on states are **closure**(I) and **goto**(I, X), where I is a set of items and X is a grammar symbol (terminal or nonterminal). **Closure** adds more items to a set of items when there is a dot to the left of a nonterminal; **goto** moves the dot past the symbol X in all items.

Closure$(I) =$
    repeat
        for any item $A \rightarrow \alpha.X\beta$ in I
            for any production $X \rightarrow \gamma$
                $I \leftarrow I \cup \{X \rightarrow .\gamma\}$
    until I does not change.
    return I

Goto$(I, X) =$
    set J to the empty set
    for any item $A \rightarrow \alpha.X\beta$ in I
        add $A \rightarrow \alpha X.\beta$ to J
    return Closure(J)

Now here is the algorithm for LR(0) parser construction. First, augment the grammar with an auxiliary start production $S' \rightarrow S\$$. Let T be the set of states seen so far, and E the set of (shift or goto) edges found so far.

Initialize T to $\{$**Closure**$(\{S' \rightarrow .S\$\})\}$
Initialize E to empty.
repeat
        for each state I in T
            for each item $A \rightarrow \alpha.X\beta$ in I
                let J be **Goto**(I, X)
                $T \leftarrow T \cup \{J\}$
                $E \leftarrow E \cup \{I \xrightarrow{X} J\}$
until E and T did not change in this iteration

However, for the symbol $\$$ we do not compute **Goto**$(I, \$)$; instead we will make an **accept** action.

For Grammar 3.20 this is illustrated in Figure 3.21.

Now we can compute set R of LR(0) reduce actions:

$R \leftarrow \{\}$
for each state I in T
    for each item $A \rightarrow \alpha.$ in I
        $R \leftarrow R \cup \{(I, A \rightarrow \alpha)\}$

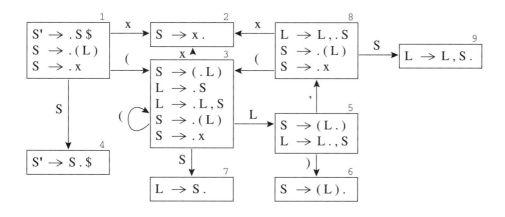

FIGURE 3.21. LR(0) states for Grammar 3.20.

	(	)	x	,	$	S	L
1	s3		s2			g4	
2	r2	r2	r2	r2	r2		
3	s3		s2			g7	g5
4					a		
5		s6		s8			
6	r1	r1	r1	r1	r1		
7	r3	r3	r3	r3	r3		
8	s3		s2			g9	
9	r4	r4	r4	r4	r4		

TABLE 3.22. LR(0) parsing table for Grammar 3.20.

We can now construct a parsing table for this grammar (Table 3.22). For each edge $I \overset{X}{\to} J$ where X is a terminal, we put the action *shift J* at position (I, X) of the table; if X is a nonterminal, we put *goto J* at position (I, X). For each state I containing an item $S' \to S.\$$ we put an *accept* action at $(I, \$)$. Finally, for a state containing an item $A \to \gamma.$ (production n with the dot at the end), we put a *reduce n* action at (I, Y) for every token Y.

In principle, since LR(0) needs no lookahead, we just need a single action for each state: A state will shift or reduce, but not both. In practice, since we need to know what state to shift into, we have rows headed by state numbers and columns headed by grammar symbols.

$_0$ $S \rightarrow E\,\$$ $_2$ $E \rightarrow T$

$_1$ $E \rightarrow T + E$ $_3$ $T \rightarrow x$

GRAMMAR 3.23.

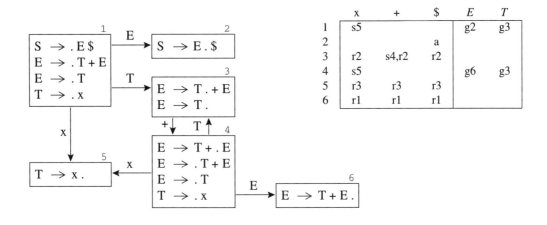

	x	+	$	E	T
1	s5			g2	g3
2			a		
3	r2	s4,r2	r2		
4	s5			g6	g3
5	r3	r3	r3		
6	r1	r1	r1		

FIGURE 3.24.   LR(0) states and parsing table for Grammar 3.23.

SLR PARSER GENERATION

Let us attempt to build an LR(0) parsing table for Grammar 3.23. The LR(0) states and parsing table are shown in Figure 3.24.

In state 3, on symbol +, there is a duplicate entry: The parser must shift into state 4 and also reduce by production 2. This is a conflict and indicates that the grammar is not LR(0) – it cannot be parsed by an LR(0) parser. We will need a more powerful parsing algorithm.

A simple way of constructing better-than-LR(0) parsers is called SLR, which stands for simple LR. Parser construction for SLR is almost identical to that for LR(0), except that we put reduce actions into the table only where indicated by the FOLLOW set.

Here is the algorithm for putting reduce actions into an SLR table:

$R \leftarrow \{\}$
for each state I in T
    for each item $A \rightarrow \alpha.$ in I
        for each token X in FOLLOW(A)
            $R \leftarrow R \cup \{(I,\ X,\ A \rightarrow \alpha)\}$

	x	+	$	E	T
1	s5			g2	g3
2			a		
3		s4	r2		
4	s5			g6	g3
5		r3	r3		
6			r1		

FIGURE 3.25. SLR parsing table for Grammar 3.23.

The action $(I, X, A \rightarrow \alpha)$ indicates that in state I, on lookahead symbol X, the parser will reduce by rule $A \rightarrow \alpha$.

Thus, for Grammar 3.23 we use the same LR(0) state diagram (Figure 3.24), but we put fewer reduce actions into the SLR table, as shown in Figure 3.25.

The SLR class of grammars is precisely those grammars whose SLR parsing table contains no conflicts (duplicate entries). Grammar 3.23 belongs to this class, as do many useful programming-language grammars.

LR(1) ITEMS; LR(1) PARSING TABLE

Even more powerful than SLR is the LR(1) parsing algorithm. Most programming languages whose syntax is describable by a context-free grammar have an LR(1) grammar.

The algorithm for constructing an LR(1) parsing table is similar to that for LR(0), but the notion of an *item* is more sophisticated. An LR(1) item consists of a *grammar production*, a *right-hand-side position* (represented by the dot), and a *lookahead symbol*. The idea is that an item $(A \rightarrow \alpha.\beta, \ x)$ indicates that the sequence α is on top of the stack, and at the head of the input is a string derivable from βx.

An LR(1) state is a set of LR(1) items, and there are **Closure** and **Goto** operations for LR(1) that incorporate the lookahead:

Closure$(I) =$
 repeat
  for any item $(A \rightarrow \alpha.X\beta, z)$ in I
   for any production $X \rightarrow \gamma$
    for any $w \in \mathrm{FIRST}(\beta z)$
     $I \leftarrow I \cup \{(X \rightarrow .\gamma, \ w)\}$
 until I does not change
 return I

Goto$(I, X) =$
 $J \leftarrow \{\}$
 for any item $(A \rightarrow \alpha.X\beta, \ z)$ in I
  add $(A \rightarrow \alpha X.\beta, \ z)$ to J
 return Closure(J).

The start state is the closure of the item $(S' \rightarrow .S \, \$, \, ?)$, where the lookahead symbol ? will not matter, because the end-of-file marker will never be shifted.

The reduce actions are chosen by this algorithm:

$R \leftarrow \{\}$
for each state I in T
    for each item $(A \rightarrow \alpha. \, , \, z)$ in I
        $R \leftarrow R \cup \{(I, z, A \rightarrow \alpha)\}$

The action $(I, z, A \rightarrow \alpha)$ indicates that in state I, on lookahead symbol z, the parser will reduce by rule $A \rightarrow \alpha$.

Grammar 3.26 is not SLR (see Exercise 3.9), but it is in the class of LR(1) grammars. Figure 3.27 shows the LR(1) states for this grammar; in the figure, where there are several items with the same production but different lookahead, as at left below, we have abbreviated as at right:

$S' \rightarrow . \, S \, \$$	?
$S \rightarrow . \, V \, = \, E$	$\$$
$S \rightarrow . \, E$	$\$$
$E \rightarrow . \, V$	$\$$
$V \rightarrow . \, x$	$\$$
$V \rightarrow . \, * \, E$	$\$$
$V \rightarrow . \, x$	$=$
$V \rightarrow . \, * \, E$	$=$

$S' \rightarrow . \, S \, \$$	?
$S \rightarrow . \, V \, = \, E$	$\$$
$S \rightarrow . \, E$	$\$$
$E \rightarrow . \, V$	$\$$
$V \rightarrow . \, x$	$\$, =$
$V \rightarrow . \, * \, E$	$\$, =$

The LR(1) parsing table derived from this state graph is Table 3.28a. Wherever the dot is at the end of a production (as in state 3 of Figure 3.27, where it is at the end of production $E \rightarrow V$), then there is a *reduce* action for that production in the LR(1) table, in the row corresponding to the state number and the column corresponding to the lookahead of the item (in this case, the lookahead is $\$$). Whenever the dot is to the left of a terminal symbol or nonterminal, there is a corresponding shift or goto action in the LR(1) parsing table, just as there would be in an LR(0) table.

LALR(1) PARSING TABLES

LR(1) parsing tables can be very large, with many states. A smaller table can be made by merging any two states whose items are identical except for lookahead sets. The result parser is called an LALR(1) parser, for *lookahead LR(1)*.

0	$S' \rightarrow S\ \$$	3	$E \rightarrow V$
1	$S \rightarrow V = E$	4	$V \rightarrow x$
2	$S \rightarrow E$	5	$V \rightarrow {}^* E$

GRAMMAR 3.26. A grammar capturing the essence of expressions, variables, and pointer-dereference (by the *) operator in the C language.

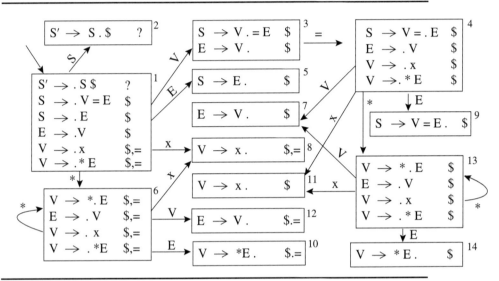

FIGURE 3.27. LR(1) states for Grammar 3.26.

(a) LR(1)

	x	*	=	$	S	E	V
1	s8	s6			g2	g5	g3
2				a			
3			s4	r3			
4	s11	s13				g9	g7
5				r2			
6	s8	s6				g10	g12
7				r3			
8			r4	r4			
9				r1			
10			r5	r5			
11				r4			
12			r3	r3			
13	s11	s13				g14	g7
14				r5			

(b) LALR(1)

	x	*	=	$	S	E	V
1	s8	s6			g2	g5	g3
2				a			
3			s4	r3			
4	s8	s6				g9	g7
5				r2			
6	s8	s6				g10	g7
7			r3	r3			
8			r4	r4			
9				r1			
10			r5	r5			

TABLE 3.28. LR(1) and LALR(1) parsing tables for Grammar 3.26.

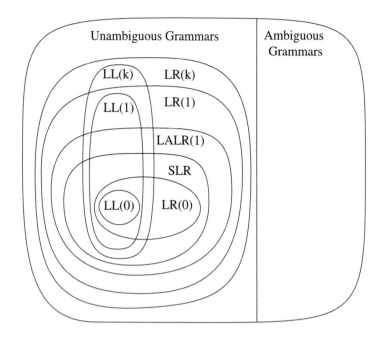

FIGURE 3.29.   A hierarchy of grammar classes.

For example, the items in states 6 and 13 of the LR(1) parser for Grammar 3.26 (Figure 3.27) are identical if the lookahead sets are ignored. Also, states 7 and 12 are identical except for lookahead, as are states 8 and 11 and states 10 and 14. Merging these pairs of states gives the LALR(1) parsing table shown in Table 3.28b.

For some grammars, the LALR(1) table contains reduce-reduce conflicts where the LR(1) table has none, but in practice the difference matters little. What does matter is that the LALR(1) parsing table requires less memory to represent than the LR(1) table, since there can be many fewer states.

HIERARCHY OF GRAMMAR CLASSES

A grammar is said to be LALR(1) if its LALR(1) parsing table contains no conflicts. All SLR grammars are LALR(1), but not vice versa. Figure 3.29 shows the relationship between several classes of grammars.

Any reasonable programming language has a LALR(1) grammar, and there are many parser-generator tools available for LALR(1) grammars. For this reason, LALR(1) has become a standard for programming languages and for automatic parser generators.

LR PARSING OF AMBIGUOUS GRAMMARS

Many programming languages have grammar rules such as

$S \rightarrow$ if E then S else S
$S \rightarrow$ if E then S
$S \rightarrow$ other

which allow programs such as

```
if a then if b then s1 else s2
```

Such a program could be understood in two ways:

```
(1)         if a then { if b then s1 else s2 }
(2)         if a then { if b then s1 } else s2
```

In most programming languages, an `else` must match the most recent possible `then`, so interpretation *(1)* is correct. In the LR parsing table there will be a shift-reduce conflict:

$S \rightarrow$ if E then S .	else
$S \rightarrow$ if E then S . else S	*(any)*

Shifting corresponds to interpretation *(1)* and reducing to interpretation *(2)*.

The ambiguity can be eliminated by introducing auxiliary nonterminals M (for *matched statement*) and U (for *unmatched statement*):

$S \rightarrow M$
$S \rightarrow U$
$M \rightarrow$ if E then M else M
$M \rightarrow$ other
$U \rightarrow$ if E then S
$U \rightarrow$ if E then M else U

But instead of rewriting the grammar, we can leave the grammar unchanged and tolerate the shift-reduce conflict. In constructing the parsing table this conflict should be resolved by shifting, since we prefer interpretation *(1)*.

1   $P \rightarrow L$

2   $S \rightarrow$ id : = id
3   $S \rightarrow$ while id do S
4   $S \rightarrow$ begin L end
5   $S \rightarrow$ if id then S
6   $S \rightarrow$ if id then S else S

7   $L \rightarrow S$
8   $L \rightarrow L$; S

GRAMMAR 3.30.

It is often possible to use ambiguous grammars by resolving shift-reduce conflicts in favor of shifting or reducing, as appropriate. But it is best to use this technique sparingly, and only in cases (such as the *dangling-else* described here, and operator-precedence to be described on page 74) that are well understood. Most shift-reduce conflicts, and probably all reduce-reduce conflicts, should not be resolved by fiddling with the parsing table. They are symptoms of an ill-specified grammar, and they should be resolved by eliminating ambiguities.

3.4   USING PARSER GENERATORS

The task of constructing a parser is simple enough to be automated. In the previous chapter we described the lexical-analyzer aspects of JavaCC and SableCC. Here we will discuss the parser-generator aspects of these tools. Documentation for JavaCC and SableCC are available via this book's Web site.

JAVACC
JavaCC is an LL(k) parser generator. Productions are of the form:

```
void Assignment() : {} { Identifier() "=" Expression() ";" }
```

where the left-hand side is `Assignment()`; the right-hand side is enclosed between the last two curly brackets; `Assignment()`, `Identifier()`, and `Expression()` are nonterminal symbols; and `"="` and `";"` are terminal symbols.

Grammar 3.30 can be represented as a JavaCC grammar as shown in Gram-

```
PARSER_BEGIN(MyParser)
  public class MyParser {}
PARSER_END(MyParser)

SKIP :
{ " " | "\t" | "\n" }

TOKEN :
{ < WHILE: "while" >
| < BEGIN: "begin" >
| < END: "end" >
| < DO: "do" >
| < IF: "if" >
| < THEN: "then" >
| < ELSE: "else" >
| < SEMI: ";" >
| < ASSIGN: "=" >
| < ID: ["a"-"z"](["a"-"z"] | ["0"-"9"])* >
}

void Prog() :
{}
{ StmList() <EOF> }

void StmList() :
{}
{ Stm() StmListPrime() }

void StmListPrime() :
{}
{ ( ";" Stm() StmListPrime() )? }

void Stm() :
{}
{ <ID> "=" <ID>
| "while" <ID> "do" Stm()
| "begin" StmList() "end"
| LOOKAHEAD(5)   /* we need to lookahead till we see "else" */
  "if" <ID> "then" Stm()
| "if" <ID> "then" Stm() "else" Stm()
}
```

GRAMMAR 3.31. JavaCC version of Grammar 3.30.

mar 3.31. Notice that if we had written the production for StmList() in the style of Grammar 3.30, that is,

```
void StmList() :
{}
{ Stm()
| StmList( ) ";" Stm()
}
```

then the grammar would be left recursive. In that case, JavaCC would give the following error:

```
Left recursion detected: "StmList... --> StmList..."
```

We used the techniques mentioned earlier to remove the left recursion and arrive at Grammar 3.31.

SABLECC

SableCC is an LALR(1) parser generator. Productions are of the form:

```
assignment = identifier assign expression semicolon ;
```

where the left-hand side is assignment; the right-hand side is enclosed between = and ;; assignment, identifier, and expression are nonterminal symbols; and assign and semicolon are terminal symbols that are defined in an earlier part of the syntax specification.

Grammar 3.30 can be represented as a SableCC grammar as shown in Grammar 3.32. When there is more than one alternative, SableCC requires a name for each alternative. A name is given to an alternative in the grammar by prefixing the alternative with an identifier between curly brackets. Also, if the same grammar symbol appears twice in the same alternative of a production, SableCC requires a name for at least one of the two elements. Element names are specified by prefixing the element with an identifier between square brackets followed by a colon.

SableCC reports shift-reduce and reduce-reduce conflicts. A shift-reduce conflict is a choice between shifting and reducing; a reduce-reduce conflict is a choice of reducing by two different rules.

SableCC will report that the Grammar 3.32 has a shift-reduce conflict. The conflict can be examined by reading the detailed error message SableCC produces, as shown in Figure 3.33.

```
Tokens
    while = 'while';
    begin = 'begin';
    end = 'end';
    do = 'do';
    if = 'if';
    then = 'then';
    else = 'else';
    semi = ';';
    assign = '=';
    whitespace = (' ' | '\t' | '\n')+;
    id = ['a'..'z'](['a'..'z'] | ['0'..'9'])*;
Ignored Tokens
    whitespace;
Productions
    prog = stmlist;

    stm =   {assign} [left]:id assign [right]:id |
            {while} while id do stm |
            {begin} begin stmlist end |
            {if_then} if id then stm |
            {if_then_else} if id then [true_stm]:stm else [false_stm]:stm;

    stmlist = {stmt} stm |
              {stmtlist} stmlist semi stm;
```

GRAMMAR 3.32. SableCC version of Grammar 3.30.

```
shift/reduce conflict in state [stack: TIf TId TThen PStm *] on TElse in {
        [ PStm = TIf TId TThen PStm * TElse PStm ] (shift),
        [ PStm = TIf TId TThen PStm * ] followed by TElse (reduce)
}
```

FIGURE 3.33. SableCC shift-reduce error message for Grammar 3.32.

SableCC prefixes productions with an uppercase 'P' and tokens with an uppercase 'T', and replaces the first letter with an uppercase when it makes the objects for the tokens and productions. This is what you see on the stack in the error message in Figure 3.33. So on the stack we have tokens for if, id, then, and a production that matches a stm, and now we have an else token. Clearly this reveals that the conflict is caused by the familiar dangling else.

In order to resolve this conflict we need to rewrite the grammar, removing the ambiguity as in Grammar 3.34.

```
Productions
    prog = stmlist;

    stm =   {stm_without_trailing_substm}
                stm_without_trailing_substm |
            {while} while id do stm |
            {if_then} if id then stm |
            {if_then_else} if id then stm_no_short_if
                        else [false_stm]:stm;

    stm_no_short_if = {stm_without_trailing_substm}
                        stm_without_trailing_substm |
                    {while_no_short_if}
                        while id do stm_no_short_if |
                {if_then_else_no_short_if}
                    if id then [true_stm]:stm_no_short_if
                        else [fals_stm]:stm_no_short_if;

    stm_without_trailing_substm  =  {assign} [left]:id assign [right]:id |
                                    {begin} begin stmlist end ;

    stmlist = {stmt} stm | {stmtlist} stmlist semi stm;
```

GRAMMAR 3.34. SableCC productions of Grammar 3.32 with conflicts resolved.

PRECEDENCE DIRECTIVES

No ambiguous grammar is LR(k) for any k; the LR(k) parsing table of an ambiguous grammar will always have conflicts. However, ambiguous grammars can still be useful if we can find ways to resolve the conflicts.

For example, Grammar 3.5 is highly ambiguous. In using this grammar to describe a programming language, we intend it to be parsed so that $*$ and $/$ bind more tightly than $+$ and $-$, and that each operator associates to the left. We can express this by rewriting the unambiguous Grammar 3.8.

But we can avoid introducing the T and F symbols and their associated "trivial" reductions $E \rightarrow T$ and $T \rightarrow F$. Instead, let us start by building the LR(1) parsing table for Grammar 3.5, as shown in Table 3.35. We find many conflicts. For example, in state 13 with lookahead $+$ we find a conflict between *shift into state 8* and *reduce by rule 3*. Two of the items in state 13 are

$$
\begin{array}{ll}
E \rightarrow E * E\,. & + \\
E \rightarrow E\,. + E & (any)
\end{array}
$$

	id	num	+	-	*	/	(	)	$	E
1	s2	s3					s4			g7
2			r1	r1	r1	r1		r1	r1	
3			r2	r2	r2	r2		r2	r2	
4	s2	s3					s4			g5
5								s6		
6			r7	r7	r7	r7		r7	r7	
7			s8	s10	s12	s14			a	
8	s2	s3					s4			g9
9			s8,r5	s10,r5	s12,r5	s14,r5		r5	r5	
10	s2	s3					s4			g11
11			s8,r6	s10,r6	s12,r6	s14,r6		r6	r6	
12	s2	s3					s4			g13
13			s8,r3	s10,r3	s12,r3	s14,r3		r3	r3	
14	s2	s3					s4			g15
15			s8,r4	s10,r4	s12,r4	s14,r4		r4	r4	

TABLE 3.35.   LR parsing table for Grammar 3.5.

In this state the top of the stack is $\cdots E * E$. Shifting will lead to a stack $\cdots E * E+$ and eventually $\cdots E * E + E$ with a reduction of $E + E$ to E. Reducing now will lead to the stack $\cdots E$ and then the $+$ will be shifted. The parse trees obtained by shifting and reducing are

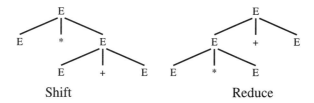

| Shift | Reduce |

If we wish $*$ to bind tighter than $+$, we should reduce instead of shift. So we fill the $(13, +)$ entry in the table with r3 and discard the s8 action.

Conversely, in state 9 on lookahead $*$, we should shift instead of reduce, so we resolve the conflict by filling the $(9, *)$ entry with s12.

The case for state 9, lookahead $+$ is

$$
\begin{array}{ll}
E \rightarrow E + E \,. & + \\
E \rightarrow E \,.\, + E & (any)
\end{array}
$$

Shifting will make the operator right-associative; reducing will make it left-associative. Since we want left associativity, we fill $(9, +)$ with r5.

Consider the expression $a - b - c$. In most programming languages, this

	+	-	*	/	
			⋮		
9	r5	r5	s12	s14	
11			s12	s14	⋯
13	r3	r3	r3	r3	
15	r4	r4			
			⋮		

TABLE 3.36.   Conflicts of Table 3.35 resolved.

associates to the left, as if written $(a - b) - c$. But suppose we believe that this expression is inherently confusing, and we want to force the programmer to put in explicit parentheses, either $(a - b) - c$ or $a - (b - c)$. Then we say that the minus operator is *nonassociative*, and we would fill the $(11, -)$ entry with an error entry.

The result of all these decisions is a parsing table with all conflicts resolved (Table 3.36).

Yacc has *precedence directives* to indicate the resolution of this class of shift-reduce conflicts. (Unfortunately, SableCC does not have precedence directives.) A series of declarations such as

```
precedence nonassoc EQ, NEQ;
precedence left PLUS, MINUS;
precedence left TIMES, DIV;
precedence right EXP;
```

indicates that + and – are left-associative and bind equally tightly; that * and / are left-associative and bind more tightly than +; that ^ is right-associative and binds most tightly; and that = and ≠ are nonassociative, and bind more weakly than +.

In examining a shift-reduce conflict such as

$$
\begin{array}{ll}
E \rightarrow E * E\,. & + \\
E \rightarrow E\,.+E & \textit{(any)}
\end{array}
$$

there is the choice of shifting a *token* and reducing by a *rule*. Should the rule or the token be given higher priority? The precedence declarations (precedence left, etc.) give priorities to the tokens; the priority of a rule is given by the last token occurring on the right-hand side of that rule. Thus the choice here is between a rule with priority * and a token with priority +; the rule has higher priority, so the conflict is resolved in favor of reducing.

```
%{   declarations of yylex and yyerror %}
%token INT PLUS MINUS TIMES UMINUS
%start exp

%left PLUS MINUS
%left TIMES
%left UMINUS
%%

exp :   INT
    |   exp PLUS exp
    |   exp MINUS exp
    |   exp TIMES exp
    |   MINUS exp     %prec UMINUS
```

GRAMMAR 3.37. Yacc grammar with precedence directives.

When the rule and token have equal priority, then a `left` precedence favors reducing, `right` favors shifting, and `nonassoc` yields an error action.

Instead of using the default "rule has precedence of its last token," we can assign a specific precedence to a rule using the `%prec` directive. This is commonly used to solve the "unary minus" problem. In most programming languages a unary minus binds tighter than any binary operator, so $-6 * 8$ is parsed as $(-6) * 8$, not $-(6 * 8)$. Grammar 3.37 shows an example.

The token UMINUS is never returned by the lexer; it's just a placeholder in the chain of `precedence` declarations. The directive `%prec UMINUS` gives the rule `exp::= MINUS exp` the highest precedence, so reducing by this rule takes precedence over shifting any operator, even a minus sign.

Precedence rules are helpful in resolving conflicts, but they should not be abused. If you have trouble explaining the effect of a clever use of precedence rules, perhaps instead you should rewrite the grammar to be unambiguous.

SYNTAX VERSUS SEMANTICS

Consider a programming language with *arithmetic expressions* such as $x + y$ and *boolean expressions* such as $x + y = z$ or $a\&(b = c)$. Arithmetic operators bind tighter than the boolean operators; there are arithmetic variables and boolean variables; and a boolean expression cannot be added to an arithmetic expression. Grammar 3.38 gives a syntax for this language.

The grammar has a reduce-reduce conflict. How should we rewrite the grammar to eliminate this conflict?

Here the problem is that when the parser sees an identifier such as a, it has

```
%token ID ASSIGN PLUS MINUS AND EQUAL
%start stm
%left OR
%left AND
%left PLUS
%%

stm : ID ASSIGN ae
    | ID ASSIGN be

be  : be OR be
    | be AND be
    | ae EQUAL ae
    | ID

ae  : ae PLUS ae
    | ID
```

GRAMMAR 3.38. Yacc grammar with precedence directives.

no way of knowing whether this is an arithmetic variable or a boolean variable – syntactically they look identical. The solution is to defer this analysis until the "semantic" phase of the compiler; it's not a problem that can be handled naturally with context-free grammars. A more appropriate grammar is

$$S \rightarrow \text{id} := E$$

$$E \rightarrow \text{id}$$
$$E \rightarrow E \mathbin{\&} E$$
$$E \rightarrow E = E$$
$$E \rightarrow E + E$$

Now the expression $a + 5\&b$ is syntactically legal, and a later phase of the compiler will have to reject it and print a semantic error message.

3.5   ERROR RECOVERY

LR(k) parsing tables contain shift, reduce, accept, and error actions. On page 58 we claimed that when an LR parser encounters an error action it stops parsing and reports failure. This behavior would be unkind to the programmer, who would like to have *all* the errors in her program reported, not just the first error.

RECOVERY USING THE ERROR SYMBOL

Local error recovery mechanisms work by adjusting the parse stack and the input *at the point where the error was detected* in a way that will allow parsing to resume. One local recovery mechanism – found in many versions of the Yacc parser generator – uses a special *error* symbol to control the recovery process. Wherever the special *error* symbol appears in a grammar rule, a sequence of erroneous input tokens can be matched.

For example, in a Yacc grammar we might have productions such as

$$exp \ \rightarrow \ ID$$
$$exp \ \rightarrow \ exp \ + \ exp$$
$$exp \ \rightarrow \ (\ exps \ )$$
$$exps \rightarrow exp$$
$$exps \rightarrow exps \ ; \ exp$$

Informally, we can specify that if a syntax error is encountered in the middle of an expression, the parser should skip to the next semicolon or right parenthesis (these are called *synchronizing tokens*) and resume parsing. We do this by adding error-recovery productions such as

$$exp \ \rightarrow \ (\ error \ )$$
$$exps \rightarrow error \ ; \ exp$$

What does the parser generator do with the *error* symbol? In parser generation, *error* is considered a terminal symbol, and shift actions are entered in the parsing table for it as if it were an ordinary token.

When the LR parser reaches an error state, it takes the following actions:

1. Pop the stack (if necessary) until a state is reached in which the action for the *error* token is *shift*.
2. Shift the *error* token.
3. Discard input symbols (if necessary) until a lookahead is reached that has a nonerror action in the current state.
4. Resume normal parsing.

In the two *error* productions illustrated above, we have taken care to follow the *error* symbol with an appropriate synchronizing token – in this case, a right parenthesis or semicolon. Thus, the "nonerror action" taken in step 3 will always *shift*. If instead we used the production $exp \rightarrow error$, the "nonerror action" would be *reduce*, and (in an SLR or LALR parser) it is possible that the original (erroneous) lookahead symbol would cause another error after the reduce action, without having advanced the input. Therefore, grammar rules that contain *error* not followed by a token should be used only when there is no good alternative.

Caution. One can attach *semantic actions* to Yacc grammar rules; whenever a rule is reduced, its semantic action is executed. Chapter 4 explains the use of semantic actions. Popping states from the stack can lead to seemingly "impossible" semantic actions, especially if the actions contain side effects. Consider this grammar fragment:

```
statements:  statements exp SEMICOLON
          |  statements error SEMICOLON
          |  /* empty */

exp : increment exp decrement
    | ID

increment:  LPAREN      {: nest=nest+1; :}
decrement:  RPAREN      {: nest=nest-1; :}
```

"Obviously" it is true that whenever a semicolon is reached, the value of `nest` is zero, because it is incremented and decremented in a balanced way according to the grammar of expressions. But if a syntax error is found after some left parentheses have been parsed, then states will be popped from the stack without "completing" them, leading to a nonzero value of `nest`. The best solution to this problem is to have side-effect-free semantic actions that build abstract syntax trees, as described in Chapter 4.

Unfortunately, neither JavaCC nor SableCC support the *error*-symbol error-recovery method, nor the kind of global error repair described below.

GLOBAL ERROR REPAIR

Global error repair finds the smallest set of insertions and deletions that would turn the source string into a syntactically correct string, *even if the insertions and deletions are not at a point where an LL or LR parser would first report an error.*

Burke-Fisher error repair. We will describe a limited but useful form of global error repair, which tries every possible single-token insertion, deletion, or replacement at every point that occurs no earlier than K tokens before the point where the parser reported the error. Thus, with $K = 15$, if the parsing

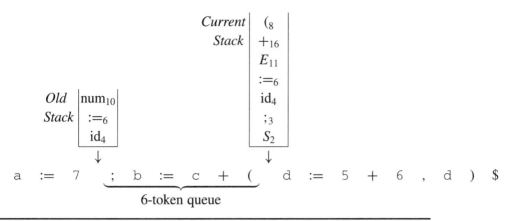

$$\begin{array}{ll} Current & (_8 \\ Stack & +_{16} \\ & E_{11} \\ & :=_6 \\ & id_4 \\ & ;_3 \\ & S_2 \end{array}$$

$$\begin{array}{ll} Old & num_{10} \\ Stack & :=_6 \\ & id_4 \end{array}$$

a := 7 ; b := c + (d := 5 + 6 , d) $

6-token queue

FIGURE 3.39.   Burke-Fisher parsing, with an error-repair queue. Figure 3.18 shows the complete parse of this string according to Table 3.19.

engine gets stuck at the 100th token of the input, then it will try every possible repair between the 85th and 100th tokens.

The correction that allows the parser to parse furthest past the original reported error is taken as the best error repair. Thus, if a single-token substitution of `var` for `type` at the 98th token allows the parsing engine to proceed past the 104th token without getting stuck, this repair is a successful one. Generally, if a repair carries the parser $R = 4$ tokens beyond where it originally got stuck, this is "good enough."

The advantage of this technique is that the LL(k) or LR(k) (or LALR, etc.) grammar is not modified at all (no *error* productions), nor are the parsing tables modified. Only the parsing engine, which interprets the parsing tables, is modified.

The parsing engine must be able to back up K tokens and reparse. To do this, it needs to remember what the parse stack looked like K tokens ago. Therefore, the algorithm maintains *two* parse stacks: the *current* stack and the *old* stack. A queue of K tokens is kept; as each new token is shifted, it is pushed on the *current* stack and also put onto the tail of the queue; simultaneously, the head of the queue is removed and shifted onto the *old* stack. With each *shift* onto the old or current stack, the appropriate reduce actions are also performed. Figure 3.39 illustrates the two stacks and queue.

Now suppose a syntax error is detected at the *current* token. For each possible insertion, deletion, or substitution of a token at any position of the queue, the Burke-Fisher error repairer makes that change to within (a copy of) the queue, then attempts to reparse from the *old* stack. The success of a modification is in how many tokens past the *current* token can be parsed; generally, if three or four new tokens can be parsed, this is considered a completely successful repair.

In a language with N kinds of tokens, there are $K + K \cdot N + K \cdot N$ possible deletions, insertions, and substitutions within the K-token window. Trying this many repairs is not very costly, especially considering that it happens only when a syntax error is discovered, not during ordinary parsing.

Semantic actions. Shift and reduce actions are tried repeatedly and discarded during the search for the best error repair. Parser generators usually perform programmer-specified semantic actions along with each reduce action, but the programmer does not expect that these actions will be performed repeatedly and discarded – they may have side effects. Therefore, a Burke-Fisher parser does not execute any of the semantic actions as reductions are performed on the *current* stack, but waits until the same reductions are performed (permanently) on the *old* stack.

This means that the lexical analyzer may be up to $K + R$ tokens ahead of the point to which semantic actions have been performed. If semantic actions affect lexical analysis – as they do in C, compiling the `typedef` feature – this can be a problem with the Burke-Fisher approach. For languages with a pure context-free grammar approach to syntax, the delay of semantic actions poses no problem.

Semantic values for insertions. In repairing an error by insertion, the parser needs to provide a semantic value for each token it inserts, so that semantic actions can be performed as if the token had come from the lexical analyzer. For punctuation tokens no value is necessary, but when tokens such as numbers or identifiers must be inserted, where can the value come from? The ML-Yacc parser generator, which uses Burke-Fischer error correction, has a `%value` directive, allowing the programmer to specify what value should be used when inserting each kind of token:

```
%value ID   ("bogus")
%value INT (1)
%value STRING  ("")
```

Programmer-specified substitutions. Some common kinds of errors cannot be repaired by the insertion or deletion of a single token, and sometimes a particular single-token insertion or substitution is very commonly required and should be tried first. Therefore, in an ML-Yacc grammar specification the programmer can use the `%change` directive to suggest error corrections to be tried first, before the default "delete or insert each possible token" repairs.

```
%change      EQ -> ASSIGN  |  ASSIGN -> EQ
        |    SEMICOLON ELSE -> ELSE    |    -> IN INT END
```

Here the programmer is suggesting that users often write "`; else`" where they mean "`else`" and so on. These particular error corrections are often useful in parsing the ML programming language.

The insertion of `in 0 end` is a particularly important kind of correction, known as a *scope closer*. Programs commonly have extra left parentheses or right parentheses, or extra left or right brackets, and so on. In ML, another kind of nesting construct is `let ··· in ··· end`. If the programmer forgets to close a scope that was opened by a left parenthesis, then the automatic single-token insertion heuristic can close this scope where necessary. But to close a `let` scope requires the insertion of three tokens, which will not be done automatically unless the compiler-writer has suggested "change *nothing* to `in 0 end`" as illustrated in the `%change` command above.

PROGRAM   PARSING

Use JavaCC or SableCC to implement a parser for the MiniJava language. Do it by extending the specification from the corresponding exercise in the previous chapter. Appendix A describes the syntax of MiniJava.

FURTHER READING

Conway [1963] describes a predictive (recursive-descent) parser, with a notion of FIRST sets and left-factoring. LL(k) parsing theory was formalized by Lewis and Stearns [1968].

LR(k) parsing was developed by Knuth [1965]; the SLR and LALR techniques by DeRemer [1971]; LALR(1) parsing was popularized by the development and distribution of Yacc [Johnson 1975] (which was not the first parser generator, or "compiler-compiler," as can be seen from the title of the cited paper).

Figure 3.29 summarizes many theorems on subset relations between grammar classes. Heilbrunner [1981] shows proofs of several of these theorems, including LL(k) $\subset$ LR(k) and LL(1) $\not\subset$ LALR(1) (see Exercise 3.14). Backhouse [1979] is a good introduction to theoretical aspects of LL and LR parsing.

Aho et al. [1975] showed how deterministic LL or LR parsing engines can handle ambiguous grammars, with ambiguities resolved by precedence directives (as described in Section 3.4).

Burke and Fisher [1987] invented the error-repair tactic that keeps a K-token queue and two parse stacks.

EXERCISES

3.1 Translate each of these regular expressions into a context-free grammar.

a. $((xy^*x)|(yx^*y))$?

b. $((0|1)^{+\,"}\,.\,{}^{"}(0|1)^*)|((0|1)^{*\,"}\,.\,{}^{"}(0|1)^+)$

*3.2 Write a grammar for English sentences using the words

```
time, arrow, banana, flies, like, a, an, the, fruit
```

and the semicolon. Be sure to include all the senses (noun, verb, etc.) of each word. Then show that this grammar is ambiguous by exhibiting more than one parse tree for "time flies like an arrow; fruit flies like a banana."

3.3 Write an unambiguous grammar for each of the following languages. **Hint:** One way of verifying that a grammar is unambiguous is to run it through Yacc and get no conflicts.

a. Palindromes over the alphabet $\{a, b\}$ (strings that are the same backward and forward).

b. Strings that match the regular expression $a*b*$ and have more a's than b's.

c. Balanced parentheses and square brackets. Example: ([] (() [()][]))

*d. Balanced parentheses and brackets, where a closing bracket also closes any outstanding open parentheses (up to the previous open bracket). Example: [([] (() [(][])]. **Hint:** First, make the language of balanced parentheses and brackets, where extra open parentheses are allowed; then make sure this nonterminal must appear within brackets.

e. All subsets and permutations (without repetition) of the keywords `public final static synchronized transient`. (Then comment on how best to handle this situation in a real compiler.)

f. Statement blocks in Pascal or ML where the semicolons *separate* the statements:

```
( statement ; ( statement ; statement ) ; statement )
```

g. Statement blocks in C where the semicolons *terminate* the statements:

```
{ expression; { expression; expression; } expression; }
```

3.4 Write a grammar that accepts the same language as Grammar 3.1, but that is suitable for LL(1) parsing. That is, eliminate the ambiguity, eliminate the left recursion, and (if necessary) left-factor.

3.5 Find nullable, FIRST, and FOLLOW sets for this grammar; then construct the LL(1) parsing table.

0   $S' \rightarrow S \ \$$

1   $S \rightarrow$

2   $S \rightarrow X \ S$

3   $B \rightarrow \backslash \ \text{begin} \ \{ \ \text{WORD} \ \}$

4   $E \rightarrow \backslash \ \text{end} \ \{ \ \text{WORD} \ \}$

5   $X \rightarrow B \ S \ E$

6   $X \rightarrow \{ \ S \ \}$

7   $X \rightarrow \text{WORD}$

8   $X \rightarrow \text{begin}$

9   $X \rightarrow \text{end}$

10 $X \rightarrow \backslash \ \text{WORD}$

3.6 a. Calculate nullable, FIRST, and FOLLOW for this grammar:

$S \rightarrow u \ B \ D \ z$
$B \rightarrow B \ v$
$B \rightarrow w$
$D \rightarrow E \ F$
$E \rightarrow y$
$E \rightarrow$
$F \rightarrow x$
$F \rightarrow$

b. Construct the LL(1) parsing table.

c. Give evidence that this grammar is not LL(1).

d. Modify the grammar **as little as possible** to make an LL(1) grammar that accepts the same language.

*3.7 a. Left-factor this grammar.

0   $S \rightarrow G \ \$$

1   $G \rightarrow P$

2   $G \rightarrow P \ G$

3   $P \rightarrow \text{id} \ : \ R$

4   $R \rightarrow$

5   $R \rightarrow \text{id} \ R$

b. Show that the resulting grammar is LL(2). You can do this by constructing FIRST sets (etc.) containing two-symbol strings; but it is simpler to construct an LL(1) parsing table and then argue convincingly that any conflicts can be resolved by looking ahead one more symbol.

c. Show how the `tok` variable and `advance` function should be altered for recursive-descent parsing with two-symbol lookahead.

d. Use the grammar class hierarchy (Figure 3.29) to show that the (left-factored) grammar is LR(2).

e. Prove that no string has two parse trees according to this (left-factored) grammar.

3.8 Make up a tiny grammar containing left recursion, and use it to demonstrate that left recursion is not a problem for LR parsing. Then show a small example comparing growth of the LR parse stack with left recursion versus right recursion.

3.9 Diagram the LR(0) states for Grammar 3.26, build the SLR parsing table, and identify the conflicts.

3.10 Diagram the LR(1) states for the grammar of Exercise 3.7 (without left-factoring), and construct the LR(1) parsing table. Indicate clearly any conflicts.

3.11 Construct the LR(0) states for this grammar, and then determine whether it is an SLR grammar.

$$0 \quad S \to B \; \$$$

$$1 \quad B \to \text{id} \; P$$
$$2 \quad B \to \text{id} \; (\; E \;]$$

$$3 \quad P \to$$
$$4 \quad P \to (\; E \;)$$

$$5 \quad E \to B$$
$$6 \quad E \to B \; , \; E$$

3.12 a. Build the LR(0) DFA for this grammar:

$$0 \quad S \to E \; \$$$

$$1 \quad E \to \text{id}$$
$$2 \quad E \to \text{id} \; (\; E \;)$$
$$3 \quad E \to E \; + \; \text{id}$$

b. Is this an LR(0) grammar? Give evidence.

c. Is this an SLR grammar? Give evidence.

d. Is this an LR(1) grammar? Give evidence.

3.13 Show that this grammar is LALR(1) but not SLR:

$$0 \quad S \to X \; \$$$
$$1 \quad X \to M \; a$$
$$2 \quad X \to b \; M \; c$$

$$3 \quad X \to d \; c$$
$$4 \quad X \to b \; d \; a$$
$$5 \quad M \to d$$

3.14 Show that this grammar is LL(1) but not LALR(1):

1	$S \rightarrow (X$	5	$X \rightarrow F \,]$
2	$S \rightarrow E \,]$	6	$E \rightarrow A$
3	$S \rightarrow F \,)$	7	$F \rightarrow A$
4	$X \rightarrow E \,)$	8	$A \rightarrow$

*3.15 Feed this grammar to Yacc; from the output description file, construct the LALR(1) parsing table for this grammar, with duplicate entries where there are conflicts. For each conflict, show whether shifting or reducing should be chosen so that the different kinds of expressions have "conventional" precedence. Then show the Yacc-style precedence directives that resolve the conflicts this way.

0 $S \rightarrow E \,\$$

1 $E \rightarrow$ while E do E
2 $E \rightarrow$ id $:= E$
3 $E \rightarrow E + E$
4 $E \rightarrow$ id

*3.16 Explain how to resolve the conflicts in this grammar, using precedence directives, or grammar transformations, or both. Use Yacc or SableCC as a tool in your investigations, if you like.

		3	$B \rightarrow +$
1	$E \rightarrow$ id	4	$B \rightarrow -$
2	$E \rightarrow E \, B \, E$	5	$B \rightarrow \times$
		6	$B \rightarrow /$

*3.17 Prove that Grammar 3.8 cannot generate parse trees of the form shown in Figure 3.9. **Hint:** What nonterminals could possibly be where the $?X$ is shown? What does that tell us about what could be where the $?Y$ is shown?

4

Abstract Syntax

ab-stract: disassociated from any specific instance

Webster's Dictionary

A compiler must do more than recognize whether a sentence belongs to the language of a grammar – it must do something useful with that sentence. The *semantic actions* of a parser can do useful things with the phrases that are parsed.

In a recursive-descent parser, semantic action code is interspersed with the control flow of the parsing actions. In a parser specified in JavaCC, semantic actions are fragments of Java program code attached to grammar productions. SableCC, on the other hand, automatically generates syntax trees as it parses.

4.1 SEMANTIC ACTIONS

Each terminal and nonterminal may be associated with its own type of semantic value. For example, in a simple calculator using Grammar 3.37, the type associated with exp and INT might be int; the other tokens would not need to carry a value. The type associated with a token must, of course, match the type that the lexer returns with that token.

For a rule $A \rightarrow B\ C\ D$, the semantic action must return a value whose type is the one associated with the nonterminal A. But it can build this value from the values associated with the matched terminals and nonterminals B, C, D.

RECURSIVE DESCENT

In a recursive-descent parser, the semantic actions are the values returned by parsing functions, or the side effects of those functions, or both. For each ter-

```
class Token {int kind; Object val;
             Token(int k, Object v) {kind=k; val=v;}
           }
final int EOF=0, ID=1, NUM=2, PLUS=3, MINUS=4,  ...

int lookup(String id) {  ...  }

int F_follow[] = { PLUS, TIMES, RPAREN, EOF };

int F() {switch (tok.kind) {
        case ID:   int i=lookup((String)(tok.val)); advance(); return i;
        case NUM:  int i=((Integer)(tok.val)).intValue();
                     advance(); return i;
        case LPAREN: eat(LPAREN);
                     int i = E();
                     eatOrSkipTo(RPAREN, F_follow);
                     return i;
        case EOF:
        default:   print("expected ID, NUM, or left-paren");
                   skipto(F_follow); return 0;
        }}

int T_follow[] = { PLUS, RPAREN, EOF };

int T() {switch (tok.kind) {
        case ID:
        case NUM:
        case LPAREN: return Tprime(F());
        default: print("expected ID, NUM, or left-paren");
                 skipto(T_follow);
                 return 0;
        }}

int Tprime(int a)  {switch (tok.kind) {
        case TIMES: eat(TIMES); return Tprime(a*F());
        case PLUS:
        case RPAREN:
        case EOF:  return a;
        default:  ...
        }}

void eatOrSkipTo(int expected, int[] stop) {
   if (tok.kind==expected)
        eat(expected);
   else {print(...); skipto(stop);}
}
```

PROGRAM 4.1.   Recursive-descent interpreter for part of Grammar 3.15.

```
void Start() :
{ int i; }
{ i=Exp() <EOF>   { System.out.println(i); }
}
int Exp() :
{ int a,i; }
{ a=Term()
  ( "+" i=Term() { a=a+i; }
  | "-" i=Term() { a=a-i; }
  )*
  { return a; }
}
int Term() :
{ int a,i; }
{ a=Factor()
  ( "*" i=Factor() { a=a*i; }
  | "/" i=Factor() { a=a/i; }
  )*
  { return a; }
}
int Factor() :
{ Token t; int i; }
{ t=<IDENTIFIER>        { return lookup(t.image); }
| t=<INTEGER_LITERAL> { return Integer.parseInt(t.image); }
| "(" i=Exp() ")"       { return i; }
}
```

PROGRAM 4.2.   JavaCC version of a variant of Grammar 3.15.

---

minal and nonterminal symbol, we associate a *type* (from the implementation language of the compiler) of *semantic values* representing phrases derived from that symbol.

Program 4.1 is a recursive-descent interpreter for part of Grammar 3.15. The tokens ID and NUM must now carry values of type `string` and `int`, respectively. We will assume there is a lookup table mapping identifiers to integers. The type associated with E, T, F, etc., is `int`, and the semantic actions are easy to implement.

The semantic action for an artificial symbol such as T' (introduced in the elimination of left recursion) is a bit tricky. Had the production been $T \rightarrow T * F$, then the semantic action would have been

```
int a = T(); eat(TIMES); int b=F(); return a*b;
```

With the rearrangement of the grammar, the production $T' \rightarrow *FT'$ is missing the left operand of the $*$. One solution is for T to pass the left operand as an argument to T', as shown in Program 4.1.

AUTOMATICALLY GENERATED PARSERS

A parser specification for JavaCC consists of a set of grammar rules, each annotated with a semantic action that is a Java statement. Whenever the generated parser reduces by a rule, it will execute the corresponding semantic action fragment.

Program 4.2 shows how this works for a variant of Grammar 3.15. Every INTEGER_CONSTANT terminal and every nonterminal (except Start) carries a value. To access this value, give the terminal or nonterminal a name in the grammar rule (such as i in Program 4.2), and access this name as a variable in the semantic action.

SableCC, unlike JavaCC, has no way to attach action code to productions. However, SableCC automatically generates syntax tree classes, and a parser generated by SableCC will build syntax trees using those classes. For JavaCC, there are several companion tools, including JJTree and JTB (the Java Tree Builder), which, like SableCC, generate syntax tree classes and insert action code into the grammar for building syntax trees.

4.2　　ABSTRACT PARSE TREES

It is possible to write an entire compiler that fits within the semantic action phrases of a JavaCC or SableCC parser. However, such a compiler is difficult to read and maintain, and this approach constrains the compiler to analyze the program in exactly the order it is parsed.

To improve modularity, it is better to separate issues of syntax (parsing) from issues of semantics (type-checking and translation to machine code). One way to do this is for the parser to produce a *parse tree* – a data structure that later phases of the compiler can traverse. Technically, a parse tree has exactly one leaf for each token of the input and one internal node for each grammar rule reduced during the parse.

Such a parse tree, which we will call a *concrete parse tree,* representing the *concrete syntax* of the source language, may be inconvenient to use directly. Many of the punctuation tokens are redundant and convey no information – they are useful in the input string, but once the parse tree is built, the structure

$$E \rightarrow E + E$$
$$E \rightarrow E - E$$
$$E \rightarrow E * E$$
$$E \rightarrow E / E$$
$$E \rightarrow \text{id}$$
$$E \rightarrow \text{num}$$

GRAMMAR 4.3.   Abstract syntax of expressions.

---

of the tree conveys the structuring information more conveniently.

Furthermore, the structure of the parse tree may depend too much on the grammar! The grammar transformations shown in Chapter 3 – factoring, elimination of left recursion, elimination of ambiguity – involve the introduction of extra nonterminal symbols and extra grammar productions for technical purposes. These details should be confined to the parsing phase and should not clutter the semantic analysis.

An *abstract syntax* makes a clean interface between the parser and the later phases of a compiler (or, in fact, for the later phases of other kinds of program-analysis tools such as dependency analyzers). The abstract syntax tree conveys the phrase structure of the source program, with all parsing issues resolved but without any semantic interpretation.

Many early compilers did not use an abstract syntax data structure because early computers did not have enough memory to represent an entire compilation unit's syntax tree. Modern computers rarely have this problem. And many modern programming languages (ML, Modula-3, Java) allow forward reference to identifiers defined later in the same module; using an abstract syntax tree makes compilation easier for these languages. It may be that Pascal and C require clumsy *forward* declarations because their designers wanted to avoid an extra compiler pass on the machines of the 1970s.

Grammar 4.3 shows an abstract syntax of the expression language is Grammar 3.15. This grammar is completely impractical for parsing: The grammar is quite ambiguous, since precedence of the operators is not specified.

However, Grammar 4.3 is not meant for parsing. The parser uses the *concrete syntax* to build a parse tree for the *abstract syntax*. The semantic analysis phase takes this *abstract syntax tree*; it is not bothered by the ambiguity of the grammar, since it already has the parse tree!

The compiler will need to represent and manipulate abstract syntax trees as

```
Exp Start() :
  { Exp e; }
  { e=Exp() { return e; }
  }
Exp Exp() :
  { Exp e1,e2; }
  { e1=Term()
      ( "+" e2=Term() { e1=new  PlusExp(e1,e2); }
      | "-" e2=Term() { e1=new MinusExp(e1,e2); }
      )*
    { return e1; }
  }
Exp Term() :
  { Exp e1,e2; }
  { e1=Factor()
      ( "*" e2=Factor() { e1=new  TimesExp(e1,e2); }
      | "/" e2=Factor() { e1=new DivideExp(e1,e2); }
      )*
    { return e1; }
  }
Exp Factor() :
  { Token t; Exp e; }
  { ( t=<IDENTIFIER>        { return new Identifier(t.image); } |
      t=<INTEGER_LITERAL> { return new IntegerLiteral(t.image); } |
      "(" e=Exp() ")"       { return e; } )
  }
```

PROGRAM 4.4. Building syntax trees for expressions.

data structures. In Java, these data structures are organized according to the principles outlined in Section 1.3: an abstract class for each nonterminal, a subclass for each production, and so on. In fact, the classes of Program 4.5 are abstract syntax classes for Grammar 4.3. An alternate arrangement, with all the different binary operators grouped into an OpExp class, is also possible.

Let us write an interpreter for the expression language in Grammar 3.15 by first building syntax trees and then interpreting those trees. Program 4.4 is a JavaCC grammar with semantic actions that produce syntax trees. Each class of syntax-tree nodes contains an eval function; when called, such a function will return the value of the represented expression.

POSITIONS

In a one-pass compiler, lexical analysis, parsing, and semantic analysis (type-checking) are all done simultaneously. If there is a type error that must be reported to the user, the *current* position of the lexical analyzer is a reason-

```
public abstract class Exp {
   public abstract int eval();
}
public class PlusExp extends Exp {
   private Exp e1,e2;
   public PlusExp(Exp a1, Exp a2) { e1=a1; e2=a2; }
   public int eval() {
       return e1.eval()+e2.eval();
   }
}
public class MinusExp extends Exp {
   private Exp e1,e2;
   public MinusExp(Exp a1, Exp a2) { e1=a1; e2=a2; }
   public int eval() {
       return e1.eval()-e2.eval();
   }
}
public class TimesExp extends Exp {
   private Exp e1,e2;
   public TimesExp(Exp a1, Exp a2) { e1=a1; e2=a2; }
   public int eval() {
       return e1.eval()*e2.eval();
   }
}
public class DivideExp extends Exp {
   private Exp e1,e2;
   public DivideExp(Exp a1, Exp a2) { e1=a1; e2=a2; }
   public int eval() {
       return e1.eval()/e2.eval();
   }
}
public class Identifier extends Exp {
   private String f0;
   public Identifier(String n0) { f0 = n0; }
   public int eval() {
       return lookup(f0);
   }
}
public class IntegerLiteral extends Exp {
   private String f0;
   public IntegerLiteral(String n0) { f0 = n0; }
   public int eval() {
       return Integer.parseInt(f0);
   }
}
```

PROGRAM 4.5. Exp class for Program 4.4.

---

able approximation of the source position of the error. In such a compiler, the lexical analyzer keeps a "current position" global variable, and the error-message routine just prints the value of that variable with each message.

A compiler that uses abstract-syntax-tree data structures need not do all the parsing and semantic analysis in one pass. This makes life easier in many ways, but slightly complicates the production of semantic error messages. The lexer reaches the end of file before semantic analysis even begins; so if a semantic error is detected in traversing the abstract syntax tree, the *current* position of the lexer (at end of file) will not be useful in generating a line number for the error message. Thus, the source-file position of each node of the abstract syntax tree must be remembered, in case that node turns out to contain a semantic error.

To remember positions accurately, the abstract-syntax data structures must be sprinkled with `pos` fields. These indicate the position, within the original source file, of the characters from which these abstract-syntax structures were derived. Then the type-checker can produce useful error messages. (The syntax constructors we will show in Figure 4.9 do not have `pos` fields; any compiler that uses these exactly as given will have a hard time producing accurately located error messages.)

The lexer must pass the source-file positions of the beginning and end of each token to the parser. We can augment the types `Exp`, etc. with a `position` field; then each constructor must take a `pos` argument to initialize this field. The positions of leaf nodes of the syntax tree can be obtained from the tokens returned by the lexical analyzer; internal-node positions can be derived from the positions of their subtrees. This is tedious but straightforward.

4.3   VISITORS

Each abstract syntax class of Program 4.5 has a constructor for building syntax trees, and an `eval` method for returning the value of the represented expression. This is an *object-oriented* style of programming. Let us consider an alternative.

Suppose the code for evaluating expressions is written *separately* from the abstract syntax classes. We might do that by examining the syntax-tree data structure by using `instanceof` and by fetching public class variables that represent subtrees. This is a *syntax separate from interpretations* style of programming.

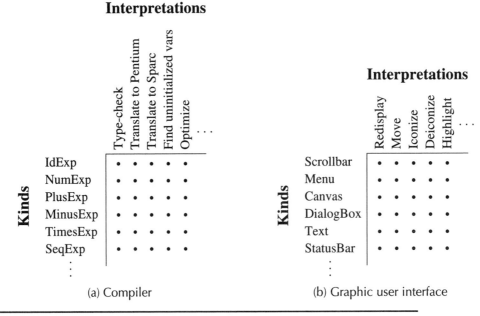

(a) Compiler   (b) Graphic user interface

FIGURE 4.6.   Orthogonal directions of modularity.

The choice of style affects the modularity of the compiler. In a situation such as this, we have several *kinds* of objects: compound statements, assignment statements, print statements, and so on. And we also may have several different *interpretations* of these objects: type-check, translate to Pentium code, translate to Sparc code, optimize, interpret, and so on.

Each *interpretation* must be applied to each *kind*; if we add a new kind, we must implement each interpretation for it; and if we add a new interpretation, we must implement it for each kind. Figure 4.6 illustrates the orthogonality of kinds and interpretations – for compilers, and for graphic user interfaces, where the *kinds* are different widgets and gadgets, and the *interpretations* are move, hide, and redisplay commands.

If the *syntax separate from interpretations* style is used, then it is easy and modular to add a new *interpretation:* One new function is written, with clauses for the different kinds all grouped logically together. On the other hand, it will not be modular to add a new *kind*, since a new clause must be added to every interpretation function.

With the *object-oriented* style, each interpretation is just a *method* in all the classes. It is easy and modular to add a new *kind:* All the interpretations of that kind are grouped together as methods of the new class. But it is not

```
public abstract class Exp {
   public abstract int accept(Visitor v);
}
public class PlusExp extends Exp {
   public Exp e1,e2;
   public PlusExp(Exp a1, Exp a2) { e1=a1; e2=a2; }
   public int accept(Visitor v) {
       return v.visit(this);
   }
}
public class MinusExp extends Exp {
   public Exp e1,e2;
   public MinusExp(Exp a1, Exp a2) { e1=a1; e2=a2; }
   public int accept(Visitor v) {
       return v.visit(this);
   }
}
public class TimesExp extends Exp {
   public Exp e1,e2;
   public TimesExp(Exp a1, Exp a2) { e1=a1; e2=a2; }
   public int accept(Visitor v) {
       return v.visit(this);
   }
}
public class DivideExp extends Exp {
   public Exp e1,e2;
   public DivideExp(Exp a1, Exp a2) { e1=a1; e2=a2; }
   public int accept(Visitor v) {
       return v.visit(this);
   }
}
public class Identifier extends Exp {
   public String f0;
   public Identifier(String n0) { f0 = n0; }
   public int accept(Visitor v) {
       return v.visit(this);
   }
}
public class IntegerLiteral extends Exp {
   public String f0;
   public IntegerLiteral(String n0) { f0 = n0; }
   public int accept() {
       return v.visit(this);
   }
}
```

PROGRAM 4.7.   Syntax classes with accept methods.

```
public interface Visitor {
    public int visit(PlusExp n);
    public int visit(MinusExp n);
    public int visit(TimesExp n);
    public int visit(DivideExp n);
    public int visit(Identifier n);
    public int visit(IntegerLiteral n);
}

public class Interpreter implements Visitor {
    public int visit(PlusExp n) {
        return n.e1.accept(this)+n.e2.accept(this);
    }
    public int visit(MinusExp n) {
        return n.e1.accept(this)-n.e2.accept(this);
    }
    public int visit(TimesExp n) {
        return n.e1.accept(this)*n.e2.accept(this);
    }
    public int visit(DivideExp n) {
        return n.e1.accept(this)/n.e2.accept(this);
    }
    public int visit(Identifier n) {
        return lookup(n.f0);
    }
    public int visit(IntegerLiteral n) {
        return Integer.parseInt(n.f0);
    }
}
```

PROGRAM 4.8. An interpreter visitor.

modular to add a new *interpretation:* A new method must be added to every class.

For graphic user interfaces, each application will want to make its own kinds of widgets; it is impossible to predetermine one set of widgets for everyone to use. On the other hand, the set of common operations (interpretations) is fixed: The window manager demands that each widget support only a certain interface. Thus, the *object-oriented* style works well, and the *syntax separate from interpretations* style would not be as modular.

For programming languages, on the other hand, it works very well to fix a syntax and then provide many interpretations of that syntax. If we have a compiler where one interpretation is *translate to Pentium* and we wish to port that compiler to the Sparc, then not only must we add operations for generating Sparc code but we might also want to remove (in this configuration) the Pentium code-generation functions. This would be very inconvenient in the object-oriented style, requiring each class to be edited. In the *syntax separate from interpretations* style, such a change is modular: We remove a Pentium-related module and add a Sparc module.

We prefer a syntax-separate-from-interpretations style. Fortunately, we can use this style without employing `instanceof` expressions for accessing syntax trees. Instead, we can use a technique known as the Visitor pattern. A visitor implements an interpretation; it is an object which contains a `visit` method for each syntax-tree class. Each syntax-tree class should contain an `accept` method. An `accept` method serves as a hook for all interpretations. It is called by a visitor and it has just one task: It passes control back to an appropriate method of the visitor. Thus, control goes back and forth between a visitor and the syntax-tree classes.

Intuitively, the visitor calls the `accept` method of a node and asks "what is your class?" The `accept` method answers by calling the corresponding `visit` method of the visitor. Code for the running example, using visitors, is given in Programs 4.7 and 4.8. Every visitor implements the interface `Visitor`. Notice that each `accept` method takes a visitor as an argument, and that each `visit` method takes a syntax-tree-node object as an argument.

In Programs 4.7 and 4.8, the `visit` and `accept` methods all return `int`. Suppose we want instead to return `String`. In that case, we can add an appropriate `accept` method to each syntax tree class, and we can write a new visitor class in which all `visit` methods return `String`.

The main difference between the object-oriented style and the syntax-separate-from-interpretations style is that, for example, the interpreter code in Program 4.5 is in the `eval` methods while in Program 4.8 it is in the `Interpreter` visitor.

In summary, with the Visitor pattern we can add a new interpretation without editing and recompiling existing classes, provided that each of the appropriate classes has an `accept` method. The following table summarizes some advantages of the Visitor pattern:

	Frequent type casts?	Frequent recompilation?
Instanceof and type casts	Yes	No
Dedicated methods	No	Yes
The Visitor pattern	No	No

ABSTRACT SYNTAX FOR MiniJava

Figure 4.9 shows classes for the abstract syntax of MiniJava. The meaning of each constructor in the abstract syntax should be clear after a careful study of Appendix A, but there are a few points that merit explanation.

Only the constructors are shown in Figure 4.9; the object field variables correspond exactly to the names of the constructor arguments. Each of the six list classes is implemented in the same way, for example:

```
public class ExpList {
    private Vector list;
    public ExpList() {
        list = new Vector();
    }
    public void addElement(Exp n) {
        list.addElement(n);
    }
    public Exp elementAt(int i)  {
        return (Exp)list.elementAt(i);
    }
    public int size() {
        return list.size();
    }
}
```

Each of the nonlist classes has an accept method for use with the visitor pattern. The interface `Visitor` is shown in Program 4.10.

We can construct a syntax tree by using nested `new` expressions. For example, we can build a syntax tree for the MiniJava statement:

```
x = y.m(1,4+5);
```

using the following Java code:

```
ExpList el = new ExpList();
el.addElement(new IntegerLiteral(1));
el.addElement(new Plus(new IntegerLiteral(4),
                    new IntegerLiteral(5)));
Statement s = new Assign(new Identifier("x"),
                    new Call(new IdentifierExp("y"),
                        new Identifier("m"),
                        el));
```

SableCC enables automatic generation of code for syntax tree classes, code for building syntax trees, and code for template visitors. For JavaCC, a companion tool called the Java Tree Builder (JTB) enables the generation of sim-

```
package syntaxtree;
```

Program(MainClass m, ClassDeclList cl)
MainClass(Identifier i1, Identifier i2, Statement s)

```
abstract class ClassDecl
```
ClassDeclSimple(Identifier i, VarDeclList vl, MethodDeclList ml)
ClassDeclExtends(Identifier i, Identifier j,
                              VarDeclList vl, MethodDeclList ml)   *see Ch.14*

VarDecl(Type t, Identifier i)
MethodDecl(Type t, Identifier i, FormalList fl, VarDeclList vl,
                    StatementList sl, Exp e)
Formal(Type t, Identifier i)

```
abstract class Type
```
IntArrayType() **BooleanType**() **IntegerType**() **IdentifierType**(String s)

```
abstract class Statement
```
Block(StatementList sl)
If(Exp e, Statement s1, Statement s2)
While(Exp e, Statement s)
Print(Exp e)
Assign(Identifier i, Exp e)
ArrayAssign(Identifier i, Exp e1, Exp e2)

```
abstract class Exp
```
And(Exp e1, Exp e2)
LessThan(Exp e1, Exp e2)
Plus(Exp e1, Exp e2) **Minus**(Exp e1, Exp e2) **Times**(Exp e1, Exp e2)
ArrayLookup(Exp e1, Exp e2)
ArrayLength(Exp e)
Call(Exp e, Identifier i, ExpList el)
IntegerLiteral(int i)
True()
False()
IdentifierExp(String s)
This()
NewArray(Exp e)
NewObject(Identifier i)
Not(Exp e)

Identifier(String s)

list classes
ClassDeclList() **ExpList**() **FormalList**() **MethodDeclList**() **StatementList**() **VarDeclList**()

FIGURE 4.9.   Abstract syntax for the MiniJava language.

```
public interface Visitor {
  public void visit(Program n);
  public void visit(MainClass n);
  public void visit(ClassDeclSimple n);
  public void visit(ClassDeclExtends n);
  public void visit(VarDecl n);
  public void visit(MethodDecl n);
  public void visit(Formal n);
  public void visit(IntArrayType n);
  public void visit(BooleanType n);
  public void visit(IntegerType n);
  public void visit(IdentifierType n);
  public void visit(Block n);
  public void visit(If n);
  public void visit(While n);
  public void visit(Print n);
  public void visit(Assign n);
  public void visit(ArrayAssign n);
  public void visit(And n);
  public void visit(LessThan n);
  public void visit(Plus n);
  public void visit(Minus n);
  public void visit(Times n);
  public void visit(ArrayLookup n);
  public void visit(ArrayLength n);
  public void visit(Call n);
  public void visit(IntegerLiteral n);
  public void visit(True n);
  public void visit(False n);
  public void visit(IdentifierExp n);
  public void visit(This n);
  public void visit(NewArray n);
  public void visit(NewObject n);
  public void visit(Not n);
  public void visit(Identifier n);
}
```

PROGRAM 4.10. MiniJava visitor

ilar code. The advantage of using such tools is that once the grammar is written, one can go straight on to writing visitors that operate on syntax trees. The disadvantage is that the syntax trees supported by the generated code may be less abstract than one could desire.

PROGRAM

ABSTRACT SYNTAX

Add semantic actions to your parser to produce abstract syntax for the Mini-Java language. Syntax-tree classes are available in `$MINIJAVA/chap4`, together with a `PrettyPrintVisitor`. If you use JavaCC, you can use JTB to generate the needed code automatically. Similarly, with SableCC, the needed code can be generated automatically.

FURTHER READING

Many compilers mix recursive-descent parsing code with semantic-action code, as shown in Program 4.1; Gries [1971] and Fraser and Hanson [1995] are ancient and modern examples. Machine-generated parsers with semantic actions (in special-purpose "semantic-action mini-languages") attached to the grammar productions were tried out in 1960s [Feldman and Gries 1968]; Yacc [Johnson 1975] was one of the first to permit semantic action fragments to be written in a conventional, general-purpose programming language.

The notion of *abstract syntax* is due to McCarthy [1963], who designed the abstract syntax for Lisp [McCarthy et al. 1962]. The abstract syntax was intended to be used for writing programs until designers could get around to creating a concrete syntax with human-readable punctuation (instead of **L**ots of **I**rritating **S**illy **P**arentheses), but programmers soon got used to programming directly in abstract syntax.

The search for a theory of programming-language semantics, and a notation for expressing semantics in a compiler-compiler, led to ideas such as *denotational semantics* [Stoy 1977]. The semantic interpreter shown in Programs 4.4 and 4.5 is inspired by ideas from denotational semantics, as is the idea of separating concrete syntax from semantics using the abstract syntax as a clean interface.

EXERCISES

4.1 Write a package of Java classes to express the abstract syntax of regular expressions.

4.2 Extend Grammar 3.15 such that a program is a sequence of either assignment statements or print statements. Each assignment statement assigns an expression to an implicitly-declared variable; each print statement prints the value of an expression. Extend the interpreter in Program 4.1 to handle the new language.

4.3 Write a JavaCC version of the grammar from Exercise 4.2. Insert Java code for interpreting programs, in the style of Program 4.2.

4.4 Modify the JavaCC grammar from Exercise 4.3 to contain Java code for building syntax trees, in the style of Program 4.4. Write two interpreters for the language: one in object-oriented style and one that uses visitors.

4.5 In `$MINIJAVA/chap4/handcrafted/visitor`, there is a file with a visitor `PrettyPrintVisitor.java` for pretty printing syntax trees. Improve the pretty printing of nested `if` and `while` statements.

4.6 The visitor pattern in Program 4.7 has `accept` methods that return `int`. If one wanted to write some visitors that return integers, others that return class *A*, and yet others that return class *B*, one could modify all the classes in Program 4.7 to add two more `accept` methods, but this would not be very modular. Another way is to make the visitor return `Object` and cast each result, but this loses the benefit of compile-time type-checking. But there is a third way.

Modify Program 4.7 so that all the `accept` methods return `void`, and write two extensions of the `Visitor` class: one that computes an `int` for each `Exp`, and the other that computes a `float` for each `Exp`. Since the `accept` method will return `void`, the visitor object must have an instance variable into which each `accept` method can place its result. Explain why, if one then wanted to write a visitor that computed an object of class *C* for each `Exp`, no more modification of the `Exp` subclasses would be necessary.

5

Semantic Analysis

se-man-tic: of or relating to meaning in language

Webster's Dictionary

The *semantic analysis* phase of a compiler connects variable definitions to their uses, checks that each expression has a correct type, and translates the abstract syntax into a simpler representation suitable for generating machine code.

5.1   SYMBOL TABLES

This phase is characterized by the maintenance of *symbol tables* (also called *environments*) mapping identifiers to their types and locations. As the declarations of types, variables, and functions are processed, these identifiers are bound to "meanings" in the symbol tables. When *uses* (nondefining occurrences) of identifiers are found, they are looked up in the symbol tables.

Each local variable in a program has a *scope* in which it is visible. For example, in a MiniJava method m, all formal parameters and local variables declared in m are visible only until the end of m. As the semantic analysis reaches the end of each scope, the identifier bindings local to that scope are discarded.

An environment is a set of *bindings* denoted by the $\mapsto$ arrow. For example, we could say that the environment σ_0 contains the bindings $\{g \mapsto string, a \mapsto int\}$, meaning that the identifier a is an integer variable and g is a string variable.

Consider a simple example in the Java language:

```
1 class C {
2   int a; int b; int c;
3   public void m(){
4     System.out.println(a+c);
5     int j = a+b;
6     String a = "hello";
7     System.out.println(a);
8     System.out.println(j);
9     System.out.println(b);
10  }
11 }
```

Suppose we compile this class in the environment σ_0. The field declarations on line 2 give us the table σ_1 equal to $\sigma_0 + \{a \mapsto \text{int}, b \mapsto \text{int}, c \mapsto \text{int}\}$, that is, σ_0 extended with new bindings for a, b, and c. The identifiers in line 4 can be looked up in σ_1. At line 5, the table $\sigma_2 = \sigma_1 + \{j \mapsto \text{int}\}$ is created; and at line 6, $\sigma_3 = \sigma_2 + \{a \mapsto \text{String}\}$ is created.

How does the $+$ operator for tables work when the two environments being "added" contain different bindings for the same symbol? When σ_2 and $\{a \mapsto \text{String}\}$ map a to int and String, respectively? To make the scoping rules work the way we expect them to in real programming languages, we want $\{a \mapsto \text{String}\}$ to take precedence. So we say that $X + Y$ for tables is not the same as $Y + X$; bindings in the right-hand table override those in the left.

The identifiers in lines 7, 8, and 9 can be looked up in σ_3. Finally, at line 10, we discard σ_3 and go back to σ_1. And at line 11 we discard σ_1 and go back to σ_0.

How should this be implemented? There are really two choices. In a *functional* style, we make sure to keep σ_1 in pristine condition while we create σ_2 and σ_3. Then when we need σ_1 again, it's rested and ready.

In an *imperative* style, we modify σ_1 until it becomes σ_2. This *destructive update* "destroys" σ_1; while σ_2 exists, we cannot look things up in σ_1. But when we are done with σ_2, we can *undo* the modification to get σ_1 back again. Thus, there is a single global environment σ which becomes $\sigma_0, \sigma_1, \sigma_2, \sigma_3, \sigma_1, \sigma_0$ at different times and an "undo stack" with enough information to remove the destructive updates. When a symbol is added to the environment, it is also added to the undo stack; at the end of scope (e.g., at line 10), symbols popped from the undo stack have their latest binding removed from σ (and their previous binding restored).

Either the functional or imperative style of environment management can be used regardless of whether the language being compiled or the implemen-

```
structure M = struct                 package M;
   structure E = struct              class E {
      val a = 5;                        static int a = 5;
   end                                }
   structure N = struct              class N {
      val b = 10                        static int b = 10;
      val a = E.a + b                   static int a = E.a + b;
   end                                }
   structure D = struct              class D {
      val d = E.a + N.a                 static int d = E.a + N.a;
   end                                }
end
```

(a) An example in ML   (b) An example in Java

FIGURE 5.1.   Several active environments at once.

tation language of the compiler is a "functional" or "imperative" or "object-oriented" language.

MULTIPLE SYMBOL TABLES

In some languages there can be several active environments at once: Each module, or class, or record in the program has a symbol table σ of its own.

In analyzing Figure 5.1, let σ_0 be the base environment containing predefined functions, and let

$$\sigma_1 = \{a \mapsto int\}$$
$$\sigma_2 = \{E \mapsto \sigma_1\}$$
$$\sigma_3 = \{b \mapsto int, a \mapsto int\}$$
$$\sigma_4 = \{N \mapsto \sigma_3\}$$
$$\sigma_5 = \{d \mapsto int\}$$
$$\sigma_6 = \{D \mapsto \sigma_5\}$$
$$\sigma_7 = \sigma_2 + \sigma_4 + \sigma_6$$

In ML, the N is compiled using environment $\sigma_0 + \sigma_2$ to look up identifiers; D is compiled using $\sigma_0 + \sigma_2 + \sigma_4$, and the result of the analysis is $\{M \mapsto \sigma_7\}$.

In Java, forward reference is allowed (so inside N the expression $D.d$ would be legal), so E, N, and D are all compiled in the environment σ_7; for this program the result is still $\{M \mapsto \sigma_7\}$.

```
class Bucket {String key; Object binding; Bucket next;
      Bucket(String k, Object b, Bucket n) {key=k; binding=b; next=n;}
}

class HashT {
   final int SIZE = 256;
   Bucket table[] = new Bucket[SIZE];

   private int hash(String s) {
        int h=0;
        for(int i=0; i<s.length(); i++)
           h=h*65599+s.charAt(i);
        return h;
   }

   void insert(String s, Binding b) {
        int index=hash(s)%SIZE
        table[index]=new Bucket(s,b,table[index]);
   }

   Object lookup(String s) {
        int index=hash(s)%SIZE
        for (Binding b = table[index]; b!=null; b=b.next)
          if (s.equals(b.key)) return b.binding;
        return null;
   }

   void pop(String s) {
        int index=hash(s)%SIZE
        table[index]=table[index].next;
   }
}
```

PROGRAM 5.2.   Hash table with external chaining.

EFFICIENT IMPERATIVE SYMBOL TABLES

Because a large program may contain thousands of distinct identifiers, symbol tables must permit efficient lookup.

Imperative-style environments are usually implemented using hash tables, which are very efficient. The operation $\sigma' = \sigma + \{a \mapsto \tau\}$ is implemented by inserting τ in the hash table with key a. A simple *hash table with external chaining* works well and supports deletion easily (we will need to delete $\{a \mapsto \tau\}$ to recover σ at the end of the scope of a).

Program 5.2 implements a simple hash table. The ith bucket is a linked list of all the elements whose keys hash to i mod SIZE.

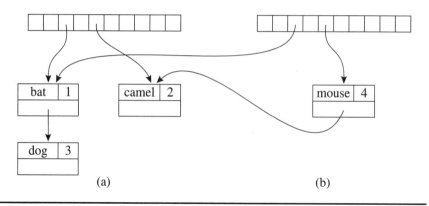

(a)   (b)

FIGURE 5.3.   Hash tables.

Consider $\sigma + \{a \mapsto \tau_2\}$ when σ contains $a \mapsto \tau_1$ already. The `insert` function leaves $a \mapsto \tau_1$ in the bucket and puts $a \mapsto \tau_2$ earlier in the list. Then, when $\mathrm{pop}(a)$ is done at the end of a's scope, σ is restored. Of course, `pop` works only if bindings are inserted and popped in a stacklike fashion.

An industrial-strength implementation would improve on this in several ways; see Exercise 5.1.

EFFICIENT FUNCTIONAL SYMBOL TABLES

In the functional style, we wish to compute $\sigma' = \sigma + \{a \mapsto \tau\}$ in such a way that we still have σ available to look up identifiers. Thus, instead of "altering" a table by adding a binding to it we create a new table by computing the "sum" of an existing table and a new binding. Similarly, when we add $7 + 8$ we don't alter the 7 by adding 8 to it; we create a new value, 15 – and the 7 is still available for other computations.

However, nondestructive update is not efficient for hash tables. Figure 5.3a shows a hash table implementing mapping m_1. It is fast and efficient to add *mouse* to the fifth slot; just make the *mouse* record point at the (old) head of the fifth linked list, and make the fifth slot point to the *mouse* record. But then we no longer have the mapping m_1: We have destroyed it to make m_2. The other alternative is to copy the array, but still share all the old buckets, as shown in Figure 5.3b. But this is not efficient: The array in a hash table should be quite large, proportional in size to the number of elements, and we cannot afford to copy it for each new entry in the table.

By using binary search trees we can perform such "functional" additions to search trees efficiently. Consider, for example, the search tree in Figure 5.4,

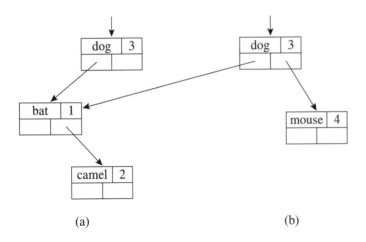

(a)   (b)

FIGURE 5.4.   Binary search trees.

---

which represents the mapping

$$m_1 = \{bat \mapsto 1, \; camel \mapsto 2, \; dog \mapsto 3\}.$$

We can add the binding *mouse* $\mapsto$ 4, creating the mapping m_2 without destroying the mapping m_1, as shown in Figure 5.4b. If we add a new node at depth d of the tree, we must create d new nodes – but we don't need to copy the whole tree. So creating a new tree (that shares some structure with the old one) can be done as efficiently as looking up an element: in $\log(n)$ time for a balanced tree of n nodes. This is an example of a *persistent data structure;* a persistent *red-black* tree can be kept balanced to guarantee $\log(n)$ access time (see Exercise 1.1c, and also page 276).

SYMBOLS

The hash table of Program 5.2 must examine every character of the string s for the `hash` operation, and then again each time it compares s against a string in the ith bucket. To avoid unnecessary string comparisons, we can convert each string to a `symbol`, so that all the different occurrences of any given string convert to the same symbol object.

The `Symbol` module implements symbols and has these important properties:

- Comparing symbols for equality is fast (just pointer or integer comparison).
- Extracting an integer hash key is fast (in case we want to make a hash table mapping symbols to something else).

```
package Symbol;

public class Symbol {
  public String toString();
  public static Symbol symbol(String s);
}

public class Table {
  public Table();
  public void put(Symbol key, Object value);
  public Object get(Symbol key);
  public void beginScope();
  public void endScope();
  public java.util.Enumeration keys();
}
```

PROGRAM 5.5.   The interface of package `Symbol`.

- Comparing two symbols for "greater-than" (in some arbitrary ordering) is fast (in case we want to make binary search trees).

Even if we intend to make functional-style environments mapping symbols to bindings, we can use a destructive-update hash table to map strings to symbols: We need this to make sure the second occurrence of "abc" maps to the same symbol as the first occurrence. Program 5.5 shows the interface of the `Symbol` module.

Environments are implemented in the `Symbol.Table` class as `Tables` mapping `Symbols` to bindings. We want different notions of `binding` for different purposes in the compiler – type bindings for types, value bindings for variables and functions – so we let the bindings be `Object`, though in any given table every binding should be a type binding, or every binding should be a value binding, and so on.

To implement the `Symbol` class (Program 5.6), we rely on the `intern()` method of the `java.lang.String` class to give us a unique object for any given character sequence; we can map from `Symbol` to `String` by having each symbol contain a string variable, but the reverse mapping must be done using a hash table (we use `java.util.Hashtable`).

To handle the "undo" requirements of destructive update, the interface function `beginScope` remembers the current state of the table, and `endScope` restores the table to where it was at the most recent `beginScope` that has not already been ended.

An imperative table is implemented using a hash table. When the binding

```
package Symbol;
public class Symbol {
   private String name;
   private Symbol(String n) {name=n; }
   private static java.util.Dictionary dict = new java.util.Hashtable();

   public String toString() {return name;}

   public static Symbol symbol(String n) {
        String u = n.intern();
        Symbol s = (Symbol)dict.get(u);
        if (s==null) {s = new Symbol(u); dict.put(u,s); }
        return s;
   }
}
```

PROGRAM 5.6. Symbol table implementation.

$x \mapsto b$ is entered (`table.put(x,b)`), x is hashed into an index i, and a `Binder` object $x \mapsto b$ is placed at the head of the linked list for the ith bucket. If the table had already contained a binding $x \mapsto b'$, that would still be in the bucket, hidden by $x \mapsto b$. This is important because it will support the implementation of *undo* (`beginScope` and `endScope`).

The key x is not a character string, but is the `Symbol` object itself.

There must also be an auxiliary stack, showing in what order the symbols were "pushed" into the symbol table. When $x \mapsto b$ is entered, then x is pushed onto this stack. A `beginScope` operation pushes a special marker onto the stack. Then, to implement `endScope`, symbols are popped off the stack down to and including the topmost marker. As each symbol is popped, the head binding in its bucket is removed.

The auxiliary stack can be integrated into the `Binder` by having a global variable `top` showing the most recent `Symbol` bound in the table. Then "pushing" is accomplished by copying `top` into the `prevtop` field of the `Binder`. Thus, the "stack" is threaded through the binders.

If we wanted to use functional-style symbol tables, the `Table` interface might look like this:

```
public class Table {
   public Table();
   public Table put(Symbol key, Object value);
   public Object get(Symbol key);
   public java.util.Enumeration keys();
}
```

```
class B {
    C f;   int [] j;   int q;
    public int start(int p, int q) {
        int ret;   int a;
        /* ... */
        return ret;
    }
    public boolean stop(int p) {
            /* ... */
        retun false;
    }
}

class C {
    /* ... */
}
```

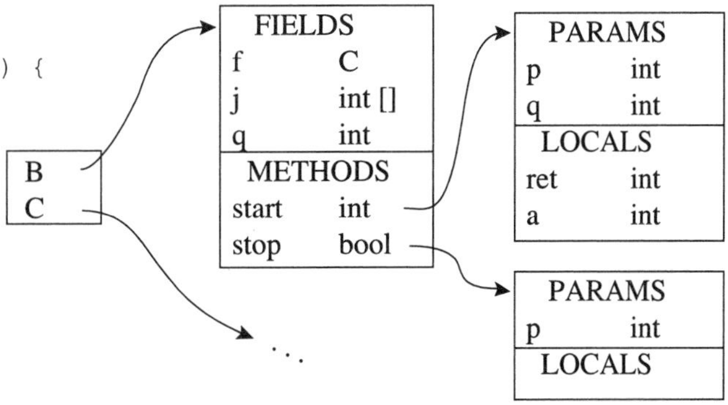

	FIELDS		PARAMS	
	f	C	p	int
	j	int []	q	int
B	q	int	LOCALS	
C	METHODS		ret	int
	start	int	a	int
	stop	bool		

PARAMS	
p	int
LOCALS	

FIGURE 5.7.   A MiniJava Program and its symbol table

The `put` function would return a new table without modifying the old one. We wouldn't need `beginScope` and `endScope`, because we could keep an old version of the table even as we use the new version.

5.2   TYPE-CHECKING MiniJava

With what should a symbol table be filled – that is, what is a `binding`? To enable type-checking of MiniJava programs, the symbol table should contain all declared type information:

- each variable name and formal-parameter name should be bound to its type;
- each method name should be bound to its parameters, result type, and local variables; and
- each class name should be bound to its variable and method declarations.

For example, consider Figure 5.7, which shows a program and its symbol table. The two class names B and C are each mapped to two tables for fields and methods. In turn, each method is mapped to both its result type and tables with its formal parameters and local variables.

The primitive types in MiniJava are `int` and `boolean`; all other types are either integer array, written `int []`, or class names. For simplicity, we

```
class ErrorMsg {
  boolean anyErrors;
  void complain(String msg) {
    anyErrors = true;
    System.out.println(msg);
  }
}

// Type t;
// Identifier i;
public void visit(VarDecl n) {

  Type t =  n.t.accept(this);
  String id =  n.i.toString();

  if (currMethod == null) {
    if (!currClass.addVar(id,t))
      error.complain(id + "is already defined in " + currClass.getId());
  } else if (!currMethod.addVar(id,t))
      error.complain(id + "is already defined in "
          + currClass.getId() + "." + currMethod.getId());
}
```

PROGRAM 5.8. A `visit` method for variable declarations

choose to represent each type as a string, rather than as a symbol; this allows us to test type equality by doing string comparison.

Type-checking of a MiniJava program proceeds in two phases. First, we build the symbol table, and then we type-check the statements and expressions. During the second phase, the symbol table is consulted for each identifier that is found. It is convenient to use two phases because, in Java and MiniJava, the classes are mutually recursive. If we tried to do type-checking in a single phase, then we might need to type-check a call to a method that is not yet entered into the symbol table. To avoid such situations, we use an approach with two phases.

The first phase of the type-checker can be implemented by a visitor that visits nodes in a MiniJava syntaxtree and builds a symbol table. For instance, the visit method in Program 5.8 handles variable declarations. It will add the variable name and type to a data structure for the current class which later will be added to the symbol table. Notice that the visit method checks whether a variable is declared more than once and, if so, then it prints an appropriate error message.

```
// Exp e1,e2;
public Type visit(Plus n) {
   if (! (n.e1.accept(this) instanceof IntegerType) )
      error.complain("Left side of LessThan must be of type integer");
   if (! (n.e2.accept(this) instanceof IntegerType) )
      error.complain("Right side of LessThan must be of type integer");
   return new IntegerType();
}
```

PROGRAM 5.9.   A `visit` method for plus expressions

The second phase of the type-checker can be implemented by a visitor that type-checks all statements and expressions. The result type of each visit method is `String`, for representing MiniJava types. The idea is that when the visitor visits an expression, then it returns the type of that expression. If the expression does not type-check, then the type-check is terminated with an error message.

Let's take a simple case: an addition expression $e_1 + e_2$. In MiniJava, both operands must be integers (the type-checker must check this) and the result will be an integer (the type-checker will return this type). The visit method for addition is easy to implement; see Program 5.9.

In most languages, addition is *overloaded*: The + operator stands for either integer addition or real addition. If the operands are both integers, the result is integer; if the operands are both real, the result is real. And in many languages if one operand is an integer and the other is real, the integer is implicitly converted into a real, and the result is real. Of course, the compiler will have to make this conversion explicit in the machine code it generates.

For an assignment statement, it must be checked that the left-hand side and the right-hand side have the same type. When we allow extension of classes, the requirement is less strict: It is sufficient to check that the right-hand side is a subtype of the left-hand side.

For method calls, it is necessary to look up the method identifier in the symbol table to get the parameter list and the result type. For a call `e.m(...)`, where `e` has type `C`, we look up the definition of `m` in class `C`. The parameter types must then be matched against the arguments in the function-call expression. The result type of the method becomes the type of the method call as a whole.

Every kind of statement and expression has its own type-checking rules, but in all the cases we have not already described, the rules can be derived by reference to the Java Language Specification.

ERROR HANDLING

When the type-checker detects a type error or an undeclared identifier, it should print an error message and continue – because the programmer would like to be told of all the errors in the program. To recover after an error, it's often necessary to build data structures as if a valid expression had been encountered. For example, type-checking

```
{int i = new C();
 int j = i + i;
 ...
}
```

even though the expression `new C()` doesn't match the type required to initialize an integer, it is still useful to enter `i` in the symbol table as an integer so that the rest of the program can be type-checked.

If the type-checking phase detects errors, then the compiler should not produce a compiled program as output. This means that the later phases of the compiler – translation, register allocation, etc. – will not be executed. It will be easier to implement the later phases of the compiler if they are not required to handle invalid inputs. Thus, if at all possible, all errors in the input program should be detected in the front end of the compiler (parsing and type-checking).

PROGRAM   **TYPE-CHECKING**

Design a set of visitors which type-checks a MiniJava program and produces any appropriate error messages about mismatching types or undeclared identifiers.

EXERCISES

5.1   Improve the hash table implementation of Program 5.2: Double the size of the array when the average bucket length grows larger than 2 (so `table` is now a pointer to a dynamically allocated array). To double an array, allocate a bigger one and rehash the contents of the old array; then discard the old array.

***5.2 In many applications, we want a + operator for environments that does more than add one new binding; instead of $\sigma' = \sigma + \{a \mapsto \tau\}$, we want $\sigma' = \sigma_1 + \sigma_2$, where σ_1 and σ_2 are arbitrary environments (perhaps overlapping, in which case bindings in σ_2 take precedence).

We want an efficient algorithm and data structure for environment "adding." Balanced trees can implement $\sigma + \{a \mapsto \tau\}$ efficiently (in $\log(N)$ time, where N is the size of σ), but take $O(N)$ to compute $\sigma_1 + \sigma_2$ if σ_1 and σ_2 are both about size N.

To abstract the problem, solve the general nondisjoint integer-set union problem. The input is a set of commands of the form,

$$s_1 = \{4\} \qquad \text{(define singleton set)}$$
$$s_2 = \{7\}$$
$$s_3 = s_1 \cup s_2 \text{ (nondestructive union)}$$
$$6 \overset{?}{\in} s_3 \qquad \text{(membership test)}$$
$$s_4 = s_1 \cup s_3$$
$$s_5 = \{9\}$$
$$s_6 = s_4 \cup s_5$$
$$7 \overset{?}{\in} s_2$$

An efficient algorithm is one that can process an input of N commands, answering all membership queries, in less than $o(N^2)$ time.

*a. Implement an algorithm that is efficient when a typical set union $a \leftarrow b \cup c$ has b much smaller than c [Brown and Tarjan 1979].

***b. Design an algorithm that is efficient even in the worst case, or prove that this can't be done (see Lipton et al. [1997] for a lower bound in a restricted model).

6

Activation Records

stack: an orderly pile or heap

Webster's Dictionary

In almost any modern programming language, a function may have *local* variables that are created upon entry to the function. Several invocations of the function may exist at the same time, and each invocation has its own *instantiations* of local variables.

In the Java method

```
int f(int x) {
   int y = x+x;
   if (y<10)
      return f(y);
   else
      return y-1;
}
```

a new instantiation of x is created (and initialized by f's caller) each time that f is called. Because there are recursive calls, many of these x's exist simultaneously. Similarly, a new instantiation of y is created each time the body of f is entered.

In many languages (including C, Pascal, and Java), local variables are destroyed when a function returns. Since a function returns only after all the functions it has called have returned, we say that function calls behave in last-in-first-out (LIFO) fashion. If local variables are created on function entry and destroyed on function exit, then we can use a LIFO data structure – a stack – to hold them.

```
fun f(x) =                          int (*)() f(int x) {
   let fun g(y) = x+y                   int g(int y) {return x+y;}
   in g                                 return g;
   end                              }

val h = f(3)                        int (*h)() = f(3);
val j = f(4)                        int (*j)() = f(4);

val z = h(5)                        int z = h(5);
val w = j(7)                        int w = j(7);
```

(a) Written in ML   (b) Written in pseudo-C

PROGRAM 6.1.   An example of higher-order functions.

HIGHER-ORDER FUNCTIONS

But in languages supporting both nested functions *and* function-valued variables, it may be necessary to keep local variables after a function has returned! Consider Program 6.1: This is legal in ML, but of course in C one cannot really nest the function g inside the function f.

When $f(3)$ is executed, a new local variable x is created for the activation of function f. Then g is returned as the result of $f(x)$; but g has not yet been called, so y is not yet created.

At this point f has returned, but it is too early to destroy x, because when $h(5)$ is eventually executed it will need the value $x = 3$. Meanwhile, $f(4)$ is entered, creating a *different* instance of x, and it returns a *different* instance of g in which $x = 4$.

It is the combination of *nested functions* (where inner functions may use variables defined in the outer functions) and *functions returned as results* (or stored into variables) that causes local variables to need lifetimes longer than their enclosing function invocations.

Pascal has nested functions, but it does not have functions as returnable values. C has functions as returnable values, but not nested functions. So these languages can use stacks to hold local variables.

ML, Scheme, and several other languages have both nested functions and functions as returnable values (this combination is called *higher-order functions*). So they cannot use stacks to hold all local variables. This complicates the implementation of ML and Scheme – but the added expressive power of higher-order functions justifies the extra implementation effort.

For the remainder of this chapter we will consider languages with stackable local variables and postpone discussion of higher-order functions to Chapter 15. Notice that while Java allows nesting of functions (via inner classes), MiniJava does not.

6.1 STACK FRAMES

The simplest notion of a *stack* is a data structure that supports two operations, *push* and *pop*. However, it turns out that local variables are pushed in large batches (on entry to functions) and popped in large batches (on exit). Furthermore, when local variables are created they are not always initialized right away. Finally, after many variables have been pushed, we want to continue accessing variables deep within the stack. So the abstract *push* and *pop* model is just not suitable.

Instead, we treat the stack as a big array, with a special register – the *stack pointer* – that points at some location. All locations beyond the stack pointer are considered to be garbage, and all locations before the stack pointer are considered to be allocated. The stack usually grows only at the entry to a function, by an increment large enough to hold all the local variables for that function, and, just before the exit from the function, shrinks by the same amount. The area on the stack devoted to the local variables, parameters, return address, and other temporaries for a function is called the function's *activation record* or *stack frame*. For historical reasons, run-time stacks usually start at a high memory address and grow toward smaller addresses. This can be rather confusing: Stacks grow downward and shrink upward, like icicles.

The design of a frame layout takes into account the particular features of an instruction set architecture and the programming language being compiled. However, the manufacturer of a computer often prescribes a "standard" frame layout to be used on that architecture, where possible, by all compilers for all programming languages. Sometimes this layout is not the most convenient one for a particular programming language or compiler. But by using the "standard" layout, we gain the considerable benefit that functions written in one language can call functions written in another language.

Figure 6.2 shows a typical stack frame layout. The frame has a set of *incoming arguments* (technically these are part of the previous frame but they are at a known offset from the frame pointer) passed by the caller. The *return address* is created by the CALL instruction and tells where (within the calling function) control should return upon completion of the current func-

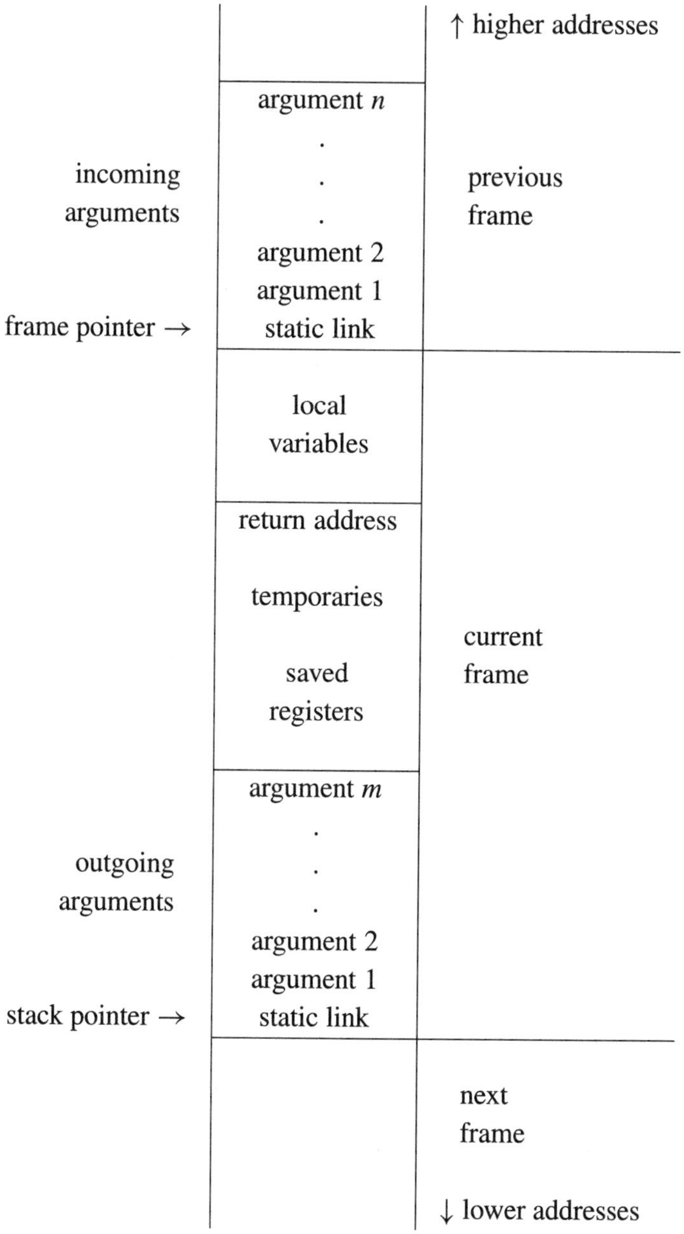

	↑ higher addresses
argument *n*	
incoming .	previous
arguments .	frame
.	
argument 2	
argument 1	
frame pointer → static link	
local	
variables	
return address	
temporaries	
	current
	frame
saved	
registers	
argument *m*	
.	
outgoing .	
arguments .	
argument 2	
argument 1	
stack pointer → static link	
	next
	frame
	↓ lower addresses

FIGURE 6.2. A stack frame.

tion. Some *local variables* are in this frame; other local variables are kept in machine registers. Sometimes a local variable kept in a register needs to be *saved* into the frame to make room for other uses of the register; there is an area in the frame for this purpose. Finally, when the current function calls other functions, it can use the *outgoing argument* space to pass parameters.

THE FRAME POINTER

Suppose a function $g(\ldots)$ calls the function $f(a_1, \ldots, a_n)$. We say g is the *caller* and f is the *callee*. On entry to f, the stack pointer points to the first argument that g passes to f. On entry, f allocates a frame by simply subtracting the frame size from the stack pointer SP.

The old SP becomes the current *frame pointer* FP. In some frame layouts, FP is a separate register; the old value of FP is saved in memory (in the frame) and the new FP becomes the old SP. When f exits, it just copies FP back to SP and fetches back the saved FP. This arrangement is useful if f's frame size can vary, or if frames are not always contiguous on the stack. But if the frame size is fixed, then for each function f the FP will always differ from SP by a known constant, and it is not necessary to use a register for FP at all – FP is a "fictional" register whose value is always SP+*framesize*.

Why talk about a frame pointer at all? Why not just refer to all variables, parameters, etc., by their offset from SP, if the frame size is constant? The frame size is not known until quite late in the compilation process, when the number of memory-resident temporaries and saved registers is determined. But it is useful to know the offsets of formal parameters and local variables much earlier. So, for convenience, we still talk about a frame pointer. And we put the formals and locals right near the frame pointer at offsets that are known *early*; the temporaries and saved registers go farther away, at offsets that are known *later*.

REGISTERS

A modern machine has a large set of *registers* (typically 32 of them). To make compiled programs run fast, it's useful to keep local variables, intermediate results of expressions, and other values in registers instead of in the stack frame. Registers can be directly accessed by arithmetic instructions; on most machines, accessing memory requires separate *load* and *store* instructions. Even on machines whose arithmetic instructions can access memory, it is faster to access registers.

A machine (usually) has only one set of registers, but many different procedures and functions need to use registers. Suppose a function f is using register r to hold a local variable and calls procedure g, which also uses r for its own calculations. Then r must be saved (stored into a stack frame) before g uses it and restored (fetched back from the frame) after g is finished using it. But is it f's responsibility to save and restore the register, or g's? We say that r is a *caller-save* register if the caller (in this case, f) must save and restore the register, and r is *callee-save* if it is the responsibility of the callee (in this case, g).

On most machine architectures, the notion of caller-save or callee-save register is not something built into the hardware, but is a convention described in the machine's reference manual. On the MIPS computer, for example, registers 16–23 are preserved across procedure calls (callee-save), and all other registers are not preserved across procedure calls (caller-save).

Sometimes the saves and restores are unnecessary. If f knows that the value of some variable x will not be needed after the call, it may put x in a caller-save register *and not save it* when calling g. Conversely, if f has a local variable i that is needed before and after several function calls, it may put i in some callee-save register r_i, and save r_i just once (upon entry to f) and fetch it back just once (before returning from f). Thus, the wise selection of a caller-save or callee-save register for each local variable and temporary can reduce the number of stores and fetches a program executes. We will rely on our register allocator to choose the appropriate kind of register for each local variable and temporary value.

PARAMETER PASSING

On most machines whose calling conventions were designed in the 1970s, function arguments were passed on the stack.[1] But this causes needless memory traffic. Studies of actual programs have shown that very few functions have more than four arguments, and almost none have more than six. Therefore, parameter-passing conventions for modern machines specify that the first k arguments (for $k = 4$ or $k = 6$, typically) of a function are passed in registers $r_p, ..., r_{p+k-1}$, and the rest of the arguments are passed in memory.

Now, suppose $f(a_1, \ldots, a_n)$ (which received its parameters in $r_1, \ldots, r_n$, for example) calls $h(z)$. It must pass the argument z in r_1; so f saves the old contents of r_1 (the value a_1) in its stack frame before calling h. But there is the memory traffic that was supposedly avoided by passing arguments in

---

[1] Before about 1960, they were passed not on the stack but in statically allocated blocks of memory, which precluded the use of recursive functions.

registers! How has the use of registers saved any time?

There are four answers, any or all of which can be used at the same time:

1. Some procedures don't call other procedures – these are called *leaf* procedures. What proportion of procedures are leaves? Well, if we make the (optimistic) assumption that the average procedure calls either no other procedures or calls at least two others, then we can describe a "tree" of procedure calls in which there are more leaves than internal nodes. This means that *most* procedures called are leaf procedures.

   Leaf procedures need not write their incoming arguments to memory. In fact, often they don't need to allocate a stack frame at all. This is an important savings.

2. Some optimizing compilers use *interprocedural register allocation*, analyzing all the functions in an entire program at once. Then they assign different procedures different registers in which to receive parameters and hold local variables. Thus $f(x)$ might receive x in r_1, but call $h(z)$ with z in r_7.

3. Even if f is not a leaf procedure, it might be finished with all its use of the argument x by the time it calls h (technically, x is a dead variable at the point where h is called). Then f can overwrite r_1 without saving it.

4. Some architectures have *register windows*, so that each function invocation can allocate a fresh set of registers without memory traffic.

If f needs to write an incoming parameter into the frame, where in the frame should it go? Ideally, f's frame layout should matter only in the implementation of f. A straightforward approach would be for the caller to pass arguments $a_1, ..., a_k$ in registers and $a_{k+1}, ..., a_n$ at the end of its own frame – the place marked *outgoing arguments* in Figure 6.2 – which become the *incoming arguments* of the callee. If the callee needed to write any of these arguments to memory, it would write them to the area marked *local variables*.

The C programming language actually allows you to take the address of a formal parameter and guarantees that all the formal parameters of a function are at consecutive addresses! This is the `varargs` feature that `printf` uses. Allowing programmers to take the address of a parameter can lead to a *dangling reference* if the address outlives the frame – as the address of x will in `int *f(int x){return &x;}` – and even when it does not lead to bugs, the consecutive-address rule for parameters constrains the compiler and makes stack-frame layout more complicated. To resolve the contradiction that parameters are passed in registers, but have addresses too, the first k parameters are passed in registers; but any parameter whose address is taken must be written to a memory location on entry to the function. To satisfy `printf`, the memory locations into which register arguments are written must all be consecutive with the memory locations in which arguments $k+1, k+2$, etc., are written. Therefore, C programs can't have some of the arguments saved in one place and some saved in another – they must all be saved contiguously.

So in the standard calling convention of many modern machines the *calling* function reserves space for the register arguments in its own frame, next to the place where it writes argument $k+1$. But the calling function does not actually write anything there; that space is written into *by the called function*, and only if the called function needs to write arguments into memory for any reason.

A more dignified way to take the address of a local variable is to use *call-by-reference*. With call-by-reference, the programmer does not explicitly manipulate the address of a variable x. Instead, if x is passed as the argument to $f(y)$, where y is a "by-reference" parameter, the compiler generates code to pass the address of x instead of the contents of x. At any use of y within the function, the compiler generates an extra pointer dereference. With call-by-reference, there can be no "dangling reference," since y must disappear when f returns, and f returns before x's scope ends.

RETURN ADDRESSES

When function g calls function f, eventually f must return. It needs to know where to go back to. If the *call* instruction within g is at address a, then (usually) the right place to return to is $a+1$, the next instruction in g. This is called the *return address*.

On 1970s machines, the return address was pushed on the stack by the *call* instruction. Modern science has shown that it is faster and more flexible to pass the return address in a register, avoiding memory traffic and also avoiding the need to build any particular stack discipline into the hardware.

On modern machines, the *call* instruction merely puts the return address (the address of the instruction after the call) in a designated register. A non-leaf procedure will then have to write it to the stack (unless interprocedural register allocation is used), but a leaf procedure will not.

FRAME-RESIDENT VARIABLES

So a modern procedure-call convention will pass function parameters in registers, pass the return address in a register, and return the function result in a register. Many of the local variables will be allocated to registers, as will the intermediate results of expression evaluation. Values are written to memory (in the stack frame) only when necessary for one of these reasons:

- the variable will be passed by reference, so it must have a memory address (or, in the C language the & operator is anywhere applied to the variable);
- the variable is accessed by a procedure nested inside the current one;[2]
- the value is too big to fit into a single register;[3]
- the variable is an array, for which address arithmetic is necessary to extract components;
- the register holding the variable is needed for a specific purpose, such as parameter passing (as described above), though a compiler may move such values to other registers instead of storing them in memory;
- or there are so many local variables and temporary values that they won't all fit in registers, in which case some of them are "spilled" into the frame.

We will say that a variable *escapes* if it is passed by reference, its address is taken (using C's & operator), or it is accessed from a nested function.

When a formal parameter or local variable is declared, it's convenient to assign it a location – either in registers or in the stack frame – right at that point in processing the program. Then, when occurrences of that variable are found in expressions, they can be translated into machine code that refers to the right location. Unfortunately, the conditions in our list don't manifest themselves early enough. When the compiler first encounters the declaration of a variable, it doesn't yet know whether the variable will ever be passed by reference, accessed in a nested procedure, or have its address taken; and it doesn't know how many registers the calculation of expressions will require (it might be desirable to put some local variables in the frame instead of in registers). An industrial-strength compiler must assign provisional locations to all formals and locals, and decide later which of them should really go in registers.

STATIC LINKS

In languages that allow nested function declarations (such as Pascal, ML, and Java), the inner functions may use variables declared in outer functions. This language feature is called *block structure*. For example, consider Program 6.3, which is written with a Pascal-like syntax. The function write refers to the outer variable output, and indent refers to outer variables n and output. To make this work, the function indent must have access not only to its own frame (for variables i and s) but also to the frames of show (for variable n) and prettyprint (for variable output).

---

[2]However, with register allocation across function boundaries, local variables accessed by inner functions can sometimes go in registers, as long as the inner function knows where to look.

[3]However, some compilers spread out a large value into several registers for efficiency.

```
1      type tree = {key: string, left: tree, right: tree}
2
3      function prettyprint(tree: tree) : string =
4       let
5           var output := ""
6
7           function write(s: string) =
8               output := concat(output,s)
9
10          function show(n:int, t: tree) =
11            let function indent(s: string) =
12                      (for i := 1 to n
13                        do write(" ");
14                      output := concat(output,s); write("\n"))
15             in if t=nil then indent(".")
16                 else (indent(t.key);
17                      show(n+1,t.left);
18                      show(n+1,t.right))
19            end
20
21       in show(0,tree); output
22      end
```

PROGRAM 6.3.   Nested functions.

There are several methods to accomplish this:

- Whenever a function f is called, it can be passed a pointer to the frame of the function statically enclosing f; this pointer is the *static link*.
- A global array can be maintained, containing – in position i – a pointer to the frame of the most recently entered procedure whose *static nesting depth* is i. This array is called a *display*.
- When g calls f, each variable of g that is actually accessed by f (or by any function nested inside f) is passed to f as an extra argument. This is called *lambda lifting*.

We will describe in detail only the method of static links. Which method should be used in practice? See Exercise 6.6.

Whenever a function f is called, it is passed a pointer to the stack frame of the "current" (most recently entered) activation of the function g that *immediately encloses* f in the text of the program.

For example, in Program 6.3:

Line #

21 prettyprint calls show, passing prettyprint's own frame pointer as show's static link.

10 `show` stores its static link (the address of `prettyprint`'s frame) into its own frame.

15 `show` calls `indent`, passing its own frame pointer as `indent`'s static link.

17 `show` calls `show`, passing its own static link (not its own frame pointer) as the static link.

12 `indent` uses the value *n* from `show`'s frame. To do so, it fetches at an appropriate offset from `indent`'s static link (which points at the frame of `show`).

13 `indent` calls `write`. It must pass the frame pointer of `prettyprint` as the static link. To obtain this, it first fetches at an offset from its own static link (from `show`'s frame), the static link that had been passed to `show`.

14 `indent` uses the variable `output` from `prettyprint`'s frame. To do so it starts with its own static link, then fetches `show`'s, then fetches `output`.[4]

So on each procedure call or variable access, a chain of zero or more fetches is required; the length of the chain is just the *difference* in static nesting depth between the two functions involved.

<table><tr><td>**6.2**</td><td></td></tr></table>

FRAMES IN THE MiniJava COMPILER

What sort of stack frames should the MiniJava compiler use? Here we face the fact that every target-machine architecture will have a different standard stack frame layout. If we want MiniJava functions to be able to call C functions, we should use the standard layout. But we don't want the specifics of any particular machine intruding on the implementation of the translation module of the MiniJava compiler.

Thus we must use *abstraction*. Just as the `Symbol` module provides a clean interface, and hides the internal representation of `Symbol.Table` from its clients, we must use an abstract representation for frames.

The frame interface will look something like this:

```
package Frame;
import Temp.Temp; import Temp.Label;

public abstract class Access { ··· }
public abstract class AccessList {···head;···tail;··· }
```

---

[4]This program would be cleaner if `show` called `write` here instead of manipulating `output` directly, but it would not be as instructive.

```
public abstract class Frame {
   abstract public Frame newFrame(Label name,
                                  Util.BoolList formals);
            public Label name;
            public AccessList formals;
   abstract public Access allocLocal(boolean escape);
    /* ... other stuff, eventually ... */
}
```

The abstract class `Frame` is implemented by a module specific to the target machine. For example, if compiling to the MIPS architecture, there would be

```
package Mips;
class Frame extends Frame.Frame { ··· }
```

In general, we may assume that the machine-independent parts of the compiler have access to this implementation of `Frame`; for example,

```
// in class Main.Main:
Frame.Frame frame = new Mips.Frame(···);
```

In this way the rest of the compiler may access `frame` without knowing the identity of the target machine (except an occurrence of the word Mips here and there).

The class `Frame` holds information about formal parameters and local variables allocated in this frame. To make a new frame for a function f with k formal parameters, call `newFrame(`f, l`)`, where l is a list of k booleans: `true` for each parameter that escapes and `false` for each parameter that does not. (In MiniJava, no parameters ever escape.) The result will be a `Frame` object. For example, consider a three-argument function named g whose first argument escapes (needs to be kept in memory). Then

```
frame.newFrame(g, new BoolList(true,
                  new BoolList(false,
                    new BoolList(false, null))))
```

returns a new frame object.

The `Access` class describes formals and locals that may be in the frame or in registers. This is an *abstract data type*, so its implementation as a pair of subclasses is visible only inside the `Frame` module:

```
package Mips;
class InFrame extends Frame.Access {int offset; ··· }
class InReg   extends Frame.Access {Temp temp; ··· }
```

InFrame(X) indicates a memory location at offset X from the frame pointer; InReg(t_{84}) indicates that it will be held in "register" t_{84}. Frame.Access is an abstract data type, so outside of the module the InFrame and InReg constructors are not visible. Other modules manipulate accesses using interface functions to be described in the next chapter.

The formals field is a list of k "accesses" denoting the locations where the formal parameters will be kept at run time, as seen from inside the callee. Parameters may be seen differently by the caller and the callee. For example, if parameters are passed on the stack, the caller may put a parameter at offset 4 from the stack pointer, but the callee sees it at offset 4 from the frame pointer. Or the caller may put a parameter into register 6, but the callee may want to move it out of the way and always access it from register 13. On the Sparc architecture, with register windows, the caller puts a parameter into register o1, but the save instruction shifts register windows so the callee sees this parameter in register i1.

Because this "shift of view" depends on the calling conventions of the target machine, it must be handled by the Frame module, starting with new-Frame. For each formal parameter, newFrame must calculate two things:

- How the parameter will be seen from inside the function (in a register, or in a frame location).
- What instructions must be produced to implement the "view shift."

For example, a frame-resident parameter will be seen as "memory at offset X from the frame pointer," and the view shift will be implemented by copying the stack pointer to the frame pointer on entry to the procedure.

REPRESENTATION OF FRAME DESCRIPTIONS
The implementation module Frame is supposed to keep the representation of Frame objects secret from any clients of the Frame module. But really it's an object holding:

- the locations of all the formals,
- instructions required to implement the "view shift,"
- the number of locals allocated so far,
- and the label at which the function's machine code is to begin (see page 131).

Table 6.4 shows the formals of the three-argument function g (see page 127) as newFrame would allocate them on three different architectures: the Pentium, MIPS, and Sparc. The first parameter escapes, so it needs to be InFrame

		Pentium	MIPS	Sparc
	1	InFrame(8)	InFrame(0)	InFrame(68)
Formals	2	InFrame(12)	InReg(t_{157})	InReg(t_{157})
	3	InFrame(16)	InReg(t_{158})	InReg(t_{158})
View		$M[\text{sp} + 0] \leftarrow \text{fp}$	$\text{sp} \leftarrow \text{sp} - K$	save %sp,-K,%sp
Shift		$\text{fp} \leftarrow \text{sp}$	$M[\text{sp} + K + 0] \leftarrow \text{r4}$	$M[\text{fp} + 68] \leftarrow \text{i0}$
		$\text{sp} \leftarrow \text{sp} - K$	$t_{157} \leftarrow \text{r5}$	$t_{157} \leftarrow \text{i1}$
			$t_{158} \leftarrow \text{r6}$	$t_{158} \leftarrow \text{i2}$

TABLE 6.4. Formal parameters for $g(x_1, x_2, x_3)$ where x_1 escapes.

on all three machines. The remaining parameters are InFrame on the Pentium, but InReg on the other machines.

The freshly created temporaries t_{157} and t_{158}, and the *move* instructions that copy r4 and r5 into them (or on the Sparc, i1 and i2), may seem superfluous. Why shouldn't the body of g just access these formals directly from the registers in which they arrive? To see why not, consider

```
void m(int x, int y) { h(y,y); h(x,x); }
```

If x stays in "parameter register 1" throughout m, and y is passed to h in parameter register 1, then there is a problem.

The register allocator will eventually choose which machine register should hold t_{157}. If there is no interference of the type shown in function m, then (on the MIPS) the allocator will take care to choose register r4 to hold t_{157} and r5 to hold t_{158}. Then the *move* instructions will be unnecessary and will be deleted at that time.

See also pages 157 and 251 for more discussion of the view shift.

LOCAL VARIABLES

Some local variables are kept in the frame; others are kept in registers. To allocate a new local variable in a frame f, the translation phase calls

```
f.allocLocal(false)
```

This returns an InFrame access with an offset from the frame pointer. For example, to allocate two local variables on the Sparc, allocLocal would be called twice, returning successively InFrame(-4) and InFrame(-8), which are standard Sparc frame-pointer offsets for local variables.

The boolean argument to `allocLocal` specifies whether the new variable escapes and needs to go in the frame; if it is false, then the variable can be allocated in a register. Thus, `f.allocLocal(false)` might create `InReg(`t_{481}`)`.

For MiniJava, that no variables escape. This is because in MiniJava:

- there is no nesting of classes and methods;
- it is not possible to take the address of a variable;
- integers and booleans are passed by value; and
- objects, including integer arrays, can be represented as pointers that are also passed by value.

The calls to `allocLocal` need not come immediately after the frame is created. In many languages, there may be variable-declaration blocks nested inside the body of a function. For example,

```
void f()
{int v=6;
 print(v);
 {int v=7;
  print(v);
 }
 print(v);
 {int v=8;
  print(v);
 }
 print(v);
}
```

In this case there are three different variables v. The program will print the sequence 6 7 6 8 6. As each variable declaration is encountered in processing the program, we will allocate a temporary or new space in the frame, associated with the name v. As each `end` (or closing brace) is encountered, the association with v will be forgotten – but the space is still reserved in the frame. Thus, there will be a distinct temporary or frame slot for every variable declared within the entire function.

The register allocator will use as few registers as possible to represent the temporaries. In this example, the second and third v variables (initialized to 7 and 8) could be held in the same register. A clever compiler might also optimize the size of the frame by noticing when two frame-resident variables could be allocated to the same slot.

TEMPORARIES AND LABELS

The compiler's translation phase will want to choose registers for parameters and local variables, and choose machine-code addresses for procedure bodies. But it is too early to determine exactly which registers are available, or exactly where a procedure body will be located. We use the word *temporary* to mean a value that is temporarily held in a register, and the word *label* to mean some machine-language location whose exact address is yet to be determined – just like a label in assembly language.

Temps are abstract names for local variables; labels are abstract names for static memory addresses. The Temp module manages these two distinct sets of names.

```
package Temp;
public class Temp {
  public String toString();
  public Temp();
}
public class Label {
  public String toString();
  public Label();
  public Label(String s);
  public Label(Symbol s);
}
public class TempList  {···}
public class LabelList {···}
```

new Temp.Temp() returns a new temporary from an infinite set of temps. new Temp.Label() returns a new label from an infinite set of labels. And new Temp.Label(*string*) returns a new label whose assembly-language name is *string*.

When processing the declaration m(···), a label for the address of m's machine code can be produced by new Temp.Label(). It's tempting to call new Temp.Label("m") instead – the assembly-language program will be easier to debug if it uses the label m instead of L213 – but unfortunately there could be two different methods named m in different classes. A better idea is to call new Temp.Label("C"+"$"+"m"), where C is the name of the class in which the method m occurs.

MANAGING STATIC LINKS

The Frame module should be independent of the specific source language being compiled. Many source languages, including MiniJava, do not have nested function declarations; thus, Frame should not know anything about static links. Instead, this is the responsibility of the translation phase. The translation phase would know that each frame contains a static link. The static link `would be` passed to a function in a register and stored into the frame. Since the static link behaves so much like a formal parameter, we can treat it as one (as much as possible).

PROGRAM   FRAMES

If you are compiling for the Sparc, implement the `Sparc` package containing `Sparc/SparcFrame.java`. If compiling for the MIPS, implement the `Mips` package, and so on.

If you are working on a RISC machine (such as MIPS or Sparc) that passes the first k parameters in registers and the rest in memory, keep things simple by handling *only* the case where there are k or fewer parameters.

Supporting files available in `$MINIJAVA/chap6` include:

`Temp/*` The module supporting temporaries and labels.
`Util/BoolList.java` The class for lists of booleans.

Optional: Handle functions with more than k formal parameters.

FURTHER READING

The use of a single contiguous stack to hold variables and return addresses dates from Lisp [McCarthy 1960] and Algol [Naur et al. 1963]. Block structure (the nesting of functions) and the use of static links are also from Algol.

Computers and compilers of the 1960s and '70s kept most program variables in memory, so that there was less need to worry about which variables escaped (needed addresses). The VAX, built in 1978, had a procedure-call instruction that assumed all arguments were pushed on the stack, and itself pushed program counter, frame pointer, argument pointer, argument count, and callee-save register mask on the stack [Leonard 1987].

With the RISC revolution [Patterson 1985] came the idea that procedure calling can be done with much less memory traffic. Local variables should be kept in registers by default; storing and fetching should be done *as needed*, driven by "spilling" in the register allocator [Chaitin 1982].

Most procedures don't have more than five arguments and five local variables [Tanenbaum 1978]. To take advantage of this, Chow et al. [1986] and

Hopkins [1986] designed calling conventions optimized for the common case: The first four arguments are passed in registers, with the (rare) extra arguments passed in memory; compilers use both caller- and callee-save registers for local variables; leaf procedures don't even need stack frames of their own if they can operate within the caller-save registers; and even the return address need not always be pushed on the stack.

EXERCISES

6.1 Using the C compiler of your choice (or a compiler for another language), compile some small test functions into assembly language. On Unix this is usually done by `cc -S`. Turn on all possible compiler optimizations. Then evaluate the compiled programs by these criteria:

a. Are local variables kept in registers?

b. If local variable b is live across more than one procedure call, is it kept in a callee-save register? Explain how doing this would speed up the following program:

```
int f(int a) {int b; b=a+1; g(); h(b); return b+2;}
```

c. If local variable x is never live across a procedure call, is it properly kept in a caller-save register? Explain how doing this would speed up the following program:

```
void h(int y) {int x; x=y+1; f(y); f(2);}
```

6.2 If you have a C compiler that passes parameters in registers, make it generate assembly language for this function:

```
extern void h(int, int);
void m(int x, int y) {h(y,y); h(x,x);}
```

Clearly, if arguments to $m(x, y)$ arrive in registers r_{arg1} and r_{arg2}, and arguments to h must be passed in r_{arg1} and r_{arg2}, then x cannot stay in r_{arg1} during the marshalling of arguments to $h(y, y)$. Explain when and how your C compiler moves x out of the r_{arg1} register so as to call $h(y, y)$.

6.3 For each of the variables a, b, c, d, e in this C program, say whether the variable should be kept in memory or a register, and why.

```
int f(int a, int b)
{ int c[3], d, e;
  d=a+1;
  e=g(c, &b);
  return e+c[1]+b;
}
```

*6.4 How much memory should this program use?

```
int f(int i) {int j,k; j=i*i; k=i?f(i-1):0; return k+j;}
void main() {f(100000);}
```

a. Imagine a compiler that passes parameters in registers, wastes no space providing "backup storage" for parameters passed in registers, does not use static links, and in general makes stack frames as small as possible. How big should each stack frame for f be, in words?

b. What is the maximum memory use of this program, with such a compiler?

c. Using your favorite C compiler, compile this program to assembly language and report the size of f's stack frame.

d. Calculate the total memory use of this program with the real C compiler.

e. Quantitatively and comprehensively explain the discrepancy between (a) and (c).

f. Comment on the likelihood that the designers of this C compiler considered deeply recursive functions important in real programs.

*6.5 Instead of (or in addition to) using static links, there are other ways of getting access to nonlocal variables. One way is just to leave the variable in a register!

```
function f() : int =
  let var a := 5
      function g() : int =
          (a+1)
   in g()+g()
  end
```

If a is left in register r_7 (for example) while g is called, then g can just access it from there.

What properties must a local variable, the function in which it is defined, and the functions in which it is used, have for this trick to work?

*6.6 A *display* is a data structure that may be used as an alternative to static links for maintaining access to nonlocal variables. It is an array of frame pointers, indexed by static nesting depth. Element D_i of the display always points to the most recently called function whose static nesting depth is i.

The bookkeeping performed by a function f, whose static nesting depth is i, looks like:

Copy D_i to *save location* in stack frame
Copy frame pointer to D_i
   $\cdots$ body of f $\cdots$
Copy *save location* back to D_i

In Program 6.3, function `prettyprint` is at depth 1, `write` and `show` are at depth 2, and so on.

a. Show the sequence of machine instructions required to fetch the variable `output` into a register at line 14 of Program 6.3, using static links.

b. Show the machine instructions required if a display were used instead.

c. When variable x is declared at depth d_1 and accessed at depth d_2, how many instructions does the static-link method require to fetch x?

d. How many does the display method require?

e. How many instructions does static-link maintenance require for a procedure entry and exit (combined)?

f. How many instructions does display maintenance require for procedure entry and exit?

Should we use displays instead of static links? Perhaps; but the issue is more complicated. For languages such as Pascal with block structure but no function variables, displays work well.

But the full expressive power of block structure is obtained when functions can be returned as results of other functions, as in Scheme and ML. For such languages, there are more issues to consider than just variable-access time and procedure entry-exit cost: there is closure-building cost, and the problem of avoiding useless data kept live in closures. Chapter 15 explains some of the issues.

7

Translation to Intermediate Code

trans-late: to turn into one's own or another language

Webster's Dictionary

The semantic analysis phase of a compiler must translate abstract syntax into abstract machine code. It can do this after type-checking, or at the same time.

Though it is possible to translate directly to real machine code, this hinders portability and modularity. Suppose we want compilers for N different source languages, targeted to M different machines. In principle this is $N \cdot M$ compilers (Figure 7.1a), a large implementation task.

An *intermediate representation* (IR) is a kind of abstract machine language that can express the target-machine operations without committing to too much machine-specific detail. But it is also independent of the details of the source language. The *front end* of the compiler does lexical analysis, parsing, semantic analysis, and translation to intermediate representation. The *back end* does optimization of the intermediate representation and translation to machine language.

A portable compiler translates the source language into IR and then translates the IR into machine language, as illustrated in Figure 7.1b. Now only N front ends and M back ends are required. Such an implementation task is more reasonable.

Even when only one front end and one back end are being built, a good IR can modularize the task, so that the front end is not complicated with machine-specific details, and the back end is not bothered with information specific to one source language. Many different kinds of IR are used in compilers; for this compiler we have chosen simple expression trees.

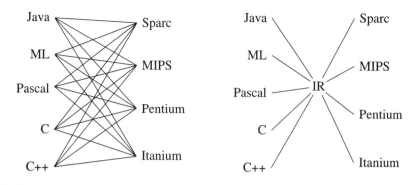

FIGURE 7.1. Compilers for five languages and four target machines: (a) without an IR, (b) with an IR.

7.1 INTERMEDIATE REPRESENTATION TREES

The intermediate representation tree language is defined by the package `Tree`, containing abstract classes `Stm` and `Exp` and their subclasses, as shown in Figure 7.2.

A good intermediate representation has several qualities:

- It must be convenient for the semantic analysis phase to produce.
- It must be convenient to translate into real machine language, for all the desired target machines.
- Each construct must have a clear and simple meaning, so that optimizing transformations that rewrite the intermediate representation can easily be specified and implemented.

Individual pieces of abstract syntax can be complicated things, such as array subscripts, procedure calls, and so on. And individual "real machine" instructions can also have a complicated effect (though this is less true of modern RISC machines than of earlier architectures). Unfortunately, it is not always the case that complex pieces of the abstract syntax correspond exactly to the complex instructions that a machine can execute.

Therefore, the intermediate representation should have individual components that describe only extremely simple things: a single fetch, store, add, move, or jump. Then any "chunky" piece of abstract syntax can be translated into just the right set of abstract machine instructions; and groups of abstract machine instructions can be clumped together (perhaps in quite different clumps) to form "real" machine instructions.

```
package Tree;

abstract class Exp
 CONST(int value)
 NAME(Label label)
 TEMP(Temp.Temp temp)
 BINOP(int binop, Exp left, Exp right)
 MEM(Exp exp)
 CALL(Exp func, ExpList args)
 ESEQ(Stm stm, Exp exp)

abstract class Stm
 MOVE(Exp dst, Exp src)
 EXP(Exp exp)
 JUMP(Exp exp, Temp.LabelList targets)
 CJUMP(int relop, Exp left, Exp right, Label iftrue, Label iffalse)
 SEQ(Stm left, Stm right)
 LABEL(Label label)
```

other classes:
ExpList(Exp head, ExpList tail)
StmList(Stm head, StmList tail)

other constants:
```
final static int BINOP.PLUS, BINOP.MINUS, BINOP.MUL, BINOP.DIV, BINOP.AND,
    BINOP.OR, BINOP.LSHIFT, BINOP.RSHIFT, BINOP.ARSHIFT, BINOP.XOR;

final static int CJUMP.EQ, CJUMP.NE, CJUMP.LT, CJUMP.GT, CJUMP.LE,
        CJUMP.GE, CJUMP.ULT, CJUMP.ULE, CJUMP.UGT, CJUMP.UGE;
```

FIGURE 7.2.   Intermediate representation trees.

Here is a description of the meaning of each tree operator. First, the expressions (Exp), which stand for the computation of some value (possibly with side effects):

CONST(i) The integer constant i.

NAME(n) The symbolic constant n (corresponding to an assembly language label).

TEMP(t) Temporary t. A temporary in the abstract machine is similar to a register in a real machine. However, the abstract machine has an infinite number of temporaries.

BINOP(o, e_1, e_2) The application of binary operator o to operands e_1, e_2. Subexpression e_1 is evaluated before e_2. The integer arithmetic operators are PLUS, MINUS, MUL, DIV; the integer bitwise logical operators are AND, OR, XOR; the integer logical shift operators are LSHIFT, RSHIFT; the integer arithmetic right-shift is ARSHIFT. The MiniJava language has only one logical operator, but the intermediate language is meant to be independent of any source language; also, the logical operators might be used in implementing other features of MiniJava.

MEM(e) The contents of *wordSize* bytes of memory starting at address e (where *wordSize* is defined in the `Frame` module). Note that when MEM is used as the left child of a MOVE, it means "store," but anywhere else it means "fetch."

CALL(f, l) A procedure call: the application of function f to argument list l. The subexpression f is evaluated before the arguments which are evaluated left to right.

ESEQ(s, e) The statement s is evaluated for side effects, then e is evaluated for a result.

The statements (`stm`) of the tree language perform side effects and control flow:

MOVE(TEMP t, e) Evaluate e and move it into temporary t.

MOVE(MEM(e_1), e_2) Evaluate e_1, yielding address a. Then evaluate e_2, and store the result into *wordSize* bytes of memory starting at a.

EXP(e) Evaluate e and discard the result.

JUMP($e, labs$) Transfer control (jump) to address e. The destination e may be a literal label, as in NAME(lab), or it may be an address calculated by any other kind of expression. For example, a C-language `switch(i)` statement may be implemented by doing arithmetic on i. The list of labels `labs` specifies all the possible locations that the expression e can evaluate to; this is necessary for dataflow analysis later. The common case of jumping to a known label l is written as JUMP(NAME l, new `LabelList`(l, `null`)), but the JUMP class has an extra constructor so that this can be abbreviated as JUMP(l).

CJUMP(o, e_1, e_2, t, f) Evaluate e_1, e_2 in that order, yielding values a, b. Then compare a, b using the relational operator o. If the result is `true`, jump to t; otherwise jump to f. The relational operators are EQ and NE for integer equality and nonequality (signed or unsigned); signed integer inequalities LT, GT, LE, GE; and unsigned integer inequalities ULT, ULE, UGT, UGE.

SEQ(s_1, s_2) The statement s_1 followed by s_2.

LABEL(n) Define the constant value of name n to be the current machine code address. This is like a label definition in assembly language. The value NAME(n) may be the target of jumps, calls, etc.

It is almost possible to give a formal semantics to the `Tree` language. However, there is no provision in this language for procedure and function definitions – we can specify only the body of each function. The procedure entry and exit sequences will be added later as special "glue" that is different for each target machine.

7.2 TRANSLATION INTO TREES

Translation of abstract syntax expressions into intermediate trees is reasonably straightforward; but there are many cases to handle. We will cover the translation of various language constructs, including many from MiniJava.

KINDS OF EXPRESSIONS

The MiniJava grammar has clearly distinguished statements and expressions. However, in languages such as C, the distinction is blurred; for example, an assignment in C can be used as an expression. When translating such languages, we will have to ask the following question. What should the representation of an abstract-syntax expression be in the `Tree` language? At first it seems obvious that it should be `Tree.Exp`. However, this is true only for certain kinds of expressions, the ones that compute a value. Expressions that return no value are more naturally represented by `Tree.Stm`. And expressions with boolean values, such as $a > b$, might best be represented as a conditional jump – a combination of `Tree.Stm` and a pair of destinations represented by `Temp.Label`s.

It is better instead to ask, "how might the expression be used?" Then we can make the right kind of *methods* for an object-oriented interface to expressions. Both for MiniJava and other languages, we end up with `Translate.Exp`, not the same class as `Tree.Exp`, having three methods:

```
package Translate;
public abstract class Exp {
   abstract Tree.Exp unEx();
   abstract Tree.Stm unNx();
   abstract Tree.Stm unCx(Temp.Label t, Temp.Label f);
}
```

Ex stands for an "expression," represented as a `Tree.Exp`.

Nx stands for "no result," represented as a `Tree` statement.

Cx stands for "conditional," represented as a function from label-pair to statement. If you pass it a true destination and a false destination, it will make a statement that evaluates some conditionals and then jumps to one of the destinations (the statement will never "fall through").

For example, the MiniJava statement

```
if (a<b && c<d) {
      // true block
}
else {
      // false block
}
```

might translate to a `Translate.Exp` whose `unCx` method is roughly like

```
Tree.Stm unCx(Label t, Label f) {
  Label z = new Label();
  return new SEQ(new CJUMP(CJUMP.LT,a,b,z,f),
             new SEQ(new LABEL(z),
                 new CJUMP(CJUMP.LT,c,d,t,f)));
}
```

The abstract class `Translate.Exp` can be instantiated by several subclasses: `Ex` for an ordinary expression that yields a single value, `Nx` for an expression that yields no value, and `Cx` for a "conditional" expression that jumps to either t or f:

```
class Ex extends Exp {
   Tree.Exp exp;
   Ex(Tree.Exp e) {exp=e;}
   Tree.Exp unEx() {return exp;}
   Tree.Stm unNx() { ···?··· }
   Tree.Stm unCx(Label t, Label f) { ···?··· }
}
class Nx extends Exp {
   Tree.Stm stm;
   Nx(Tree.Stm s) {stm=s;}
   Tree.Exp unEx() { ···?··· }
   Tree.Stm unNx() {return stm;}
   Tree.Stm unCx(Label t, Label f) { ···?··· }
}
```

But what does the `unNx` method of an `Ex` do? We have a simple `Tree.Exp` that yields a value, and we are asked to produce a `Tree.Stm` that produces no value. There is a conversion operator `Tree.EXP`, and `unNx` must apply it:

```
class Ex extends Exp {
  Tree.Exp exp;
   ⋮
  Tree.Stm unNx() {return new Tree.EXP(exp); }
   ⋮
}
```

```
abstract class Cx extends Exp {
  Tree.Exp unEx() {
    Temp r = new Temp();
    Label t = new Label();
    Label f = new Label();

    return new Tree.ESEQ(
            new Tree.SEQ(new Tree.MOVE(new Tree.TEMP(r),
                                       new Tree.CONST(1)),
                new Tree.SEQ(unCx(t,f),
                  new Tree.SEQ(new Tree.LABEL(f),
                    new Tree.SEQ(new Tree.MOVE(new Tree.TEMP(r),
                                               new Tree.CONST(0)),
                      new Tree.LABEL(t))))),
                new Tree.TEMP(r));
  }

  abstract Tree.Stm unCx(Label t, Label f);

  Tree.Stm unNx() { ··· }
}
```

PROGRAM 7.3. The Cx class.

Each kind of `Translate.Exp` class must have similar conversion methods. For example, the MiniJava statement

```
flag = (a<b && c<d);
```

requires the `unEx` method of a `Cx` object so that a 1 (for true) or 0 (for false) can be stored into `flag`.

Program 7.3 shows the class `Cx`. The `unEx` method is of particular interest. To convert a "conditional" into a "value expression," we invent a new temporary r and new labels t and f. Then we make a `Tree.Stm` that moves the value 1 into r, and a conditional jump $unCx(t, f)$ that implements the conditional. If the condition is false, then 0 is moved into r; if it is true, then execution proceeds at t and the second move is skipped. The result of the whole thing is just the temporary r containing zero or one.

The `unCx` method is still abstract: We will discuss this later, with the translation of comparison operators. But the `unEx` and `unNx` methods can still be implemented in terms of the `unCx` method. We have shown `unEx`; we will leave `unNx` (which is simpler) as an exercise.

The `unCx` method of class `Ex` is left as an exercise. It's helpful to have `unCx` treat the cases of CONST 0 and CONST 1 specially, since they have particularly simple and efficient translations. Class Nx's unEx and unCx methods need not be implemented, since these cases should never occur in compiling a well-typed MiniJava program.

SIMPLE VARIABLES

For a simple variable v declared in the current procedure's stack frame, we translate it as

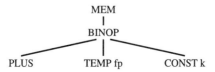

MEM(BINOP(PLUS, TEMP fp, CONST k))

where k is the offset of v within the frame and TEMP fp is the frame-pointer register. For the MiniJava compiler we make the simplifying assumption that all variables are the same size – the natural word size of the machine.

The Frame class holds all machine-dependent definitions; here we add to it a frame-pointer register FP and a constant whose value is the machine's natural word size:

```
package Frame;
public class Frame {
    :
    abstract public Temp FP();
    abstract public int wordSize();
}
public abstract class Access {
    public abstract Tree.Exp exp(Tree.Exp framePtr);
}
```

In this and later chapters, we will abbreviate BINOP(PLUS, e_1, e_2) as $+(e_1, e_2)$, so the tree above would be shown as

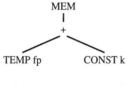

$+$(TEMP fp, CONST k)

The `exp` method of `Frame.Access` is used by `Translate` to turn a `Frame.Access` into the `Tree` expression. The `Tree.Exp` argument is the address of the stack frame that the `Access` lives in. Thus, for an access a such as $\text{InFrame}(k)$, we have

```
a.exp(new TEMP(frame.FP())) =
            MEM(BINOP(PLUS,TEMP(frame.FP()),CONST(k)))
```

If a is a register access such as $\text{InReg}(t_{832})$, then the frame-address argument to `a.exp()` will be discarded, and the result will be simply TEMP t_{832}.

An l-value such as v or $a[i]$ or $p.next$ can appear either on the left side or the right side of an assignment statement – l stands for *left*, to distinguish from r-values, which can appear only on the right side of an assignment. Fortunately, both MEM and TEMP nodes can appear on the left of a MOVE node.

ARRAY VARIABLES

For the rest of this chapter we will not specify all the interface functions of `Translate`, as we have done for `simpleVar`. But the rule of thumb just given applies to all of them: There should be a `Translate` function to handle array subscripts, one for record fields, one for each kind of expression, and so on.

Different programming languages treat array-valued variables differently.

In Pascal, an array variable stands for the contents of the array – in this case all 12 integers. The Pascal program

```
var a,b : array[1..12] of integer
begin
      a := b
end;
```

copies the contents of array a into array b.

In C, there is no such thing as an array variable. There are pointer variables; arrays are like "pointer constants." Thus, this is illegal:

```
{int a[12], b[12];
 a = b;
}
```

but this is quite legal:

```
{int a[12], *b;
 b = a;
}
```

The statement b = a does not copy the elements of *a*; instead, it means that *b* now points to the beginning of the array *a*.

In MiniJava (as in Java and ML), array variables behave like pointers. MiniJava has no named array constants as in C, however. Instead, new array values are created (and initialized) by the construct new int[n]; where *n* is the number of elements, and 0 is the initial value of each element. In the program

```
int [] a;
a = new int[12];
b = new int[12];
a = b;
```

the array variable *a* ends up pointing to the same 12 zeros as the variable *b*; the original 12 zeros allocated for *a* are discarded.

MiniJava objects are also pointers. Object assignment, like array assignment, is pointer assignment and does not copy all the fields (see below). This is also true of other object-oriented and functional programming languages, which try to blur the syntactic distinction between pointers and objects. In C or Pascal, however, a record value is "big," and record assignment means copying all the fields.

STRUCTURED *L*-VALUES

An *l*-value is the result of an expression that can occur on the *left* of an assignment statement, such as x or p.y or a[i+2]. An *r*-value is one that can only appear on the *right* of an assignment, such as a+3 or f(x). That is, an *l*-value denotes a *location* that can be assigned to, and an *r*-value does not.

Of course, an *l*-value can occur on the right of an assignment statement; in this case the *contents* of the location are implicitly taken.

We say that an integer or pointer value is a "scalar," since it has only one component. Such a value occupies just one word of memory and can fit in a register. All the variables and *l*-values in MiniJava are scalar. Even a MiniJava array or object variable is really a pointer (a kind of scalar); the *Java Language Reference Manual* may not say so explicitly, because it is talking about Java semantics instead of Java implementation.

In C or Pascal there are structured *l*-values – structs in C, arrays and records in Pascal – that are not scalar. To implement a language with "large" variables such as the arrays and records in C or Pascal requires a bit of extra work. In a C compiler, the access type would require information about the size of the variable. Then, the MEM operator of the TREE intermediate language would need to be extended with a notion of size:

```
package Tree;
abstract class Exp
 MEM(Exp exp, int size)
```

The translation of a local variable into an IR tree would look like

$$\text{MEM}(+(\text{TEMP fp}, \text{ CONST } k_n), \ S)$$

where the S indicates the size of the object to be fetched or stored (depending on whether this tree appears on the left or right of a MOVE).

Leaving out the size on MEM nodes makes the MiniJava compiler easier to implement, but limits the generality of its intermediate representation.

SUBSCRIPTING AND FIELD SELECTION

To subscript an array in Pascal or C (to compute $a[i]$), just calculate the address of the ith element of a: $(i-l) \times s + a$, where l is the lower bound of the index range, s is the size (in bytes) of each array element, and a is the base address of the array elements. If a is global, with a compile-time constant address, then the subtraction $a - s \times l$ can be done at compile time.

Similarly, to select field f of a record l-value a (to calculate $a.f$), simply add the constant field offset of f to the address a.

An array variable a is an l-value; so is an array subscript expression $a[i]$, even if i is not an l-value. To calculate the l-value $a[i]$ from a, we do arithmetic on the address of a. Thus, in a Pascal compiler, the translation of an l-value (particularly a structured l-value) should *not* be something like

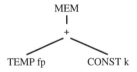

but should instead be the `Tree` expression representing the base address of the array:

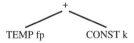

What could happen to this l-value?

- A particular element might be subscripted, yielding a (smaller) *l*-value. A "+" node would add the index times the element size to the *l*-value for the base of the array.
- The *l*-value (representing the entire array) might be used in a context where an *r*-value is required (e.g., passed as a by-value parameter, or assigned to another array variable). Then the *l*-value is *coerced* into an *r*-value by applying the MEM operator to it.

In the MiniJava language, there are no structured, or "large," *l*-values. This is because all object and array values are really pointers to object and array structures. The "base address" of the array is really the contents of a pointer variable, so MEM is required to fetch this base address.

Thus, if *a* is a memory-resident array variable represented as MEM(*e*), then the contents of address *e* will be a one-word pointer value *p*. The contents of addresses p, $p + W$, $p + 2W$, ... (where *W* is the word size) will be the elements of the array (all elements are one word long). Thus, *a*[*i*] is just

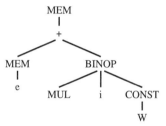

$$\text{MEM}(+(\text{MEM}(e), \text{BINOP}(\text{MUL}, i, \text{CONST } W)))$$

***l*-values and MEM nodes.** Technically, an *l*-value (or *assignable variable*) should be represented as an *address* (without the top MEM node in the diagram above). Converting an *l*-value to an *r*-value (when it is used in an expression) means *fetching* from that address; assigning to an *l*-value means *storing* to that address. We are attaching the MEM node to the *l*-value before knowing whether it is to be fetched or stored; this works only because in the `Tree` intermediate representation, MEM means both *store* (when used as the left child of a MOVE) and *fetch* (when used elsewhere).

A SERMON ON SAFETY

Life is too short to spend time chasing down irreproducible bugs, and money is too valuable to waste on the purchase of flaky software. When a program has a bug, it should detect that fact as soon as possible and announce that fact (or take corrective action) before the bug causes any harm.

Some bugs are very subtle. But it should not take a genius to detect an out-of-bounds array subscript: If the array bounds are $L..H$, and the subscript is i, then $i < L$ or $i > H$ is an array bounds error. Furthermore, computers are well-equipped with hardware able to compute the condition $i > H$. For several decades now, we have known that compilers can automatically emit the code to test this condition. There is no excuse for a compiler that is unable to emit code for checking array bounds. Optimizing compilers can often *safely* remove the checks by compile-time analysis; see Section 18.4.

One might say, by way of excuse, "but the language in which I program has the kind of address arithmetic that makes it impossible to know the bounds of an array." Yes, and the man who shot his mother and father threw himself upon the mercy of the court because he was an orphan.

In some rare circumstances, a portion of a program demands blinding speed, and the timing budget does not allow for bounds checking. In such a case, it would be best if the optimizing compiler could analyze the subscript expressions and prove that the index will always be within bounds, so that an explicit bounds check is not necessary. If that is not possible, perhaps it is reasonable in these rare cases to allow the programmer to explicitly specify an unchecked subscript operation. But this does not excuse the compiler from checking all the other subscript expressions in the program.

Needless to say, the compiler should check pointers for `nil` before dereferencing them, too.[1]

ARITHMETIC

Integer arithmetic is easy to translate: Each arithmetic operator corresponds to a `Tree` operator.

The `Tree` language has no unary arithmetic operators. Unary negation of integers can be implemented as subtraction from zero; unary complement can be implemented as XOR with all ones.

Unary floating-point negation cannot be implemented as subtraction from zero, because many floating-point representations allow a *negative zero*. The negation of negative zero is positive zero, and vice versa. Thus, the `Tree` language does not support unary negation very well.

Fortunately, the MiniJava language doesn't support floating-point numbers; but in a real compiler, a new operator would have to be added for floating negation.

---

[1] A different way of checking for `nil` is to unmap page 0 in the virtual-memory page tables, so that attempting to fetch/store fields of a `nil` record results in a page fault.

CONDITIONALS

The result of a comparison operator will be a Cx expression: a statement s that will jump to any true-destination and false-destination you specify.

Making "simple" Cx expressions from comparison operators is easy with the CJUMP operator. However, the whole point of the Cx representation is that conditional expressions can be combined easily with the MiniJava operator &&. Therefore, an expression such as x<5 will be translated as $Cx(s_1)$, where

$$s_1(t, f) = \text{CJUMP}(\text{LT}, x, \text{CONST}(5), t, f)$$

for any labels t and f.

To do this, we extend the Cx class to make a subclass RelCx that has private fields to hold the left and right expressions (in this case x and 5) and the comparison operator (in this case Tree.CJUMP.LT). Then we override the unCx method to generate the CJUMP from these data. It is not necessary to make unEx and unNx methods, since these will be inherited from the parent Cx class.

The most straightforward thing to do with an if-expression

if e_1 then e_2 else e_3

is to treat e_1 as a Cx expression, and e_2 and e_3 as Ex expressions. That is, use the unCx method of e_1 and the unEx of e_2 and e_3. Make two labels t and f to which the conditional will branch. Allocate a temporary r, and after label t, move e_2 to r; after label f, move e_3 to r. Both branches should finish by jumping to a newly created "join" label.

This will produce perfectly correct results. However, the translated code may not be very efficient at all. If e_2 and e_3 are both "statements" (expressions that return no value), then their representation is likely to be Nx, not Ex. Applying unEx to them will work – a coercion will automatically be applied – but it might be better to recognize this case specially.

Even worse, if e_2 or e_3 is a Cx expression, then applying the unEx coercion to it will yield a horrible tangle of jumps and labels. It is much better to recognize this case specially.

For example, consider

if $x < 5$ then $a > b$ else 0

As shown above, $x < 5$ translates into $Cx(s_1)$; similarly, $a > b$ will be translated as $Cx(s_2)$ for some s_2. The whole if-statement should come out approximately as

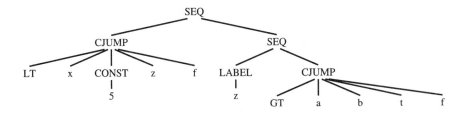

$$\text{SEQ}(s_1(z, f), \ \text{SEQ}(\text{LABEL } z, s_2(t, f)))$$

for some new label z.

Therefore, the translation of an **if** requires a new subclass of Exp:

```
class IfThenElseExp extends Exp {
    Exp cond, a, b;
    Label t = new Label();
    Label f = new Label();
    Label join = new Label();
    IfThenElseExp(Exp cc, Exp aa, Exp bb) {
            cond=cc; a=aa; b=bb;
    }
    Tree.Stm unCx(Label tt, Label ff) {  ···  }
    Tree.Exp unEx() {  ···  }
    Tree.Stm unNx() {  ···  }
}
```

The labels t and f indicate the beginning of the then-clause and else-clause, respectively. The labels tt and ff are quite different: These are the places to which conditions inside the then-clause (or else-clause) must jump, depending on the truth of those subexpressions.

STRINGS

A string literal is typically implemented as the constant address of a segment of memory initialized to the proper characters. In assembly language, a label is used to refer to this address from the middle of some sequence of instructions. At some other place in the assembly-language program, the *definition* of that label appears, followed by the assembly-language pseudo-instruction to reserve and initialize a block of memory to the appropriate characters.

For each string literal lit, a translator must make a new label lab, and return the tree Tree.NAME(lab). It should also put the assembly-language fragment frame.string(lab,lit) onto a global list of such fragments to be handed to the code emitter. "Fragments" are discussed further on page 157.

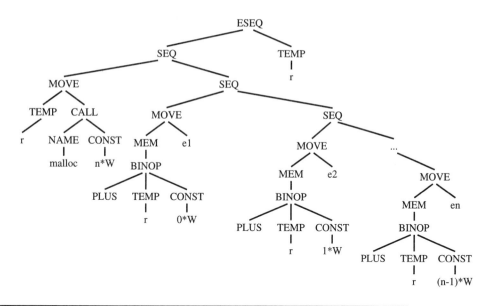

FIGURE 7.4.   Object initialization.

All string operations are performed in functions provided by the runtime system; these functions heap-allocate space for their results, and return pointers. Thus, the compiler (almost) doesn't need to know what the representation is, as long as it knows that each string pointer is exactly one word long. We say "almost" because string literals must be represented.

In Pascal, strings are fixed-length arrays of characters; literals are padded with blanks to make them fit. This is not very useful. In C, strings are pointers to variable-length, zero-terminated sequences. This is much more useful, though a string containing a zero byte cannot be represented.

RECORD AND ARRAY CREATION

Imagine a language construct $\{e_1, e_2, ..., e_n\}$ which creates an n-element record initialized to the values of expressions e_i. This is like an object constructor that initializes all the instance variables of the object. Such a record may outlive the procedure activation that creates it, so it cannot be allocated on the stack. Instead, it must be allocated on the *heap*. If there is no provision for freeing records (or strings), industrial-strength systems should have a *garbage collector* to reclaim unreachable records (see Chapter 13).

The simplest way to create a record is to call an external memory-allocation function that returns a pointer to an n-word area into a new temporary r. Then a series of MOVE trees can initialize offsets $0, 1W, 2W, ..., (n-1)W$ from r with the translations of expressions e_i. Finally, the result of the whole expression is TEMP(r), as shown in Figure 7.4.

In an industrial compiler, calling `malloc` (or its equivalent) on every record creation might be too slow; see Section 13.7.

Array creation is very much like record creation, except that all the fields are initialized to the same value. The external `initArray` function can take the array length and the initializing value as arguments, see later.

In MiniJava we can create an array of integers by the construct

```
new int [exp]
```

where `exp` is an expression that evaluates to an integer. This will create an integer array of a length determined by the value of `exp` and with each value initialized to zero.

To translate array creation, the compiler needs to perform the following steps:

1. Determine how much space is needed for the array. This can be calculated by:

((length of the array) + 1) × (size of an integer, e.g., 4).

The reason we add one to the length of the array is that we want to store the length of the array along with the array. This is needed for bounds checking and to determine the length at run time.
2. Call an external function to get space on the heap. The call will return a pointer to the beginning of the array.
3. Generate code for saving the length of the array at offset 0.
4. Generate code for initializing each of the values in the array to zero starting at offset 4.

Calling runtime-system functions. To call an external function named `init-Array` with arguments a, b, simply generate a CALL such as

```
static Label initArray = new Label("initArray");
new CALL(new NAME(initArray),
        new Tree.ExpList(a, new Tree.ExpList(b, null)));
```

This refers to an external function `initArray` which is written in a language such as C or assembly language – it cannot be written in MiniJava because MiniJava has no mechanism for manipulating raw memory.

To implement 7, the `Translate` phase should generate a move instruction

MOVE(RV, body)

that puts the result of evaluating the body in the return value (RV) location specified by the machine-specific `frame` structure:

```
package Frame;
public abstract class Frame {
    ⋮
    abstract public Temp RV();
}
```

Item 4 (moving incoming formal parameters), and 5 and 8 (the saving and restoring of callee-save registers), are part of the *view shift* described on page 128. They should be done by a function in the `Frame` module:

```
package Frame;
public abstract class Frame {
    ⋮
    abstract public Tree.Stm procEntryExit1(Tree.Stm body);
}
```

The implementation of this function will be discussed on page 251. `Translate` should apply it to each procedure body (items 5–7) as it is translated.

FRAGMENTS

Given a function definition comprising an already-translated `body` expression, the `Translate` phase should produce a descriptor for the function containing this necessary information:

frame: The frame descriptor containing machine-specific information about local variables and parameters;

body: The result returned from `procEntryExit1`.

Call this pair a *fragment* to be translated to assembly language. It is the second kind of fragment we have seen; the other was the assembly-language pseudo-instruction sequence for a string literal. Thus, it is useful to define (in the `Translate` interface) a `frag` datatype:

```
package Translate;
public abstract class Frag {  public Frag next; }
public ProcFrag(Tree.Stm body, Frame.Frame frame);
public DataFrag(String data);
```

```
class Vehicle {
    int position;
    int gas;
    int move (int x) {
        position = position + x;
        return position;
    }
    int fill (int y) {
        gas = gas + y;
        return gas;
    }
}
```

PROGRAM 7.5.   A MiniJava program.

```
public class Translate {
    :
    private Frag frags;    // linked list of accumulated fragments
    public void procEntryExit(Exp body);
    public Frag getResult();
}
```

The semantic analysis phase calls upon new Translate.Level(···) in processing a function header. Later it calls other methods of Translate to translate the body of the function. Finally the semantic analyzer calls procEntryExit, which has the *side effect* of remembering a ProcFrag.

All the remembered fragments go into a private fragment list within Translate; then getResult can be used to extract the fragment list.

CLASSES AND OBJECTS

Figure 7.5 shows a MiniJava class Vehicle with two instance variables position and gas, and two methods move and fill. We can create multiple Vehicle objects. Each Vehicle object will have its own position and gas variables. Two Vehicle objects can have different values in their variables, and in MiniJava, only the methods of an object can access the variables of that object. The translation of new Vehicle() is much like the translation of record creation and can be done in two steps:

1. Generate code for allocating heap space for all the instance variables; in this case we need to allocate 8 bytes (2 integers, each of size, say, 4).
2. Iterate through the memory locations for those variables and initialize them— in this case, they should both be initialized to 0.

Methods and the *this* pointer. Method calls in MiniJava are similar to function calls; but first, we must determine the class in which the method is declared and look up the method in that class. Second, we need to address the following question. Suppose we have multiple `Vehicle` objects and we want to call a method on one of them; how do we ensure that the implementation knows for which object we are calling the method? The solution is to pass that object as an extra argument to the method; that argument is the *this* pointer. For a method call

```
Vehicle v;
...
v.move();
```

the `Vehicle` object in variable `v` will be the *this* pointer when calling the `move` method.

The translation of method declarations is much like the translation of functions, but we need to avoid name clashes among methods with the same name that are declared in different classes. We can do that by choosing a naming scheme such that the name of the translated method is the concatenation of the class name and the method name. For example, the translation of `move` can be given the name `Vehicle_move`.

Accessing variables. In MiniJava, variables can be accessed from methods in the same class. Variables are accessed via the *this* pointer; thus, the translation of a variable reference is like field selection for records. The position of the variable in the object can be looked up in the symbol table for the class.

PROGRAM

TRANSLATION TO TREES

Design a set of visitors which translate a MiniJava program into intermediate representation trees.

Supporting files in `$MINIJAVA/chap7` include:

`Tree/*` Data types for the `Tree` language.
`Tree/Print.java` Functions to display trees for debugging.

A simpler translator. To simplify the implementation of the translator, you may do without the `Ex`, `Nx`, `Cx` constructors. The entire translation can be done with ordinary value expressions. This means that there is only one `Exp` class (without subclasses); this class contains one field of type `Tree.Exp` and only an `unEx()` method. Instead of $Nx(s)$, use $Ex(ESEQ(s, CONST\ 0))$. For conditionals, instead of a `Cx`, use an expression that just evaluates to 1 or 0.

The intermediate representation trees produced from this kind of naive translation will be bulkier and slower than a "fancy" translation. But they *will* work correctly, and in principle a fancy back-end optimizer might be able to clean up the clumsiness. In any case, a clumsy but correct translator is better than a fancy one that doesn't work.

EXERCISES

7.1 Suppose a certain compiler translates all statements and expressions into Tree.Exp trees, and does not use the Nx and Cx constructors to represent expressions in different ways. Draw a picture of the IR tree that results from each of the following MiniJava statements and expressions.

a. a+5

b. b[i+1]

c. a<b, which should be implemented by making an ESEQ whose left-hand side moves a 1 or 0 into some newly defined temporary, and whose right-hand side is the temporary.

d. a = x+y; which should be translated with an EXP node at the top.

e. if (a<b) c=a; else c=b; translated using the a<b tree from part (c) above; the whole statement will therefore be rather clumsy and inefficient.

f. if (a<b) c=a; else c=b; translated in a less clumsy way.

7.2 Translate each of these MiniJava statements and expressions into IR trees, but using the Ex, Nx, and Cx constructors as appropriate. In each case, just draw pictures of the trees; an Ex tree will be a Tree Exp, an Nx tree will be a Tree Stm, and a Cx tree will be a Stm with holes labeled *true* and *false* into which labels can later be placed.

a. a+5;

b. b[i+1]=0;

c. while (a<0) a=a+1;

d. a<b moves a 1 or 0 into some newly defined temporary, and whose right-hand side is the temporary.

e. a = x+y;

f. if (a<b) c=a; else c=b;

7.3 Using the C compiler of your choice (or a compiler for another language), translate some functions to assembly language. On Unix this is done with the -S option to the C compiler.

Then identify all the components of the calling sequence (items 1–11), and explain what each line of assembly language does (especially the pseudo-instructions that comprise items 1 and 11). Try one small function that returns without much computation (a *leaf* function), and one that calls another function before eventually returning.

7.4 The `Tree` intermediate language has no operators for floating-point variables. Show how the language would look with new binops for floating-point arithmetic, and new relops for floating-point comparisons. You may find it useful to introduce a variant of MEM nodes to describe fetching and storing floating-point values.

*7.5 The `Tree` intermediate language has no provision for data values that are not exactly one word long. The C programming language has signed and unsigned integers of several sizes, with conversion operators among the different sizes. Augment the intermediate language to accommodate several sizes of integers, with conversions among them.

Hint: Do not distinguish signed values from unsigned values in the intermediate trees, but do distinguish between signed operators and unsigned operators. See also Fraser and Hanson [1995], Sections 5.5 and 9.1.

8

Basic Blocks and Traces

ca-non-i-cal: reduced to the simplest or clearest schema
possible

Webster's Dictionary

The trees generated by the semantic analysis phase must be translated into assembly or machine language. The operators of the `Tree` language are chosen carefully to match the capabilities of most machines. However, there are certain aspects of the tree language that do not correspond exactly with machine languages, and some aspects of the `Tree` language interfere with compile-time optimization analyses.

For example, it's useful to be able to evaluate the subexpressions of an expression in any order. But the subexpressions of `Tree.exp` can contain side effects – ESEQ and CALL nodes that contain assignment statements and perform input/output. If tree expressions did not contain ESEQ and CALL nodes, then the order of evaluation would not matter.

Some of the mismatches between `Trees` and machine-language programs are

- The CJUMP instruction can jump to either of two labels, but real machines' conditional jump instructions fall through to the next instruction if the condition is false.
- ESEQ nodes within expressions are inconvenient, because they make different orders of evaluating subtrees yield different results.
- CALL nodes within expressions cause the same problem.
- CALL nodes within the argument-expressions of other CALL nodes will cause problems when trying to put arguments into a fixed set of formal-parameter registers.

Why does the `Tree` language allow ESEQ and two-way CJUMP, if they are so troublesome? Because they make it much more convenient for the `Translate` (translation to intermediate code) phase of the compiler.

We can take any tree and rewrite it into an equivalent tree without any of the cases listed above. Without these cases, the only possible parent of a SEQ node is another SEQ; all the SEQ nodes will be clustered at the top of the tree. This makes the SEQs entirely uninteresting; we might as well get rid of them and make a linear list of `Tree.Stms`.

The transformation is done in three stages: First, a tree is rewritten into a list of *canonical trees* without SEQ or ESEQ nodes; then this list is grouped into a set of *basic blocks*, which contain no internal jumps or labels; then the basic blocks are ordered into a set of *traces* in which every CJUMP is immediately followed by its `false` label.

Thus the module `Canon` has these tree-rearrangement functions:

```
package Canon;
public class Canon {
  static public Tree.StmList linearize(Tree.Stm s);
}
public class BasicBlocks {
  public StmListList blocks;
  public Temp.Label done;
  public BasicBlocks(Tree.StmList stms);
}
StmListList(Tree.StmList head, StmListList tail);
public class TraceSchedule {
  public TraceSchedule(BasicBlocks b);
  public Tree.StmList stms;
}
```

`Linearize` removes the ESEQs and moves the CALLs to top level. Then `BasicBlocks` groups statements into sequences of straight-line code. Finally, `TraceSchedule` orders the blocks so that every CJUMP is followed by its `false` label.

8.1   CANONICAL TREES

Let us define *canonical trees* as having these properties:

1. No SEQ or ESEQ.
2. The parent of each CALL is either EXP(...) or MOVE(TEMP t, ...).

TRANSFORMATIONS ON ESEQ

How can the ESEQ nodes be eliminated? The idea is to lift them higher and higher in the tree, until they can become SEQ nodes.

Figure 8.1 gives some useful identities on trees.

Identity (1) is obvious. So is identity (2): Statement s is to be evaluated; then e_1; then e_2; then the sum of the expressions is returned. If s has side effects that affect e_1 or e_2, then either the left-hand side or the right-hand side of the first equation will execute those side effects before the expressions are evaluated.

Identity (3) is more complicated, because of the need not to interchange the evaluations of s and e_1. For example, if s is MOVE(MEM(x), y) and e_1 is BINOP(PLUS, MEM(x), z), then the program will compute a different result if s is evaluated before e_1 instead of after. Our goal is simply to pull s out of the BINOP expression; but now (to preserve the order of evaluation) we must pull e_1 out of the BINOP with it. To do so, we assign e_1 into a new temporary t, and put t inside the BINOP.

It may happen that s causes no side effects that can alter the result produced by e_1. This will happen if the temporaries and memory locations assigned by s are not referenced by e_1 (and s and e_1 don't both perform external I/O). In this case, identity (4) can be used.

We cannot always tell if two expressions commute. For example, whether MOVE(MEM(x), y) commutes with MEM(z) depends on whether $x = z$, which we cannot always determine at compile time. So we *conservatively approximate* whether statements commute, saying either "they definitely do commute" or "perhaps they don't commute." For example, we know that any statement "definitely commutes" with the expression CONST(n), so we can use identity (4) to justify special cases like

$$\text{BINOP}(op, \text{CONST}(n), \text{ESEQ}(s, e)) = \text{ESEQ}(s, \text{BINOP}(op, \text{CONST}(n), e)).$$

The `commute` function estimates (very naively) whether a statement commutes with an expression:

```
static boolean commute(Tree.Stm a, Tree.Exp b) {
    return isNop(a)
        || b instanceof Tree.NAME
        || b instanceof Tree.CONST;
}
```

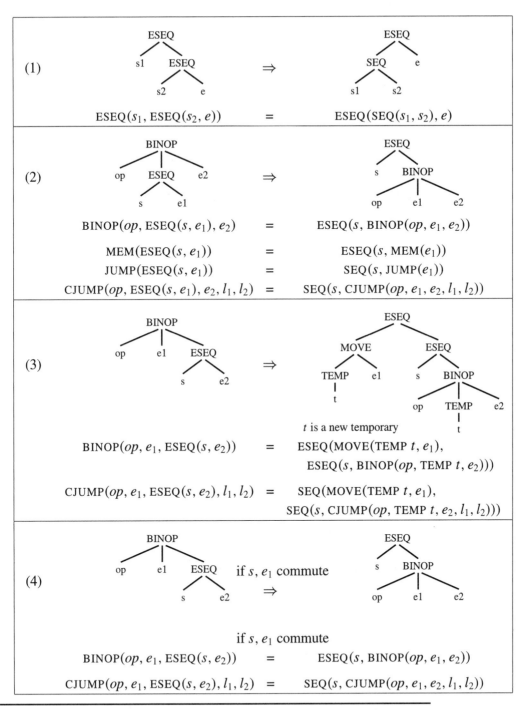

$$(1) \quad \mathrm{ESEQ}(s_1, \mathrm{ESEQ}(s_2, e)) \quad = \quad \mathrm{ESEQ}(\mathrm{SEQ}(s_1, s_2), e)$$

$$(2)$$
$$\mathrm{BINOP}(op, \mathrm{ESEQ}(s, e_1), e_2) \quad = \quad \mathrm{ESEQ}(s, \mathrm{BINOP}(op, e_1, e_2))$$
$$\mathrm{MEM}(\mathrm{ESEQ}(s, e_1)) \quad = \quad \mathrm{ESEQ}(s, \mathrm{MEM}(e_1))$$
$$\mathrm{JUMP}(\mathrm{ESEQ}(s, e_1)) \quad = \quad \mathrm{SEQ}(s, \mathrm{JUMP}(e_1))$$
$$\mathrm{CJUMP}(op, \mathrm{ESEQ}(s, e_1), e_2, l_1, l_2) \quad = \quad \mathrm{SEQ}(s, \mathrm{CJUMP}(op, e_1, e_2, l_1, l_2))$$

$$(3)$$

t is a new temporary

$$\mathrm{BINOP}(op, e_1, \mathrm{ESEQ}(s, e_2)) \quad = \quad \mathrm{ESEQ}(\mathrm{MOVE}(\mathrm{TEMP}\ t, e_1),$$
$$\mathrm{ESEQ}(s, \mathrm{BINOP}(op, \mathrm{TEMP}\ t, e_2)))$$

$$\mathrm{CJUMP}(op, e_1, \mathrm{ESEQ}(s, e_2), l_1, l_2) \quad = \quad \mathrm{SEQ}(\mathrm{MOVE}(\mathrm{TEMP}\ t, e_1),$$
$$\mathrm{SEQ}(s, \mathrm{CJUMP}(op, \mathrm{TEMP}\ t, e_2, l_1, l_2)))$$

$$(4) \quad \text{if } s, e_1 \text{ commute}$$

if s, e_1 commute

$$\mathrm{BINOP}(op, e_1, \mathrm{ESEQ}(s, e_2)) \quad = \quad \mathrm{ESEQ}(s, \mathrm{BINOP}(op, e_1, e_2))$$
$$\mathrm{CJUMP}(op, e_1, \mathrm{ESEQ}(s, e_2), l_1, l_2) \quad = \quad \mathrm{SEQ}(s, \mathrm{CJUMP}(op, e_1, e_2, l_1, l_2))$$

FIGURE 8.1.   Identities on trees (see also Exercise 8.1).

```
static boolean isNop(Tree.Stm a) {
   return  a instanceof Tree.EXP
           && ((Tree.EXP)a).exp instanceof Tree.CONST;
}
```

A constant commutes with any statement, and the empty statement commutes with any expression. Anything else is assumed not to commute.

GENERAL REWRITING RULES

In general, for each kind of `Tree` statement or expression we can identify the subexpressions. Then we can make rewriting rules, similar to the ones in Figure 8.1, to pull the ESEQs out of the statement or expression.

For example, in $[e_1, e_2, \text{ESEQ}(s, e_3)]$, the statement s must be pulled leftward past e_2 and e_1. If they commute, we have $(s; [e_1, e_2, e_3])$. But suppose e_2 does not commute with s; then we must have

$$(\text{SEQ}(\text{MOVE}(t_1, e_1), \text{SEQ}(\text{MOVE}(t_2, e_2), s)); \quad [\text{TEMP}(t_1), \text{TEMP}(t_2), e_3])$$

Or if e_2 commutes with s but e_1 does not, we have

$$(\text{SEQ}(\text{MOVE}(t_1, e_1), s); \quad [\text{TEMP}(t_1), \ e_2, \ e_3])$$

The `reorder` function takes a list of expressions and returns a pair of (statement, expression-list). The statement contains all the things that must be executed before the expression-list. As shown in these examples, this includes all the statement-parts of the ESEQs, as well as any expressions to their left with which they did not commute. When there are no ESEQs at all we will use EXP(CONST 0), which does nothing, as the statement.

Algorithm. Step one is to make a "subexpression-extraction" method for each kind. Step two is to make a "subexpression-insertion" method: Given an ESEQ-clean version of each subexpression, this builds a new version of the expression or statement.

These will be methods of the `Tree.Exp` and `Tree.Stm` classes:

```
package Tree;
abstract public class Exp {
      abstract public ExpList kids();
      abstract public Exp build(ExpList kids);
}
```

```
abstract public class Stm {
        abstract public ExpList kids();
        abstract public Stm build(ExpList kids);
}
```

Each subclass `Exp` or `Stm` must implement the methods; for example,

```
package Tree;
public class BINOP extends Exp {
  public int binop;
  public Exp left, right;
  public BINOP(int b, Exp l, Exp r) {binop=b; ···}
  public final static int PLUS=0, MINUS=1, MUL=2, DIV=3,
          AND=4,OR=5,LSHIFT=6,RSHIFT=7,ARSHIFT=8,XOR=9;
  public ExpList kids() {return new ExpList(left,
                                   new ExpList(right,null));}
  public Exp build(ExpList kids) {
    return new BINOP(binop,kids.head,kids.tail.head);
  }
}
```

Other subclasses have similar (or even simpler) `kids` and `build` methods. Using these `build` methods, we can write functions

```
static Tree.Stm do_stm(Tree.Stm s)
static Tree.ESEQ do_exp (Tree.Exp e)
```

that pull all the ESEQs out of a statement or expression, respectively. That is, `do_stm` uses `s.kids()` to get the immediate subexpressions of `s`, which will be an expression-list l. It then pulls all the ESEQs out of l recursively, yielding a clump of side-effecting statements s_1 and a cleaned-up list l'. Then SEQ(s_1, `s.build`(l')) constructs a new statement, like the original `s` but with no ESEQs. These functions rely on auxiliary functions `reorder_stm` and `reorder_exp` for help; see also Exercise 8.3.

The left-hand operand of the MOVE statement is not considered a subexpression, because it is the *destination* of the statement – its value is not used by the statement. However, if the destination is a memory location, then the *address* acts like a source. Thus we have,

```
public class MOVE extends Stm {
  public Exp dst, src;
  public MOVE(Exp d, Exp s) {dst=d; src=s;}
  public ExpList kids() {
    if (dst instanceof MEM)
      return new ExpList(((MEM)dst).exp,
                         new ExpList(src,null));
    else return new ExpList(src,null);
  }
  public Stm build(ExpList kids) {
    if (dst instanceof MEM)
     return new MOVE(new MEM(kids.head), kids.tail.head);
    else return new MOVE(dst, kids.head);
  }
}
```

Now, given a list of "kids," we pull the ESEQs out, from right to left.

MOVING CALLS TO TOP LEVEL

The `Tree` language permits CALL nodes to be used as subexpressions. However, the actual implementation of CALL will be that each function returns its result in the same dedicated return-value register TEMP(RV). Thus, if we have

$$\text{BINOP}(\text{PLUS}, \text{CALL}(\ldots), \text{CALL}(\ldots))$$

the second call will overwrite the RV register before the PLUS can be executed.

We can solve this problem with a rewriting rule. The idea is to assign each return value immediately into a fresh temporary register, that is

$$\text{CALL}(\textit{fun}, \textit{args}) \quad \rightarrow \quad \text{ESEQ}(\text{MOVE}(\text{TEMP } t, \text{CALL}(\textit{fun}, \textit{args})), \text{TEMP } t)$$

Now the ESEQ-eliminator will percolate the MOVE up outside of its containing BINOP (etc.) expressions.

This technique will generate a few extra MOVE instructions, which the register allocator (Chapter 11) can clean up.

The rewriting rule is implemented as follows: `reorder` replaces any occurrence of CALL(f, $\textit{args}$) by

$$\text{ESEQ}(\text{MOVE}(\text{TEMP } t_{\text{new}}, \text{CALL}(f, \textit{args})), \text{ TEMP } t_{\text{new}})$$

and calls itself again on the ESEQ. But `do_stm` recognizes the pattern

$$\text{MOVE}(\text{TEMP } t_{\text{new}}, \text{CALL}(f, \textit{args}))$$

and does not call `reorder` on the CALL node in that case, but treats the f and *args* as the children of the MOVE node. Thus, `reorder` never "sees" any CALL that is already the immediate child of a MOVE. Occurrences of the pattern EXP(CALL(f, *args*)) are treated similarly.

A LINEAR LIST OF STATEMENTS

Once an entire function body s_0 is processed with `do_stm`, the result is a tree s_0' where all the SEQ nodes are near the top (never underneath any other kind of node). The `linearize` function repeatedly applies the rule

$$\text{SEQ}(\text{SEQ}(a, b), c) = \text{SEQ}(a, \text{SEQ}(b, c))$$

The result is that s_0' is linearized into an expression of the form

$$\text{SEQ}(s_1, \text{SEQ}(s_2, \ldots, \text{SEQ}(s_{n-1}, s_n) \ldots))$$

Here the SEQ nodes provide no structuring information at all, and we can just consider this to be a simple list of statements,

$$s_1, s_2, \ldots, s_{n-1}, s_n$$

where none of the s_i contain SEQ or ESEQ nodes.

These rewrite rules are implemented by `linearize`, with an auxiliary function `linear`:

```
static Tree.StmList linear(Tree.SEQ s, Tree.StmList l) {
  return linear(s.left,linear(s.right,l));
}
static Tree.StmList linear(Tree.Stm s, Tree.StmList l) {
  if (s instanceof Tree.SEQ) return linear((Tree.SEQ)s,l);
  else return new Tree.StmList(s,l);
}
static public Tree.StmList linearize(Tree.Stm s) {
  return linear(do_stm(s), null);
}
```

8.2 TAMING CONDITIONAL BRANCHES

Another aspect of the `Tree` language that has no direct equivalent in most machine instruction sets is the two-way branch of the CJUMP instruction. The `Tree` language CJUMP is designed with two target labels for convenience in translating into trees and analyzing trees. On a real machine, the conditional jump either transfers control (on a `true` condition) or "falls through" to the next instruction.

To make the trees easy to translate into machine instructions, we will re-arrange them so that every CJUMP($cond, l_t, l_f$) is immediately followed by LABEL(l_f), its "false branch." Each such CJUMP can be directly implemented on a real machine as a conditional branch to label l_t.

We will make this transformation in two stages: First, we take the list of canonical trees and form them into *basic blocks*; then we order the basic blocks into a *trace*. The next sections will define these terms.

BASIC BLOCKS

In determining where the jumps go in a program, we are analyzing the program's *control flow*. Control flow is the sequencing of instructions in a program, ignoring the data values in registers and memory, and ignoring the arithmetic calculations. Of course, not knowing the data values means we cannot know whether the conditional jumps will go to their true or false labels; so we simply say that such jumps can go either way.

In analyzing the control flow of a program, any instruction that is not a jump has an entirely uninteresting behavior. We can lump together any sequence of nonbranch instructions into a basic block and analyze the control flow between basic blocks.

A *basic block* is a sequence of statements that is always entered at the beginning and exited at the end, that is:

- The first statement is a LABEL.
- The last statement is a JUMP or CJUMP.
- There are no other LABELs, JUMPs, or CJUMPs.

The algorithm for dividing a long sequence of statements into basic blocks is quite simple. The sequence is scanned from beginning to end; whenever a LABEL is found, a new block is started (and the previous block is ended); whenever a JUMP or CJUMP is found, a block is ended (and the next block is started). If this leaves any block not ending with a JUMP or CJUMP, then a JUMP to the next block's label is appended to the block. If any block has been left without a LABEL at the beginning, a new label is invented and stuck there.

We will apply this algorithm to each function-body in turn. The procedure "epilogue" (which pops the stack and returns to the caller) will not be part of this body, but is intended to follow the last statement. When the flow of program execution reaches the end of the last block, the epilogue should follow. But it is inconvenient to have a "special" block that must come last and that has no JUMP at the end. Thus, we will invent a new label done – intended to mean the beginning of the epilogue – and put a JUMP(NAME done) at the end of the last block.

In the MiniJava compiler, the class `Canon.BasicBlocks` implements this simple algorithm.

TRACES

Now the basic blocks can be arranged in any order, and the result of executing the program will be the same – every block ends with a jump to the appropriate place. We can take advantage of this to choose an ordering of the blocks satisfying the condition that each CJUMP is followed by its false label.

At the same time, we can also arrange that many of the unconditional JUMPs are immediately followed by their target label. This will allow the deletion of these jumps, which will make the compiled program run a bit faster.

A *trace* is a sequence of statements that could be consecutively executed during the execution of the program. It can include conditional branches. A program has many different, overlapping traces. For our purposes in arranging CJUMPs and false-labels, we want to make a set of traces that exactly covers the program: Each block must be in exactly one trace. To minimize the number of JUMPs from one trace to another, we would like to have as few traces as possible in our covering set.

A very simple algorithm will suffice to find a covering set of traces. The idea is to start with some block – the beginning of a trace – and follow a possible execution path – the rest of the trace. Suppose block b_1 ends with a JUMP to b_4, and b_4 has a JUMP to b_6. Then we can make the trace b_1, b_4, b_6.

But suppose b_6 ends with a conditional jump CJUMP($cond, b_7, b_3$). We cannot know at compile time whether b_7 or b_3 will be next. But we can assume that some execution will follow b_3, so let us imagine it is that execution that we are simulating. Thus, we append b_3 to our trace and continue with the rest of the trace after b_3. The block b_7 will be in some other trace.

Algorithm 8.2 (which is similar to `Canon.TraceSchedule`) orders the blocks into traces as follows: It starts with some block and follows a chain of jumps, marking each block and appending it to the current trace. Eventually it comes to a block whose successors are all marked, so it ends the trace and picks an unmarked block to start the next trace.

Put all the blocks of the program into a list Q.

while Q is not empty

>   Start a new (empty) trace, call it T.
>
>   Remove the head element b from Q.
>
>   **while** b is not marked
>
> >   Mark b; append b to the end of the current trace T.
> >
> >   Examine the successors of b (the blocks to which b branches);
> >
> >   **if** there is any unmarked successor c
> >
> > > $b \leftarrow c$
>
>   End the current trace T.

ALGORITHM 8.2. Generation of traces.

FINISHING UP

An efficient compiler will keep the statements grouped into basic blocks, because many kinds of analysis and optimization algorithms run faster on (relatively few) basic blocks than on (relatively many) individual statements. For the MiniJava compiler, however, we seek simplicity in the implementation of later phases. So we will flatten the ordered list of traces back into one long list of statements.

At this point, most (but not all) CJUMPs will be followed by their true or false label. We perform some minor adjustments:

- Any CJUMP immediately followed by its false label we let alone (there will be many of these).
- For any CJUMP followed by its true label, we switch the true and false labels and negate the condition.
- For any CJUMP($cond, a, b, l_t, l_f$) followed by neither label, we invent a new false label l'_f and rewrite the single CJUMP statement as three statements, just to achieve the condition that the CJUMP is followed by its false label:

  > CJUMP($cond, a, b, l_t, l'_f$)
  > LABEL l'_f
  > JUMP(NAME l_f)

The trace-generating algorithm will tend to order the blocks so that many of the unconditional JUMPs are immediately followed by their target labels. We can remove such jumps.

prologue statements	*prologue statements*	*prologue statements*
~~JUMP(NAME *test*)~~	~~JUMP(NAME *test*)~~	JUMP(NAME *test*)
LABEL(*test*)	LABEL(*test*)	LABEL(*body*)
CJUMP($>, i, N, done, body$)	CJUMP($\leq, i, N, body, done$)	*loop body statements*
LABEL(*body*)	LABEL(*done*)	~~JUMP(NAME *test*)~~
loop body statements	*epilogue statements*	LABEL(*test*)
JUMP(NAME *test*)	LABEL(*body*)	CJUMP($\leq, i, N, body, done$)
LABEL(*done*)	*loop body statements*	LABEL(*done*)
epilogue statements	JUMP(NAME *test*)	*epilogue statements*
(a)	(b)	(c)

FIGURE 8.3.   Different trace coverings for the same program.

OPTIMAL TRACES

For some applications of traces, it is important that any frequently executed sequence of instructions (such as the body of a loop) should occupy its own trace. This helps not only to minimize the number of unconditional jumps, but also may help with other kinds of optimizations, such as register allocation and instruction scheduling.

Figure 8.3 shows the same program organized into traces in different ways. Figure 8.3a has a CJUMP and a JUMP in every iteration of the **while**-loop; Figure 8.3b uses a different trace covering, also with CJUMP and a JUMP in every iteration. But Figure 8.3c shows a better trace covering, with no JUMP in each iteration.

The MiniJava compiler's Canon module doesn't attempt to optimize traces around loops, but it is sufficient for the purpose of cleaning up the Tree-statement lists for generating assembly code.

FURTHER READING

The rewrite rules of Figure 8.1 are an example of a *term rewriting system*; such systems have been much studied [Dershowitz and Jouannaud 1990].

Fisher [1981] shows how to cover a program with traces so that frequently executing paths tend to stay within the same trace. Such traces are useful for program optimization and scheduling.

EXERCISES

*8.1 The rewriting rules in Figure 8.1 are a subset of the rules necessary to eliminate all ESEQs from expressions. Show the right-hand side for each of the following incomplete rules:

a. MOVE(TEMP t, ESEQ(s, e)) $\Rightarrow$

b. MOVE(MEM(ESEQ(s, e_1)), e_2) $\Rightarrow$

c. MOVE(MEM(e_1), ESEQ(s, e_2)) $\Rightarrow$

d. EXP(ESEQ(s, e)) $\Rightarrow$

e. EXP(CALL(ESEQ(s, e), $args$)) $\Rightarrow$

f. MOVE(TEMP t, CALL(ESEQ(s, e), $args$)) $\Rightarrow$

g. EXP(CALL(e_1, [e_2, ESEQ(s, e_3), e_4])) $\Rightarrow$

In some cases, you may need two different right-hand sides depending on whether something commutes (just as parts (3) and (4) of Figure 8.1 have different right-hand sides for the same left-hand sides).

8.2 Draw each of the following expressions as a tree diagram, and then apply the rewriting rules of Figure 8.1 and Exercise 8.1, as well as the CALL rule on page 168.

a. MOVE(MEM(ESEQ(SEQ(CJUMP(LT, TEMP$_i$, CONST$_0$, L_{out}, L_{ok}), LABEL$_{ok}$), TEMP$_i$)), CONST$_1$)

b. MOVE(MEM(MEM(NAME$_a$)), MEM(CALL(TEMP$_f$, [])))

c. BINOP(PLUS, CALL(NAME$_f$, [TEMP$_x$]), CALL(NAME$_g$, [ESEQ(MOVE(TEMP$_x$, CONST$_0$), TEMP$_x$)]))

*8.3 The directory $MINIJAVA/chap8 contains an implementation of every algorithm described in this chapter. Read and understand it.

8.4 A primitive form of the commute test is shown on page 164. This function is conservative: If interchanging the order of evaluation of the expressions will change the result of executing the program, this function will definitely return false; but if an interchange is harmless, commute might return true or false.

Write a more powerful version of commute that returns true in more cases, but is still conservative. Document your program by drawing pictures of (pairs of) expression trees on which it will return true.

*8.5 The left-hand side of a MOVE node really represents a destination, not an expression. Consequently, the following rewrite rule is *not* a good idea:

$$\text{MOVE}(e_1, \text{ESEQ}(s, e_2)) \rightarrow \text{SEQ}(s, \text{MOVE}(e_1, e_2)) \qquad \text{if } s, e_1 \text{ commute}$$

Write a statement matching the left side of this rewrite rule that produces a different result when rewritten.

Hint: It is very reasonable to say that the statement MOVE(TEMP$_a$, TEMP$_b$) commutes with expression TEMP$_b$ (if a and b are not the same), since TEMP$_b$ yields the same value whether executed before or after the MOVE.

Conclusion: The only subexpression of MOVE(TEMP$_a$, e) is e, and the subexpressions of MOVE(MEM(e_1), e_2) are [e_1, e_2]; we should not say that a is a subexpression of MOVE(a, b).

8.6 Break this program into basic blocks.

1	$m \leftarrow 0$		9	$x \leftarrow M[r]$
2	$v \leftarrow 0$		10	$s \leftarrow s + x$
3	if $v \geq n$ goto 15		11	if $s \leq m$ goto 13
4	$r \leftarrow v$		12	$m \leftarrow s$
5	$s \leftarrow 0$		13	$r \leftarrow r + 1$
6	if $r < n$ goto 9		14	goto 6
7	$v \leftarrow v + 1$		15	return m
8	goto 3			

8.7 Express the basic blocks of Exercise 8.6 as statements in the `Tree` intermediate form, and use Algorithm 8.2 to generate a set of traces.

9

Instruction Selection

in-struc-tion: a code that tells a computer to perform a
particular operation

Webster's Dictionary

The intermediate representation (Tree) language expresses only one operation in each tree node: memory fetch or store, addition or subtraction, conditional jump, and so on. A real machine instruction can often perform several
of these primitive operations. For example, almost any machine can perform
an add and a fetch in the same instruction, corresponding to the tree

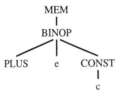

Finding the appropriate machine instructions to implement a given intermediate representation tree is the job of the *instruction selection* phase of a
compiler.

TREE PATTERNS

We can express a machine instruction as a fragment of an IR tree, called a *tree
pattern*. Then instruction selection becomes the task of tiling the tree with a
minimal set of tree patterns.

For purposes of illustration, we invent an instruction set: the *Jouette* architecture. The arithmetic and memory instructions of *Jouette* are shown in
Figure 9.1. On this machine, register r_0 always contains zero.

Name	Effect	Trees
—	r_i	TEMP
ADD	$r_i \leftarrow r_j + r_k$	+
MUL	$r_i \leftarrow r_j \times r_k$	*
SUB	$r_i \leftarrow r_j - r_k$	-
DIV	$r_i \leftarrow r_j / r_k$	/
ADDI	$r_i \leftarrow r_j + c$	+ (CONST) ; + (CONST) ; CONST
SUBI	$r_i \leftarrow r_j - c$	- (CONST)
LOAD	$r_i \leftarrow M[r_j + c]$	MEM/+/CONST ; MEM/+/CONST ; MEM/CONST ; MEM
STORE	$M[r_j + c] \leftarrow r_i$	MOVE/MEM/+/CONST CONST ; MOVE/MEM/+/CONST ; MOVE/MEM/CONST ; MOVE/MEM
MOVEM	$M[r_j] \leftarrow M[r_i]$	MOVE/MEM MEM

FIGURE 9.1. Arithmetic and memory instructions. The notation $M[x]$ denotes the memory word at address x.

Each instruction above the double line in Figure 9.1 produces a result in a register. The very first entry is not really an instruction, but expresses the idea that a TEMP node is implemented as a register, so it can "produce a result in a register" without executing any instructions at all. The instructions below the double line do not produce results in registers, but are executed only for side effects on memory.

For each instruction, the tree patterns it implements are shown. Some instructions correspond to more than one tree pattern; the alternate patterns are obtained for commutative operators (+ and *), and in some cases where a register or constant can be zero (LOAD and STORE). In this chapter we abbre-

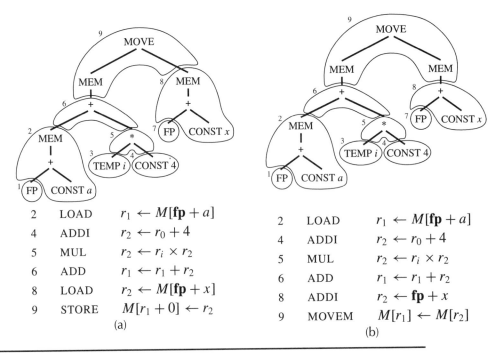

2	LOAD	$r_1 \leftarrow M[\mathbf{fp} + a]$
4	ADDI	$r_2 \leftarrow r_0 + 4$
5	MUL	$r_2 \leftarrow r_i \times r_2$
6	ADD	$r_1 \leftarrow r_1 + r_2$
8	LOAD	$r_2 \leftarrow M[\mathbf{fp} + x]$
9	STORE	$M[r_1 + 0] \leftarrow r_2$

(a)

2	LOAD	$r_1 \leftarrow M[\mathbf{fp} + a]$
4	ADDI	$r_2 \leftarrow r_0 + 4$
5	MUL	$r_2 \leftarrow r_i \times r_2$
6	ADD	$r_1 \leftarrow r_1 + r_2$
8	ADDI	$r_2 \leftarrow \mathbf{fp} + x$
9	MOVEM	$M[r_1] \leftarrow M[r_2]$

(b)

FIGURE 9.2.   A tree tiled in two ways.

viate the tree diagrams slightly: BINOP(PLUS, x, y) nodes will be written as $+(x, y)$, and the actual values of CONST and TEMP nodes will not always be shown.

The fundamental idea of instruction selection using a tree-based intermediate representation is *tiling* the IR tree. The *tiles* are the set of tree patterns corresponding to legal machine instructions, and the goal is to cover the tree with nonoverlapping tiles.

For example, the MiniJava-language expression such as $a[i] := x$, where i is a register variable and a and x are frame-resident, results in a tree that can be tiled in many different ways. Two tilings, and the corresponding instruction sequences, are shown in Figure 9.2 (remember that a is really the frame offset of the pointer to an array). In each case, tiles 1, 3, and 7 do not correspond to any machine instructions, because they are just registers (TEMPs) already containing the right values.

Finally – assuming a "reasonable" set of tile patterns – it is always possible to tile the tree with tiny tiles, each covering only one node. In our example, such a tiling looks like this:

ADDI	$r_1 \leftarrow r_0 + a$
ADD	$r_1 \leftarrow \mathbf{fp} + r_1$
LOAD	$r_1 \leftarrow M[r_1 + 0]$
ADDI	$r_2 \leftarrow r_0 + 4$
MUL	$r_2 \leftarrow r_i \times r_2$
ADD	$r_1 \leftarrow r_1 + r_2$
ADDI	$r_2 \leftarrow r_0 + x$
ADD	$r_2 \leftarrow \mathbf{fp} + r_2$
LOAD	$r_2 \leftarrow M[r_2 + 0]$
STORE	$M[r_1 + 0] \leftarrow r_2$

For a reasonable set of patterns, it is sufficient that each individual Tree node correspond to some tile. It is usually possible to arrange for this; for example, the LOAD instruction can be made to cover just a single MEM node by using a constant of 0, and so on.

OPTIMAL AND OPTIMUM TILINGS

The best tiling of a tree corresponds to an instruction sequence of least cost: the shortest sequence of instructions. Or if the instructions take different amounts of time to execute, the least-cost sequence has the lowest total time.

Suppose we could give each kind of instruction a cost. Then we could define an *optimum* tiling as the one whose tiles sum to the lowest possible value. An *optimal* tiling is one where no two adjacent tiles can be combined into a single tile of lower cost. If there is some tree pattern that can be split into several tiles of lower combined cost, then we should remove that pattern from our catalog of tiles before we begin.

Every *optimum* tiling is also *optimal*, but not vice versa. For example, suppose every instruction costs one unit, except for MOVEM, which costs m units. Then either Figure 9.2a is optimum (if $m > 1$) or Figure 9.2b is optimum (if $m < 1$) or both (if $m = 1$); but both trees are optimal.

Optimum tiling is based on an idealized cost model. In reality, instructions are not self-contained with individually attributable costs; nearby instructions interact in many ways, as discussed in Chapter 20.

9.1   ALGORITHMS FOR INSTRUCTION SELECTION

There are good algorithms for finding optimum and optimal tilings, but the algorithms for optimal tilings are simpler, as you might expect.

Complex instruction set computers (CISC) have instructions that accomplish several operations each. The tiles for these instructions are quite large, and the difference between optimum and optimal tilings – while never very large – is at least sometimes noticeable.

Most architectures of modern design are *reduced instruction set computers (RISC)*. Each RISC instruction accomplishes just a small number of operations (all the *Jouette* instructions except MOVEM are typical RISC instructions). Since the tiles are small and of uniform cost, there is usually no difference at all between optimum and optimal tilings. Thus, the simpler tiling algorithms suffice.

MAXIMAL MUNCH

The algorithm for optimal tiling is called *maximal munch*. It is quite simple. Starting at the root of the tree, find the largest tile that fits. Cover the root node – and perhaps several other nodes near the root – with this tile, leaving several subtrees. Now repeat the same algorithm for each subtree.

As each tile is placed, the instruction corresponding to that tile is generated. The maximal munch algorithm generates the instructions *in reverse order* – after all, the instruction at the root is the first to be generated, but it can only execute after the other instructions have produced operand values in registers.

The "largest tile" is the one with the most nodes. For example, the tile for ADD has one node, the tile for SUBI has two nodes, and the tiles for STORE and MOVEM have three nodes each.

If two tiles of equal size match at the root, then the choice between them is arbitrary. Thus, in the tree of Figure 9.2, STORE and MOVEM both match, and either can be chosen.

Maximal munch is quite straightforward to implement in Java. Simply write two recursive functions, munchStm for statements and munchExp for expressions. Each clause of munchExp will match one tile. The clauses are ordered in order of tile preference (biggest tiles first).

Program 9.3 is a partial example of a *Jouette* code generator based on the maximal munch algorithm. Executing this program on the tree of Figure 9.2 will match the first clause of munchStm; this will call munchExp to emit all the instructions for the operands of the STORE, followed by the STORE itself. Program 9.3 does not show how the registers are chosen and operand syntax is specified for the instructions; we are concerned here only with the pattern-matching of tiles.

```
void munchMove(MEM dst, Exp src) {
  // MOVE(MEM(BINOP(PLUS, e1, CONST(i))), e2)
  if (dst.exp instanceof BINOP && ((BINOP)dst.exp).oper==BINOP.PLUS
         && ((BINOP)dst.exp).right instanceof CONST)
     {munchExp(((BINOP)dst.exp).left); munchExp(src); emit("STORE");}
  // MOVE(MEM(BINOP(PLUS, CONST(i), e1)), e2)
  else if (dst.exp instanceof BINOP && ((BINOP)dst.exp).oper==BINOP.PLUS
         && ((BINOP)dst.exp).left instanceof CONST)
     {munchExp(((BINOP)dst.exp).right); munchExp(src); emit("STORE");}
  // MOVE(MEM(e1), MEM(e2))
  else if (src instanceof MEM)
     {munchExp(dst.exp); munchExp(((MEM)src).exp); emit("MOVEM");}
  // MOVE(MEM(e1), e2)
  else
     {munchExp(dst.exp); munchExp(src); emit("STORE");}
}
void munchMove(TEMP dst, Exp src) {
  // MOVE(TEMP(t1), e)
  munchExp(src); emit("ADD");
}
void munchMove(Exp dst, Exp src) {
  // MOVE(d, e)
  if (dst instanceof MEM) munchMove((MEM)dst,src);
  else if (dst instanceof TEMP) munchMove((TEMP)dst,src);
}
void munchStm(Stm s) {
  if (s instanceof MOVE) munchMove(((MOVE)s).dst, ((MOVE)s).src);
  :
  : // CALL, JUMP, CJUMP  unimplemented here
}


void munchExp(Exp)
MEM(BINOP(PLUS, e1, CONST(i)))  ⇒  munchExp(e1); emit("LOAD");
MEM(BINOP(PLUS, CONST(i), e1))  ⇒  munchExp(e1); emit("LOAD");
MEM(CONST(i))  ⇒  emit("LOAD");
MEM(e1)  ⇒  munchExp(e1); emit("LOAD");
BINOP(PLUS, e1, CONST(i))  ⇒  munchExp(e1); emit("ADDI");
BINOP(PLUS, CONST(i), e1)  ⇒  munchExp(e1); emit("ADDI");
CONST(i)  ⇒  munchExp(e1); emit("ADDI");
BINOP(PLUS, e1, CONST(i))  ⇒  munchExp(e1); emit("ADD");
TEMP(t)  ⇒  {}
```

PROGRAM 9.3. Maximal Munch in Java.

If, for each node-type in the `Tree` language, there exists a single-node tile pattern, then maximal munch cannot get "stuck" with no tile to match some subtree.

DYNAMIC PROGRAMMING

Maximal munch always finds an optimal tiling, but not necessarily an optimum. A dynamic-programming algorithm can find the optimum. In general, dynamic programming is a technique for finding optimum solutions for a whole problem based on the optimum solution of each subproblem; here the subproblems are the tilings of the subtrees.

The dynamic-programming algorithm assigns a *cost* to every node in the tree. The cost is the sum of the instruction costs of the best instruction sequence that can tile the subtree rooted at that node.

This algorithm works bottom-up, in contrast to maximal munch, which works top-down. First, the costs of all the children (and grandchildren, etc.) of node n are found recursively. Then, each tree pattern (tile kind) is matched against node n.

Each tile has zero or more *leaves*. In Figure 9.1 the leaves are represented as edges whose bottom ends exit the tile. The leaves of a tile are places where subtrees can be attached.

For each tile t of cost c that matches at node n, there will be zero or more subtrees s_i corresponding to the leaves of the tile. The cost c_i of each subtree has already been computed (because the algorithm works bottom-up). So the cost of matching tile t is just $c + \sum c_i$.

Of all the tiles t_j that match at node n, the one with the minimum-cost match is chosen, and the (minimum) cost of node n is thus computed. For example, consider this tree:

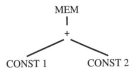

The only tile that matches CONST 1 is an ADDI instruction with cost 1. Similarly, CONST 2 has cost 1. Several tiles match the + node:

Tile	Instruction	Tile Cost	Leaves Cost	Total Cost
+	ADD	1	1+1	3
+ CONST	ADDI	1	1	2
+ CONST	ADDI	1	1	2

The ADD tile has two leaves, but the ADDI tile has only one leaf. In matching the first ADDI pattern, we are saying "though we computed the cost of tiling CONST 2, we are not going to use that information." If we choose to use the first ADDI pattern, then CONST 2 will not be the root of any tile, and its cost will be ignored. In this case, either of the two ADDI tiles leads to the minimum cost for the + node, and the choice is arbitrary. The + node gets a cost of 2.

Now, several tiles match the MEM node:

Tile	Instruction	Tile Cost	Leaves Cost	Total Cost
MEM |	LOAD	1	2	3
MEM | + /\ CONST	LOAD	1	1	2
MEM | + /\ CONST	LOAD	1	1	2

Either of the last two matches will be optimum.

Once the cost of the root node (and thus the entire tree) is found, the *instruction emission* phase begins. The algorithm is as follows:

Emission(node n): for each leaf l_i of the tile selected at node n, perform Emission(l_i). Then emit the instruction matched at node n.

Emission(n) does *not* recur on the children of node n, but on the *leaves of the tile* that matched at n. For example, after the dynamic-programming algorithm finds the optimum cost of the simple tree above, the emission phase emits

ADDI $r_1 \leftarrow r_0 + 1$
LOAD $r_1 \leftarrow M[r_1 + 2]$

but no instruction is emitted for any tile rooted at the + node, because this was not a leaf of the tile matched at the root.

TREE GRAMMARS

For machines with complex instruction sets and several classes of registers and addressing modes, there is a useful generalization of the dynamic-program-

Name	Effect	Trees
—	r_i	TEMP
ADD	$d_i \leftarrow d_j + d_k$	d + (d, d)
MUL	$d_i \leftarrow d_j \times d_k$	d * (d, d)
SUB	$d_i \leftarrow d_j - d_k$	d - (d, d)
DIV	$d_i \leftarrow d_j / d_k$	d / (d, d)
ADDI	$d_i \leftarrow d_j + c$	d + (d, CONST) d + (CONST, d) d CONST
SUBI	$d_i \leftarrow d_j - c$	d - (d, CONST)
MOVEA	$d_j \leftarrow a_i$	d a
MOVED	$a_j \leftarrow d_i$	a d
LOAD	$d_i \leftarrow M[a_j + c]$	d MEM + (a, CONST) d MEM + (CONST, a) d MEM CONST d MEM a
STORE	$M[a_j + c] \leftarrow d_i$	MOVE (MEM +(a,CONST), d) MOVE (MEM +(CONST,a), d) MOVE (MEM CONST, d) MOVE (MEM a, d)
MOVEM	$M[a_j] \leftarrow M[a_i]$	MOVE (MEM a, MEM a)

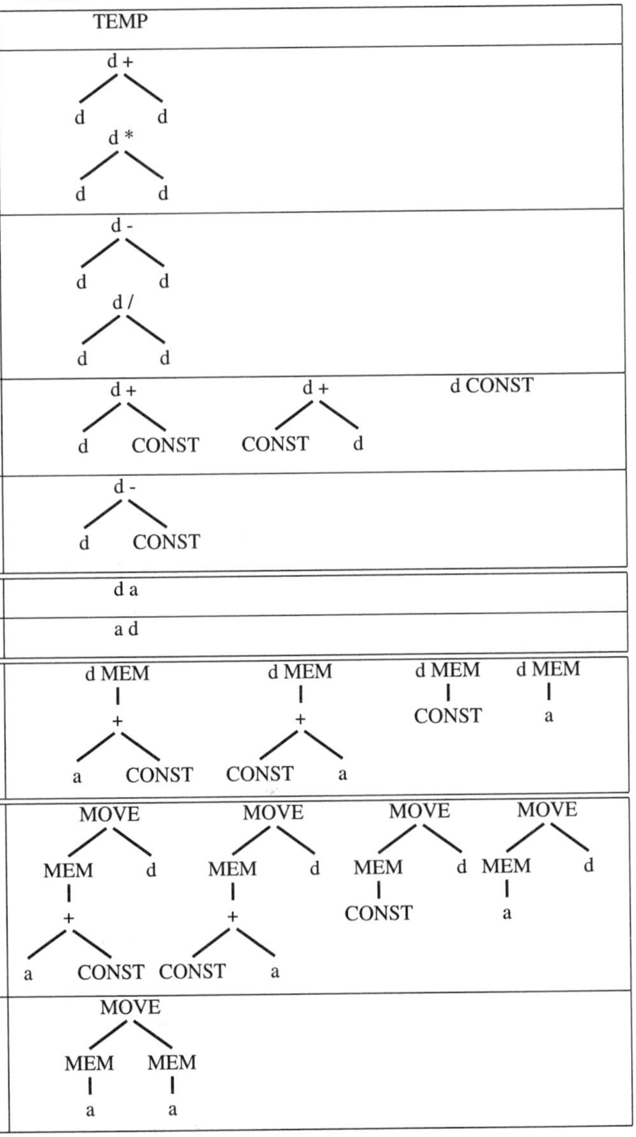

FIGURE 9.4. The *Schizo-Jouette* architecture.

ming algorithm. Suppose we make a brain-damaged version of *Jouette* with two classes of registers: *a* registers for addressing, and *d* registers for "data." The instruction set of the *Schizo-Jouette* machine (loosely based on the Motorola 68000) is shown in Figure 9.4.

The root and leaves of each tile must be marked with *a* or *d* to indicate which kind of register is implied. Now, the dynamic-programming algorithm must keep track, for each node, of the min-cost match as an *a* register, *and also* the min-cost match as a *d* register.

At this point it is useful to use a context-free grammar to describe the tiles; the grammar will have nonterminals *s* (for statements), *a* (for expressions calculated into an *a* register), and *d* (for expressions calculated into a *d* register). Section 3.1 describes the use of context-free grammars for source-language syntax; here we use them for quite a different purpose.

The grammar rules for the LOAD, MOVEA, and MOVED instructions might look like this:

$$d \rightarrow \text{MEM}(+(a, \text{CONST}))$$
$$d \rightarrow \text{MEM}(+(\text{CONST}, a))$$
$$d \rightarrow \text{MEM}(\text{CONST})$$
$$d \rightarrow \text{MEM}(a)$$
$$d \rightarrow a$$
$$a \rightarrow d$$

Such a grammar is highly ambiguous: There are many different parses of the same tree (since there are many different instruction sequences implementing the same expression). For this reason, the parsing techniques described in Chapter 3 are not very useful in this application. However, a generalization of the dynamic-programming algorithm works quite well: The minimum-cost match at each node *for each nonterminal of the grammar* is computed.

Though the dynamic-programming algorithm is conceptually simple, it becomes messy to write down directly in a general-purpose programming language such as Java. Thus, several tools have been developed. These *code-generator generators* process grammars that specify machine instruction sets; for each rule of the grammar, a cost and an action are specified. The costs are used to find the optimum tiling, and then the actions of the matched rules are used in the *emission* phase.

Like Yacc and Lex, the output of a code-generator generator is usually a program in C or Java that operates a table-driven matching engine with the action fragments (written in C or Java) inserted at the appropriate points.

Such tools are quite convenient. Grammars can specify addressing modes of treelike CISC instructions quite well. A typical grammar for the VAX has 112 rules and 20 nonterminal symbols; and one for the Motorola 68020 has

141 rules and 35 nonterminal symbols. However, instructions that produce more than one result – such as autoincrement instructions on the VAX – are difficult to express using tree patterns.

Code-generator generators are probably overkill for RISC machines. The tiles are quite small, there aren't very many of them, and there is little need for a grammar with many nonterminal symbols.

FAST MATCHING

Maximal munch and the dynamic-programming algorithm must examine, for each node, all the tiles that match at that node. A tile matches if each nonleaf node of the tile is labeled with the same operator (MEM, CONST, etc.) as the corresponding node of the tree.

The naive algorithm for matching would be to examine each tile in turn, checking each node of the tile against the corresponding part of the tree. However, there are better approaches. To match a tile at node n of the tree, the label at n can be used in a `case` statement:

```
match(n) {
  switch (label(n)) {
    case MEM: · · ·
    case BINOP: · · ·
    case CONST: · · ·
  }
```

Once the clause for one label (such as MEM) is selected, only those patterns rooted in that label remain in consideration. Another `case` statement can use the label of the child of n to begin distinguishing among those patterns.

The organization and optimization of decision trees for pattern matching is beyond the scope of this book. However, for better performance the naive sequence of clauses in function `munchExp` should be rewritten as a sequence of comparisons that never looks twice at the same tree node.

EFFICIENCY OF TILING ALGORITHMS

How expensive are maximal munch and dynamic programming?

Let us suppose that there are T different tiles, and that the average matching tile contains K nonleaf (labeled) nodes. Let K' be the largest number of nodes that ever need to be examined to see which tiles match at a given subtree; this is approximately the same as the size of the largest tile. And suppose that, on the average, T' different patterns (tiles) match at each tree node. For a typical RISC machine we might expect $T = 50$, $K = 2$, $K' = 4$, $T' = 5$.

Suppose there are N nodes in the input tree. Then maximal munch will have to consider matches at only N/K nodes because, once a "munch" is made at the root, no pattern-matching needs to take place at the nonleaf nodes of the tile.

To find all the tiles that match at one node, at most K' tree nodes must be examined; but (with a sophisticated decision tree) each of these nodes will be examined only once. Then each of the successful matches must be compared to see if its cost is minimal. Thus, the matching at each node costs $K' + T'$, for a total cost proportional to $(K' + T')N/K$.

The dynamic-programming algorithm must find all the matches at *every* node, so its cost is proportional to $(K' + T')N$. However, the constant of proportionality is higher than that of maximal munch, since dynamic programming requires two tree-walks instead of one.

Since K, K', and T' are constant, the running time of all of these algorithms is linear. In practice, measurements show that these instruction selection algorithms run very quickly compared to the other work performed by a real compiler – even lexical analysis is likely to take more time than instruction selection.

9.2   CISC MACHINES

A typical modern RISC machine has

1. 32 registers,
2. only one class of integer/pointer registers,
3. arithmetic operations only between registers,
4. "three-address" instructions of the form $r_1 \leftarrow r_2 \oplus r_3$,
5. load and store instructions with only the M[reg+const] addressing mode,
6. every instruction exactly 32 bits long,
7. one result or effect per instruction.

Many machines designed between 1970 and 1985 are *complex instruction set computers (CISC)*. Such computers have more complicated addressing modes that encode instructions in fewer bits, which was important when computer memories were smaller and more expensive. Typical features found on CISC machines include

1. few registers (16, or 8, or 6);
2. registers divided into different classes, with some operations available only on certain registers;

3. arithmetic operations can access registers or memory through "addressing modes";
4. "two-address" instructions of the form $r_1 \leftarrow r_1 \oplus r_2$;
5. several different addressing modes;
6. variable-length instructions, formed from variable-length opcode plus variable-length addressing modes;
7. instructions with side effects such as "autoincrement" addressing modes.

Most computer architectures designed since 1990 are RISC machines, but most general-purpose computers installed since 1990 are CISC machines: the Intel 80386 and its descendants (486, Pentium).

The Pentium, in 32-bit mode, has six general-purpose registers, a stack pointer, and a frame pointer. Most instructions can operate on all six registers, but the multiply and divide instructions operate only on the eax register. In contrast to the "three-address" instructions found on RISC machines, Pentium arithmetic instructions are generally "two-address," meaning that the destination register must be the same as the first source register. Most instructions can have either two register operands ($r_1 \leftarrow r_1 \oplus r_2$), or one register and one memory operand, for example $M[r_1 + c] \leftarrow M[r_1 + c] \oplus r_2$ or $r_1 \leftarrow r_1 \oplus M[r_2 + c]$, but not $M[r_1 + c_1] \leftarrow M[r_1 + c_1] \oplus M[r_2 + c_2]$

We will cut through these Gordian knots as follows:

1. **Few registers:** We continue to generate TEMP nodes freely, and assume that the register allocator will do a good job.
2. **Classes of registers:** The multiply instruction on the Pentium requires that its left operand (and therefore destination) must be the eax register. The high-order bits of the result (useless to a MiniJava program) are put into register edx. The solution is to move the operands and result explicitly; to implement $t_1 \leftarrow t_2 \times t_3$:

mov eax, t_2	eax $\leftarrow t_2$
mul t_3	eax $\leftarrow$ eax $\times t_3$; edx $\leftarrow$ *garbage*
mov t_1, eax	t_1 $\leftarrow$ eax

This looks very clumsy; but one job that the register allocator performs is to eliminate as many move instructions as possible. If the allocator can assign t_1 or t_3 (or both) to register eax, then it can delete one or both of the move instructions.

3. **Two-address instructions:** We solve this problem in the same way as we solve the previous one: by adding extra move instructions. To implement $t_1 \leftarrow$

$t_2 + t_3$ we produce

mov t_1, t_2	$t_1 \leftarrow t_2$
add t_1, t_3	$t_1 \leftarrow t_1 + t_3$

Then we hope that the register allocator will be able to allocate t_1 and t_2 to the same register, so that the move instruction will be deleted.

4. **Arithmetic operations can address memory:** The instruction selection phase turns every TEMP node into a "register" reference. Many of these "registers" will actually turn out to be memory locations. The *spill* phase of the register allocator must be made to handle this case efficiently; see Chapter 11.

The alternative to using memory-mode operands is simply to fetch all the operands into registers before operating and store them back to memory afterwards. For example, these two sequences compute the same thing:

mov eax, [ebp $-$ 8]	
add eax, ecx	add [ebp $-$ 8], ecx
mov [ebp $-$ 8], eax	

The sequence on the right is more concise (and takes less machine-code space), but *the two sequences are equally fast*. The load, register-register add, and store take 1 cycle each, and the memory-register add takes 3 cycles. On a highly pipelined machine such as the Pentium Pro, simple cycle counts are not the whole story, but the result will be the same: The processor has to perform the load, add, and store, no matter how the instructions specify them.

The sequence on the left has one significant disadvantage: It trashes the value in register eax. Therefore, we should try to use the sequence on the right when possible. But the issue here turns into one of register allocation, not of instruction speed; so we defer its solution to the register allocator.

5. **Several addressing modes:** An addressing mode that accomplishes six things typically takes six steps to execute. Thus, these instructions are often no faster than the multi-instruction sequences they replace. They have only two advantages: They "trash" fewer registers (such as the register eax in the previous example), and they have a shorter instruction encoding. With some work, tree-matching instruction selection can be made to select CISC addressing modes, but programs can be just as fast using the simple RISC-like instructions.

6. **Variable-length instructions:** This is not really a problem for the compiler; once the instructions are selected, it is a trivial (though tedious) matter for the assembler to emit the encodings.

7. **Instructions with side effects:** Some machines have an "autoincrement" memory fetch instruction whose effect is

$$r_2 \leftarrow M[r_1]; \quad r_1 \leftarrow r_1 + 4$$

This instruction is difficult to model using tree patterns, since it produces two results. There are three solutions to this problem:

(a) Ignore the autoincrement instructions, and hope they go away. This is an increasingly successful solution, as few modern machines have multiple-side-effect instructions.

(b) Try to match special idioms in an ad hoc way, within the context of a tree pattern-matching code generator.

(c) Use a different instruction algorithm entirely, one based on DAG patterns instead of tree patterns.

Several of these solutions depend critically on the register allocator to eliminate move instructions and to be smart about spilling; see Chapter 11.

9.3 INSTRUCTION SELECTION FOR THE MiniJava COMPILER

Pattern-matching of "tiles" is simple (if tedious) in Java, as shown in Program 9.3. But this figure does not show what to do with each pattern match. It is all very well to print the name of the instruction, but which registers should these instructions use?

In a tree tiled by instruction patterns, the root of each tile will correspond to some intermediate result held in a register. Register allocation is the act of assigning register numbers to each such node.

The instruction selection phase can simultaneously do register allocation. However, many aspects of register allocation are independent of the particular target-machine instruction set, and it is a shame to duplicate the register-allocation algorithm for each target machine. Thus, register allocation should come either before or after instruction selection.

Before instruction selection, it is not even known which tree nodes will need registers to hold their results, since only the roots of tiles (and not other labeled nodes within tiles) require explicit registers. Thus, register allocation before instruction selection cannot be very accurate. But some compilers do it anyway, to avoid the need to describe machine instructions without the real registers filled in.

We will do register allocation after instruction selection. The instruction selection phase will generate instructions without quite knowing which registers the instructions use.

ABSTRACT ASSEMBLY LANGUAGE INSTRUCTIONS

We will invent a data type for "assembly language instruction without register assignments," called `Assem.Instr`:

```
package Assem;
import Temp.TempList;

public abstract class Instr {
  public String assem;
  public abstract TempList use();
  public abstract TempList def();
  public abstract Targets jumps();
  public String format(Temp.TempMap m);
}

public Targets(Temp.LabelList labels);

public OPER(String assem, TempList dst, TempList src,
            Temp.LabelList jump);
public OPER(String assem, TempList dst, TempList src);
public MOVE(String assem, Temp dst, Temp src);
public LABEL(String assem, Temp.Label label);
```

An OPER holds an assembly language instruction `assem`, a list of operand registers `src`, and a list of result registers `dst`. Any of these lists may be empty. Operations that always fall through to the next instruction are constructed with `OPER(assem,dst,src)` and the `jumps()` method will return `null`; other operations have a list of "target" labels to which they may jump (this list must explicitly include the next instruction if it is possible to fall through to it). The `use()` method returns the `src` list, and the `def()` method returns the `dst` list, either of which may be `null`.

A LABEL is a point in a program to which jumps may go. It has an `assem` component showing how the label will look in the assembly language program and a `label` component identifying which label symbol was used.

A MOVE is like an OPER, but must perform only data transfer. Then, if the `dst` and `src` temporaries are assigned to the same register, the MOVE can later be deleted. The `use()` method returns a singleton list `src`, and the `def()` method returns a singleton list `dst`.

Calling *i*.`format`(*m*) formats an assembly instruction as a string; *m* is an object implementing the `TempMap` interface, which contains a method to give the register assignment (or perhaps just the name) of every temp.

```
package Temp;
public interface TempMap {
    public String tempMap(Temp.Temp t);
}
```

Machine independence. The `Assem.Instr` class is *independent* of the chosen target-machine assembly language (though it is tuned for machines with only one class of register). If the target machine is a Sparc, then the `assem` strings will be Sparc assembly language. We will use *Jouette* assembly language for illustration.

For example, the tree

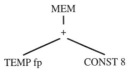

could be translated into *Jouette* assembly language as

```
new OPER("LOAD 'd0 <- M['s0+8]",
        new TempList(new Temp(), null),
        new TempList(frame.FP(), null));
```

This instruction needs some explanation. The actual assembly language of *Jouette*, after register allocation, might be

```
LOAD r1 <- M[r27+8]
```

assuming that register r_{27} is the frame pointer `fp` and that the register allocator decided to assign the new temp to register r_1. But the `Assem` instruction does not know about register assignments; instead, it just talks of the sources and destination of each instruction. This LOAD instruction has one source register, which is referred to as `'s0`, and one destination register, referred to as `'d0`.

Another example will be useful. The tree

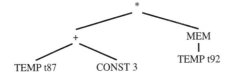

could be translated as

assem	*dst*	*src*
ADDI 'd0 <- 's0+3	t908	t87
LOAD 'd0 <- M['s0+0]	t909	t92
MUL 'd0 <- 's0*'s1	t910	t908,t909

where t908, t909, and t910 are temporaries newly chosen by the instruction selector.

After register allocation the assembly language might look like:

```
ADDI   r1 <- r12+3
LOAD   r2 <- M[r13+0]
MUL    r1 <- r1 * r2
```

The `string` of an `instr` may refer to *source registers* 's0, 's1, ... 's$(k-1)$, and *destination* registers 'd0, 'd1, etc. Jumps are OPER instructions that refer to labels 'j0, 'j1, etc. Conditional jumps, which may branch away or fall through, typically have two labels in the `jump` list but refer to only one of them in the `assem` string.

Two-address instructions. Some machines have arithmetic instructions with two operands, where one of the operands is both a source and a destination. The instruction add t1,t2, which has the effect of $t_1 \leftarrow t_1 + t_2$, can be described as

assem	*dst*	*src*
add 'd0,'s1	t1	t1, t2

where 's0 is implicitly, but not explicitly, mentioned in the `assem` string.

PRODUCING ASSEMBLY INSTRUCTIONS

Now it is a simple matter to write the right-hand sides of the pattern-matching clauses that "munch" `Tree` expressions into `Assem` instructions. We will show some examples from the *Jouette* code generator, but the same ideas apply to code generators for real machines.

The functions `munchStm` and `munchExp` will produce `Assem` instructions, bottom-up, as side effects. `MunchExp` returns the temporary in which the result is held.

```
Temp.Temp munchExp(Tree.Exp e);
void      munchStm(Tree.Stm s);
```

The "actions" of the `munchExp` clauses of Program 9.3 can be written as shown in Programs 9.5 and 9.6.

```
TempList L(Temp h, TempList t) {return new TempList(h,t);}

munchStm(SEQ(a,b))
    {munchStm(a); munchStm(b);}
munchStm(MOVE(MEM(BINOP(PLUS,e1,CONST(i))),e2))
    emit(new OPER("STORE M['s0+" + i + "] <- 's1\n",
               null, L(munchExp(e1), L(munchExp(e2), null))));
munchStm(MOVE(MEM(BINOP(PLUS,CONST(i),e1)),e2))
    emit(new OPER("STORE M['s0+" + i + "] <- 's1\n",
               null, L(munchExp(e1), L(munchExp(e2), null))));
munchStm(MOVE(MEM(e1),MEM(e2)))
    emit(new OPER("MOVE  M['s0] <- M['s1]\n",
               null, L(munchExp(e1), L(munchExp(e2), null))));
munchStm(MOVE(MEM(CONST(i)),e2))
    emit(new OPER("STORE M[r0+" + i + "] <- 's0\n",
               null, L(munchExp(e2), null)));
munchStm(MOVE(MEM(e1),e2))
    emit(new OPER("STORE M['s0] <- 's1\n",
               null, L(munchExp(e1), L(munchExp(e2), null))));
munchStm(MOVE(TEMP(i), e2))
    emit(new OPER("ADD    'd0 <- 's0 + r0\n",
               L(i,null), L(munchExp(e2), null)));
munchStm(LABEL(lab))
    emit(new Assem.LABEL(lab.toString() + ":\n", lab));
```

PROGRAM 9.5.   Assem-instructions for munchStm.

The emit function just accumulates a list of instructions to be returned later, as shown in Program 9.7.

PROCEDURE CALLS

Procedure calls are represented by EXP(CALL(f, $args$)), and function calls by MOVE(TEMP t, CALL(f, $args$)). These trees can be matched by tiles such as

```
munchStm(EXP(CALL(e,args)))
    {Temp r = munchExp(e); TempList l = munchArgs(0,args);
     emit(new OPER("CALL 's0\n",calldefs,L(r,l)));}
```

In this example, munchArgs generates code to move all the arguments to their correct positions, in outgoing parameter registers and/or in memory. The integer parameter to munchArgs is i for the ith argument; munchArgs will recur with $i + 1$ for the next argument, and so on.

What munchArgs returns is a list of all the temporaries that are to be passed to the machine's CALL instruction. Even though these temps are never

```
munchExp(MEM(BINOP(PLUS,e1,CONST(i))))
    Temp r = new Temp();
    emit(new OPER("LOAD 'd0 <- M['s0+" + i + "]\n",
                L(r,null), L(munchExp(e1),null)));
    return r;
munchExp(MEM(BINOP(PLUS,CONST(i),e1)))
    Temp r = new Temp();
    emit(new OPER("LOAD 'd0 <- M['s0+" + i + "]\n",
                L(r,null), L(munchExp(e1),null)));
    return r;
munchExp(MEM(CONST(i)))
    Temp r = new Temp();
    emit(new OPER("LOAD 'd0 <- M[r0+" + i + "]\n",
            L(r,null), null));
    return r;
munchExp(MEM(e1))
    Temp r = new Temp();
    emit(new OPER("LOAD 'd0 <- M['s0+0]\n",
                L(r,null), L(munchExp(e1),null)));
    return r;
munchExp(BINOP(PLUS,e1,CONST(i)))
    Temp r = new Temp();
    emit(new OPER("ADDI 'd0 <- 's0+" + i + "\n",
                L(r,null), L(munchExp(e1),null)));
    return r;
munchExp(BINOP(PLUS,CONST(i),e1))
    Temp r = new Temp();
    emit(new OPER("ADDI 'd0 <- 's0+" + i + "\n",
                L(r,null), L(munchExp(e1),null)));
    return r;
munchExp(CONST(i))
    Temp r = new Temp();
    emit(new OPER("ADDI 'd0 <- r0+" + i + "\n",
                null, L(munchExp(e1),null)));
    return r;
munchExp(BINOP(PLUS,e1,e2))
    Temp r = new Temp();
    emit(new OPER("ADD  'd0 <- 's0+'s1\n",
                L(r,null),L(munchExp(e1),L(munchExp(e2),null))));
    return r;
munchExp(TEMP(t))
    return t;
```

PROGRAM 9.6.   Assem-instructions for munchExp.

```
package Jouette;
public class Codegen {
  Frame frame;
  public Codegen(Frame f) {frame=f;}

  private Assem.InstrList ilist=null, last=null;

  private void emit(Assem.Instr inst) {
    if (last!=null)
      last = last.tail = new Assem.InstrList(inst,null);
    else last = ilist = new Assem.InstrList(inst,null);
  }

  void      munchStm(Tree.Stm s) { ··· }
  Temp.Temp munchExp(Tree.Exp s) { ··· }

  Assem.InstrList codegen(Tree.Stm s) {
      Assem.InstrList l;
      munchStm(s);
      l=ilist;
      ilist=last=null;
      return l;
  }
}

package Frame;
public class Frame {
  ...
  public Assem.InstrList codegen(Tree.Stm stm); {
      return (new Codegen(this)).codegen(stm);
  }
}
```

PROGRAM 9.7. The Codegen class.

written explicitly in assembly language, they should be listed as "sources" of the instruction, so that liveness analysis (Chapter 10) can see that their values need to be kept up to the point of call.

A CALL is expected to "trash" certain registers – the caller-save registers, the return-address register, and the return-value register. This list of calldefs should be listed as "destinations" of the CALL, so that the later phases of the compiler know that something happens to them here.

In general, any instruction that has the side effect of writing to another register requires this treatment. For example, the Pentium's multiply instruction writes to register edx with useless high-order result bits, so edx and eax are both listed as destinations of this instruction. (The high-order bits can be very useful for programs written in assembly language to do multiprecision arithmetic, but most programming languages do not support any way to access them.)

IF THERE'S NO FRAME POINTER

In a stack frame layout such as the one shown in Figure 6.2, the frame pointer points at one end of the frame and the stack pointer points at the other. At each procedure call, the stack pointer register is copied to the frame pointer register, and then the stack pointer is incremented by the size of the new frame.

Many machines' calling conventions do not use a frame pointer. Instead, the "virtual frame pointer" is always equal to stack pointer plus frame size. This saves time (no copy instruction) and space (one more register usable for other purposes). But our `Translate` phase has generated trees that refer to this fictitious frame pointer. The `codegen` function must replace any reference to FP+k with SP $+ k + fs$, where fs is the frame size. It can recognize these patterns as it munches the trees.

However, to replace them it must know the value of fs, which cannot yet be known because register allocation is not known. Assuming the function f is to be emitted at label L14 (for example), `codegen` can just put `sp+L14_framesize` in its assembly instructions and hope that the prologue for f (generated by `Frame.procEntryExit3`) will include a definition of the assembly language constant `L14_framesize`. Codegen is passed the `frame` argument (Program 9.7) so that it can learn the name L14.

Implementations that have a "real" frame pointer won't need this hack and can ignore the `frame` argument to `codegen`. But why would an implementation use a real frame pointer when it wastes time and space to do so? The answer is that this permits the frame size to grow and shrink even after it is first created; some languages have permitted dynamic allocation of arrays within the stack frame (e.g., using `alloca` in C). Calling-convention designers now tend to avoid dynamically adjustable frame sizes, however.

PROGRAM   INSTRUCTION SELECTION

Implement the translation to Assem-instructions for your favorite instruction set (let μ stand for *Sparc, Mips, Alpha, Pentium,* etc.) using maximal munch. If you would like to generate code for a RISC machine, but you have no RISC computer on which to test it, you may wish to use SPIM (a MIPS simulator implemented by James Larus), described on the Web page for this book.

First write the class μ.Codegen implementing the "maximal munch" translation algorithm from IR trees to the Assem data structure.

Use the Canon module (described in Chapter 8) to simplify the trees before applying your Codegen module to them. Use the format function to translate the resulting Assem trees to μ assembly language. Since you won't have done register assignment, just pass new Temp.DefaultMap() to format as the translation function from temporaries to strings.

```
package Temp;
public class DefaultMap implements TempMap {
        public String tempMap(Temp.Temp t) {
            return t.toString();
        }
}
```

This will produce "assembly" language that does not use register names at all: The instructions will use names such as t3, t283, and so on. But some of these temps are the "built-in" ones created by the Frame module to stand for particular machine registers (see page 143), such as Frame.FP. The assembly language will be easier to read if these registers appear with their natural names (e.g., fp instead of t1).

The Frame module must provide a mapping from the special temps to their names, and nonspecial temps to null:

```
package Frame;
public class Frame implements Temp.TempMap {
    ⋮
    abstract public String tempMap(Temp temp);
}
```

Then, for the purposes of displaying your assembly language prior to register allocation, make a new TempMap function that first tries frame.tempMap, and if that returns null, resorts to Temp.toString().

REGISTER LISTS

Make the following lists of registers; for each register, you will need a string for its assembly language representation and a Temp.Temp for referring to it in Tree and Assem data structures.

specialregs a list of μ registers used to implement "special" registers such as RV and FP and also the stack pointer SP, the return-address register RA, and (on some machines) the zero register ZERO. Some machines may have other special registers;

argregs a list of μ registers in which to pass outgoing arguments (including the static link);

calleesaves a list of μ registers that the called procedure (callee) must preserve unchanged (or save and restore);

callersaves a list of μ registers that the callee may trash.

The four lists of registers must not overlap, and must include any register that might show up in Assem instructions. These lists are not public, but they are useful internally for both Frame and Codegen – for example, to implement munchArgs and to construct the calldefs list.

Implement the procEntryExit2 function of the μ.Frame class.

```
package Frame;
class Frame implements Temp.TempMap {
    ⋮
   abstract public Assem.InstrList procEntryExit2(
                                Assem.InstrList body);
}
```

This function appends a "sink" instruction to the function body to tell the register allocator that certain registers are live at procedure exit. In the case of the *Jouette* machine, this is simply:

```
package Jouette;
class Frame extends Frame.Frame {
    ⋮
  static TempList returnSink =
                 L(ZERO, L(RA, L(SP, calleeSaves)));

  static Assem.InstrList append(Assem.InstrList a,
                              Assem.InstrList b) {
        if (a==null) return b;
        else {Assem.InstrList p;
             for(p=a; p.tail!=null; p=p.tail) {}
             p.tail=b;
             return a;
        }
    }
}
```

```
public Assem.InstrList procEntryExit2(
                              Assem.InstrList body) {
   return append(body,
     new Assem.InstrList(
           new Assem.OPER("", null, returnSink),null));
  }
}
```

meaning that the temporaries *zero*, *return-address*, *stack pointer*, and all the callee-saves registers are still live at the end of the function. Having *zero* live at the end means that it is live throughout, which will prevent the register allocator from trying to use it for some other purpose. The same trick works for any other special registers the machine might have.

Files available in $MINIJAVA/chap9 include:

Canon/* Canonicalization and trace generation.
Assem/* The Assem module.
Main/Main.java A Main module that you may wish to adapt.

Your code generator will handle only the body of each procedure or function, but not the procedure entry/exit sequences. Use a "scaffold" version of Frame.procEntryExit3 function:

```
package μ;
class Frame extends Frame.Frame {
    ⋮
    public Frame.Proc procEntryExit3(Assem.InstrList body) {
        return new Frame.Proc(
            "PROCEDURE " + name.toString() + "\n",
            body,
            "END " + name.toString() + "\n");
    }
}
```

FURTHER READING

Cattell [1980] expressed machine instructions as tree patterns, invented the maximal munch algorithm for instruction selection, and built a *code-generator generator* to produce an instruction selection function from a tree-pattern description of an instruction set. Glanville and Graham [1978] expressed the tree patterns as productions in LR(1) grammars, which allows the maximal munch algorithm to use multiple nonterminal symbols to represent different classes of registers and addressing modes. But grammars describing instruction sets are inherently ambiguous, leading to problems with the LR(1) approach; Aho et al. [1989] use dynamic programming to parse the tree grammars, which solves the ambiguity problem, and describe the *Twig* automatic code-generator generator. The dynamic programming can be done at compiler-construction time instead of code-generation time [Pelegri-Llopart and Graham 1988]; using this technique, the *BURG* tool [Fraser et al. 1992] has an interface similar to Twig's but generates code much faster.

EXERCISES

9.1 For each of the following expressions, draw the tree and generate *Jouette*-machine instructions using maximal munch. Circle the tiles (as in Figure 9.2), but number them *in the order that they are munched*, and show the sequence of *Jouette* instructions that results.

a. MOVE(MEM(+(+(CONST$_{1000}$, MEM(TEMP$_x$)), TEMP$_{fp}$)), CONST$_0$)

b. BINOP(MUL, CONST$_5$, MEM(CONST$_{100}$))

*9.2 Consider a machine with the following instruction:
```
mult const1(src1), const2(src2), dst3
```
$r_3 \leftarrow M[r_1 + \text{const}_1] * M[r_2 + \text{const}_2]$
On this machine, r_0 is always 0, and $M[1]$ always contains 1.

a. Draw all the tree patterns corresponding to this instruction (and its special cases).

b. Pick **one** of the bigger patterns and show how to write a Java if-statement to match it, with the `Tree` representation used for the MiniJava compiler.

9.3 The *Jouette* machine has control-flow instructions as follows:

BRANCHGE	if $r_i \geq 0$ goto L
BRANCHLT	if $r_i < 0$ goto L
BRANCHEQ	if $r_i = 0$ goto L
BRANCHNE	if $r_i \neq 0$ goto L
JUMP	goto r_i

where the JUMP instruction goes to an address contained in a register.
Use these instructions to implement the following tree patterns:

Assume that a CJUMP is always followed by its false label. Show the best way to implement each pattern; in some cases you may need to use more than one instruction or make up a new temporary. How do you implement CJUMP(GT, . . .) without a BRANCHGT instruction?

10

Liveness Analysis

live: of continuing or current interest

Webster's Dictionary

The front end of the compiler translates programs into an intermediate language with an unbounded number of temporaries. This program must run on a machine with a bounded number of registers. Two temporaries a and b can fit into the same register, if a and b are never "in use" at the same time. Thus, many temporaries can fit in few registers; if they don't all fit, the excess temporaries can be kept in memory.

Therefore, the compiler needs to analyze the intermediate-representation program to determine which temporaries are in use at the same time. We say a variable is *live* if it holds a value that may be needed in the future, so this analysis is called *liveness* analysis.

To perform analyses on a program, it is often useful to make a *control-flow graph*. Each statement in the program is a node in the flow graph; if statement x can be followed by statement y, there is an edge from x to y. Graph 10.1 shows the flow graph for a simple loop.

Let us consider the liveness of each variable (Figure 10.2). A variable is live if its current value will be used in the future, so we analyze liveness by working from the future to the past. Variable b is used in statement 4, so b is live on the $3 \rightarrow 4$ edge. Since statement 3 does not assign into b, then b is also live on the $2 \rightarrow 3$ edge. Statement 2 assigns into b. That means that the contents of b on the $1 \rightarrow 2$ edge are not needed by anyone; b is dead on this edge. So the *live range* of b is $\{2 \rightarrow 3, \ 3 \rightarrow 4\}$.

The variable a is an interesting case. It's live from $1 \rightarrow 2$, and again from $4 \rightarrow 5 \rightarrow 2$, but not from $2 \rightarrow 3 \rightarrow 4$. Although a has a perfectly

$$a \leftarrow 0$$
$$L_1 : b \leftarrow a + 1$$
$$c \leftarrow c + b$$
$$a \leftarrow b * 2$$
$$\text{if } a < N \text{ goto } L_1$$
$$\text{return } c$$

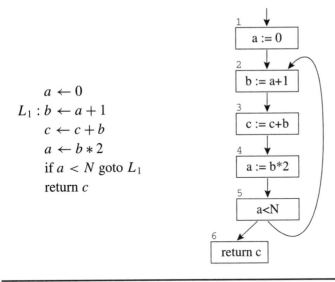

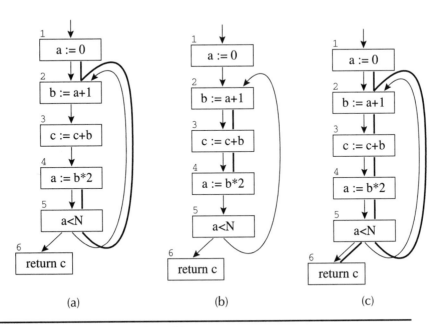

GRAPH 10.1.   Control-flow graph of a program.

FIGURE 10.2.   Liveness of variables a, b, c.

well-defined value at node 3, that value will not be needed again before a is assigned a new value.

The variable c is live on entry to this program. Perhaps it is a formal parameter. If it is a local variable, then liveness analysis has detected an uninitialized variable; the compiler could print a warning message for the programmer.

Once all the live ranges are computed, we can see that only two registers are needed to hold a, b, and c, since a and b are never live at the same time. Register 1 can hold both a and b, and register 2 can hold c.

10.1   SOLUTION OF DATAFLOW EQUATIONS

Liveness of variables "flows" around the edges of the control-flow graph; determining the live range of each variable is an example of a *dataflow* problem. Chapter 17 will discuss several other kinds of dataflow problems.

Flow-graph terminology. A flow-graph node has *out-edges* that lead to *successor* nodes, and *in-edges* that come from *predecessor* nodes. The set $pred[n]$ is all the predecessors of node n, and $succ[n]$ is the set of successors.

In Graph 10.1 the out-edges of node 5 are $5 \rightarrow 6$ and $5 \rightarrow 2$, and $succ[5] = \{2, 6\}$. The in-edges of 2 are $5 \rightarrow 2$ and $1 \rightarrow 2$, and $pred[2] = \{1, 5\}$.

Uses and defs. An assignment to a variable or temporary *defines* that variable. An occurrence of a variable on the right-hand side of an assignment (or in other expressions) *uses* the variable. We can speak of the *def* of a variable as the set of graph nodes that define it; or the *def* of a graph node as the set of variables that it defines; and similarly for the *use* of a variable or graph node. In Graph 10.1, $def(3) = \{c\}$, $use(3) = \{b, c\}$.

Liveness. A variable is *live* on an edge if there is a directed path from that edge to a *use* of the variable that does not go through any *def*. A variable is *live-in* at a node if it is live on any of the in-edges of that node; it is *live-out* at a node if it is live on any of the out-edges of the node.

CALCULATION OF LIVENESS
Liveness information (*live-in* and *live-out*) can be calculated from *use* and *def* as follows:

$$in[n] = use[n] \cup (out[n] - def[n])$$
$$out[n] = \bigcup_{s \in succ[n]} in[s]$$

EQUATIONS 10.3. Dataflow equations for liveness analysis.

---

for each n
    $in[n] \leftarrow \{\}; \ out[n] \leftarrow \{\}$
repeat
    for each n
        $in'[n] \leftarrow in[n]; \ out'[n] \leftarrow out[n]$
        $in[n] \leftarrow use[n] \cup (out[n] - def[n])$
        $out[n] \leftarrow \bigcup_{s \in succ[n]} in[s]$
until $in'[n] = in[n]$ and $out'[n] = out[n]$ for all n

ALGORITHM 10.4. Computation of liveness by iteration.

---

1. If a variable is in $use[n]$, then it is *live-in* at node n. That is, if a statement uses a variable, the variable is live on entry to that statement.
2. If a variable is *live-in* at a node n, then it is *live-out* at all nodes m in $pred[n]$.
3. If a variable is *live-out* at node n, and not in $def[n]$, then the variable is also *live-in* at n. That is, if someone needs the value of a at the end of statement n, and n does not provide that value, then a's value is needed even on entry to n.

These three statements can be written as Equations 10.3 on sets of variables. The live-in sets are an array $in[n]$ indexed by node, and the live-out sets are an array $out[n]$. That is, $in[n]$ is all the variables in $use[n]$, plus all the variables in $out[n]$ and not in $def[n]$. And $out[n]$ is the union of the live-in sets of all successors of n.

Algorithm 10.4 finds a solution to these equations by iteration. As usual, we initialize $in[n]$ and $out[n]$ to the the empty set $\{\}$, for all n, then repeatedly treat the equations as assignment statements until a fixed point is reached.

Table 10.5 shows the results of running the algorithm on Graph 10.1. The columns 1st, 2nd, etc., are the values of in and out on successive iterations of the **repeat** loop. Since the 7th column is the same as the 6th, the algorithm terminates.

We can speed the convergence of this algorithm significantly by ordering the nodes properly. Suppose there is an edge $3 \rightarrow 4$ in the graph. Since $in[4]$

	use	def	1st in	1st out	2nd in	2nd out	3rd in	3rd out	4th in	4th out	5th in	5th out	6th in	6th out	7th in	7th out
1		a				a		a		ac	c	ac	c	ac	c	ac
2	a	b	a		a	bc	ac	bc	ac	bc	ac	bc	ac	bc	ac	bc
3	bc	c	bc		bc	b	bc	b	bc	b	bc	b	bc	bc	bc	bc
4	b	a	b		b	a	b	a	b	ac	bc	ac	bc	ac	bc	ac
5	a		a	a	a	ac	ac	ac	ac	ac	ac	ac	ac	ac	ac	ac
6	c		c		c		c		c		c		c		c	

TABLE 10.5. Liveness calculation following forward control-flow edges.

	use	def	1st out	1st in	2nd out	2nd in	3rd out	3rd in
6	c			c		c		c
5	a		c	ac	ac	ac	ac	ac
4	b	a	ac	bc	ac	bc	ac	bc
3	bc	c	bc	bc	bc	bc	bc	bc
2	a	b	bc	ac	bc	ac	bc	ac
1		a	ac	c	ac	c	ac	c

TABLE 10.6. Liveness calculation following reverse control-flow edges.

is computed from *out*[4], and *out*[3] is computed from *in*[4], and so on, we should compute the in and out sets in the order *out*[4] → *in*[4] → *out*[3] → *in*[3]. But in Table 10.5, just the opposite order is used in each iteration! We have waited as long as possible (in each iteration) to make use of information gained from the previous iteration.

Table 10.6 shows the computation, in which each **for** loop iterates from 6 to 1 (approximately following the *reversed* direction of the flow-graph arrows), and in each iteration the out sets are computed before the in sets. By the end of the second iteration, the fixed point has been found; the third iteration just confirms this.

When solving dataflow equations by iteration, the order of computation should follow the "flow." Since liveness flows *backward* along control-flow arrows, and from "out" to "in," so should the computation.

Ordering the nodes can be done easily by depth-first search, as shown in Section 17.4.

Basic blocks. Flow-graph nodes that have only one predecessor and one successor are not very interesting. Such nodes can be merged with their predecessors and successors; what results is a graph with many fewer nodes, where each node represents a basic block. The algorithms that operate on flow graphs, such as liveness analysis, go much faster on the smaller graphs. Chapter 17 explains how to adjust the dataflow equations to use basic blocks. In this chapter we keep things simple.

One variable at a time. Instead of doing dataflow "in parallel" using set equations, it can be just as practical to compute dataflow for one variable at a time as information about that variable is needed. For liveness, this would mean repeating the dataflow traversal once for each temporary. Starting from each *use* site of a temporary t, and tracing backward (following *predecessor* edges of the flow graph) using depth-first search, we note the liveness of t at each flow-graph node. The search stops at any definition of the temporary. Although this might seem expensive, many temporaries have very short live ranges, so the searches terminate quickly and do not traverse the entire flow graph for most variables.

REPRESENTATION OF SETS

There are at least two good ways to represent sets for dataflow equations: as arrays of bits or as sorted lists of variables.

If there are N variables in the program, the bit-array representation uses N bits for each set. Calculating the union of two sets is done by *or*-ing the corresponding bits at each position. Since computers can represent K bits per word (with $K = 32$ typical), one set-union operation takes N/K operations.

A set can also be represented as a linked list of its members, sorted by any totally ordered key (such as variable name). Calculating the union is done by merging the lists (discarding duplicates). This takes time proportional to the size of the sets being unioned.

Clearly, when the sets are sparse (fewer than N/K elements, on the average), the sorted-list representation is asymptotically faster; when the sets are dense, the bit-array representation is better.

TIME COMPLEXITY

How fast is iterative dataflow analysis?

A program of size N has at most N nodes in the flow graph, and at most N variables. Thus, each live-in set (or live-out set) has at most N elements;

(a) Matrix   (b) Graph

FIGURE 10.9.   Representations of interference.

registers $r_1, \ldots, r_k$. A condition that prevents a and b from being allocated to the same register is called an *interference*.

The most common kind of interference is caused by overlapping live ranges: When a and b are both live at the same program point, then they cannot be put in the same register. But there are some other causes of interference: for example, when a must be generated by an instruction that cannot address register r_1, then a and r_1 interfere.

Interference information can be expressed as a matrix; Figure 10.9a has an **x** marking interferences of the variables in Graph 10.1. The interference matrix can also be expressed as an undirected graph (Figure 10.9b), with a node for each variable, and edges connecting variables that interfere.

Special treatment of MOVE instructions. In static liveness analysis, we can give MOVE instructions special consideration. It is important not to create artifical interferences between the source and destination of a move. Consider the program:

$t \leftarrow s$ (*copy*)

$\vdots$

$x \leftarrow \ldots s \ldots$ (*use of s*)

$\vdots$

$y \leftarrow \ldots t \ldots$ (*use of t*)

After the copy instruction both s and t are live, and normally we would make an interference edge (s, t) since t is being defined at a point where s is live. But we do not need separate registers for s and t, since they contain the same value. The solution is just not to add an interference edge (t, s) in this case. Of course, if there is a later (nonmove) definition of t while s is still live, that will create the interference edge (t, s).

Therefore, the way to add interference edges for each new definition is

```
package Graph;

public class Graph {
  public Graph();
  public NodeList nodes();
  public Node newNode();
  public void addEdge(Node from, Node to);
  public void rmEdge(Node from, Node to);
  public void show(java.io.PrintStream out);
}

public class Node {
    public Node(Graph g);
    public NodeList succ();
    public NodeList pred();
    public NodeList adj();
    public int outDegree();
    public int inDegree();
    public int degree();
    public boolean goesTo(Node n);
    public boolean comesFrom(Node n);
    public boolean adj(Node n);
    public String toString();
}
```

PROGRAM 10.10. The `Graph` abstract data type.

1. At any nonmove instruction that *defines* a variable a, where the *live-out* variables are $b_1, \ldots, b_j$, add interference edges $(a, b_1), \ldots, (a, b_j)$.
2. At a move instruction $a \leftarrow c$, where variables $b_1, \ldots, b_j$ are *live-out*, add interference edges $(a, b_1), \ldots, (a, b_j)$ for any b_i that is *not* the same as c.

10.2   LIVENESS IN THE MiniJava COMPILER

The flow analysis for the MiniJava compiler is done in two stages: First, the control flow of the `Assem` program is analyzed, producing a control-flow graph; then, the liveness of variables in the control-flow graph is analyzed, producing an interference graph.

GRAPHS

To represent both kinds of graphs, let's make a `Graph` abstract data type (Program 10.10).

The constructor `Graph()` creates an empty directed graph; `g.newNode()` makes a new node within a graph *g*. A directed edge from *n* to *m* is created by `g.addEdge(n,m)`; after that, *m* will be found in the list `n.succ()` and *n* will be in `m.pred()`. When working with undirected graphs, the function `adj` is useful: $m.\text{adj}() = m.\text{succ}() \cup m.\text{pred}()$.

To delete an edge, use `rmEdge`. To test whether *m* and *n* are the same node, use `m==n`.

When using a graph in an algorithm, we want each node to represent something (an instruction in a program, for example). To make mappings from nodes to the things they are supposed to represent, we use a `Hashtable`. The following idiom associates information *x* with node *n* in a mapping `mytable`.

```
java.util.Dictionary mytable = new java.util.Hashtable();
  ···   mytable.put(n,x);
```

CONTROL-FLOW GRAPHS

The `FlowGraph` package manages control-flow graphs. Each instruction (or basic block) is represented by a node in the flow graph. If instruction *m* can be followed by instruction *n* (either by a jump or by falling through), then there will be an edge (m, n) in the graph.

```
public abstract class FlowGraph extends Graph.Graph {
    public abstract TempList def(Node node);
    public abstract TempList use(Node node);
    public abstract boolean isMove(Node node);
    public void show(java.io.PrintStream out);
}
```

Each `Node` of the flow graph represents an instruction (or, perhaps, a basic block). The `def()` method tells what temporaries are defined at this node (destination registers of the instruction). `use()` tells what temporaries are used at this node (source registers of the instruction). `isMove` tells whether this instruction is a MOVE instruction, one that could be deleted if the `def` and `use` were identical.

The `AssemFlowGraph` class provides an implementation of `FlowGraph` for `Assem` instructions.

```
package FlowGraph;
public class AssemFlowGraph extends FlowGraph {
    public Instr instr(Node n);
    public AssemFlowGraph(Assem.InstrList instrs);
}
```

The constructor `AssemFlowGraph` takes a list of instructions and returns a flow graph. In making the flow graph, the `jump` fields of the `instrs` are used in creating control-flow edges, and the `use` and `def` information (obtained from the `src` and `dst` fields of the `instrs`) is attached to the nodes by means of the `use` and `def` methods of the `flowgraph`.

Information associated with the nodes. For a flow graph, we want to associate some *use* and *def* information with each node in the graph. Then the liveness-analysis algorithm will also want to remember *live-in* and *live-out* information at each node. We could make room in the `Node` class to store all of this information. This would work well and would be quite efficient. However, it may not be very modular. Eventually we may want to do other analyses on flow graphs, which remember other kinds of information about each node. We may not want to modify the data structure (which is a widely used interface) for each new analysis.

Instead of storing the information *in* the nodes, a more modular approach is to say that a graph is a graph, and that a flow graph is a graph along with separately packaged auxiliary information (tables, or functions mapping nodes to whatever). Similarly, a dataflow algorithm on a graph does not need to modify dataflow information *in* the nodes, but modifies its own privately held mappings.

There may be a trade-off here between efficiency and modularity, since it may be faster to keep the information *in* the nodes, accessible by a simple pointer-traversal instead of a hash-table or search-tree lookup.

LIVENESS ANALYSIS

The `RegAlloc` package has an abstract class `InterferenceGraph` to indicate which pairs of temporaries cannot share a register:

```
package RegAlloc;
abstract public class InterferenceGraph extends Graph.Graph{
    abstract public Graph.Node tnode(Temp.Temp temp);
    abstract public Temp.Temp gtemp(Node node);
    abstract public MoveList moves();
    public int spillCost(Node node);
}
```

The method `tnode` relates a `Temp` to a `Node`, and `gtemp` is the inverse map. The method `moves` tells what MOVE instructions are associated with this graph (this is a hint about what pairs of temporaries to try to allocate to the same register). The `spillCost(n)` is an estimate of how many extra instructions would be executed if n were kept in memory instead of in registers; for a naive spiller, it suffices to return 1 for every n.

The class Liveness produces an interference graph from a flow graph:

```
package RegAlloc;
public class Liveness extends InterferenceGraph {
    public Liveness(FlowGraph flow);
}
```

In the implementation of the Liveness module, it is useful to maintain a data structure that remembers what is live at the exit of each flow-graph node:

```
private java.util.Dictionary liveMap =
                        new java.util.Hashtable();
```

where the keys are nodes and objects are TempLists. Given a flow-graph node n, the set of live temporaries at that node can be looked up in a global liveMap.

Having calculated a complete liveMap, we can now construct an interference graph. At each flow node n where there is a newly defined temporary $d \in def(n)$, and where temporaries $\{t_1, t_2, \ldots\}$ are in the liveMap, we just add interference edges $(d, t_1), (d, t_2), \ldots$. For MOVEs, these edges will be safe but suboptimal; pages 213–214 describe a better treatment.

What if a newly defined temporary is not live just after its definition? This would be the case if a variable is defined but never used. It would seem that there's no need to put it in a register at all; thus it would not interfere with any other temporaries. But if the defining instruction is going to execute (perhaps it is necessary for some other side effect of the instruction), then it *will* write to some register, and that register had better not contain any other live variable. Thus, zero-length live ranges *do* interfere with any live ranges that overlap them.

PROGRAM   CONSTRUCTING FLOW GRAPHS

Implement the AssemFlowGraph class that turns a list of Assem instructions into a flow graph. Use the abstract classes Graph.Graph and Flow-Graph.FlowGraph provided in $MINIJAVA/chap10.

PROGRAM   LIVENESS

Implement the Liveness module. Use either the set-equation algorithm with the array-of-boolean or sorted-list-of-temporaries representation of sets, or the one-variable-at-a-time method.

EXERCISES

10.1 Perform flow analysis on the program of Exercise 8.6:

a. Draw the control-flow graph.

b. Calculate live-in and live-out at each statement.

c. Construct the register interference graph.

**10.2 Prove that Equations 10.3 have a least fixed point and that Algorithm 10.4 always computes it.

    Hint: We know the algorithm refuses to terminate until it has a fixed point. The questions are whether (a) it must eventually terminate, and (b) the fixed point it computes is smaller than all other fixed points. For (a) show that the sets can only get bigger. For (b) show by induction that at any time the *in* and *out* sets are subsets of those in any possible fixed point. This is clearly true initially, when *in* and *out* are both empty; show that each step of the algorithm preserves the invariant.

*10.3 Analyze the asymptotic complexity of the one-variable-at-a-time method of computing dataflow information.

*10.4 Analyze the worst-case asymptotic complexity of making an interference graph, for a program of size N (with at most N variables and at most N control-flow nodes). Assume the dataflow analysis is already done and that *use*, *def*, and *live-out* information for each node can be queried in constant time. What representation of graph adjacency matrices should be used for efficiency?

10.5 The DEC Alpha architecture places the following restrictions on floating-point instructions, for programs that wish to recover from arithmetic exceptions:

1. Within a basic block (actually, in any sequence of instructions not separated by a *trap-barrier* instruction), no two instructions should write to the same destination register.

2. A source register of an instruction cannot be the same as the destination register of that instruction or any later instruction in the basic block.

$r_1 + r_5 \rightarrow r_4$	$r_1 + r_5 \rightarrow r_4$	$r_1 + r_5 \rightarrow r_3$	$r_1 + r_5 \rightarrow r_4$
$r_3 \times r_2 \rightarrow r_4$	$r_4 \times r_2 \rightarrow r_1$	$r_4 \times r_2 \rightarrow r_4$	$r_4 \times r_2 \rightarrow r_6$
violates rule 1.	*violates rule 2.*	*violates rule 2.*	*OK*

Show how to express these restrictions in the register interference graph.

11

Register Allocation

reg-is-ter: a device for storing small amounts of data
al-lo-cate: to apportion for a specific purpose

Webster's Dictionary

The `Translate`, `Canon`, and `Codegen` phases of the compiler assume that there are an infinite number of registers to hold temporary values and that MOVE instructions cost nothing. The job of the register allocator is to assign the many temporaries to a small number of machine registers, and, where possible, to assign the source and destination of a MOVE to the same register so that the MOVE can be deleted.

From an examination of the control and dataflow graph, we derive an *interference graph*. Each node in the interference graph represents a temporary value; each edge (t_1, t_2) indicates a pair of temporaries that cannot be assigned to the same register. The most common reason for an interference edge is that t_1 and t_2 are live at the same time. Interference edges can also express other constraints; for example, if a certain instruction $a \leftarrow b \oplus c$ cannot produce results in register r_{12} on our machine, we can make a interfere with r_{12}.

Next we *color* the interference graph. We want to use as few colors as possible, but no pair of nodes connected by an edge may be assigned the same color. Graph coloring problems derive from the old mapmakers' rule that adjacent countries on a map should be colored with different colors. Our "colors" correspond to registers: If our target machine has K registers, and we can K-color the graph (color the graph with K colors), then the coloring is a valid register assignment for the interference graph. If there is no K-coloring, we will have to keep some of our variables and temporaries in memory instead of registers; this is called *spilling*.

11.1   COLORING BY SIMPLIFICATION

Register allocation is an NP-complete problem (except in special cases, such as expression trees); graph coloring is also NP-complete. Fortunately there is a linear-time approximation algorithm that gives good results; its principal phases are **Build**, **Simplify**, **Spill**, and **Select**.

Build: Construct the interference graph. We use dataflow analysis to compute the set of temporaries that are simultaneously live at each program point, and we add an edge to the graph for each pair of temporaries in the set. We repeat this for all program points.

Simplify: We color the graph using a simple heuristic. Suppose the graph G contains a node m with fewer than K neighbors, where K is the number of registers on the machine. Let G' be the graph $G - \{m\}$ obtained by removing m. If G' can be colored, then so can G, for when m is added to the colored graph G', the neighbors of m have at most $K - 1$ colors among them, so a free color can always be found for m. This leads naturally to a stack-based (or recursive) algorithm for coloring: We repeatedly remove (and push on a stack) nodes of degree less than K. Each such simplification will decrease the degrees of other nodes, leading to more opportunity for simplification.

Spill: Suppose at some point during simplification the graph G has nodes only of *significant degree*, that is, nodes of degree $\geq K$. Then the *simplify* heuristic fails, and we mark some node for spilling. That is, we choose some node in the graph (standing for a temporary variable in the program) and decide to represent it in memory, not registers, during program execution. An optimistic approximation to the effect of spilling is that the spilled node does not interfere with any of the other nodes remaining in the graph. It can therefore be removed and pushed on the stack, and the simplify process continued.

Select: We assign colors to nodes in the graph. Starting with the empty graph, we rebuild the original graph by repeatedly adding a node from the top of the stack. When we add a node to the graph, there must be a color for it, as the premise for removing it in the simplify phase was that it could always be assigned a color provided the remaining nodes in the graph could be successfully colored.

When *potential spill* node n that was pushed using the *Spill* heuristic is

11.2   COALESCING

It is easy to eliminate redundant move instructions with an interference graph. If there is no edge in the interference graph between the source and destination of a move instruction, then the move can be eliminated. The source and destination nodes are *coalesced* into a new node whose edges are the union of those of the nodes being replaced.

In principle, any pair of nodes not connected by an interference edge could be coalesced. This aggressive form of copy propagation is very successful at eliminating move instructions. Unfortunately, the node being introduced is more constrained than those being removed, as it contains a union of edges. Thus, it is quite possible that a graph, colorable with K colors before coalescing, may no longer be K-colorable after reckless coalescing. We wish to coalesce only where it is *safe* to do so, that is, where the coalescing will not render the graph uncolorable. Both of the following strategies are safe:

Briggs: Nodes a and b can be coalesced if the resulting node ab will have fewer than K neighbors of significant degree (i.e., having $\geq K$ edges). The coalescing is guaranteed not to turn a K-colorable graph into a non-K-colorable graph, because after the simplify phase has removed all the insignificant-degree nodes from the graph, the coalesced node will be adjacent only to those neighbors that were of significant degree. Since there are fewer than K of these, *simplify* can then remove the coalesced node from the graph. Thus if the original graph was colorable, the conservative coalescing strategy does not alter the colorability of the graph.

George: Nodes a and b can be coalesced if, for every neighbor t of a, either t already interferes with b or t is of insignificant degree. This coalescing is safe, by the following reasoning. Let S be the set of insignificant-degree neighbors of a in the original graph. If the coalescing were not done, *simplify* could remove all the nodes in S, leaving a reduced graph G_1. If the coalescing is done, then *simplify* can remove all the nodes in S, leaving a graph G_2. But G_2 is a subgraph of G_1 (the node ab in G_2 corresponds to the node b in G_1), and thus must be at least as easy to color.

These strategies are *conservative*, because there are still safe situations in which they will fail to coalesce. This means that the program may perform some unnecessary MOVE instructions – but this is better than spilling!

Interleaving simplification steps with conservative coalescing eliminates most move instructions, while still guaranteeing not to introduce spills. The coalesce, simplify, and spill procedures should be alternated until the graph is empty, as shown in Figure 11.4.

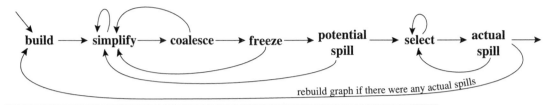

FIGURE 11.4.   Graph coloring with coalescing.

These are the phases of a register allocator with coalescing:

Build: Construct the interference graph, and categorize each node as either *move-related* or *non-move-related*. A move-related node is one that is either the source or destination of a move instruction.

Simplify: One at a time, remove non-move-related nodes of low ($< K$) degree from the graph.

Coalesce: Perform conservative coalescing on the reduced graph obtained in the simplification phase. Since the degrees of many nodes have been reduced by *simplify*, the conservative strategy is likely to find many more moves to coalesce than it would have in the initial interference graph. After two nodes have been coalesced (and the move instruction deleted), if the resulting node is no longer move-related, it will be available for the next round of simplification. *Simplify* and *coalesce* are repeated until only significant-degree or move-related nodes remain.

Freeze: If neither *simplify* nor *coalesce* applies, we look for a move-related node of low degree. We *freeze* the moves in which this node is involved: That is, we give up hope of coalescing those moves. This causes the node (and perhaps other nodes related to the frozen moves) to be considered non-move-related, which should enable more simplification. Now, *simplify* and *coalesce* are resumed.

Spill: If there are no low-degree nodes, we select a significant-degree node for potential spilling and push it on the stack.

Select: Pop the entire stack, assigning colors.
    Consider Graph 11.1; nodes b, c, d, and j are the only move-related nodes. The initial work list used in the simplify phase must contain only non-move-

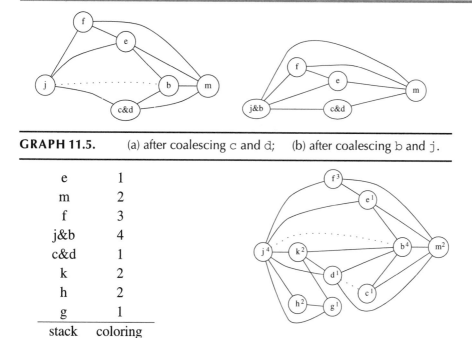

GRAPH 11.5.   (a) after coalescing c and d;   (b) after coalescing b and j.

stack	coloring
e	1
m	2
f	3
j&b	4
c&d	1
k	2
h	2
g	1

FIGURE 11.6.   A coloring, with coalescing, for Graph 11.1.

related nodes and consists of nodes g, h, and f. Once again, after removal of g, h, and k we obtain Graph 11.2.

We could continue the simplification phase further; however, if we invoke a round of coalescing at this point, we discover that c and d are indeed coalesceable as the coalesced node has only two neighbors of significant degree: m and b. The resulting graph is shown in Graph 11.5a, with the coalesced node labeled as c&d.

From Graph 11.5a we see that it is possible to coalesce b and j as well. Nodes b and j are adjacent to two neighbors of significant degree, namely m and e. The result of coalescing b and j is shown in Graph 11.5b.

After coalescing these two moves, there are no more move-related nodes, and therefore no more coalescing is possible. The simplify phase can be invoked one more time to remove all the remaining nodes. A possible assignment of colors is shown in Figure 11.6.

Some moves are neither coalesced nor frozen. Instead, they are *constrained*. Consider the graph x, y, z, where (x, z) is the only interference edge and there are two moves $x \leftarrow y$ and $y \leftarrow z$. Either move is a candidate for coalescing. But after x and y are coalesced, the remaining move $xy \leftarrow z$ cannot be coalesced because of the interference edge (xy, z). We say this move is *constrained*, and we remove it from further consideration: It no longer causes nodes to be treated as move-related.

SPILLING

If spilling is necessary, *build* and *simplify* must be repeated on the whole program. The simplest version of the algorithm discards any coalescences found if *build* must be repeated. Then it is easy to see that coalescing does not increase the number of spills in any future round of *build*. A more efficient algorithm preserves any coalescences done *before the first potential spill was discovered*, but discards (uncoalesces) any coalescences done after that point.

Coalescing of spills. On a machine with many registers (> 20), there will usually be few spilled nodes. But on a six-register machine (such as the Intel Pentium), there will be many spills. The front end may have generated many temporaries, and transformations such as SSA (described in Chapter 19) may split them into many more temporaries. If each spilled temporary lives in its own stack-frame location, then the frame may be quite large.

Even worse, there may be many move instructions involving pairs of spilled nodes. But to implement $a \leftarrow b$ when a and b are both spilled temporaries requires a fetch-store sequence, $t \leftarrow M[b_{\text{loc}}]; \ M[a_{\text{loc}}] \leftarrow t$. This is expensive, and also defines a temporary t that itself may cause other nodes to spill.

But many of the spill pairs are never live simultaneously. Thus, they may be graph-colored, with coalescing! In fact, because there is no fixed limit to the number of stack-frame locations, we can coalesce aggressively, without worrying about how many high-degree neighbors the spill nodes have. The algorithm is thus:

1. Use liveness information to construct the interference graph for spilled nodes.
2. While there is any pair of noninterfering spilled nodes connected by a move instruction, coalesce them.
3. Use *simplify* and *select* to color the graph. There is no (further) spilling in this coloring; instead, *simplify* just picks the lowest-degree node, and *select* picks the first available color, without any predetermined limit on the number of colors.
4. The colors correspond to activation-record locations for the spilled variables.

This should be done *before* generating the spill instructions and regenerating the register-temporary interference graph, so as to avoid creating fetch-store sequences for coalesced moves of spilled nodes.

11.3 PRECOLORED NODES

Some temporaries are *precolored* – they represent machine registers. The front end generates these when interfacing to standard calling conventions across module boundaries, for example. For each actual register that is used for some specific purpose, such as the frame pointer, standard-argument-1-register, standard-argument-2-register, and so on, the `Codegen` or `Frame` module should use the particular temporary that is permanently bound to that register (see also page 251). For any given color (that is, for any given machine register) there should be only one precolored node of that color.

The *select* and *coalesce* operations can give an ordinary temporary the same color as a precolored register, as long as they don't interfere, and in fact this is quite common. Thus, a standard calling-convention register can be reused inside a procedure as a temporary variable. Precolored nodes may be coalesced with other (non-precolored) nodes using conservative coalescing.

For a K-register machine, there will be K precolored nodes that all interfere with each other. Those of the precolored nodes that are not used explicitly (in a parameter-passing convention, for example) will not interfere with any ordinary (non-precolored) nodes; but a machine register used explicitly will have a live range that interferes with any other variables that happen to be live at the same time.

We cannot *simplify* a precolored node – this would mean pulling it from the graph in the hope that we can assign it a color later, but in fact we have no freedom about what color to assign it. And we should not spill precolored nodes to memory, because the machine registers are by definition *registers*. Thus, we should treat them as having "infinite" degree.

TEMPORARY COPIES OF MACHINE REGISTERS

The coloring algorithm works by calling *simplify, coalesce,* and *spill* until only the precolored nodes remain, and then the *select* phase can start adding the other nodes (and coloring them).

Because precolored nodes do not spill, the front end must be careful to keep their live ranges short. It can do this by generating MOVE instructions to move values to and from precolored nodes. For example, suppose r_7 is a callee-save register; it is "defined" at procedure entry and "used" at procedure exit. Instead of being kept in a precolored register throughout the procedure (Figure 11.7a), it can be moved into a fresh temporary and then moved back enter: def(r_7)   enter: def(r_7)

                                                                $t_{231} \leftarrow r_7$

(a) $\vdots$ (b) $\vdots$

                                                                $r_7 \leftarrow t_{231}$

exit: use(r_7)   exit: use(r_7)

| **FIGURE 11.7.** | Moving a callee-save register to a fresh temporary. |

(Figure 11.7b). If there is *register pressure* (a high demand for registers) in this function, t_{231} will spill; otherwise t_{231} will be coalesced with r_7 and the MOVE instructions will be eliminated.

CALLER-SAVE AND CALLEE-SAVE REGISTERS

A local variable or compiler temporary that is not live across any procedure call should usually be allocated to a caller-save register, because in this case no saving and restoring of the register will be necessary at all. On the other hand, any variable that is live across several procedure calls should be kept in a callee-save register, since then only one save/restore will be necessary (on entry/exit from the calling procedure).

How can the register allocator allocate variables to registers using this criterion? Fortunately, a graph-coloring allocator can do this very naturally, as a byproduct of ordinary coalescing and spilling. All the callee-save registers are considered live on entry to the procedure, and are *used* by the return instruction. The CALL instructions in the Assem language have been annotated to *define* (interfere with) all the caller-save registers. If a variable is not live across a procedure call, it will tend to be allocated to a caller-save register.

If a variable x is live across a procedure call, then it interferes with all the caller-save (precolored) registers, *and* it interferes with all the new temporaries (such as t_{231} in Figure 11.7) created for callee-save registers. Thus, a spill will occur. Using the common spill-cost heuristic that spills a node with high degree but few uses, the node chosen for spilling will not be x but t_{231}. Since t_{231} is spilled, r_7 will be available for coloring x (or some other variable). Essentially, the callee saves the callee-save register by spilling t_{231}.

EXAMPLE WITH PRECOLORED NODES

A worked example will illustrate the issues of register allocation with precolored nodes, callee-save registers, and spilling.

```
int f(int a, int b) {
    int d=0;
    int e=a;
    do {d = d+b;
        e = e-1;
    } while (e>0);
    return d;
}
```

enter: $c \leftarrow r_3$
$a \leftarrow r_1$
$b \leftarrow r_2$
$d \leftarrow 0$
$e \leftarrow a$
loop: $d \leftarrow d + b$
$e \leftarrow e - 1$
if $e > 0$ goto loop
$r_1 \leftarrow d$
$r_3 \leftarrow c$
return $(r_1, r_3$ *live out*$)$

(a)   (b)

PROGRAM 11.8. A C function and its translation into instructions

---

A C compiler is compiling Program 11.8a for a target machine with three registers; r_1 and r_2 are caller-save, and r_3 is callee-save. The code generator has therefore made arrangements to preserve the value of r_3 explicitly, by copying it into the temporary c and back again.

The instruction-selection phase has produced the instruction list of Program 11.8b. The interference graph for this function is shown at right.

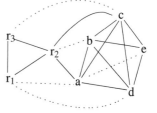

The register allocation proceeds as follows (with $K = 3$):

1. In this graph, there is no opportunity for *simplify* or *freeze* (because all the non-precolored nodes have degree $\geq K$). Any attempt to *coalesce* would produce a coalesced node adjacent to K or more significant-degree nodes. Therefore we must *spill* some node. We calculate spill priorities as follows:

Node	Uses+Defs outside loop		Uses+Defs within loop		Degree		Spill priority
a	(2	+ 10 ×	0	) /	4	=	0.50
b	(1	+ 10 ×	1	) /	4	=	2.75
c	(2	+ 10 ×	0	) /	6	=	0.33
d	(2	+ 10 ×	2	) /	4	=	5.50
e	(1	+ 10 ×	3	) /	3	=	10.33

Node c has the lowest priority – it interferes with many other temporaries but is rarely used – so it should be spilled first. Spilling c, we obtain the graph at right.

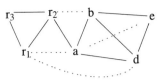

2. We can now coalesce a and e, since the resulting node will be adjacent to fewer than K significant-degree nodes (after coalescing, node d will be low-degree, though it is significant-degree right now). No other *simplify* or *coalesce* is possible now.

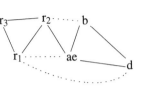

3. Now we could coalesce $ae\&r_1$ or coalesce $b\&r_2$. Let us do the latter.

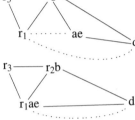

4. We can now coalesce either $ae\&r_1$ or coalesce $d\&r_1$. Let us do the former.

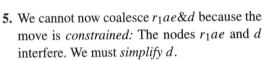

5. We cannot now coalesce $r_1ae\&d$ because the move is *constrained:* The nodes r_1ae and d interfere. We must *simplify* d.

6. Now we have reached a graph with only precolored nodes, so we pop nodes from the stack and assign colors to them. First we pick d, which can be assigned color r_3. Nodes a, b, and e have already been assigned colors by coalescing. But node c, which was a *potential spill,* turns into an *actual spill* when it is popped from the stack, since no color can be found for it.

7. Since there was spilling in this round, we must rewrite the program to include spill instructions. For each use (or definition) of c, we make up a new temporary, and fetch (or store) it immediately beforehand (or afterward).

enter: $c_1 \leftarrow r_3$
$\qquad M[c_{\text{loc}}] \leftarrow c_1$
$\qquad a \leftarrow r_1$
$\qquad b \leftarrow r_2$
$\qquad d \leftarrow 0$
$\qquad e \leftarrow a$
loop: $\quad d \leftarrow d + b$
$\qquad e \leftarrow e - 1$
$\qquad$ if $e > 0$ goto loop
$\qquad r_1 \leftarrow d$
$\qquad c_2 \leftarrow M[c_{\text{loc}}]$
$\qquad r_3 \leftarrow c_2$
$\qquad$ return

8. Now we build a new interference graph:

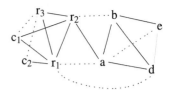

9. Graph-coloring proceeds as follows. We can immediately coalesce $c_1 \& r_3$ and then $c_2 \& r_3$.

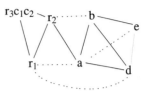

10. Then, as before, we can coalesce $a \& e$ and then $b \& r_2$.

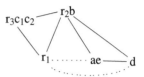

11. As before, we can coalesce $ae \& r_1$ and then simplify d.

12. Now we start popping from the stack: We select color r_3 for d, and this was the only node on the stack – all other nodes were coalesced or precolored. The coloring is shown at right.

Node	Color
a	r_1
b	r_2
c	r_3
d	r_3
e	r_1

13. Now we can rewrite the program using the register assignment.

enter: $r_3 \leftarrow r_3$
$M[c_{\mathrm{loc}}] \leftarrow r_3$
$r_1 \leftarrow r_1$
$r_2 \leftarrow r_2$
$r_3 \leftarrow 0$
$r_1 \leftarrow r_1$
loop: $r_3 \leftarrow r_3 + r_2$
$r_1 \leftarrow r_1 - 1$
if $r_1 > 0$ goto loop
$r_1 \leftarrow r_3$
$r_3 \leftarrow M[c_{\mathrm{loc}}]$
$r_3 \leftarrow r_3$
return

14. Finally, we can delete any move instruction whose source and destination are the same; these are the result of coalescing.

$$
\begin{aligned}
\text{enter:} \quad & M[c_{\text{loc}}] \leftarrow r_3 \\
& r_3 \leftarrow 0 \\
\text{loop:} \quad & r_3 \leftarrow r_3 + r_2 \\
& r_1 \leftarrow r_1 - 1 \\
& \text{if } r_1 > 0 \text{ goto loop} \\
& r_1 \leftarrow r_3 \\
& r_3 \leftarrow M[c_{\text{loc}}] \\
& \text{return}
\end{aligned}
$$

The final program has only one uncoalesced move instruction.

11.4   GRAPH-COLORING IMPLEMENTATION

The graph-coloring algorithm needs to query the interference-graph data structure frequently. There are two kinds of queries:

1. Get all the nodes adjacent to node X; and
2. Tell if X and Y are adjacent.

An adjacency list (per node) can answer query 1 quickly, but not query 2 if the lists are long. A two-dimensional bit matrix indexed by node numbers can answer query 2 quickly, but not query 1. Therefore, we need both data structures to (redundantly) represent the interference graph. If the graph is very sparse, a hash table of integer pairs may be better than a bit matrix.

The adjacency lists of machine registers (precolored nodes) can be very large; because they're used in standard calling conventions, they interfere with any temporaries that happen to be live near *any* of the procedure-calls in the program. But we don't need to represent the adjacency list for a precolored node, because adjacency lists are used only in the *select* phase (which does not apply to precolored nodes) and in the Briggs coalescing test. To save space and time, we do not explicitly represent the adjacency lists of the machine registers. We coalesce an ordinary node a with a machine register r using the George coalescing test, which needs the adjacency list of a but not of r.

To test whether two ordinary (non-precolored) nodes can be coalesced, the algorithm shown here uses the Briggs coalescing test.

Associated with each move-related node is a count of the moves it is involved in. This count is easy to maintain and is used to test if a node is no longer move-related. Associated with all nodes is a count of the number of neighbors currently in the graph. This is used to determine whether a node is of significant degree during coalescing, and whether a node can be removed from the graph during simplification.

It is important to be able to quickly perform each *simplify* step (removing a low-degree non-move-related node), each *coalesce* step, and each *freeze* step. To do this, we maintain four work lists:

- Low-degree non-move-related nodes *(simplifyWorklist)*;
- Move instructions that might be coalesceable *(worklistMoves)*;
- Low-degree move-related nodes *(freezeWorklist)*;
- High-degree nodes *(spillWorklist)*.

Using these work lists, we avoid quadratic time blowup in finding coalesceable nodes.

DATA STRUCTURES

The algorithm maintains these data structures to keep track of graph nodes and move edges:

Node work lists, sets, and stacks. The following lists and sets are always *mutually disjoint* and every node is always in exactly one of the sets or lists.

precolored: machine registers, preassigned a color.

initial: temporary registers, not precolored and not yet processed.

simplifyWorklist: list of low-degree non-move-related nodes.

freezeWorklist: low-degree move-related nodes.

spillWorklist: high-degree nodes.

spilledNodes: nodes marked for spilling during this round; initially empty.

coalescedNodes: registers that have been coalesced; when $u \leftarrow v$ is coalesced, v is added to this set and u put back on some work list (or vice versa).

coloredNodes: nodes successfully colored.

selectStack: stack containing temporaries removed from the graph.

Since membership in these sets is often tested, the representation of each node should contain an enumeration value telling which set it is in. Since nodes must frequently be added to and removed from these sets, each set can be represented by a doubly linked list of nodes. Initially (on entry to Main), and on exiting RewriteProgram, only the sets *precolored* and *initial* are nonempty.

Move sets. There are five sets of move instructions, and every move is in exactly one of these sets (after Build through the end of Main).

coalescedMoves: moves that have been coalesced.

constrainedMoves: moves whose source and target interfere.

frozenMoves: moves that will no longer be considered for coalescing.

worklistMoves: moves enabled for possible coalescing.

activeMoves: moves not yet ready for coalescing.

Like the node work lists, the move sets should be implemented as doubly linked lists, with each move containing an enumeration value identifying which set it belongs to.

When a node x changes from significant to low-degree, the moves associated with its neighbors must be added to the move work list. Moves that were blocked with too many significant neighbors might now be enabled for coalescing.

Other data structures.

adjSet: the set of interference edges (u, v) in the graph; if $(u, v) \in$ adjSet, then $(v, u) \in$ adjSet.

adjList: adjacency list representation of the graph; for each non-precolored temporary u, adjList[u] is the set of nodes that interfere with u.

degree: an array containing the current degree of each node.

moveList: a mapping from a node to the list of moves it is associated with.

alias: when a move (u, v) has been coalesced, and v put in coalescedNodes, then alias(v) = u.

color: the color chosen by the algorithm for a node; for precolored nodes this is initialized to the given color.

INVARIANTS

After Build, the following invariants always hold:

Degree invariant.

$$(u \in \text{simplifyWorklist} \cup \text{freezeWorklist} \cup \text{spillWorklist}) \Rightarrow$$
$$\text{degree}(u) = |\text{adjList}(u) \cap (\text{precolored} \cup \text{simplifyWorklist}$$
$$\cup \text{freezeWorklist} \cup \text{spillWorklist})|$$

Simplify worklist invariant. Either u has been selected for spilling, or

$$(u \in \text{simplifyWorklist}) \Rightarrow$$
$$\text{degree}(u) < K \wedge \text{moveList}[u] \cap (\text{activeMoves} \cup \text{worklistMoves}) = \{\}$$

Freeze worklist invariant.

$$(u \in \text{freezeWorklist}) \Rightarrow$$
$$\text{degree}(u) < K \wedge \text{moveList}[u] \cap (\text{activeMoves} \cup \text{worklistMoves}) \neq \{\}$$

Spill worklist invariant.

$$(u \in \text{spillWorklist}) \;\Rightarrow\; \text{degree}[u] \geq K$$

PROGRAM CODE

The algorithm is invoked using the procedure *Main*, which loops (via tail recursion) until no spills are generated.

> **procedure** Main()
>   LivenessAnalysis()
>   Build()
>   MakeWorklist()
>   **repeat**
>   **if** simplifyWorklist $\neq$ {} **then** Simplify()
>   **else if** worklistMoves $\neq$ {} **then** Coalesce()
>   **else if** freezeWorklist $\neq$ {} **then** Freeze()
>   **else if** spillWorklist $\neq$ {} **then** SelectSpill()
>   **until** simplifyWorklist = {} $\wedge$ worklistMoves = {}
> $\wedge$ freezeWorklist = {} $\wedge$ spillWorklist = {}
>   AssignColors()
>   **if** spilledNodes $\neq$ {} **then**
>   RewriteProgram(spilledNodes)
>   Main()

If *AssignColors* spills, then *RewriteProgram* allocates memory locations for the spilled temporaries and inserts store and fetch instructions to access them. These stores and fetches are to newly created temporaries (with tiny live ranges), so the main loop must be performed on the altered graph.

> **procedure** Build ()
>   **forall** $b \in$ blocks in program
>   **let** live = liveOut(b)
>   **forall** $I \in$ instructions(b) in reverse order
>   **if** isMoveInstruction(I) **then**
>   live $\leftarrow$ live\use(I)
>   **forall** $n \in$ def(I) $\cup$ use(I)
>   moveList[n] $\leftarrow$ moveList[n] $\cup$ {I}
>   worklistMoves $\leftarrow$ worklistMoves $\cup$ {I}
>   live $\leftarrow$ live $\cup$ def(I)
>   **forall** $d \in$ def(I)
>   **forall** $l \in$ live
>   AddEdge(l, d)
>   live $\leftarrow$ use(I) $\cup$ (live\def(I))

Procedure *Build* constructs the interference graph (and bit matrix) using the results of static liveness analysis, and also initializes the *worklistMoves* to contain all the moves in the program.

procedure AddEdge(u, v)
    if ((u, v) $\notin$ adjSet) $\wedge$ ($u \neq v$) **then**
        adjSet $\leftarrow$ adjSet $\cup$ {(u, v), (v, u)}
        if $u \notin$ precolored **then**
            adjList[u] $\leftarrow$ adjList[u] $\cup$ {v}
            degree[u] $\leftarrow$ degree[u] + 1
        if $v \notin$ precolored **then**
            adjList[v] $\leftarrow$ adjList[v] $\cup$ {u}
            degree[v] $\leftarrow$ degree[v] + 1

procedure MakeWorklist()
    forall $n \in$ initial
        initial $\leftarrow$ initial \ {n}
        if degree[n] $\geq K$ **then**
            spillWorklist $\leftarrow$ spillWorklist $\cup$ {n}
        else if MoveRelated(n) **then**
            freezeWorklist $\leftarrow$ freezeWorklist $\cup$ {n}
        else
            simplifyWorklist $\leftarrow$ simplifyWorklist $\cup$ {n}

function Adjacent(n)
    adjList[n] \ (selectStack $\cup$ coalescedNodes)

function NodeMoves (n)
    moveList[n] $\cap$ (activeMoves $\cup$ worklistMoves)

function MoveRelated(n)
    NodeMoves(n) $\neq$ {}

procedure Simplify()
    let $n \in$ simplifyWorklist
    simplifyWorklist $\leftarrow$ simplifyWorklist \ {n}
    push(n, selectStack)
    forall m $\in$ Adjacent(n)
        DecrementDegree(m)

Removing a node from the graph involves decrementing the degree of its *current* neighbors. If the *degree* of a neighbor is already less than $K - 1$, then the neighbor must be move-related, and is not added to the `simplifyWork-list`. When the degree of a neighbor transitions from K to $K - 1$, moves associated with *its* neighbors may be enabled.

procedure DecrementDegree(*m*)
    let d = degree[m]
    degree[m] $\leftarrow$ d-1
    if $d = K$ **then**
        EnableMoves($\{m\} \cup$ Adjacent(m))
        spillWorklist $\leftarrow$ spillWorklist $\setminus \{m\}$
        if MoveRelated(m) **then**
            freezeWorklist $\leftarrow$ freezeWorklist $\cup \{m\}$
        else
            simplifyWorklist $\leftarrow$ simplifyWorklist $\cup \{m\}$

procedure EnableMoves(nodes)
    forall $n \in$ nodes
        forall $m \in$ NodeMoves(n)
            if $m \in$ activeMoves **then**
                activeMoves $\leftarrow$ activeMoves $\setminus \{m\}$
                worklistMoves $\leftarrow$ worklistMoves $\cup \{m\}$

Only moves in the *worklistMoves* are considered in the coalesce phase. When a move is coalesced, it may no longer be move-related and can be added to the simplify work list by the procedure *AddWorkList*. *OK* implements the heuristic used for coalescing a precolored register. *Conservative* implements the conservative coalescing heuristic.

procedure AddWorkList(u)
    if ($u \notin$ precolored $\wedge$ not(MoveRelated(u)) $\wedge$ degree[u] < K) **then**
        freezeWorklist $\leftarrow$ freezeWorklist $\setminus \{u\}$
        simplifyWorklist $\leftarrow$ simplifyWorklist $\cup \{u\}$

function OK(*t*,*r*)
    degree[t] < $K \vee t \in$ precolored $\vee (t, r) \in$ adjSet

function Conservative(nodes)
    let $k = 0$
    forall $n \in$ nodes
        if degree[n] $\geq K$ **then** $k \leftarrow k + 1$
    return ($k < K$)

procedure Coalesce()
    let $m_{(=copy(x,y))} \in$ worklistMoves
    $x \leftarrow$ GetAlias(x)
    $y \leftarrow$ GetAlias(y)
    if $y \in$ precolored **then**
        let $(u, v) = (y, x)$
    else
        let $(u, v) = (x, y)$
    worklistMoves $\leftarrow$ worklistMoves $\setminus \{m\}$
    if $(u = v)$ **then**
        coalescedMoves $\leftarrow$ coalescedMoves $\cup \{m\}$
        AddWorkList(u)
    else if $v \in$ precolored $\vee$ $(u, v) \in$ adjSet **then**
        constrainedMoves $\leftarrow$ constrainedMoves $\cup \{m\}$
        AddWorkList(u)
        AddWorkList(v)
    else if $u \in$ precolored $\wedge$ $(\forall t \in$ Adjacent(v), OK(t, u))
            $\vee$ $u \notin$ precolored $\wedge$
                Conservative(Adjacent(u) $\cup$ Adjacent(v)) **then**
        coalescedMoves $\leftarrow$ coalescedMoves $\cup \{m\}$
        Combine(u,v)
        AddWorkList(u)
    else
        activeMoves $\leftarrow$ activeMoves $\cup \{m\}$

procedure Combine(u,v)
    if $v \in$ freezeWorklist **then**
        freezeWorklist $\leftarrow$ freezeWorklist $\setminus \{v\}$
    else
        spillWorklist $\leftarrow$ spillWorklist $\setminus \{v\}$
    coalescedNodes $\leftarrow$ coalescedNodes $\cup \{v\}$
    alias[v] $\leftarrow u$
    moveList[u] $\leftarrow$ moveList[u] $\cup$ moveList[v]
    EnableMoves(v)
    forall $t \in$ Adjacent(v)
        AddEdge(t,u)
        DecrementDegree(t)
    if degree[u] $\geq K \wedge u \in$ freezeWorkList
        freezeWorkList $\leftarrow$ freezeWorkList $\setminus \{u\}$
        spillWorkList $\leftarrow$ spillWorkList $\cup \{u\}$

function GetAlias (*n*)
    if *n* ∈ coalescedNodes **then**
        GetAlias(alias[*n*])
    else *n*

procedure Freeze()
    let *u* ∈ freezeWorklist
    freezeWorklist ← freezeWorklist \ {*u*}
    simplifyWorklist ← simplifyWorklist ∪ {*u*}
    FreezeMoves(*u*)

procedure FreezeMoves(*u*)
    forall $m_{(=copy(x,y))}$ ∈ NodeMoves(*u*)
        if GetAlias(*y*)=GetAlias(*u*) **then**
            v ← GetAlias(*x*)
        else
            v ← GetAlias(*y*)
        activeMoves ← activeMoves \ {*m*}
        frozenMoves ← frozenMoves ∪ {*m*}
        if *v* ∈ freezeWorklist ∧ NodeMoves(*v*) = {} **then**
            freezeWorklist ← freezeWorklist \ {*v*}
            simplifyWorklist ← simplifyWorklist ∪ {*v*}

procedure SelectSpill()
    let *m* ∈ spillWorklist *selected using favorite heuristic*
        Note: avoid choosing nodes that are the tiny live ranges
        resulting from the fetches of previously spilled registers
    spillWorklist ← spillWorklist \ {*m*}
    simplifyWorklist ← simplifyWorklist ∪ {*m*}
    FreezeMoves(*m*)

procedure AssignColors()
    while SelectStack not empty
        let n = pop(SelectStack)
        okColors $\leftarrow$ {0, ..., K-1}
        forall $w \in$ adjList[n]
            if GetAlias(w) $\in$ (coloredNodes $\cup$ precolored) **then**
                okColors $\leftarrow$ okColors \ {color[GetAlias(w)]}
        if okColors $=$ {} **then**
            spilledNodes $\leftarrow$ spilledNodes $\cup$ {n}
        else
            coloredNodes $\leftarrow$ coloredNodes $\cup$ {n}
            let $c \in$ okColors
            color[n] $\leftarrow c$
    forall $n \in$ coalescedNodes
        color[n] $\leftarrow$ color[GetAlias(n)]

procedure RewriteProgram()
    Allocate memory locations for each $v \in$ spilledNodes,
    Create a new temporary v_i for each definition and each use,
    In the program *(instructions)*, insert a store after each
    definition of a v_i, a fetch before each use of a v_i.
    Put all the v_i into a set newTemps.
    spilledNodes $\leftarrow$ {}
    initial $\leftarrow$ coloredNodes $\cup$ coalescedNodes $\cup$ newTemps
    coloredNodes $\leftarrow$ {}
    coalescedNodes $\leftarrow$ {}

We show a variant of the algorithm in which all coalesces are discarded if the program must be rewritten to incorporate spill fetches and stores. For a faster algorithm, keep all the coalesces found before the first call to `Select-Spill` and rewrite the program to eliminate the coalesced move instructions and temporaries.

In principle, a heuristic could be used to select the freeze node; the *Freeze* shown above picks an arbitrary node from the freeze work list. But freezes are not common, and a selection heuristic is unlikely to make a significant difference.

function SimpleAlloc(t)

    for each nontrivial tile u that is a child of t

        SimpleAlloc(u)

    for each nontrivial tile u that is a child of t

        $n \leftarrow n - 1$

    $n \leftarrow n + 1$

    assign r_n to hold the value at the root of t

ALGORITHM 11.9. Simple register allocation on trees.

11.5   REGISTER ALLOCATION FOR TREES

Register allocation for expression trees is much simpler than for arbitrary flow graphs. We do not need global dataflow analysis or interference graphs. Suppose we have a tiled tree such as in Figure 9.2a. This tree has two *trivial* tiles, the TEMP nodes *fp* and *i*, which we assume are already in registers r_{fp} and r_i. We wish to label the roots of the nontrivial tiles (the ones corresponding to instructions, i.e., 2, 4, 5, 6, 8) with registers from the list $r_1, r_2, \ldots, r_k$.

Algorithm 11.9 traverses the tree in postorder, assigning a register to the root of each tile. With n initialized to zero, this algorithm applied to the root (tile 9) produces the allocation {tile2 $\mapsto r_1$, tile4 $\mapsto r_2$, tile5 $\mapsto r_2$, tile6 $\mapsto r_1$, tile8 $\mapsto r_2$, tile9 $\mapsto r_1$}. The algorithm can be combined with Maximal Munch, since both algorithms are doing the same bottom-up traversal.

But this algorithm will not always lead to an optimal allocation. Consider the following tree, where each tile is shown as a single node:

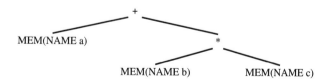

The SimpleAlloc function will use three registers for this expression (as shown at left on the next page), but by reordering the instructions we can do the computation using only two registers (as shown at right):

function Label(t)
    for each tile u that is a child of t
        Label(u)
    if t is trivial
        then $need[t] \leftarrow 0$
    else if t has two children, u_{left} and u_{right}
        then if $need[u_{\text{left}}] = need[u_{\text{right}}]$
                then $need[t] \leftarrow 1 + need[u_{\text{left}}]$
                else $need[t] \leftarrow \max(1, need[u_{\text{left}}], need[u_{\text{right}}])$
    else if t has one child, u
        then $need[t] \leftarrow \max(1, need[u])$
    else if t has no children
        then $need[t] \leftarrow 1$

ALGORITHM 11.10. Sethi-Ullman labeling algorithm.

$$
\begin{aligned}
r_1 &\leftarrow M[a] \\
r_2 &\leftarrow M[b] \\
r_3 &\leftarrow M[c] \\
r_2 &\leftarrow r_2 \times r_3 \\
r_1 &\leftarrow r_1 + r_2
\end{aligned}
\qquad\qquad
\begin{aligned}
r_1 &\leftarrow M[b] \\
r_2 &\leftarrow M[c] \\
r_1 &\leftarrow r_1 \times r_2 \\
r_2 &\leftarrow M[a] \\
r_1 &\leftarrow r_2 + r_1
\end{aligned}
$$

Using dynamic programming, we can find the optimal ordering for the instructions. The idea is to label each tile with the number of registers it needs during its evaluation. Suppose a tile t has two nontrivial children u_{left} and u_{right} that require n and m registers, respectively, for their evaluation. If we evaluate u_{left} first, and hold its result in one register while we evaluate u_{right}, then we have needed $\max(n, 1+m)$ registers for the whole expression rooted at t. Conversely, if we evaluate u_{right} first, then we need $\max(1+n, m)$ registers. Clearly, if $n > m$, we should evaluate u_{left} first, and if $n < m$, we should evaluate u_{right} first. If $n = m$, we will need $n + 1$ registers no matter which subexpression is evaluated first.

Algorithm 11.10 labels each tile t with $need[t]$, the number of registers needed to evaluate the subtree rooted at t. It can be generalized to handle tiles with more than two children. Maximal Munch should identify – but not emit – the tiles, simultaneously with the labeling of Algorithm 11.10. The next pass emits *Assem* instructions for the tiles; wherever a tile has more than one

function SethiUllman(t, n)
  if t has two children, u_{left} and u_{right}
    if $need[u_{\text{left}}] \geq K \ \wedge need[u_{\text{right}}] \geq K$
      SethiUllman($u_{\text{right}}, 0$)
      $n \leftarrow n - 1$
      spill: emit instruction to store $reg[u_{\text{right}}]$
      SethiUllman($u_{\text{left}}, 0$)
      unspill: $reg[u_{\text{right}}] \leftarrow$ "r_1"; emit instruction to fetch $reg[u_{\text{right}}]$
    else if $need[u_{\text{left}}] \geq need[u_{\text{right}}]$
      SethiUllman(u_{left}, n)
      SethiUllman($u_{\text{right}}, n + 1$)
    else $need[u_{\text{left}}] < need[u_{\text{right}}]$
      SethiUllman(u_{right}, n)
      SethiUllman(u_{left}, n)
    $reg[t] \leftarrow$ "r_n"
    emit OPER($instruction[t]$, $reg[t]$, [$reg[u_{\text{left}}]$, $reg[u_{\text{right}}]$])
  else if t has one child, u
    SethiUllman(u, n)
    $reg[t] \leftarrow$ "r_n"
    emit OPER($instruction[t]$, $reg[t]$, $[reg[u]]$)
  else if t is nontrivial but has no children
    $reg[t] \leftarrow$ "r_n"
    emit OPER($instruction[t]$, $reg[t]$, [ ])
  else if t is a trivial node TEMP(r_i)
    $reg[t] \leftarrow$ "r_i"

ALGORITHM 11.11. Sethi-Ullman register allocation for trees.

---

child, the subtrees must be emitted in decreasing order of register *need*.

Algorithm 11.10 can profitably be used in a compiler that uses graph-coloring register allocation. Emitting the subtrees in decreasing order of *need* will minimize the number of simultaneously live temporaries and reduce the number of spills.

In a compiler without graph-coloring register allocation, Algorithm 11.10 is used as a pre-pass to Algorithm 11.11, which assigns registers as the trees are emitted and also handles spilling cleanly. This takes care of register allocation for the internal nodes of expression trees; allocating registers for explicit TEMPs of the *Tree* language would have to be done in some other way. In general, such a compiler would keep almost all program variables in the stack frame, so there would not be many of these explicit TEMPs to allocate.

PROGRAM GRAPH COLORING

Implement graph-coloring register allocation as two modules: `Color`, which does just the graph coloring itself, and `RegAlloc`, which manages spilling and calls upon `Color` as a subroutine. To keep things simple, do not implement spilling or coalescing; this simplifies the algorithm considerably.

```
package RegAlloc;

public class RegAlloc implements Temp.TempMap {
  public Assem.InstrList instrs;
  public String tempMap(Temp temp);
  public RegAlloc(Frame.Frame f, Assem.InstrList il);
}

class Color implements TempMap {
  public TempList spills();
  public String tempMap(Temp t);
  public Color(InterferenceGraph ig,
              TempMap initial,
              TempList registers);
}
```

Given an interference graph, an `initial` allocation (precoloring) of some temporaries imposed by calling conventions, and a list of colors (`registers`), `color` produces an extension of the `initial` allocation. The resulting allocation assigns all temps used in the flow graph, making use of registers from the `registers` list.

The `initial` allocation is the `frame` (which implements a `TempMap` describing precolored temporaries); the `registers` argument is just the list of all machine registers, `Frame.registers` (see page 251). The registers in the `initial` allocation can also appear in the `registers` argument to `Color`, since it's OK to use them to color other nodes as well.

The result of `Color` is a `TempMap` (that is, `Color` implements `TempMap`) describing the register allocation, along with a list of spills. The result of `RegAlloc` – if there were no spills – is an identical `TempMap`, which can be used in final assembly-code emission as an argument to `Assem.format`.

A better `Color` interface would have a `spillCost` argument that specifies the spilling cost of each temporary. This can be just the number of uses and defs, or better yet, uses and defs weighted by occurrence in loops and nested loops. A naive `spillCost` that just returns 1 for every temporary will also work.

A simple implementation of the coloring algorithm without coalescing requires only one work list: the `simplifyWorklist`, which contains all non-precolored, nonsimplified nodes of degree less than K. Obviously, no `freezeWorklist` is necessary. No `spillWorklist` is necessary either, if we are willing to look through all the nodes in the original graph for a spill candidate every time the `simplifyWorklist` becomes empty.

With only a `simplifyWorklist`, the doubly linked representation is not necessary: This work list can be implemented as a singly linked list or a stack, since it is never accessed "in the middle."

ADVANCED PROJECT: SPILLING

Implement spilling, so that no matter how many parameters and locals a Mini-Java program has, you can still compile it.

ADVANCED PROJECT: COALESCING

Implement coalescing, to eliminate practically all the MOVE instructions from the program.

FURTHER READING

Kempe [1879] invented the simplification algorithm that colors graphs by removing vertices of degree $< K$. Chaitin [1982] formulated register allocation as a graph-coloring problem – using Kempe's algorithm to color the graph – and performed copy propagation by (nonconservatively) coalescing noninterfering move-related nodes before coloring the graph. Briggs et al. [1994] improved the algorithm with the idea of optimistic spilling, and also avoided introducing spills by using the conservative coalescing heuristic before coloring the graph. George and Appel [1996] found that there are more opportunities for coalescing if conservative coalescing is done during simplification instead of beforehand, and developed the work-list algorithm presented in this chapter.

Ershov [1958] developed the algorithm for optimal register allocation on expression trees; Sethi and Ullman [1970] generalized this algorithm and showed how it should handle spills.

EXERCISES

11.1 The following program has been compiled for a machine with three registers r_1, r_2, r_3; r_1 and r_2 are (caller-save) argument registers and r_3 is a callee-save register. Construct the interference graph and show the steps of the register allocation process in detail, as on pages 229–232. When you coalesce two nodes, say whether you are using the Briggs or George criterion.

Hint: When two nodes are connected by an interference edge *and* a move edge, you may delete the move edge; this is called *constrain* and is accomplished by the first **else if** clause of procedure *Coalesce*.

$$
\begin{array}{lll}
f: & c \leftarrow r_3 & \\
& p \leftarrow r_1 & \\
& \text{if } p = 0 \text{ goto } L_1 & \\
& r_1 \leftarrow M[p] & \\
& \text{call } f & \textit{(uses } r_1, \textit{ defines } r_1, r_2) \\
& s \leftarrow r_1 & \\
& r_1 \leftarrow M[p+4] & \\
& \text{call } f & \textit{(uses } r_1, \textit{ defines } r_1, r_2) \\
& t \leftarrow r_1 & \\
& u \leftarrow s+t & \\
& \text{goto } L_2 & \\
L_1: & u \leftarrow 1 & \\
L_2: & r_1 \leftarrow u & \\
& r_3 \leftarrow c & \\
& \text{return} & \textit{(uses } r_1, r_3)
\end{array}
$$

11.2 The table below represents a register-interference graph. Nodes 1–6 are precolored (with colors 1–6), and nodes A–H are ordinary (non-precolored). Every pair of precolored nodes interferes, and each ordinary node interferes with nodes where there is an x in the table.

	1	2	3	4	5	6	A	B	C	D	E	F	G	H
A	x	x	x	x	x	x								
B	x		x	x	x	x								
C			x	x	x	x				x	x	x	x	x
D	x		x	x	x				x		x	x	x	x
E	x		x		x	x		x	x			x	x	x
F	x		x	x		x		x	x	x			x	x
G								x	x	x	x			
H	x			x	x	x		x	x	x	x			

The following pairs of nodes are related by MOVE instructions:

$(A, 3)$ $(H, 3)$ $(G, 3)$ $(B, 2)$ $(C, 1)$ $(D, 6)$ $(E, 4)$ $(F, 5)$

Assume that register allocation must be done for an 8-register machine.

a. Ignoring the MOVE instructions, and without using the *coalesce* heuristic, color this graph using *simplify* and *spill*. Record the sequence (stack) of *simplify* and *potential-spill* decisions, show which potential spills become actual spills, and show the coloring that results.

b. Color this graph using coalescing. Record the sequence of *simplify*, *coalesce*, *freeze*, and *spill* decisions. Identify each *coalesce* as Briggs- or George-style. Show how many MOVE instructions remain.

*c. Another coalescing heuristic is *biased coloring*. Instead of using a *conservative coalescing* heuristic during simplification, run the *simplify-spill* part of the algorithm as in part (a), but in the *select* part of the algorithm,

  i.   When selecting a color for node X that is move-related to node Y, when a color for Y has already been selected, use the same color if possible (to eliminate the MOVE).

  ii. When selecting a color for node X that is move-related to node Y, when a color for Y has not yet been selected, use a color that is *not* the same as the color of any of Y's neighbors (to increase the chance of heuristic (i) working when Y is colored).

Conservative coalescing (in the *simplify* phase) has been found to be more effective than biased coloring, in general; but it might not be on this particular graph. Since the two coalescing algorithms are used in different phases, they can both be used in the same register allocator.

*d. Use both conservative coalescing and biased coloring in allocating registers. Show where biased coloring helps make the right decisions.

11.3 *Conservative coalescing* is so called because it will not introduce any (potential) spills. But can it avoid spills? Consider this graph, where the solid edges represent interferences and the dashed edge represents a MOVE:

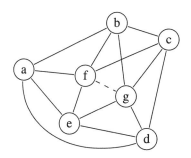

a. 4-color the graph without coalescing. Show the *select*-stack, indicating the order in which you removed nodes. Is there a potential spill? Is there an actual spill?

b. 4-color the graph with conservative coalescing. Did you use the Briggs or George criterion? Is there a potential spill? Is there an actual spill?

11.4 It has been proposed that the conservative coalescing heuristic could be simplified. In testing whether MOVE(a, b) can be coalesced, instead of asking whether the combined node ab is adjacent to $< K$ nodes of significant degree, we could simply test whether ab is adjacent to $< K$ nodes of any degree. The theory is that if ab is adjacent to many low-degree nodes, they will be removed by simplification anyway.

a. Show that this kind of coalescing cannot create any new potential spills.

b. Demonstrate the algorithm on this graph (with $K = 3$):

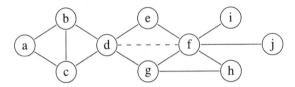

*c. Show that this test is less effective than standard conservative coalescing. **Hint:** Use the graph of Exercise 11.3, with $K = 4$.

12

Putting It All Together

de-bug: to eliminate errors in or malfunctions of

Webster's Dictionary

Chapters 2–11 have described the fundamental components of a good compiler: a *front end*, which does lexical analysis, parsing, construction of abstract syntax, type-checking, and translation to intermediate code; and a *back end*, which does instruction selection, dataflow analysis, and register allocation.

What lessons have we learned? We hope that the reader has learned about the algorithms used in different components of a compiler and the interfaces used to connect the components. But the authors have also learned quite a bit from the exercise.

Our goal was to describe a good compiler that is, to use Einstein's phrase, "as simple as possible – but no simpler." we will now discuss the thorny issues that arose in designing the MiniJava compiler.

Structured l-values. Java (and MiniJava) have no record or array variables, as C, C++, and Pascal do. Instead, all object and array values are really just pointers to heap-allocated data. Implementing structured l-values requires some care but not too many new insights.

Tree intermediate representation. The `Tree` language has a fundamental flaw: It does not describe procedure entry and exit. These are handled by opaque procedures inside the `Frame` module that generate `Tree` code. This means that a program translated to `Tree`s using, for example, the `Pentium-Frame` version of `Frame` will be different from the same program translated using `SparcFrame` – the `Tree` representation is not completely machine-independent.

Also, there is not enough information in the trees themselves to simulate the execution of an entire program, since the *view shift* (page 128) is partly done implicitly by procedure prologues and epilogues that are not represented as `Trees`. Consequently, there is not enough information to do whole-program optimization (across function boundaries).

The `Tree` representation is a *low-level* intermediate representation, useful for instruction selection and intraprocedural optimization. A *high-level* intermediate representation would preserve more of the source-program semantics, including the notions of nested functions (if applicable), nonlocal variables, object creation (as distinguished from an opaque external function call), and so on. Such a representation would be more tied to a particular family of source languages than the general-purpose `Tree` language is.

Register allocation. Graph-coloring register allocation is widely used in real compilers, but does it belong in a compiler that is supposed to be "as simple as possible"? After all, it requires the use of global dataflow (liveness) analysis, construction of interference graphs, and so on. This makes the back end of the compiler significantly bigger.

It is instructive to consider what the MiniJava compiler would be like without it. We could keep all local variables in the stack frame, fetching them into temporaries only when they are used as operands of instructions. The redundant loads within a single basic block can be eliminated by a simple intrablock liveness analysis. Internal nodes of `Tree` expressions could be assigned registers using Algorithms 11.10 and 11.9. But other parts of the compiler would become much uglier: The TEMPs introduced in canonicalizing the trees (eliminating ESEQs) would have to be dealt with in an ad hoc way, by augmenting the `Tree` language with an operator that provides explicit scope for temporary variables; the `Frame` interface, which mentions registers in many places, would now have to deal with them in more complicated ways. To be able to create arbitrarily many `temps` and `moves`, and rely on the register allocator to clean them up, greatly simplifies procedure-calling sequences and code generation.

PROGRAM   PROCEDURE ENTRY/EXIT

Implement the rest of the `Frame` module, which contains all the machine-dependent parts of the compiler: register sets, calling sequences, and activation record (frame) layout.

```
package Frame;
import Temp.Temp;

public abstract class Frame implements Temp.TempMap {
abstract public Temp RV();        (see p. 157)
abstract public Temp FP();        (p. 143)
abstract public Temp.TempList registers();
abstract public String tempMap(Temp temp);
abstract public int wordSize();   (p. 143)
abstract public Tree.Exp externalCall(String func,Tree.ExpList args);  (p. 153)
abstract public Frame newFrame(Temp.Label name,
                               Util.BoolList formals);   (p. 127)
public AccessList formals;    (p. 128)
public Temp.Label name;       (p. 127)
abstract public Access allocLocal(boolean escape);   (p. 129)
abstract public Tree.Stm procEntryExit1(Tree.Stm body);  (p. 251)
abstract public Assem.InstrList procEntryExit2(Assem.InstrList body);  (p. 199)
abstract public Proc procEntryExit3(Assem.InstrList body);
abstract public Assem.InstrList codegen(Tree.Stm stm);   (p. 196)
}
```

PROGRAM 12.1. Package Frame.

Program 12.1 shows the Frame class. Most of this interface has been described elsewhere. What remains is

registers A list of all the register names on the machine, which can be used as "colors" for register allocation.

tempMap For each machine register, the Frame module maintains a particular Temp that serves as the "precolored temporary" that stands for the register. These temps appear in the Assem instructions generated from CALL nodes, in procedure entry sequences generated by procEntryExit1, and so on. The tempMap tells the "color" of each of these precolored temps.

procEntryExit1 For each incoming register parameter, move it to the place from which it is seen from within the function. This could be a fresh temporary. One good way to handle this is for newFrame to create a sequence of Tree.MOVE statements as it creates all the formal parameter "accesses." newFrame can put this into the frame data structure, and procEntryExit1 can just concatenate it onto the procedure body.

Also concatenated to the body are statements for saving and restoring of callee-save registers (including the return-address register). If your register allocator does not implement spilling, all the callee-save (and return-address) registers should be written to the frame at the beginning of the procedure body and fetched back afterward. Therefore, procEntryExit1 should call allocLocal for each register to be saved, and generate Tree.MOVE instructions to save and restore the registers. With luck, saving and restoring the callee-save registers will give the register allocator enough headroom to work with, so that some nontrivial programs can be compiled. Of course, some programs just cannot be compiled without spilling.

If your register allocator implements spilling, then the callee-save registers should not always be written to the frame. Instead, if the register allocator needs the space, it may choose to spill only some of the callee-save registers. But "precolored" temporaries are never spilled; so procEntryExit1 should make up new temporaries for each callee-save (and return-address) register. On entry, it should move all these registers to their new temporary locations, and on exit, it should move them back. Of course, these moves (for nonspilled registers) will be eliminated by register coalescing, so they cost nothing.

procEntryExit3 Creates the procedure prologue and epilogue assembly language. First (for some machines) it calculates the size of the *outgoing parameter space* in the frame. This is equal to the maximum number of outgoing parameters of any CALL instruction in the procedure body. Unfortunately, after conversion to Assem trees the procedure calls have been separated from their arguments, so the outgoing parameters are not obvious. Either procEntryExit2 should scan the body and record this information in some new component of the frame type, or procEntryExit3 should use the maximum legal value.

Once this is known, the assembly language for procedure entry, stack-pointer adjustment, and procedure exit can be put together; these are the prologue and epilogue.

PROGRAM · MAKING IT WORK

Make your compiler generate working code that runs.

The file $MINIJAVA/chap12/runtime.c is a C-language file containing several external functions useful to your MiniJava program. These are generally reached by externalCall from code generated by your compiler. You may modify this as necessary.

Write a module Main that calls on all the other modules to produce an assembly language file prog.s for each input program prog.java. This assembly language program should be assembled (producing prog.o) and linked with runtime.o to produce an executable file.

Programming projects

After your MiniJava compiler is done, here are some ideas for further work:

12.1 Write a garbage collector (in C) for your MiniJava compiler. You will need to make some modifications to the compiler itself to add descriptors to records and stack frames (see Chapter 13).

12.2 Implement inner classes is MiniJava.

12.3 Implement dataflow analyses such as *reaching definitions* and *available expressions* and use them to implement some of the optimizations discussed in Chapter 17.

12.4 Figure out other approaches to improving the assembly language generated by your compiler. Discuss; perhaps implement.

12.5 Implement instruction scheduling to fill branch-delay and load-delay slots in the assembly language (for a machine such as the Sparc). Or discuss how such a module could be integrated into the existing compiler; what interfaces would have to change, and in what ways?

12.6 Implement "software pipelining" (instruction scheduling around loop iterations) in your compiler (see Chapter 20).

12.7 Analyze how adequate the MiniJava language itself would be for writing a compiler. What are the smallest possible additions/changes that would make it a much more useful language?

12.8 In the MiniJava language, some object types are recursive and *must* be implemented as pointers; that is, a value of that type might contain a pointer to another value of the same type (directly or indirectly). But some object types are not recursive, so they could be implemented without pointers. Modify your compiler to take advantage of this by keeping nonrecursive records in the stack frame instead of on the heap.

12.9 Similarly, some arrays have bounds that are known at compile time, are not recursive, and are not assigned to other array variables. Modify your compiler so that these arrays are implemented right in the stack frame.

12.10 Implement inline expansion of functions (see Section 15.4).

12.11 Suppose an ordinary MiniJava program were to run on a parallel machine (a multiprocessor)? How could the compiler automatically make a parallel program out of the original sequential one? Research the approaches.

PART TWO
Advanced Topics

13

Garbage Collection

gar-bage: unwanted or useless material

Webster's Dictionary

Heap-allocated records that are not reachable by any chain of pointers from program variables are *garbage*. The memory occupied by garbage should be reclaimed for use in allocating new records. This process is called *garbage collection*, and is performed not by the compiler but by the runtime system (the support programs linked with the compiled code).

Ideally, we would say that any record that is not dynamically live (will not be used in the future of the computation) is garbage. But, as Section 10.1 explains, it is not always possible to know whether a variable is live. So we will use a conservative approximation: We will require the compiler to guarantee that any *live* record is *reachable*; we will ask the compiler to minimize the number of reachable records that are *not* live; and we will preserve all reachable records, even if some of them might not be live.

Figure 13.1 shows a Java program ready to undergo garbage collection (at the point marked *garbage-collect here*). There are only three program variables in scope: p, q, and r.

13.1 MARK-AND-SWEEP COLLECTION

Program variables and heap-allocated records form a directed graph. The variables are *roots* of this graph. A node n is reachable if there is a path of directed edges $r \to \cdots \to n$ starting at some root r. A graph-search algorithm such as *depth-first search* (Algorithm 13.2) can *mark* all the reachable nodes.

```
class list {list link;
            int key; }
class tree {int key;
            tree left;
            tree right; }
class main {
 static tree maketree() { ··· }
 static void showtree(tree t) { ··· }
 static void main() {
   {list x = new list(nil,7);
    list y = new list(x,9);
    x.link = y;
   }
   {tree p = maketree();
    tree r = p.right;
    int q = r.key;
    garbage-collect here
    showtree(r);
   }
 }
}
```

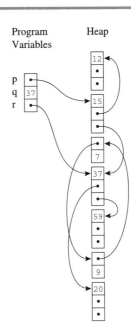

Program Variables · Heap

FIGURE 13.1. A heap to be garbage collected. Class descriptors are not shown in the diagram.

function DFS(x)
    if x is a pointer into the heap
        if record x is not marked
            mark x
            for each field f_i of record x
                DFS($x.f_i$)

ALGORITHM 13.2. Depth-first search.

Any node not marked must be garbage, and should be reclaimed. This can be done by a *sweep* of the entire heap, from its first address to its last, looking for nodes that are not marked (Algorithm 13.3). These are garbage and can be linked together in a linked list (the *freelist*). The sweep phase should also unmark all the marked nodes, in preparation for the next garbage collection.

After the garbage collection, the compiled program resumes execution. Whenever it wants to heap-allocate a new record, it gets a record from the freelist. When the freelist becomes empty, that is a good time to do another garbage collection to replenish the freelist.

Mark phase:	Sweep phase:

Mark phase:
> **for** each root v
> > DFS(v)

Sweep phase:
> $p \leftarrow$ first address in heap
> **while** $p <$ last address in heap
> > **if** record p is marked
> > > unmark p
> > **else** let f_1 be the first field in p
> > > $p.f_1 \leftarrow$ `freelist`
> > > `freelist` $\leftarrow p$
> > $p \leftarrow p+(\text{size of record } p)$

ALGORITHM 13.3. Mark-and-sweep garbage collection.

Cost of garbage collection. Depth-first search takes time proportional to the number of nodes it marks, that is, time proportional to the amount of reachable data. The sweep phase takes time proportional to the size of the heap. Suppose there are R words of reachable data in a heap of size H. Then the cost of one garbage collection is $c_1 R + c_2 H$ for some constants c_1 and c_2; for example, c_1 might be 10 instructions and c_2 might be 3 instructions.

The "good" that collection does is to replenish the freelist with $H - R$ words of usable memory. Therefore, we can compute the *amortized cost* of collection by dividing the *time spent collecting* by the *amount of garbage reclaimed*. That is, for every word that the compiled program allocates, there is an eventual garbage-collection cost of

$$\frac{c_1 R + c_2 H}{H - R}$$

If R is close to H, this cost becomes very large: Each garbage collection reclaims only a few words of garbage. If H is much larger than R, then the cost per allocated word is approximately c_2, or about 3 instructions of garbage-collection cost per word allocated.

The garbage collector can measure H (the heap size) and $H - R$ (the freelist size) directly. After a collection, if R/H is larger than 0.5 (or some other criterion), the collector should increase H by asking the operating system for more memory. Then the cost per allocated word will be approximately $c_1 + 2c_2$, or perhaps 16 instructions per word.

Using an explicit stack. The DFS algorithm is recursive, and the maximum depth of its recursion is as long as the longest path in the graph of reachable

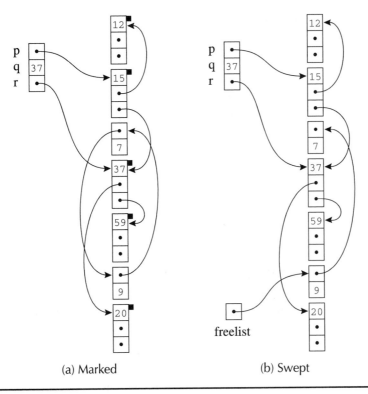

(a) Marked   (b) Swept

FIGURE 13.4.   Mark-and-sweep collection.

data. There could be a path of length H in the worst case, meaning that the stack of activation records would be larger than the entire heap!

To attack this problem, we use an explicit stack (instead of recursion), as in Algorithm 13.5. Now the stack could still grow to size H, but at least this is H words and not H activation records. Still, it is unacceptable to require auxiliary stack memory as large as the heap being collected.

Pointer reversal. After the contents of field $x.f_i$ have been pushed on the stack, Algorithm 13.5 will never again look the original location $x.f_i$. This means we can use $x.f_i$ to store one element of the stack itself! This all-too-clever idea is called *pointer reversal*, because $x.f_i$ will be made to point back to the record from which x was reached. Then, as the stack is popped, the field $x.f_i$ will be restored to its original value.

Algorithm 13.6 requires a field in each record called *done*, which indicates how many fields in that record have been processed. This takes only a few

function DFS(x)
  if x is a pointer and record x is not marked
   mark x
   $t \leftarrow 1$
   stack[t] $\leftarrow x$
   while $t > 0$
       $x \leftarrow$ stack[t]; $t \leftarrow t - 1$
       for each field f_i of record x
          if $x.f_i$ is a pointer and record $x.f_i$ is not marked
            mark $x.f_i$
            $t \leftarrow t + 1$;   stack[t] $\leftarrow x.f_i$

ALGORITHM 13.5. Depth-first search using an explicit stack.

bits per record (and it can also serve as the mark field).

The variable t serves as the top of the stack; every record x on the stack is already marked, and if $i = \text{done}[x]$, then $x.f_i$ is the "stack link" to the next node down. When popping the stack, $x.f_i$ is restored to its original value.

An array of freelists. The sweep phase is the same no matter which marking algorithm is used: It just puts the unmarked records on the freelist, and unmarks the marked records. But if records are of many different sizes, a simple linked list will not be very efficient for the allocator. When allocating a record of size n, it may have to search a long way down the list for a free block of that size.

A good solution is to have an array of several freelists, so that freelist[i] is a linked list of all records of size i. The program can allocate a node of size i just by taking the head of freelist[i]; the sweep phase of the collector can put each node of size j at the head of freelist[j].

If the program attempts to allocate from an empty freelist[i], it can try to grab a larger record from freelist[j] (for $j > i$) and split it (putting the unused portion back on freelist[$j - i$]). If this fails, it is time to call the garbage collector to replenish the freelists.

Fragmentation. It can happen that the program wants to allocate a record of size n, and there are many free records smaller than n but none of the right size. This is called *external fragmentation*. On the other hand, *internal fragmentation* occurs when the program uses a too-large record without splitting

function DFS(x)
  if x is a pointer and record x is not marked
  $t \leftarrow$ nil
  mark x; done$[x] \leftarrow 0$
  while true
      $i \leftarrow$ done$[x]$
      if $i\ <\ \#$ of fields in record x
        $y \leftarrow x.f_i$
        if y is a pointer and record y is not marked
          $x.f_i \leftarrow t$; $t \leftarrow x$; $x \leftarrow y$
          mark x; done$[x] \leftarrow 0$
        else
          done$[x] \leftarrow i + 1$
      else
        $y \leftarrow x$; $x \leftarrow t$
        if $x =$ nil **then return**
        $i \leftarrow$ done$[x]$
        $t \leftarrow x.f_i$; $x.f_i \leftarrow y$
        done$[x] \leftarrow i + 1$

ALGORITHM 13.6. Depth-first search using pointer reversal.

---

it, so that the unused memory is inside the record instead of outside.

13.2 REFERENCE COUNTS

One day a student came to Moon and said: "I understand
how to make a better garbage collector. We must keep a
reference count of the pointers to each cons."
Moon patiently told the student the following story:
    "One day a student came to Moon and said: 'I under-
    stand how to make a better garbage collector ...' "

(MIT-AI koan by Danny Hillis)

Mark-sweep collection identifies the garbage by first finding out what is reachable. Instead, it can be done directly by keeping track of how many pointers

point to each record: This is the *reference count* of the record, and it is stored with each record.

The compiler emits extra instructions so that whenever p is stored into $x.f_i$, the reference count of p is incremented, and the reference count of what $x.f_i$ previously pointed to is decremented. If the decremented reference count of some record r reaches zero, then r is put on the freelist and all the other records that r points to have their reference counts decremented.

Instead of decrementing the counts of $r.f_i$ when r is put on the freelist, it is better to do this "recursive" decrementing when r is removed from the freelist, for two reasons:

1. It breaks up the "recursive decrementing" work into shorter pieces, so that the program can run more smoothly (this is important only for interactive or real-time programs).
2. The compiler must emit code (at each decrement) to check whether the count has reached zero and put the record on the freelist, but the recursive decrementing will be done only in one place, in the allocator.

Reference counting seems simple and attractive. But there are two major problems:

1. Cycles of garbage cannot be reclaimed. In Figure 13.1, for example, there is a loop of list cells (whose keys are 7 and 9) that are not reachable from program variables; but each has a reference count of 1.
2. Incrementing the reference counts is very expensive indeed. In place of the single machine instruction $x.f_i \leftarrow p$, the program must execute

$$
\begin{aligned}
z &\leftarrow x.f_i \\
c &\leftarrow z.\text{count} \\
c &\leftarrow c - 1 \\
z.\text{count} &\leftarrow c \\
\text{if } c = 0 \text{ call } &putOnFreelist \\
x.f_i &\leftarrow p \\
c &\leftarrow p.\text{count} \\
c &\leftarrow c + 1 \\
p.\text{count} &\leftarrow c
\end{aligned}
$$

A naive reference counter will increment and decrement the counts on every assignment to a program variable. Because this would be extremely expensive, many of the increments and decrements are eliminated using dataflow analysis: As a pointer value is fetched and then propagated through local variables, the compiler can aggregate the many changes in the count to a single increment, or (if the net change is zero) no extra instructions at all. However, even with this technique there are many ref-count increments and decrements that remain, and their cost is very high.

There are two possible solutions to the "cycles" problem. The first is simply to require the programmer to explicitly break all cycles when she is done with a data structure. This is less annoying than putting explicit *free* calls (as would be necessary without any garbage collection at all), but it is hardly elegant. The other solution is to combine reference counting (for eager and nondisruptive reclamation of garbage) with an occasional mark-sweep collection (to reclaim the cycles).

On the whole, the problems with reference counting outweigh its advantages, and it is rarely used for automatic storage management in programming language environments.

13.3   COPYING COLLECTION

The reachable part of the heap is a directed graph, with records as nodes, and pointers as edges, and program variables as roots. Copying garbage collection traverses this graph (in a part of the heap called *from-space*), building an isomorphic copy in a fresh area of the heap (called *to-space*). The to-space copy is *compact*, occupying contiguous memory without fragmentation (that is, without free records interspersed with the reachable data). The roots are made to point at the to-space copy; then the entire from-space (garbage, plus the previously reachable graph) is unreachable.

Figure 13.7 illustrates the situation before and after a copying collection. Before the collection, the from-space is full of reachable nodes and garbage; there is no place left to allocate, since next has reached limit. After the collection, the area of to-space between next and limit is available for the compiled program to allocate new records. Because the new-allocation area is contiguous, allocating a new record of size n into pointer p is very easy: Just copy next to p, and increment next by n. Copying collection does not have a fragmentation problem.

Eventually, the program will allocate enough that next reaches limit; then another garbage collection is needed. The roles of from-space and to-space are swapped, and the reachable data are again copied.

Initiating a collection. To start a new collection, the pointer next is initialized to point at the beginning of to-space; as each reachable record in from-

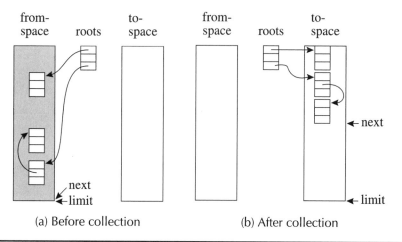

(a) Before collection   (b) After collection

FIGURE 13.7.   Copying collection.

---

function Forward(p)
    if p points to from-space
        then if $p.f_1$ points to to-space
            then return $p.f_1$
            else for each field f_i of p
                    `next.`$f_i \leftarrow p.f_i$
                $p.f_1 \leftarrow$ `next`
                `next` $\leftarrow$ `next`$+$ size of record p
                return $p.f_1$
    else return p

ALGORITHM 13.8. Forwarding a pointer.

---

space is found, it is copied to to-space at position `next`, and `next` incremented by the size of the record.

Forwarding. The basic operation of copying collection is *forwarding* a pointer; that is, given a pointer p that points to from-space, make p point to to-space (Algorithm 13.8).
    There are three cases:

1. If p points to a from-space record that has already been copied, then $p.f_1$ is a special *forwarding pointer* that indicates where the copy is. The forwarding pointer can be identified just by the fact that it points within the to-space, as

scan ← next ← beginning of to-space
for each root r
   $r ← \text{Forward}(r)$
while scan < next
   for each field f_i of record at scan
      $\text{scan}.f_i ← \text{Forward}(\text{scan}.f_i)$
   scan ← scan+ size of record at scan

ALGORITHM 13.9. Breadth-first copying garbage collection.

---

   no ordinary from-space field could point there.

2. If p points to a from-space record that has not yet been copied, then it is copied to location next; and the forwarding pointer is installed into $p.f_1$. It's all right to overwrite the f_1 field of the old record, because all the data have already been copied to the to-space at next.

3. If p is not a pointer at all, or if it points outside from-space (to a record outside the garbage-collected arena, or to to-space), then forwarding p does nothing.

Cheney's algorithm. The simplest algorithm for copying collection uses breadth-first search to traverse the reachable data (Algorithm 13.9, illustrated in Figure 13.10). First, the roots are forwarded. This copies a few records (those reachable *directly* from root pointers) to to-space, thereby incrementing next.

The area between scan and next contains records that have been copied to to-space, but whose fields have not yet been forwarded: In general, these fields point to from-space. The area between the beginning of to-space and scan contains records that have been copied *and* forwarded, so that all the pointers in this area point to to-space. The **while** loop (of Algorithm 13.9) moves scan toward next, but copying records will cause next to move also. Eventually, scan catches up with next after all the reachable data are copied to to-space.

Cheney's algorithm requires no external stack, and no pointer reversal: It uses the to-space area between scan and next as the queue of its breadth-first search. This makes it considerably simpler to implement than depth-first search with pointer reversal.

Locality of reference. However, pointer data structures copied by breadth-first have poor locality of reference: If a record at address a points to another

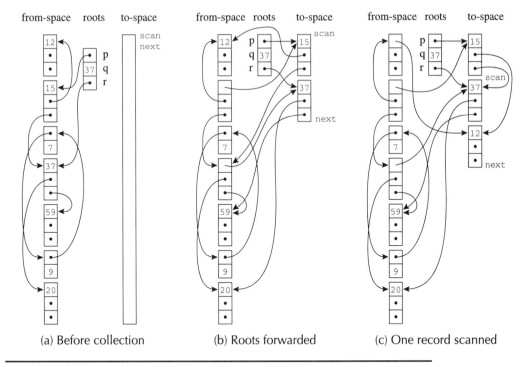

from-space   roots   to-space   from-space   roots   to-space   from-space   roots   to-space

(a) Before collection   (b) Roots forwarded   (c) One record scanned

FIGURE 13.10.   Breadth-first copying collection.

record at address b, it is likely that a and b will be far apart. Conversely, the record at $a+8$ is likely to be unrelated to the one at a. Records that are copied near each other are those whose distance from the roots are equal.

In a computer system with virtual memory, or with a memory cache, good locality of reference is important. After the program fetches address a, then the memory subsystem expects addresses near a to be fetched soon. So it ensures that the entire page or cache line containing a and nearby addresses can be quickly accessed.

Suppose the program is fetching down a chain of n pointers in a linked list. If the records in the list are scattered around memory, each on a page (or cache line) containing completely unrelated data, then we expect n difference pages or cache lines to be active. But if successive records in the chain are at adjacent addresses, then only n/k pages (cache lines) need to be active, where k records fit on each page (cache line).

Depth-first copying gives better locality, since each object a will tend to be adjacent to its first child b, unless b is adjacent to another "parent" a'. Other

function Forward(p)
   if p points to from-space
      then if $p.f_1$ points to to-space
         then return $p.f_1$
         else Chase(p); **return** $p.f_1$
      else **return** p

function Chase(p)
   repeat
      $q \leftarrow$ next
      next $\leftarrow$ next$+$ size of record p
      $r \leftarrow$ nil
      for each field f_i of record p
         $q.f_i \leftarrow p.f_i$
         if $q.f_i$ points to from-space **and** $q.f_i.f_1$ does not point to to-space
         then $r \leftarrow q.f_i$
      $p.f_1 \leftarrow q$
      $p \leftarrow r$
   until $p =$ nil

ALGORITHM 13.11. Semi-depth-first forwarding.

---

children of a may not be adjacent to a, but if the subtree b is small, then they should be nearby.

But depth-first copy requires pointer-reversal, which is inconvenient and slow. A hybrid, partly depth-first and partly breadth-first algorithm can provide acceptable locality. The basic idea is to use breadth-first copying, but whenever an object is copied, see if some child can be copied near it (Algorithm 13.11).

Cost of garbage collection. Breadth-first search (or the semi-depth-first variant) takes time proportional to the number of nodes it marks, that is, $c_3 R$ for some constant c_3 (perhaps equal to 10 instructions). There is no sweep phase, so $c_3 R$ is the total cost of collection. The heap is divided into two semi-spaces, so each collection reclaims $H/2 - R$ words that can be allocated before the next collection. The amortized cost of collection is thus

$$\frac{c_3 R}{\frac{H}{2} - R}$$

instructions per word allocated.

As H grows much larger than R, this cost approaches zero. That is, *there is no inherent lower bound to the cost of garbage collection.* In a more realistic setting, where $H = 4R$, the cost would be about 10 instructions per word allocated. This is rather costly in space and time: It requires four times as much memory as reachable data, and requires 40 instructions of overhead for every 4-word object allocated. To reduce both space and time costs significantly, we use *generational* collection.

13.4 GENERATIONAL COLLECTION

In many programs, newly created objects are likely to die soon; but an object that is still reachable after many collections will probably survive for many collections more. Therefore the collector should concentrate its effort on the "young" data, where there is a higher proportion of garbage.

We divide the heap into *generations*, with the youngest objects in generation G_0; every object in generation G_1 is older than any object in G_0; everything in G_2 is older than anything in G_1, and so on.

To collect (by mark-and-sweep or by copying) just G_0, just start from the roots and do either depth-first marking or breadth-first copying (or semi-depth-first copying). But now the roots are not just program variables: They include any pointer within $G_1, G_2, \ldots$ that points into G_0. If there are too many of these, then processing the roots will take longer than the traversal of reachable objects within G_0!

Fortunately, it is rare for an older object to point to a much younger object. In many common programming styles, when an object a is created its fields are immediately initialized; for example, they might be made to point to b and c. But b and c already exist; they are older than a. So we have a newer object pointing to an older object. The only way that an older object b could point to a newer object a is if some field of b is updated long after b is created; this turns out to be rare.

To avoid searching all of $G_1, G_2, \ldots$ for roots of G_0, we make the compiled program *remember* where there are pointers from old objects to new ones. There are several ways of remembering:

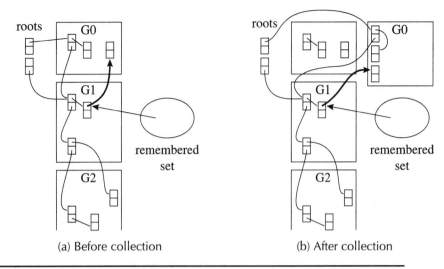

(a) Before collection · (b) After collection

FIGURE 13.12. Generational collection. The bold arrow is one of the rare pointers from an older generation to a newer one.

Remembered list: The compiler generates code, after each *update* store of the form $b.f_i \leftarrow a$, to put b into a vector of *updated objects*. Then, at each garbage collection, the collector scans the remembered list looking for old objects b that point into G_0.

Remembered set: Like the remembered list, but uses a bit within object b to record that b is already in the vector. Then the code generated by the compiler can check this bit to avoid duplicate references to b in the vector.

Card marking: Divide memory into logical "cards" of size 2^k bytes. An object can occupy part of a card or can start in the middle of one card and continue onto the next. Whenever address b is updated, the card containing that address is *marked*. There is an array of bytes that serve as marks; the byte index can be found by shifting address b right by k bits.

Page marking: This is like card marking, but if 2^k is the page size, then the computer's virtual memory system can be used instead of extra instructions generated by the compiler. Updating an old generation sets a *dirty bit* for that page. If the operating system does not make dirty bits available to user programs, then the user program can implement this by write-protecting the page and asking the operating system to refer protection violations to a user-mode fault handler that records the dirtiness and unprotects the page.

When a garbage collection begins, the remembered set tells which objects (or cards, or pages) of the old generation can possibly contain pointers into G_0; these are scanned for roots.

Algorithm 13.3 or 13.9 can be used to collect G_0: "heap" or "from-space" means G_0, "to-space" means a new area big enough to hold the reachable objects in G_0, and "roots" include program variables *and* the remembered set. Pointers to older generations are left unchanged: The marking algorithm does not mark old-generation records, and the copying algorithm copies them verbatim without forwarding them.

After several collections of G_0, generation G_1 may have accumulated a significant amount of garbage that should be collected. Since G_0 may contain many pointers into G_1, it is best to collect G_0 and G_1 together. As before, the remembered set must be scanned for roots contained in $G_2, G_3, \ldots$. Even more rarely, G_2 will be collected, and so on.

Each older generation should be exponentially bigger than the previous one. If G_0 is half a megabyte, then G_1 should be two megabytes, G_2 should be eight megabytes, and so on. An object should be promoted from G_i to G_{i+1} when it survives two or three collections of G_i.

Cost of generational collection. Without detailed empirical information about the distribution of object lifetimes, we cannot analyze the behavior of generational collection. In practice, however, it is common for the youngest generation to be less than 10% live data. With a copying collector, this means that H/R is 10 *in this generation*, so that the amortized cost per word reclaimed is $c_3 R/(10R - R)$, or about 1 instruction. If the amount of reachable data in G_0 is about 50 to 100 kilobytes, then the amount of space "wasted" by having $H = 10R$ in the youngest generation is about a megabyte. In a 50-megabyte multigeneration system, this is a small space cost.

Collecting the older generations can be more expensive. To avoid using too much space, a smaller H/R ratio can be used for older generations. This increases the time cost of an older-generation collection, but these are sufficiently rare that the overall amortized time cost is still good.

Maintaining the remembered set also takes time, approximately 10 instructions per pointer update to enter an object into the remembered set and then process that entry in the remembered set. If the program does many more updates than fresh allocations, then generational collection may be more expensive than nongenerational collection.

while there are any grey objects
   select a grey record p
  for each field f_i of p
    if record $p.f_i$ is white
      color record $p.f_i$ grey
   color record p black

ALGORITHM 13.13. Basic tricolor marking.

13.5   INCREMENTAL COLLECTION

Even if the overall garbage collection time is only a few percent of the computation time, the collector will occasionally interrupt the program for long periods. For interactive or real-time programs this is undesirable. Incremental or concurrent algorithms interleave garbage collection work with program execution to avoid long interruptions.

Terminology. The *collector* tries to collect the garbage; meanwhile, the compiled program keeps changing (mutating) the graph of reachable data, so it is called the *mutator*. An *incremental* algorithm is one in which the collector operates only when the mutator requests it; in a *concurrent* algorithm the collector can operate between or during any instructions executed by the mutator.

Tricolor marking. In a mark-sweep or copying garbage collection, there are three classes of records:

White objects are not yet visited by the depth-first or breadth-first search.
Grey objects have been visited (marked or copied), but their children have not yet been examined. In mark-sweep collection, these objects are on the stack; in Cheney's copying collection, they are between scan and next.
Black objects have been marked, and their children also marked. In mark-sweep collection, they have already been popped off the stack; in Cheney's algorithm, they have already been scanned.

The collection starts with all objects white; the collector executes Algorithm 13.13, blackening grey objects and greying their white children. Implicit in changing an object from grey to black is *removing it from the stack or queue*; implicit in greying an object is *putting it into the stack or queue*. When there are no grey objects, then all white objects must be garbage.

Algorithm 13.13 generalizes all of the mark-sweep and copying algorithms shown so far: Algorithms 13.2, 13.3, 13.5, 13.6, and 13.9.

All these algorithms preserve two natural invariants:

1. No black object points to a white object.
2. Every grey object is on the collector's (stack or queue) data structure (which we will call the *grey-set*).

While the collector operates, the mutator creates new objects (of what color?) and updates pointer fields of existing objects. If the mutator breaks one of the invariants, then the collection algorithm will not work.

Most incremental and concurrent collection algorithms are based on techniques to allow the mutator to get work done while preserving the invariants. For example:

Dijkstra, Lamport, et al. Whenever the mutator stores a white pointer a into a black object b, it colors a grey. (The compiler generates extra instructions at each store to check for this.)

Steele. Whenever the mutator stores a white pointer a into a black object b, it colors b grey (using extra instructions generated by the compiler).

Boehm, Demers, Shenker. All-black pages are marked read-only in the virtual memory system. Whenever the mutator stores *any* value into an all-black page, a page fault marks all objects on that page grey (and makes the page writable).

Baker. Whenever the mutator fetches a pointer b to a white object, it colors b grey. The mutator never possesses a pointer to a white object, so it cannot violate invariant 1. The instructions to check the color of b are generated by the compiler after every fetch.

Appel, Ellis, Li. Whenever the mutator fetches a pointer b from any virtual-memory page containing any nonblack object, a page-fault handler colors every object on the page black (making children of these objects grey). Thus the mutator never possesses a pointer to a white object.

The first three of these are *write-barrier* algorithms, meaning that each *write* (store) by the mutator must be checked to make sure an invariant is preserved. The last two are *read-barrier* algorithms, meaning that *read* (fetch) instructions are the ones that must be checked. We have seen write barriers before, for generational collection: Remembered lists, remembered sets, card marking, and page marking are all different implementations of the write barrier. Similarly, the read barrier can be implemented in software (as in Baker's algorithm) or using the virtual-memory hardware.

Any implementation of a write or read barrier must synchronize with the collector. For example, a Dijkstra-style collector might try to change a white node to grey (and put it into the grey-set) at the same time the mutator is also greying the node (and putting it into the grey-set). Thus, software implementations of the read or write barrier will need to use explicit synchronization instructions, which can be expensive.

But implementations using virtual-memory hardware can take advantage of the synchronization implicit in a page fault: If the mutator faults on a page, the operating system will ensure that no other process has access to that page before processing the fault.

13.6   BAKER'S ALGORITHM

Baker's algorithm illustrates the details of incremental collection. It is based on Cheney's copying collection algorithm, so it forwards reachable objects from from-space to to-space. Baker's algorithm is compatible with generational collection, so that the from-space and to-space might be for generation G_0, or might be $G_0 + \cdots + G_k$.

To initiate a garbage collection (which happens when an *allocate* request fails for lack of unused memory), the roles of the (previous) from-space and to-space are swapped, and all the roots are forwarded; this is called the *flip*. Then the mutator is resumed; but each time the mutator calls the allocator to get a new record, a few pointers at scan are scanned, so that scan advances toward next. Then a new record is allocated *at the end of the to-space* by decrementing limit by the appropriate amount.

The invariant is that the mutator has pointers only to to-space (never to from-space). Thus, when the mutator allocates and initializes a new record, that record need not be scanned; when the mutator stores a pointer into an old record, it is only storing a to-space pointer.

If the mutator fetches a field of a record, it might break the invariant. So each fetch is followed by two or three instructions that check whether the fetched pointer points to from-space. If so, that pointer must be *forwarded* immediately, using the standard *forward* algorithm.

For every word allocated, the allocator must advance scan by at least one word. When scan=next, the collection terminates until the next time the allocator runs out of space. If the heap is divided into two semi-spaces of size $H/2$, and $R < H/4$, then scan will catch up with next before next reaches halfway through the to-space; also by this time, no more than half the to-space will be occupied by newly allocated records.

Baker's algorithm copies no more data than is live at the flip. Records allocated during collection are not scanned, so they do not add to the cost of collection. The collection cost is thus $c_3 R$. But there is also a cost to check (at every allocation) whether incremental scanning is necessary; this is proportional to $H/2 - R$.

But the largest cost of Baker's algorithm is the extra instructions after every fetch, required to maintain the invariant. If one in every 10 instructions fetches from a heap record, and each of these fetches requires two extra instructions to test whether it is a from-space pointer, then there is at least a 20% overhead cost just to maintain the invariant. All of the incremental or concurrent algorithms that use a software write or read barrier will have a significant cost in overhead of ordinary mutator operations.

13.7   INTERFACE TO THE COMPILER

The compiler for a garbage-collected language interacts with the garbage collector by generating code that allocates records, by describing locations of roots for each garbage-collection cycle, and by describing the layout of data records on the heap. For some versions of incremental collection, the compiler must also generate instructions to implement a read or write barrier.

FAST ALLOCATION

Some programming languages, and some programs, allocate heap data (and generate garbage) very rapidly. This is especially true of programs in functional languages, where updating old data is discouraged.

The most allocation (and garbage) one could imagine a reasonable program generating is one word of allocation per store instruction; this is because each word of a heap-allocated record is usually initialized. Empirical measurements show that about one in every seven instructions executed is a store, almost regardless of programming language or program. Thus, we have (at most) $\frac{1}{7}$ word of allocation per instruction executed.

Supposing that the cost of garbage collection can be made small by proper tuning of a generational collector, there may still be a considerable cost to create the heap records. To minimize this cost, *copying collection* should be used so that the allocation space is a contiguous free region; the next free location is `next` and the end of the region is `limit`. To allocate one record of size N, the steps are

1. Call the allocate function.
2. Test $next + N < limit$? (If the test fails, call the garbage collector.)
3. Move `next` into `result`
4. Clear $M[next], M[next + 1], \ldots, M[next + N - 1]$
5. $next \leftarrow next + N$
6. Return from the allocate function.
A. Move `result` into some computationally useful place.
B. Store useful values into the record.

Steps 1 and 6 should be eliminated by *inline expanding* the allocate function at each place where a record is allocated. Step 3 can often be eliminated by combining it with step A, and step 4 can be eliminated in favor of step B (steps A and B are not numbered because they are part of the useful computation; they are not allocation overhead).

Steps 2 and 5 cannot be eliminated, but if there is more than one allocation in the same basic block (or in the same *trace*; see Section 8.2), the comparison and increment can be shared among multiple allocations. By keeping `next` and `limit` in registers, steps 2 and 5 can be done in a total of three instructions.

By this combination of techniques, the cost of allocating a record – and then eventually garbage collecting it – can be brought down to about four instructions. This means that programming techniques such as the *persistent binary search tree* (page 108) can be efficient enough for everyday use.

DESCRIBING DATA LAYOUTS

The collector must be able to operate on records of all types: `list`, `tree`, or whatever the program has declared. It must be able to determine the number of fields in each record, and whether each field is a pointer.

For statically typed languages such as Pascal, or for object-oriented languages such as Java or Modula-3, the simplest way to identify heap objects is to have the first word of every object point to a special type- or class-descriptor record. This record tells the total size of the object and the location of each pointer field.

For statically typed languages this is an overhead of one word per record to serve the garbage collector. But object-oriented languages need this descriptor pointer in every object just to implement dynamic method lookup, so that there is no additional per-object overhead attributable to garbage collection.

The type- or class-descriptor must be generated by the compiler from the static type information calculated by the semantic analysis phase of the compiler. The descriptor pointer will be the argument to the runtime system's `alloc` function.

In addition to describing every heap record, the compiler must identify to the collector every pointer-containing temporary and local variable, whether it is in a register or in an activation record. Because the set of live temporaries can change at every instruction, the *pointer map* is different at every point in the program. Therefore, it is simpler to describe the pointer map only at points where a new garbage collection can begin. These are at calls to the `alloc` function; and also, since any function call might be calling a function which in turn calls `alloc`, the pointer map must be described at each function call.

The pointer map is best keyed by return addresses: A function call at location a is best described by its return address immediately after a, because the return address is what the collector will see in the very next activation record. The data structure maps return addresses to live-pointer sets; for each pointer that is live immediately after the call, the pointer map tells its register or frame location.

To find all the roots, the collector starts at the top of the stack and scans downward, frame by frame. Each return address keys the pointer-map entry that describes the next frame. In each frame, the collector marks (or forwards, if copying collection) from the pointers in that frame.

Callee-save registers need special handling. Suppose function f calls g, which calls h. Function h knows that it saved some of the callee-save registers in its frame and mentions this fact in its pointer map; but h *does not know which of these registers are pointers*. Therefore the pointer map for g must describe which of its callee-save registers contain pointers at the call to h and which are "inherited" from f.

DERIVED POINTERS

Sometimes a compiled program has a pointer that points into the middle of a heap record, or that points before or after the record. For example, the expression a[i-2000] can be calculated internally as M[a-2000+i]:

$$t_1 \leftarrow a - 2000$$
$$t_2 \leftarrow t_1 + i$$
$$t_3 \leftarrow M[t_2]$$

If the expression $a[i-2000]$ occurs inside a loop, the compiler might choose to hoist $t_1 \leftarrow a - 2000$ outside the loop to avoid recalculating it in each iteration. If the loop also contains an `alloc`, and a garbage collection occurs while t_1 is live, will the collector be confused by a pointer t_1 that does not point to the beginning of an object, or (worse yet) that points to an unrelated object?

We say that the t_1 is *derived* from the *base* pointer a. The pointer map must identify each *derived pointer* and tell the base pointer from which it is derived. Then, when the collector relocates a to address a', it must adjust t_1 to point to address $t_1 + a' - a$.

Of course, this means that a must remain live as long as t_1 is live. Consider the loop at left, implemented as shown at right:

```
let
   var a := intarray[100] of 0

in
  for i := 1930 to 1990
    do f(a[i-2000])

end
```

$$r_1 \leftarrow 100$$
$$r_2 \leftarrow 0$$
$$\text{call alloc}$$
$$a \leftarrow r_1$$
$$t_1 \leftarrow a - 2000$$
$$i \leftarrow 1930$$
$$L_1: r_1 \leftarrow M[t_1 + i]$$
$$\text{call } f$$
$$L_2: \text{if } i \leq 1990 \text{ goto } L_1$$

If there are no other uses of a, then the temporary a appears dead after the assignment to t_1. But then the pointer map associated with the return address L_2 would not be able to "explain" t_1 adequately. Therefore, for purposes of the compiler's liveness analysis, *a derived pointer implicitly keeps its base pointer live*.

PROGRAM   DESCRIPTORS

Implement record descriptors and pointer maps for the MiniJava compiler.

For each record-type declaration, make a string literal to serve as the record descriptor. The length of the string should be equal to the number of fields in the record. The ith byte of the string should be p if the ith field of the record is a pointer (string, record, or array), or n if the ith field is a nonpointer.

The `allocRecord` function should now take the record descriptor string (pointer) instead of a length; the allocator can obtain the length from the string literal. Then `allocRecord` should store this descriptor pointer at field zero of the record. Modify the runtime system appropriately.

The user-visible fields of the record will now be at offsets $1, 2, 3, \ldots$ instead of $0, 1, 2, \ldots$; adjust the compiler appropriately.

Design a descriptor format for arrays, and implement it in the compiler and runtime system.

Implement a temp-map with a boolean for each temporary: Is it a pointer or not? Also make a similar map for the offsets in each stack frame, for frame-resident pointer variables. You will not need to handle derived pointers, as your MiniJava compiler probably does not keep derived pointers live across function calls.

For each procedure call, put a new return-address label L_{ret} immediately after the `call` instruction. For each one, make a data fragment of the form

$$L_{ptrmap327}: \quad \begin{array}{lll} \text{.word} & L_{ptrmap326} & \textit{link to previous ptr-map entry} \\ \text{.word} & L_{ret327} & \textit{key for this entry} \\ \text{.word} & \ldots & \textit{pointer map for} \\ & & \quad \textit{this return address} \\ \vdots & & \end{array}$$

and then the runtime system can traverse this linked list of pointer-map entries, and perhaps build it into a data structure of its own choosing for fast lookup of return addresses. The data-layout pseudo-instructions (`.word`, etc.) are, of course, machine-dependent.

PROGRAM GARBAGE COLLECTION

Implement a mark-sweep or copying garbage collector in the C language, and link it into the runtime system. Invoke the collector from `allocRecord` or `initArray` when the free space is exhausted.

FURTHER READING

Reference counting [Collins 1960] and mark-sweep collection [McCarthy 1960] are almost as old as languages with pointers. The pointer-reversal idea is attributed by Knuth [1967] to Peter Deutsch and to Herbert Schorr and W. M. Waite.

Fenichel and Yochelson [1969] designed the first two-space copying collector, using depth-first search; Cheney [1970] designed the algorithm that uses the unscanned nodes in to-space as the queue of a breadth-first search, and also the semi-depth-first copying that improves the locality of a linked list.

Steele [1975] designed the first concurrent mark-and-sweep algorithm. Dijkstra et al. [1978] formalized the notion of tricolor marking, and designed a concurrent algorithm that they could prove correct, trying to keep the synchronization requirements as weak as possible. Baker [1978] invented the incremental copying algorithm in which the mutator sees only to-space pointers.

Generational garbage collection, taking advantage of the fact that newer objects die quickly and that there are few old-to-new pointers, was invented by Lieberman and Hewitt [1983]; Ungar [1986] developed a simpler and more efficient *remembered set* mechanism.

The Symbolics Lisp Machine [Moon 1984] had special hardware to assist with incremental and generational garbage collection. The microcoded memory-fetch instructions enforced the invariant of Baker's algorithm; the microcoded memory-store instructions maintained the remembered set for generational collection. This collector was the first to explicitly improve locality of reference by keeping related objects on the same virtual-memory page.

As modern computers rarely use microcode, and a modern general-purpose processor embedded in a general-purpose memory hierarchy tends to be an order of magnitude faster and cheaper than a computer with special-purpose instructions and memory tags, attention turned in the late 1980s to algorithms that could be implemented with standard RISC instructions and standard virtual-memory hardware. Appel et al. [1988] use virtual memory to implement a read barrier in a truly concurrent variant of Baker's algorithm. Shaw [1988] uses virtual-memory *dirty bits* to implement a write barrier for generational collection, and Boehm et al. [1991] make the same simple write barrier serve for concurrent generational mark-and-sweep. Write barriers are cheaper to implement than read barriers, because stores to old pages are rarer than fetches from to-space, and a write barrier merely needs to set a dirty bit and continue with minimal interruption of the mutator. Sobalvarro [1988] invented the card marking technique, which uses ordinary RISC instructions without requiring interaction with the virtual-memory system.

Appel and Shao [1996] describe techniques for fast allocation of heap records and discuss several other efficiency issues related to garbage-collected systems.

Branquart and Lewi [1971] describe pointer maps communicated from a compiler to its garbage collector; Diwan et al. [1992] tie pointer maps to return addresses, show how to handle derived pointers, and compress the maps to save space.

Appel [1992, Chapter 12] shows that compilers for functional languages must be careful about closure representations; using simple static links (for example) can keep enormous amounts of data reachable, preventing the collector from reclaiming it.

Boehm and Weiser [1988] describe *conservative collection*, where the compiler does not inform the collector which variables and record fields contain pointers, so the collector must "guess." Any bit pattern pointing into the allocated heap is assumed to be a possible pointer and keeps the pointed-to record live. However, since the bit pattern might really be meant as an integer, the object cannot be moved (which would change the possible integer), and some garbage objects may not be reclaimed. Wentworth [1990] points out that such an integer may (coincidentally) point to the root of a huge garbage data structure, which therefore will not be reclaimed; so conservative collection will occasionally suffer from a disastrous space leak. Boehm [1993] describes several techniques for making these disasters unlikely: For example, if the collector ever finds an integer pointing to address X that is not a currently allocated object, it should *blacklist* that address so that the allocator will never allocate an object there. Boehm [1996] points out that even a conservative collector needs some amount of compiler assistance: If a derived pointer can point outside the bounds of an object, then its base pointer must be kept live as long as the derived pointer exists.

Page 481 discusses some of the literature on improving the cache performance of garbage-collected systems.

Cohen [1981] comprehensively surveys the first two decades of garbage-collection research; Wilson [1997] describes and discusses more recent work. Jones and Lins [1996] offer a comprehensive textbook on garbage collection.

EXERCISES

*13.1 Analyze the cost of mark-sweep versus copying collection. Assume that every record is exactly two words long, and every field is a pointer. Some pointers may point outside the collectible heap, and these are to be left unchanged.

a. Analyze Algorithm 13.6 to estimate c_1, the cost (in instructions per reachable word) of depth-first marking.

b. Analyze Algorithm 13.3 to estimate c_2, the cost (in instructions per word in the heap) of sweeping.

c. Analyze Algorithm 13.9 to estimate c_3, the cost per reachable word of copying collection.

d. There is some ratio γ so that with $H = \gamma R$ the cost of copying collection equals the cost of mark-sweep collection. Find γ.

e. For $H > \gamma R$, which is cheaper, mark-sweep or copying collection?

13.2 Run Algorithm 13.6 (pointer reversal) on the heap of Figure 13.1. Show the state of the heap; the done flags; and variables t, x, and y at the time the node containing 59 is first marked.

*13.3 Assume main calls f with callee-save registers all containing 0. Then f saves the callee-save registers it is going to use; puts pointers into some callee-save registers, integers into others, and leaves the rest untouched; and then it calls g. Now g saves some of the callee-save registers, puts some pointers and integers into them, and calls alloc, which starts a garbage collection.

a. Write functions f and g matching this description.

b. Illustrate the pointer maps of functions f and g.

c. Show the steps that the collector takes to recover the exact locations of all the pointers.

**13.4 Every object in the Java language supports a hashCode() method that returns a "hash code" for that object. Hash codes need not be unique – different objects can return the same hash code – but each object must return the same hash code every time it is called, and two objects selected at random should have only a small chance of having the same hash code.

The Java language specification says that "This is typically implemented by converting the address of the object to an integer, but this implementation technique is not required by the Java language."

Explain the problem in implementing hashCode() this way in a Java system with copying garbage collection, and propose a solution.

14

Object-Oriented Languages

ob-ject: to feel distaste for something

Webster's Dictionary

An important characteristic of object-oriented languages is the notion of *extension* or *inheritance*. If some program context (such as the formal parameter of a function or method) expects an object that supports methods m_1, m_2, m_3, then it will also accept an object that supports m_1, m_2, m_3, m_4.

14.1 CLASS EXTENSION

Program 14.1 illustrates the use of class extension in Java. Every `Vehicle` is an `Object`; every `Car` is a `Vehicle`; thus every `Car` is also an `Object`. Every `Vehicle` (and thus every `Car` and `Truck`) has an integer `position` field and a `move` method.

In addition, a `Car` has an integer `passengers` field and an `await` method. The variables in scope on entry to `await` are

`passengers` because it is a field of `Car`,
`position` because it is (implicitly) a field of `Car`,
`v` because it is a formal parameter of `await`,
`this` because it is (implicitly) a formal parameter of `await`.

At the call to `c.await(t)`, the truck `t` is bound to the formal parameter `v` of the `await` method. Then when `v.move` is called, this activates the `Truck_move` method body, not `Vehicle_move`.

We use the notation A_m to indicate a *method instance* m declared within a class A. This is not part of the Java syntax, it is just for use in discussing

```
class Vehicle {
    int position;
    void move (int x) { position = position + x; }
}
class Car extends Vehicle{
    int passengers;
    void await(Vehicle v) {
        if (v.position < position)
            v.move(position - v.position);
        else
            this.move(10);
    }
}
class Truck extends Vehicle{
    void move(int x) {
        if (x <= 55) { position = position + x; }
    }
}
class Main{
    public static void main(String args[]) {
        Truck t = new Truck();
        Car c = new Car();
        Vehicle v = c;
        c.passengers = 2;
        c.move(60);
        v.move(70);
        c.await(t);
    }
}
```

PROGRAM 14.1. An object-oriented program.

---

the semantics of Java programs. Each different declaration of a method is a different method instance. Two different method instances could have the same method name if, for example, one overrides the other.

14.2   SINGLE INHERITANCE OF DATA FIELDS

To evaluate the expression v.position, where v belongs to class Vehicle, the compiler must generate code to fetch the field position from the object (record) that v points to.

This seems simple enough: The environment entry for variable v contains

```
class A {              int a = 0;}
class B extends A {int b = 0;
                   int c = 0;}
class C extends A {int d = 0;}
class D extends B {int e = 0;}
```

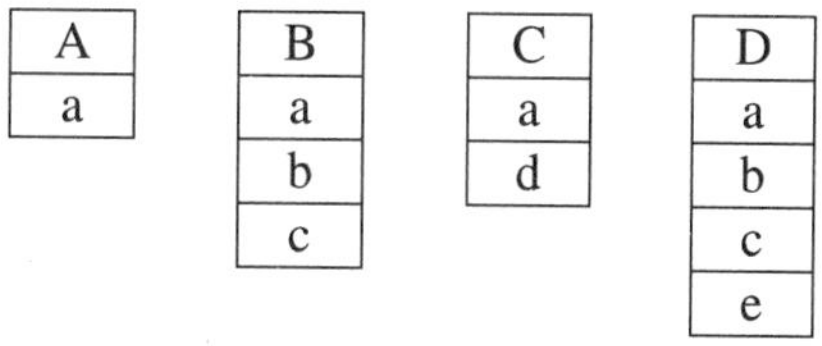

A
a

B
a
b
c

C
a
d

D
a
b
c
e

FIGURE 14.2.   Single inheritance of data fields.

(among other things) a pointer to the type (class) description of `Vehicle`; this has a list of fields and their offsets. But at run time the variable `v` could also contain a pointer to a `Car` or `Truck`; where will the `position` field be in a `Car` or `Truck` object?

Single inheritance. For *single-inheritance* languages, in which each class extends just one parent class, the simple technique of *prefixing* works well. Where B extends A, those fields of B that are inherited from A are laid out in a B record *at the beginning, in the same order they appear in* A *records*. Fields of B not inherited from A are placed afterward, as shown in Figure 14.2.

METHODS

A method instance is compiled much like a function: It turns into machine code that resides at a particular address in the instruction space. Let us say, for example, that the method instance `Truck_move` has an entry point at machine-code label `Truck_move`. In the semantic analysis phase of the compiler, each variable's environment entry contains a pointer to its class descriptor; each class descriptor contains a pointer to its parent class, and also a list of method instances; and each method instance has a machine-code label.

Static methods. Some object-oriented languages allow some methods to be declared *static*. The machine code that executes when `c.f()` is called depends on the type of the *variable* `c`, not the type of the *object* that `c` holds. To compile a method-call of the form `c.f()`, the compiler finds the class of `c`; let us suppose it is class C. Then it searches in class C for a method `f`; suppose none is found. Then it searches the parent class of C, class B, for a method `f`; then the parent class of B; and so on. Suppose in some ancestor class A it finds a static method `f`; then it can compile a function call to label `A_f`.

```
class A              {int x = 0;
                      int f() {...} }
class B extends A {int g() {...} }
class C extends B {int g() {...} }
class D extends C {int y = 0;
                      int f() {...} }
```

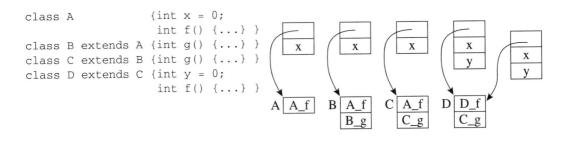

FIGURE 14.3. Class descriptors for dynamic method lookup.

Dynamic methods. This technique will not work for dynamic methods. If method f in A is a dynamic method, then it might be overridden in some class D which is a subclass of C (see Figure 14.3). But there is no way to tell at compile time if the variable c is pointing to an object of class D (in which case D_f should be called) or class C (in which case A_f should be called).

To solve this problem, the class descriptor must contain a vector with a method instance for each (nonstatic) method name. When class B inherits from A, the method table *starts with* entries for all method names known to A, and then continues with new methods declared by B. This is very much like the arrangement of fields in objects with inheritance.

Figure 14.3 shows what happens when class D overrides method f. Although the entry for f is at the beginning of D's method table, as it is also at the beginning of the ancestor class A's method table, it points to a different method-instance label because f has been overridden.

To execute c.f(), where f is a dynamic method, the compiled code must execute these instructions:

1. Fetch the class descriptor *d* at offset 0 from object c.
2. Fetch the method-instance pointer *p* from the (constant) f offset of *d*.
3. Jump to address *p*, saving return address (that is, call *p*).

14.3   MULTIPLE INHERITANCE

In languages that permit a class D to extend several parent classes A,B,C (that is, where A is not a subclass of B, or vice versa), finding field offsets and method instances is more difficult. It is impossible to put all the A fields at the beginning of D *and* to put all the B fields at the beginning of D.

```
class A { int a = 0; }
class B { int b = 0;
          int c = 0; }
class C extends A { int d = 0; }
class D extends A,B,C { int e = 0; }
```

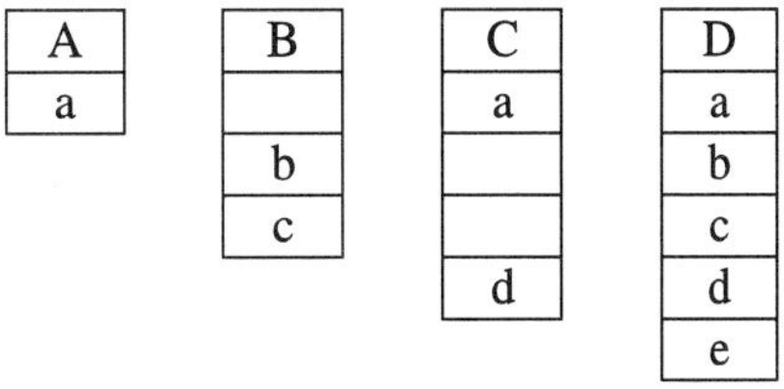

FIGURE 14.4.   Multiple inheritance of data fields.

Global graph coloring. One solution to this problem is to statically analyze all classes at once, finding some offset for each field name that can be used in every record containing that field. We can model this as a graph-coloring problem: There is a node for each distinct field name, and an edge for any two fields which coexist (perhaps by inheritance) in the same class.[1] The offsets $0, 1, 2, \ldots$ are the colors. Figure 14.4 shows an example.

The problem with this approach is that it leaves empty slots in the middle of objects, since it cannot always color the N fields of each class with colors with the first N colors. To eliminate the empty slots in objects, we pack the fields of each object and have the class descriptor tell where each field is. Figure 14.5 shows an example. We have done graph coloring on all the field names, as before, but now the "colors" are not the offsets of those fields within the *objects* but within the *descriptors*. To fetch a field a of object x, we fetch the a-word from x's descriptor; this word contains a small integer telling the position of the actual a data within x.

In this scheme, class descriptors have empty slots, but the objects do not; this is acceptable because a system with millions of objects is likely to have only dozens of class descriptors. But each data fetch (or store) requires three instructions instead of one:

1. Fetch the descriptor pointer from the object.
2. Fetch the field-offset value from the descriptor.
3. Fetch (or store) the data at the appropriate offset in the object.

In practice, it is likely that other operations on the object will have fetched the descriptor pointer already, and multiple operations on the same field (e.g., fetch then store) won't need to refetch the offset from the descriptor; common-subexpression elimination can remove much of this redundant overhead.

---

[1] *Distinct field name* does not mean simple equivalence of strings. Each fresh declaration of field or method x (where it is not overriding the x of a parent class) is really a distinct name.

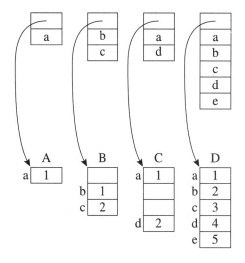

FIGURE 14.5.   Field offsets in descriptors for multiple inheritance.

Method lookup. Finding method instances in a language with multiple inheritance is just as complicated as finding field offsets. The global graph-coloring approach works well: The method names can be mixed with the field names to form nodes of a large interference graph. Descriptor entries for fields give locations within the objects; descriptor entries for methods give machine-code addresses of method instances.

Problems with dynamic linking. Any global approach suffers from the problem that the coloring (and layout of class descriptors) can be done only at link time; the job is certainly within the capability of a special-purpose linker.

However, many object-oriented systems have the capability to load new classes into a running system; these classes may be extensions (subclasses) of classes already in use. Link-time graph coloring poses many problems for a system that allows dynamic incremental linking.

Hashing. Instead of global graph coloring, we can put a hash table in each class descriptor, mapping field names to offsets and method names to method instances. This works well with separate compilation and dynamic linking.

The characters of the field names are not hashed at run time. Instead, each field name a is hashed at compile time to an integer $hash_a$ in the range $[0, N-1]$. Also, for each field name a unique run-time record (pointer) ptr_a is made.

Each class descriptor has a field-offset table Ftab of size N containing

	Modula-3	Java
Test whether object x belongs class C, or to any subclass of C.	ISTYPE(x,C)	x instanceof C
Given a variable x of class C, where x actually points to an object of class D that extends C, yield an expression whose compile-time type is class D.	NARROW(x,D)	(D)x

TABLE 14.6. Facilities for type testing and safe casting.

field-offsets and method instances, and (for purposes of collision detection) a parallel *key* table Ktab containing field-name pointers. If the class has a field x, then field-offset-table slot number hash$_x$ contains the offset for x, and key-table slot number hash$_x$ contains the pointer ptr$_x$.

To fetch a field x of object c, the compiler generates code to

1. Fetch the class descriptor d at offset 0 from object c.
2. Fetch the field name f from the address offset $d + $ Ktab $+$ hash$_x$.
3. Test whether $f = $ ptr$_x$; if so
4. Fetch the field offset k from $d + $ Ftab $+$ hash$_x$.
5. Fetch the contents of the field from $c + k$.

This algorithm has four instructions of overhead, which may still be tolerable. A similar algorithm works for dynamic method-instance lookup.

The algorithm as described does not say what to do if the test at line 3 fails. Any hash-table collision-resolution technique can be used.

14.4 TESTING CLASS MEMBERSHIP

Some object-oriented languages allow the program to test membership of an object in a class at run time, as summarized in Table 14.6.

Since each object points to its class descriptor, the address of the class descriptor can serve as a "type-tag." However, if x is an instance of D, and D extends C, then x is also an instance of C. Assuming there is no multiple inheritance, a simple way to implement x instanceof C is to generate code that performs the following loop at run time:

$$
\begin{aligned}
&t_1 \leftarrow x.\text{descriptor} \\
L_1: \quad &\textbf{if } t_1 = C \textbf{ goto } \textit{true} \\
&t_1 \leftarrow t_1.\text{super} \\
&\textbf{if } t_1 = \text{nil } \textbf{goto } \textit{false}
\end{aligned}
$$

goto L_1

where t_1.super is the superclass (parent class) of class t_1.

However, there is a faster approach using a *display* of parent classes. Assume that the class nesting depth is limited to some constant, such as 20. Reserve a 20-word block in each class descriptor. In the descriptor for a class D whose nesting depth is j, put a pointer to descriptor D in the jth slot, a pointer to D.super in the $(j - 1)$th slot, a pointer to D.super.super in slot $j - 2$, and so on up to Object in slot 0. In all slots numbered greater than j, put nil.

Now, if x is an instance of D, or of any subclass of D, then the jth slot of x's class descriptor will point to the class descriptor D. Otherwise it will not. So x instanceof D requires

1. Fetch the class descriptor d at offset 0 from object c.
2. Fetch the jth class-pointer slot from d.
3. Compare with the class descriptor D.

This works because the class-nesting depth of D is known at compile time.

Type coercions. Given a variable c of type C, it is always legal to treat c as any supertype of C – if C extends B, and variable b has type B, then the assignment $b \leftarrow c$ is legal and safe.

But the reverse is not true. The assignment $c \leftarrow b$ is safe only if b is really (at run time) an instance of C, which is not always the case. If we have $b \leftarrow$ new $B, c \leftarrow b$, followed by fetching some field of c that is part of class C but not class B, then this fetch will lead to unpredictable behavior.

Thus, safe object-oriented languages (such as Modula-3 and Java) accompany any coercion from a superclass to a subclass with a run-time type-check that raises an exception unless the run-time value is really an instance of the subclass (e.g., unless b instanceof C).

It is a common idiom to write

Modula-3:
```
IF ISTYPE(b,C)
  THEN f(NARROW(b,C))
  ELSE ...
```

Java:
```
if (b instanceof C)
    f((C)b)
else ...
```

Now there are two consecutive, identical type tests: one explicit (ISTYPE or instanceof) and one implicit (in NARROW or the cast). A good compiler will do enough flow analysis to notice that the **then**-clause is reached only if b is in fact an instance of C, so that the type-check in the narrowing operation can be eliminated.

C++ is an unsafe object-oriented language. It has a *static cast* mechanism without run-time checking; careless use of this mechanism can make the program "go wrong" in unpredictable ways. C++ also has `dynamic_cast` with run-time checking, which is like the mechanisms in Modula-3 and Java.

Typecase. Explicit `instanceof` testing, followed by a narrowing cast to a subclass, is not a wholesome "object-oriented" style. Instead of using this idiom, programmers are expected to use dynamic methods that accomplish the right thing in each subclass. Nevertheless, the test-then-narrow idiom is fairly common.

Modula-3 has a **typecase** facility that makes the idiom more beautiful and efficient (but not any more "object-oriented"):

```
TYPECASE expr
OF C₁ (v₁) => S₁
 |  C₂ (v₂) => S₂
   ⋮
 |  Cₙ (vₙ) => Sₙ
ELSE S₀
END
```

If the *expr* evaluates to an instance of class C_i, then a new variable v_i of type C_i points to the result of the *expr*, and statement S_i is executed. The declaration of v_i is implicit in the TYPECASE, and its scope covers only S_i.

If more than one of the C_i match (which can happen if, for example, one is a superclass of another), then only the first matching clause is taken. If none of the C_i match, then the ELSE clause is taken (statement S_0 is executed).

Typecase can be converted straightforwardly to a chain of **else-if**s, with each **if** doing an instance test, a narrowing, and a local variable declaration. However, if there are very many clauses, then it can take a long time to go through all the **else-if**s. Therefore it is attractive to treat it like a case (switch) statement on integers, using an indexed jump (computed goto).

That is, an ordinary case statement on integers:

ML:	C, Java:
`case i`	`switch (i) {`
`  of 0 => ` s_0	`    case 0: ` s_0 `; break;`
`	1 => ` s_1	`    case 1: ` s_1 `; break;`
`	2 => ` s_2	`    case 2: ` s_2 `; break;`
`	3 => ` s_3	`    case 3: ` s_3 `; break;`
`	4 => ` s_4	`    case 4: ` s_4 `; break;`
`	_ => ` s_d	`    default: ` s_d `;`
	`}`

is compiled as follows: First a range-check comparison is made to ensure that i is within the range of case labels (0–4, in this case); then the address of the ith statement is fetched from the ith slot of a table, and control jumps to s_i.

This approach will not work for **typecase**, because of subclassing. That is, even if we could make class descriptors be small integers instead of pointers, we cannot do an indexed jump based on the class of the object, because we will miss clauses that match superclasses of that class. Thus, Modula-3 **typecase** is implemented as a chain of **else-if**s.

Assigning integers to classes is not trivial, because separately compiled modules can each define their own classes, and we do not want the integers to clash. But a sophisticated linker might be able to assign the integers at link time.

If all the classes in the **typecase** were `final` classes (in the sense used by Java, that they cannot be extended), then this problem would not apply. Modula-3 does not have final classes; and Java does not have **typecase**. But a clever Java system might be able to recognize a chain of **else-if**s that do **instanceof** tests for a set of final classes, and generate a indexed jump.

14.5   PRIVATE FIELDS AND METHODS

True object-oriented languages can protect fields of objects from direct manipulation by other objects' methods. A *private* field is one that cannot be fetched or updated from any function or method declared outside the object; a private method is one that cannot be called from outside the object.

Privacy is enforced by the type-checking phase of the compiler. In the symbol table of c, along with each field offset and method offset, is a boolean flag indicating whether the field is private. When compiling the expression `c.f()` or `c.x`, it is a simple matter to check that field and reject accesses to private fields from any method outside the object declaration.

There are many varieties of privacy and protection. Different languages allow

- Fields and methods which are accessible only to the class that declares them.
- Fields and methods accessible to the declaring class, and to any subclasses of that class.
- Fields and methods accessible only within the same module (package, namespace) as the declaring class.
- Fields that are read-only from outside the declaring class, but writable by methods of the class.

In general, these varieties of protection can be statically enforced by compile-time type-checking, for class-based languages.

14.6 CLASSLESS LANGUAGES

Some object-oriented languages do not use the notion of **class** at all. In such a language, each object implements whatever methods and has whatever data fields it wants. Type-checking for such languages is usually *dynamic* (done at run time) instead of *static* (done at compile time).

Many objects are created by *cloning*: copying an existing object (or *template* object) and then modifying some of the fields. Thus, even in a classless language there will be groups ("pseudo-classes") of similar objects that can share descriptors. When b is created by cloning a, it can share a descriptor with a. Only if a new field is added or a method field is updated (overridden) does b require a new descriptor.

The techniques used in compiling classless languages are similar to those for class-based languages with multiple inheritance and dynamic linking: Pseudo-class descriptors contain hash tables that yield field offsets and method instances.

The same kinds of global program analysis and optimization that are used for class-based languages – finding which method instance will be called from a (dynamic) method call site – are just as useful for classless languages.

14.7 OPTIMIZING OBJECT-ORIENTED PROGRAMS

An optimization of particular importance to object-oriented languages (which also benefit from most optimizations that apply to programming languages in general) is the conversion of dynamic method calls to static method-instance calls.

Compared with an ordinary function call, at each method call site there is a dynamic method lookup to determine the method instance. For single-inheritance languages, method lookup takes only two instructions. This seems like a small cost, but:

- Modern machines can jump to constant addresses more efficiently than to addresses fetched from tables. When the address is manifest in the instruction stream, the processor is able to pre-fetch the instruction cache at the destination and direct the instruction-issue mechanism to fetch at the target of the jump. Unpredictable jumps stall the instruction-issue and -execution pipeline for several cycles.
- An optimizing compiler that does inline expansion or interprocedural analysis will have trouble analyzing the consequences of a call if it doesn't even know which method instance is called at a given site.

For multiple-inheritance and classless languages, the dynamic method-lookup cost is even higher.

Thus, optimizing compilers for object-oriented languages do global program analysis to determine those places where a method call is always calling the same method instance; then the dynamic method call can be replaced by a static function call.

For a method call c.f(), where c is of class C, *type hierarchy analysis* is used to determine which subclasses of C contain methods f that may override C_f. If there is no such method, then the method instance must be C_f.

This idea is combined with *type propagation*, a form of static dataflow analysis similar to *reaching definitions* (see Section 17.2). After an assignment $c \leftarrow$ new C, the exact class of c is known. This information can be propagated through the assignment $d \leftarrow c$, and so on. When d.f() is encountered, the type-propagation information limits the range of the type hierarchy that might contribute method instances to d.

Suppose a method f defined in class C calls method g on this. But g is a dynamic method and may be overridden, so this call requires a dynamic method lookup. An optimizing compiler may make a different copy of a method instance C_f for each subclass (e.g., D, E) that extends C. Then when the (new copy) D_f calls g, the compiler knows to call the instance D_g without a dynamic method lookup.

PROGRAM MiniJava WITH CLASS EXTENSION

Implement class extension in your MiniJava compiler.

FURTHER READING

Dahl and Nygaard's Simula-67 language [Birtwistle et al. 1973] introduced the notion of classes, objects, single inheritance, static methods, instance testing, typecase, and the *prefix* technique to implement static single inheritance. In addition it had coroutines and garbage collection.

Cohen [1991] suggested the *display* for constant-time testing of class membership.

Dynamic methods and multiple inheritance appeared in Smalltalk [Goldberg et al. 1983], but the first implementations used slow searches of parent classes to find method instances. Rose [1988] and Connor et al. [1989] discuss fast hash-based field- and method-access algorithms for multiple inheritance. The use of graph coloring in implementing multiple inheritance is due to Dixon et al. [1989]. Lippman [1996] shows how C++-style multiple inheritance is implemented.

Chambers et al. [1991] describe several techniques to make classless, dynamically typed languages perform efficiently: pseudo-class descriptors, multiple versions of method instances, and other optimizations. Diwan et al. [1996] describe optimizations for statically typed languages that can replace dynamic method calls by static function calls.

Conventional object-oriented languages choose a method instance for a call a.f(x,y) based only on the class of the method *receiver* (a) and not other arguments (x, y). Languages with *multimethods* [Bobrow et al. 1989] allow dynamic method lookup based on the types of all arguments. This would solve the problem of *orthogonal directions of modularity* discussed on page 93. Chambers and Leavens [1995] show how to do static type-checking for multimethods; Amiel et al. [1994] and Chen and Turau [1994] show how to do efficient dynamic multimethod lookup.

Nelson [1991] describes Modula-3, Stroustrup [1997] describes C++, and Arnold and Gosling [1996] describe Java.

EXERCISES

*14.1 A problem with the *display* technique (as explained on page 290) for testing class membership is that the maximum class-nesting depth N must be fixed in advance, and every class descriptor needs N words of space even if most classes are not deeply nested. Design a variant of the *display* technique that does not suffer from these problems; it will be a couple of instructions more costly than the one described on page 290.

14.2 The hash-table technique for finding field offsets and method instances in the presence of multiple inheritance is shown incompletely on page 289 – the case of $f \neq \text{ptr}_x$ is not resolved. Choose a collision-resolution technique, explain how it works, and analyze the extra cost (in instructions) in the case that $f = \text{ptr}_x$ (no collision) and $f \neq \text{ptr}_x$ (collision).

*14.3 Consider the following class hierarchy, which contains five method-call sites. The task is to show which of the method-call sites call known method instances, and (in each case) show which method instance. For example, you might say that "method-instance X_g always calls Y_f; method Z_g may call more than one instance of f."

```
class A              { int f() { return 1; } }
class B extends A { int g() { this.f(); return 2; } }
class C extends B { int f() { this.g(); return 3; } }
class D extends C { int g() { this.f(); return 4; } }
class E extends A { int g() { this.f(); return 5; } }
class F extends E { int g() { this.f(); return 6; } }
```

Do this analysis for each of the following assumptions:

a. This is the entire program, and there are no other subclasses of these modules.

b. This is part of a large program, and any of these classes may be extended elsewhere.

c. Classes C and E are local to this module, and cannot be extended elsewhere; the other classes may be extended.

*14.4 Use *method replication* to improve your analysis of the program in Exercise 14.3. That is, make *every* class override f and g. For example, in class B (which does not already override f), put a copy of method A_f, and in D put a copy of C_F:

```
class B extends A { ... int f() { return 1; } }
class D extends C { ... int f() { this.g(); return 3; } }
```

Similarly, add new instances E_f, F_f, and C_g. Now, for each set of assumptions (a), (b), and (c), show which method calls go to known static instances.

14.5 Devise an efficient implementation mechanism for any **typecase that only mentions `final` classes. A `final` class is one that cannot be extended. (In Java, there is a `final` keyword; but even in other object-oriented languages, a class that is not exported from a module is effectively `final`, and a link-time whole-program analysis can discover which classes are never extended, whether declared `final` or not.)

You may make any of the following assumptions, but state which assumptions you need to use:

a. The linker has control over the placement of class-descriptor records.

b. Class descriptors are integers managed by the linker that index into a table of descriptor records.

c. The compiler explicitly marks `final` classes (in their descriptors).

d. Code for **typecase** can be generated at link time.

e. After the program is running, no other classes and subclasses are dynamically linked into the program.

15

Functional Programming Languages

func-tion: a mathematical correspondence that assigns exactly one element of one set to each element of the same or another set

Webster's Dictionary

The mathematical notion of function is that if $f(x) = a$ "this time," then $f(x) = a$ "next time"; there is no other value equal to $f(x)$. This allows the use of *equational reasoning* familiar from algebra: If $a = f(x)$, then $g(f(x), f(x))$ is equivalent to $g(a, a)$. *Pure functional* programming languages encourage a kind of programming in which equational reasoning works, as it does in mathematics.

Imperative programming languages have similar syntax: $a \leftarrow f(x)$. But if we follow this by $b \leftarrow f(x)$, there is no guarantee that $a = b$; the function f can have *side effects* on global variables that make it return a different value each time. Furthermore, a program might assign into variable x between calls to $f(x)$, so $f(x)$ really means a different thing each time.

Higher-order functions. Functional programming languages also allow functions to be passed as arguments to other functions, or returned as results. Functions that take functional arguments are called *higher-order* functions.

Higher-order functions become particularly interesting if the language also supports *nested functions* with *lexical scope* (also called *block structure*). Lexical scope means that each function can refer to variables and parameters of any function in which it is nested. A *higher-order functional language* is one with nested scope and higher-order functions.

What is the essence of functional programming? Is it equational reasoning or is it higher-order functions? There is no clear agreement about the answer to this question. In this chapter we will discuss three different flavors of "functional" language:

FunJava The MiniJava language with higher-order functions. Because side effects are still permitted (and thus, equational reasoning won't work), this is an *impure, higher-order functional language;* other such languages are Scheme, ML, and Smalltalk.

PureFunJava A language with higher-order functions and no side effects, capturing the essence of *strict, pure functional languages* (like the pure functional subset of ML).

LazyFunJava A *nonstrict, pure functional language* that uses lazy evaluation like the language Haskell. Nonstrict pure functional languages support equational reasoning very well (see Section 15.7).

A *first-order, pure functional language* such as SISAL supports equational reasoning but not higher-order functions.

15.1   A SIMPLE FUNCTIONAL LANGUAGE

To make the new language Fun-MiniJava, we add *function types* to MiniJava:

$$
\begin{array}{rcl}
\textit{ClassDecl} & \rightarrow & \texttt{type } \textit{id} = \textit{TypeExp} \texttt{ ;} \\
\textit{TypeExp} & \rightarrow & \textit{TypeExp} \texttt{ -> } \textit{TypeExp} \\
& \rightarrow & \texttt{(} \textit{TypeList} \texttt{) -> } \textit{TypeExp} \\
& \rightarrow & \texttt{(} \textit{TypeExp} \texttt{)} \\
& \rightarrow & \textit{Type} \\
\textit{TypeList} & \rightarrow & \textit{TypeExp} \; \textit{TypeRest}^* \\
& \rightarrow & \\
\textit{TypeRest} & \rightarrow & \texttt{, } \textit{TypeExp} \\
\end{array}
$$

The type `int->String` is the type of functions that take a single integer argument and return a string result (assuming a class `String` is declared). The type `(int,String)->int[]` describes functions that take two arguments (one integer, one string) and return an array-of-integers result.

Any variable can have a functional type; functions can be passed as arguments and returned as results. Thus, the type `(int->int)->(int)->int` is perfectly legal; the `->` operator is right-associative, so this is the type of functions that take an `int->int` argument and return an `int->int` result.

We also modify the format of a CALL expression, so that the function being called is an arbitrary expression, without the .*methodname* component, and so that a method itself can be the result of an expression:

```
type intfun = int -> int;

class C {
 public intfun add(n: int) {
   public int h(int m) { return n+m; }
   return h;
 }
 public intfun twice(f: intfun) {
   public int g(int x) {return f(f(x));}
   return g;
 }
 public int test() {
   intfun addFive = add(5);
   intfun addSeven = add(7);
   int twenty = addFive(15);
   int twentyTwo = addSeven(15);
   intfun addTen = twice(addFive);
   int seventeen = twice(add(5))(7);
   intfun addTwentyFour = twice(twice(add(6)));
   return addTwentyFour(seventeen);
 }
}
```

PROGRAM 15.1. A FunJava program.

$$Exp \quad \rightarrow \quad Exp \ (\ ExpList \ )$$
$$Exp \quad \rightarrow \quad Exp \ . \ id$$

If v is an object of a class with a method int m(int[]), then the expression v.m evaluates to a function value of type (int[])->int. Evaluating v.m does not call the method.

We permit variable declarations and function (method) declarations at the beginning of a compound statement (i.e., functions are nested). We remove the if statement and add an if expression: That is, (if (E) B else C) evaluates E, and then evaluates B if E is true, otherwise evaluates C. The value of the entire if expression is the value of B or C.

$$MethodDecl \quad \rightarrow \quad \textbf{public} \ Type \ id \ (\ FormalList \ ) \ Compound$$
$$Compound \quad \rightarrow \quad \{ \ VarDecl^* \ MethodDecl^* \ Statement^* \ \textbf{return} \ Exp \ ; \ \}$$
$$Exp \quad \rightarrow \quad Compound$$
$$\rightarrow \quad \textbf{if} \ (\ Exp \ ) \ Exp \ \textbf{else} \ Exp$$

Finally, we interpret the meaning of return differently: Instead of producing the result for an entire function body, it produces the result of its own compound statement. Thus, the expression {return 3;}+{return 4;} evaluates to 7.

Program 15.1 illustrates the use of function types. The function add takes an integer argument n and returns a function h. Thus, addFive is a version of h whose n variable is 5, but addSeven is a function $h(x) = 7 + x$. The need for each different instance of h to "remember" the appropriate value for a *nonlocal* variable n motivates the implementation technique of *closures*, which is described later.

The function twice takes an argument f that is a function from int to int, and the result of twice(f) is a function g that applies f twice. Thus, addTen is a function $g(x) = addFive(addFive(x))$. Each instance of $g(x)$ needs to remember the right f value, just as each instance of h needs to remember n.

15.2   CLOSURES

In languages (such as C) without nested functions, the run-time representation of a function value can be the address of the machine code for that function. This address can be passed as an argument, stored in a variable, and so on; when it is time to call the function, the address is loaded into a machine register, and the "call to address contained in register" instruction is used.

In the Tree intermediate representation, this is easy to express. Suppose the function starts at label L_{123}; we assign the address into a variable t_{57} using

MOVE(TEMP(t_{57}), NAME(L_{123}))

and then call the function with something like

CALL(TEMP(t_{57}), ...*parameters*...).

But this will not work for nested functions; if we represent the h function by an address, in what outer frame can it access the variable n? Similarly, how does the g function access the variable f?

The solution is to represent a function variable as a *closure*: a record that contains the machine-code pointer and a way to access the necessary non-local variables. This is very much like an object with a single method (the machine-code pointer) and several instance variables. The portion of the closure giving access to values of variables is often called the *environment*.

Closures need not be based on objects; any other data structure that gives access to nonlocal variables will do. However, in this chapter we will use objects for simplicity.

HEAP-ALLOCATED ACTIVATION RECORDS

The local variables for `add` must not be destroyed when `add` returns, because n is still needed for the execution of h. To solve this problem, we can create a heap-allocated object to hold each function's local variables; then we rely on the garbage collector to reclaim the object when all references (including inner-nested function values) have disappeared.

A refinement of this technique is to save on the heap only those variables that *escape* (that are used by inner-nested functions). The stack frame will hold spilled registers, return address, and so on, and also a pointer to the *escaping-variable record*. The escaping-variable record holds (1) any local variables that an inner-nested procedure might need and (2) a pointer to the environment (escaping-variable record) provided by the enclosing function. This pointer from one closure to the closure of the statically enclosing function is called the *static link*; see Figure 15.2.

15.3   IMMUTABLE VARIABLES

The FunJava language has higher-order functions with nested scope, but it is still not really possible to use *equational reasoning* about FunJava programs. That is, $f(3)$ may return a different value each time. To remedy this situation, we prohibit *side effects* of functions: When a function is called, it must return a result without changing the "world" in any observable way.

Thus, we make a new *pure functional programming* language PureFun-Java, in which the following are prohibited:

⊘ Assignments to variables (except as initializations in variable declarations);
⊘ Assignments to fields of heap-allocated records (except initializations in the class constructor);
⊘ Calls to external functions that have visible effects: `println`.

To distinguish clearly between initializing instance variables (which is permitted) and updating instance variables (which is not), we require that every class have a constructor in a special, stereotypical form that initializes all the instance variables:

$$ClassDecl \rightarrow \textbf{class } id \ \{ \ VarDecl^* \ MethodDecl^* \ Constructor \ \}$$
$$Constructor \rightarrow \texttt{public } id \ (\ FormalList \ ) \ \{ \ Init^* \}$$
$$Init \rightarrow \textbf{this } . \ id = id$$

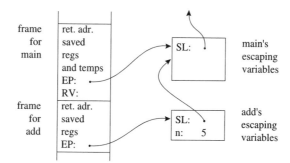

a. Inside `add`

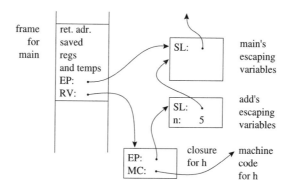

b. Back in `main`

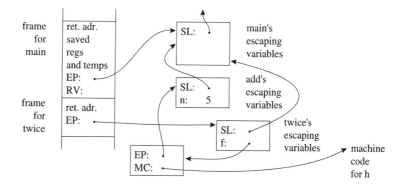

c. Inside `twice`

FIGURE 15.2. Closures for execution of `twice(add(5))`. SL=static link; RV=return value; EP=escaping-variables-pointer or environment-pointer.

This seems rather Draconian: How is the program to get any work done? To program without assignments, in a functional style, you produce new values instead of updating old ones. For example, Program 15.3 shows the implementation of binary search trees in imperative and functional styles. As explained in Section 5.1 (page 108), the imperative program updates a tree node, but the functional program returns a new tree much like the old one, though the path from the root to a "new" leaf has been copied. If we let t1 be the tree in Figure 5.4a on page 108, we can say

```
int t2 = t1.enter("mouse",4);
```

and now t1 and t2 are both available for the program to use. On the other hand, if the program returns t2 as the result of a function and discards t1, then the root node of t1 will be reclaimed by the garbage collector (the other nodes of t1 will not be reclaimed, because they are still in use by tree t2).

Similar techniques can allow functional programs to express the same wide variety of algorithms that imperative programs can, and often more clearly, expressively, and concisely.

CONTINUATION-BASED I/O

Producing new data structures instead of updating old ones makes it possible to obey the "no assignments" rules, but how is the program to do input/output? The technique of *continuation-based I/O* expresses input/output in a functional framework. As shown in Program 15.4, the predefined types and functions in PureFunJava rely on the notion of an `answer`: This is the "result" returned by the *entire program*.

MiniJava doesn't have an input function, but if it did, the type would be straightforward: something like `int readByte()`. To express this without side effects, PureFunJava's `readByte` takes an argument that is a `int-Consumer` and passes the newly read integer to that consumer. Whatever answer the consumer produces will also be the answer of the `readByte`.

Similarly, `putByte` takes a character to print as well as a *continuation* (`cont`); `putByte` outputs a character and then calls the `cont` to produce an answer.

The point of these arrangements is to allow input/output while preserving equational reasoning. Interestingly, input/output is now "visible" to the type-checker: Any function which does I/O will have `answer` in its result type.

```
class tree {
    String key; int binding; tree left; tree right;

    public tree(String key, int binding, tree left, tree right) {
        this.key=key; this.binding=binding;
        this.left=left; this.right=right;
    }

    public int look(String k) {
        int c = key.compareTo(k);
        if (c < 0)  return left.look(k);
        else if (c > 0) return right.look(k);
        else return binding;
    }

    public void enter(String k, int b) {
        int c = key.compareTo(k);
        if (c < 0)
            if (left==null)
                left = new tree(k,b,null,null);
            else left.enter(k,b);
        else if (c > 0)
            if (right==null)
                right = new tree(k,b,null,null);
            else right.enter(k,b);
        else binding=b;
    }
}
```

(a) Imperative, object-oriented Java

```
// Alternative implementation of enter
public tree enter(String k, int b) {
    int c = key.compareTo(k);
    if (c < 0)
        if (left==null)
            return new tree(k,b,null,null);
        else return left.enter(k,b);
    else if (c > 0)
        if (right==null)
            return new tree(k,b,null,null);
        else return right.enter(k,b);
    else return new tree(k,b,left,right);
}
```

(b) Functional, object-oriented Java

PROGRAM 15.3. Binary search trees implemented in two ways.

```
type answer     // a special, built-in type
type intConsumer = int -> answer
type cont = () -> answer

class ContIO {
    public answer readByte (intConsumer c);
    public answer putByte (int i, cont c);
    public answer exit();
}
```

PROGRAM 15.4. Built-in types and functions for PureFunJava.

LANGUAGE CHANGES

The following modifications of FunJava make the new language PureFun-Java:

- Add the predefined types and class shown in Program 15.4, and remove `System.out.println`.
- Assignment statements and **while** loops are deleted from the language, and each compound statement (in braces) can have only one statement after its variable declarations.

Program 15.5 shows a complete PureFunJava program that loops, reading integers and printing the factorial of each integer, until an integer larger than 12 is input.

OPTIMIZATION OF PURE FUNCTIONAL LANGUAGES

Because we have only deleted features from FunJava, and not added any new ones (except changing some predefined types), our FunJava compiler can compile PureFunJava right away. And, in general, functional-language compilers can make use of the same kinds of optimizations as imperative-language compilers: inline expansion, instruction selection, loop-invariant analysis, graph-coloring register allocation, copy propagation, and so on. Calculating the control-flow graph can be a bit more complicated, however, because much of the control flow is expressed through function calls, and some of these calls may to be function variables instead of statically defined functions.

A PureFunJava compiler can also make several kinds of optimizations that a FunJava compiler cannot, because it can take advantage of equational reasoning.

Consider this program fragment, which builds a record r and then later

```
class Factorial {
  boolean isDigit (int c) {
      return c >= 48 && c <= 48+9;   // 48 == (int)'0'
  }

  public answer getInt(intConsumer done) {
      public answer nextDigit(int accum) {
          public answer eatChar(int dig) {
              return if (isDigit(dig))
                        nextDigit(accum*10+dig-48)
                     else done(accum);
          }
          return ContIO.readByte(eatChar);
      }
      return nextDigit(0);
  }

  answer putInt(int i, cont c) {
      return if (i==0)
          c()
      else {
          int rest = i/10;
          int dig = i - rest * 10;
          public answer doDigit() { return ContIO.putByte(dig,c); }
          return putInt(rest, doDigit);
      };
  }

  int factorial (int i) {
      return if (i==0) 1 else i * factorial(i-1);
  }

  answer loop (int i) {
      return if (i > 12) ContIO.exit()
      else {
          public answer next() { return getInt(loop); }
          return putInt(factorial(i), next);
      };
  }

  public static answer main (String [] argv) {
      return getInt(loop);
  }
}
```

PROGRAM 15.5. PureFunJava program to read *i*, print *i*!.

fetches fields from it:

```
class recrd {int a; int b;
              public recrd(int a, int b) {this.a=a; this.b=b;}
}

int a1 = 5;
int b1 = 7;
recrd r = new recrd(a1,b1);

int x = f(r);

int y = r.a + r.b;
```

In a pure functional language, the compiler knows that when the computation of y refers to r.a and r.b, it is going to get the values a1 and b1. In an imperative (or impure functional) language, the computation f(r) might assign new values to the fields of r, but not in PureFunJava.

Thus, within the scope of r every occurrence of r.a can be replaced with a1, and similarly b1 can be substituted for r.b. Also, since no other part of the program can assign any new value to a1, it will contain the same value (5) for all time. Thus, 5 can be substituted for a1 everywhere, and 7 for b1. Thus, we end up with int y = 5+7, which can be turned into int y = 12; thus, 12 can be substituted for y throughout its scope.

The same kind of substitution works for imperative languages too; it's just that a compiler for an imperative language is often not sure whether a field or variable is updated between the point of definition and the point of use. Thus, it must conservatively approximate – assuming that the variable may have been modified – and thus, in most cases, the substitution cannot be performed. See also *alias analysis* (Section 17.5).

The ML language has pure functional records, which cannot be updated and on which this substitution transformation is always valid, and also has updatable reference cells, which can be assigned to and which behave like records in a conventional imperative language.

15.4   INLINE EXPANSION

Because functional programs tend to use many small functions, and especially because they pass functions from one place to another, an important optimization technique is *inline expansion* of function calls: replacing a function call with a copy of the function body.

```
class list {int head; list tail;
          public list (int head, list tail) {
               this.head=head; this.tail=tail;
          }}

type observeInt = (int,cont) -> answer;

class PrintT {
    public answer doList (observeInt f, list l, cont c) {
        return if (l===null)
           c();
        else {
           public answer doRest() {return doList(f, l.tail, c);}
           return f(l.head, doRest);
        };
    }

    public int double(int j) {return j+j;}

    public answer printDouble(int i, cont c) {
        public answer again() {return putInt(double(i), c);}
        return putInt(i, again);
    }

    public answer printTable(list l, cont c) {
        return doList(printDouble, l, c);
    }

    public static void main(string argv[]) {
        list mylist = ··· ;
        return printTable(mylist, IO.exit);
    }
}
```

PROGRAM 15.6. printTable in PureFunJava.

For example, in Program 15.6, an observeInt is any function (like the putInt of Program 15.5) that "observes" an integer and then continues. doList is a function that applies an observer f to a list l, and then continues. In this case, the observer is not putInt but printDouble, which prints i followed by $2i$. Thus, printTable prints a table of integers, each followed by its double.

For comparison, Program 15.7a is a regular Java program that does the same thing.

Program 15.6 uses a generic list-traverser, doList, for which any func-

```
class list {int head; int tail;}

class PrintT {
int double(int j) {return j+j;}          class list {int head; int tail;}

void printDouble(int i) {                class PrintT {
   putInt(i);  putInt(double(i));          void printTable(list l) {
}                                            while (l != null) {
                                               int i = l.head;
void printTable(list l) {                      putInt(i);
  while (l != null) {                          putInt(i+1);
    printDouble(l.head);                       l = l.tail;
    l = l.tail;                              }
  }                                        }
}                                        }

public static void main(...) {           public static void main(...) {
   printTable(mylist);                      printTable(mylist);
}}                                       }}
```
      (a) As written   (b) Optimized

PROGRAM 15.7. Java implementation of `printTable`.

tion can be plugged in. Although in this case `printDouble` is used, the same program could reuse `doList` for other purposes that print or "observe" all the integers in the list. But Program 15.7a lacks this flexibility – it calls `printDouble` directly.

If compiled naively, the pure functional program – which passed `print-Double` as an argument – will do many more function calls than the imperative program. By using inline expansion and tail-call optimizations (described in Section 15.6), Program 15.6 can be optimized into machine instructions equivalent to the efficient loop of Program 15.7b.

Avoiding variable capture. We must be careful about variable names when doing inlining in MiniJava (or Java), where a local declaration creates a "hole" in the scope of an outer variable:

```
   class A {
1   int x = 5
2   int function g(int y) {
3      return y+x;
    }
4   int f(int x) {
5      return g(1)+x;
    }
6   void main() { ... f(2)+x ... }
   }
```

The formal parameter x on line 4 creates a hole in the scope of the variable x declared on line 1, so that the x on line 5 refers to the formal parameter, not the variable. If we were to inline-expand the call to g(1) on line 5 by substituting the body of g for the call, we could not simply write 1+x, for then we'd have

```
4   int f(int x) {
5       return return 1+x;+x;    }
```

but the first x on line 5 is now incorrectly referring to f's parameter instead of the variable declared on line 1.

To solve this problem, we could first rename, or *α-convert*, the formal parameter of f, then perform the substitution:

```
2   int function g(int y) {          int function g(int y) {
3       return y+x;                      return y+x;
    }                                 }
4   int f(int a) {                    int f(int a) {
5       return g(1)+a;                    return {return 1+x;}+a;
    }                                 }
```

Alternately, we can rename the *actual* parameters instead of the formal parameters, and define the substitution function to avoid substituting for x inside the scope of a new definition of x.

But the best solution of all for avoiding variable capture is to have an earlier pass of the compiler rename all variables so that the same variable name is never declared twice. This simplifies reasoning about, and optimizing, the program.

By the way, the expression {return 1+x;} in line 5 is completely equivalent to the expression (1+x).

Rules for inlining. Algorithm 15.8 gives the rules for inline expansion, which can apply to imperative or functional programs. The function body B is used in place of the function call $f(\ldots)$, but within this copy of B, each actual parameter is substituted for the corresponding formal parameter. When the actual parameter is just a variable or a constant, the substitution is very simple (Algorithm 15.8a). But when the actual parameter is a nontrivial expression, we must first assign it to a new variable (Algorithm 15.8b).

For example, in Program 15.6 the function call double(i) can be replaced by a copy of j+j in which each j is replaced by the actual parameter i. Here we have used Algorithm 15.8a, since i is a variable, not a more complicated expression.

(a) When the actual parameters are simple variables $i_1, \ldots, i_n$.
 Within the scope of:

$$\texttt{int } f(a_1, \ldots, a_n)B$$

(where B is a *Compound*)
the expression

$$f(i_1, \ldots, i_n)$$

rewrites to

$$B[a_1 \mapsto i_1, \ldots, a_n \mapsto i_n]$$

(b) When the actual parameters are non-trivial expressions, not just variables. Within the scope of:

$$\texttt{int } f(a_1, \ldots, a_n)B$$

the expression $f(E_1, \ldots, E_n)$
rewrites to

$$\{ \texttt{int } i_1 = E_1;$$
$$\vdots$$
$$\texttt{int } i_n = E_n;$$
$$\texttt{return } B[a_1 \mapsto i_1, \ldots, a_n \mapsto i_n];$$
$$\}$$

where $i_1, \ldots, i_n$ are previously unused names.

ALGORITHM 15.8. Inline expansion of function bodies. We assume that no two declarations declare the same name.

Suppose we wish to inline-expand `double(g(x))`; if we improperly use Algorithm 15.8a, we obtain `g(x)+g(x)`, which computes `g(x)` twice. Even though the principle of equational reasoning assures that we will compute the same result each time, we do not wish to slow down the computation by repeating the (potentially expensive) computation `g(x)`. Instead, Algorithm 15.8b yields

```
{int i = g(x); return i+i;}
```

which computes `g(x)` only once.
 In an imperative program, not only is `g(x)+g(x)` slower than

```
{int i = g(x); return i+i;}
```

but – because `g` may have side effects – it may compute a different result! Again, Algorithm 15.8b does the right thing.

Dead function elimination. If all the calls to a function (such as `double`) have been inline-expanded, and if the function is not passed as an argument or referenced in any other way, the function itself can be deleted.

$$\boxed{\begin{array}{c} \text{int } f(a_1, \ldots, a_n) \\ B \end{array}} \quad \rightarrow \quad \boxed{\begin{array}{l} \text{int } f(a'_1, \ldots, a'_n) \\ \quad \{\, \text{int } f'(a_1, \ldots, a_n) \\ \qquad\quad B[f \mapsto f'] \\ \quad \text{return } f'(a'_1, \ldots, a'_n); \\ \quad \} \end{array}}$$

ALGORITHM 15.9. Loop-preheader transformation.

Inlining recursive functions. Inlining `doList` into `printTable` yields this new version of `printTable`:

```
public answer printTable(list l, cont c) {
    return if (l===null)
        c();
    else {
        public answer doRest() {
                return doList(printDouble, l.tail, c);
        }
        return printDouble(l.head, doRest);
    };
}
```

This is not so good: `printTable` calls `printDouble` on `l.head`, but to process `l.tail` it calls `doList` as before. Thus, we have inline-expanded *only the first iteration of the loop*. We would rather have a fully customized version of `doRest`; therefore, we do not inline-expand in this way.

For recursive functions we use a *loop-preheader* transformation (Algorithm 15.9). The idea is to split *f* into two functions: a *prelude* called from outside, and a *loop header* called from inside. Every call to the loop header will be a recursive call from within itself, except for a single call from the prelude. Applying this transformation to `doList` yields

```
public answer doList (observeInt fX, list lX, cont cX) {
    public answer doListX(observeInt f, list l, cont c) {
        return if (l==null)
            c();
        else {
            public answer doRest() {return doListX(f, l.tail, c);}
            return f(l.head, doRest);
        };
    }
    return doListX(fX,lX,cX);
}
```

If every use of f' within B is of the form $f'(E_1, \ldots, E_{i-1}, a_i, E_{i+1}, \ldots, E_n)$ such that the ith argument is always a_i, then rewrite

$$
\begin{array}{l}
\texttt{int } f(a'_1, \ldots, a'_n)\{ \\
\quad \texttt{int } f'(a_1, \ldots, a_n)B \\
\quad \texttt{return } f'(a'_1, \ldots, a'_n) \\
\}
\end{array}
\quad \rightarrow \quad
\begin{array}{l}
\texttt{int } f(a'_1, \ldots, a'_{i-1}, a_i, a'_{i+1}, \ldots, a'_n)\{ \\
\quad \textit{int } f'(a_1, \ldots, a_{i-1}, a_{i+1}, \ldots, a_n)B \\
\quad \texttt{return } f'(a'_1, \ldots, a'_{i-1}, a'_{i+1}, \ldots, a'_n) \\
\}
\end{array}
$$

where every call $f'(E_1, \ldots, E_{i-1}, a_i, E_{i+1}, \ldots, E_n)$ within B is rewritten as $f'(E_1, \ldots, E_{i-1}, E_{i+1}, \ldots, E_n)$.

ALGORITHM 15.10. Loop-invariant hoisting.

where the new doList is the prelude, and doListX is the loop header. Notice that the prelude function contains the entire loop as an internal function, so that when any call to doList is inline-expanded, a new copy of doListX comes along with it.

Loop-invariant arguments. In this example, the function doListX is passing around the values f and c that are invariant – they are the same in every recursive call. In each case, f is fX and c is cX. A *loop-invariant hoisting* transformation (Algorithm 15.10) can replace every use of f with fX, and c with cX).

Applying this transformation to doList yields

```
public answer doList (observeInt f, list lX, cont c) {
    public answer doListX(list l) {
        return if (l==null)
            c();
        else {
            public answer doRest() {return doListX(l.tail);}
            return f(l.head, doRest);
        };
    }
    return doListX(lX);
}
```

Finally, in printTable, when the call doList(printDouble,l,c) is inlined, we obtain:

```
public answer printTable(list l, cont c) {
   public answer doListX(list l) {
     return if (l==null)
         c();
     else {
         public answer doRest() {return doListX(l.tail);}
         return printDouble(l.head, doRest);
     };
   }
   return doListX(l);
}
```

Cascading inlining. In this version of `printTable`, we have `printDouble` applied to arguments (instead of just passed to `doList`), so we can inline-expand that call, yielding

```
public answer printTable(list l, cont c) {
   public answer doListX(list l) {
     return if (l==null)
         c();
     else {
         public answer doRest() {return doListX(l.tail);}
         return {
           int i = l.head;
           public answer again() {return putInt(i+i, doRest);}
           return putInt(i, again);
         };
     };
   }
   return doListX(l);
}
```

Avoiding code explosion. Inline-expansion copies function bodies. This generally makes the program bigger. If done indiscriminantly, the size of the program explodes; in fact, it is easy to construct cases where expanding one function call creates new instances that can also be expanded, ad infinitum.

There are several heuristics that can be used to control inlining:

1. Expand only those function-call sites that are very frequently executed; determine frequency either by static estimation (loop-nest depth) or by feedback from an execution profiler.
2. Expand functions with very small bodies, so that the copied function body is not much larger than the instructions that would have called the function.
3. Expand functions called only once; then *dead function elimination* will delete the original copy of the function body.

```
1    public answer printTable(list l, cont c) {
2        public answer doListX(list l) {
3            return if (l==null) c()
4                else {public answer doRest() {
5                        return doListX(l.tail);}
6                    int i = l.head;
7                    public answer again() {
8                        return putInt(i+i,doRest); }
9                    return putInt(i,again);
10       }
11       return doListX(l);
12   }
```

PROGRAM 15.11. printTable as automatically specialized.

Unnesting braces. Since the FunJava expression

$$\{ \ Decl_1 \ \texttt{return} \ \{ \ Decl_2 \ \texttt{return} \quad Exp\}\}$$

is exactly equivalent to

$$\{ \ Decl_1 \quad Decl_2 \ \texttt{return} \quad Exp\}$$

we end up with Program 15.11.

The optimizer has taken a program written with abstraction (with a general-purpose doList) and transformed it into a more efficient, special-purpose program (with a special-purpose doListX that calls putInt directly).

15.5 CLOSURE CONVERSION

A function passed as an argument is represented as a *closure*: a combination of a machine-code pointer and a means of accessing the nonlocal variables (also called *free variables*).

An example of a nonlocal variable in an object-oriented language is an instance variable of a class. A method referring to an instance variable accesses it through **this**, which is an implicit formal parameter of the method. One way to compile free-variable access for nested functions is to represent closures as objects.

The *closure conversion* phase of a functional-language compiler transforms the program so that none of the functions appears to access free (nonlocal) variables. This is done by turning each free-variable access into an instance-variable access.

Some local variables declared in a function f are also accessed by functions nested within f; we say these variables *escape*. For example, in Program 15.5, in the function putInt, the variables dig and c escape (because they are used in the inner-nested function doDigit), but the variable rest does not escape.

Given a function $f(a_1, \ldots, a_n)$ B at nesting depth d with escaping local variables (and formal parameters) $x_1, x_2, \ldots, x_n$ and nonescaping variables $y_1, \ldots, y_n$, we can rewrite into

```
f(this, a₁, ..., aₙ) {
    c272 r = newc272(this, x₁, x₂, ..., xₙ);
    return B′
}
```

The new parameter this is the closure pointer, now made into an explicit argument. The variable r is an object containing all the escaping variables *and* the enclosing closure pointer. This r becomes the closure-pointer argument when calling functions of depth $d + 1$. The class (in this case c272) has to be made up specially for each function, because the list of escaping variables (and their types) is different for each function.

Any use of a nonlocal variable (one that comes from nesting depth $< d$) within B must be transformed into an access of some offset within the record this (in the rewritten function body B').

Function values. We can represent a function value as an object with a single method (which we will call exec) and zero or more instance variables (to hold nonlocal variables). We will represent the type t1 -> t2 as the class

```
abstract class c_t1_t2 { abstract public t2 exec(t1 x); }
```

and any actual function value belonging to this type will be an extension of this class, adding instance variables and overriding exec.

Program 15.12 is the result of closure-converting Program 15.11. We can see that each function type is an abstract class, and each function is a different subclass of the abstract class. Escaping local variables are put into the closure objects of inner-nested functions. Furthermore, when functions are deeply nested, it's often useful for the closure of the inner-nested function to have a link to the enclosing function's closure for convenient access to variables of functions further out.

```
abstract class cont {
      abstract public answer exec(); }

abstract class c_list_cont_answer {
      abstract public answer exec(list l, cont c); }

class printTable extends c_list_cont_answer {
  public answer exec(list l, cont c) {
      doListX r1 = new doListX(this, c);
      return r1.exec(l);
} }

abstract class c_list_answer {
      abstract public answer exec(list l); }

class doListX extends c_list_answer {
   printTable link;
   cont c;
   public answer exec (list l) {
      return if (l==null) c.exec()
        else {doRest r2 = new doRest(this,l);
             int i = l.head;
             again r3 = new again(i,doRest);
             return putInt.exec(i,again);
}        }

abstract class c_void_answer { abstract public answer exec(); }

class doRest extends c_void_answer {
   doListX link;
   list l;
   public answer exec() {
     return doListX.exec(l);
}   }

class again extends c_void_answer {
   int i;
   doRest d;
   public answer exec() {
     return putInt(i+i, d);
}   }
```

PROGRAM 15.12. printTable after closure conversion (class constructors omitted).

15.6 EFFICIENT TAIL RECURSION

Functional programs express loops and other control flow by function calls. Where Program 15.7b has a **while** loop, Program 15.12 has a function call to doListX. Where Program 15.7b's putInt simply returns to its two points of call within printTable, Program 15.11 has continuation functions. The FunJava compiler must compile the calls to doListX, doRest, and again as efficently as the MiniJava compiler compiles loops and function returns.

Many of the function calls in Program 15.11 are in *tail position*. A function call $f(x)$ within the body of another function $g(y)$ is in tail position if "calling f is the last thing that g will do before returning." More formally, in each of the following expressions, the B_i are in tail contexts, but the C_i are not:

1. {int x = C_1; return B_1; }
2. $C_1(C_2)$
3. if C_1 B_1 else B_2
4. C_1 + C_2

For example, C_2 in expression 4 is not in a tail context, even though it seems to be "last," because after C_2 completes there will still need to be an **add** instruction. But B_1 in expression 3 is in a tail context, even though it is not "last" syntactically.

If a function call $f(x)$ is in a tail context with respect to its enclosing expression, and that expression is in a tail context, and so on all the way to the body of the enclosing function definition int $g(y)$ B, then $f(x)$ is a tail call.

Tail calls can be implemented more efficiently than ordinary calls. Given

```
int g(int y) {int x = h(y); return f(x)}
```

then h(y) is not a tail call, but f(x) is. When f(x) returns some result z, then z will also be the result returned from g. Instead of pushing a new return address for f to return to, g could just give f the return address given to g, and have f return there directly.

That is, a tail call can be implemented more like a jump than a call. The steps for a tail call are

1. Move actual parameters into argument registers.
2. Restore callee-save registers.
3. Pop the stack frame of the calling function, *if it has one.*
4. Jump to the callee.

printTable:	allocate object r1	printTable:	allocate stack frame
	jump to doListX		jump to whileL
doListX:	allocate record r2	whileL:	
	if l=nil goto doneL		if l=nil goto doneL
	i = l.head		i := l.head
	allocate object r3		
	jump to putInt		call putInt
again:	add this.i+this.i		add i+i
	jump to putInt		call putInt
doRest:	jump to doListX		jump to whileL
doneL :	jump to this.c	doneL:	return

<table>
<tr><td align="center">(a) Functional program</td><td align="center">(b) Imperative program</td></tr>
</table>

FIGURE 15.13. `printTable` as compiled.

In many cases, item 1 (moving parameters) is eliminated by the copy-propagation (coalescing) phase of the compiler. Often, items 2 and 3 are eliminated because the calling function has no stack frame – any function that can do all its computation in caller-save registers needs no frame. Thus, a tail call can be as cheap as a jump instruction.

In Program 15.12, *every* call is a tail call! Also, none of the functions in this program needs a stack frame. This need not have been true; for example, the call to `double` in Program 15.6 is not in tail position, and this nontail call only disappeared because the inline-expander did away with it.

Tail calls implemented as jumps. The compilation of Programs 15.12 and 15.7b is instructive. Figure 15.13 shows that the pure functional program and the imperative program are executing almost exactly the same instructions! The figure does not show the functional program's fetching from static-link records; and it does not show the imperative program's saving and restoring callee-save registers.

The remaining inefficiency in the functional program is that it creates three heap-allocated objects, r1, r2, r3, while the imperative program creates only one stack frame. However, more advanced closure-conversion algorithms can succeed in creating only one record (at the beginning of `print-Table`). So the difference between the two programs would be little more than a heap-record creation versus a stack-frame creation.

Allocating object on the garbage-collected heap may be more expensive than pushing and popping a stack frame. Optimizing compilers for functional languages solve this problem in different ways:

- Compile-time *escape analysis* can identify which closures do not outlive the function that creates them. These objects can be stack-allocated. In the case of `printTable`, this would make the "functional" code almost identical to the "imperative" code.
- Or heap allocation and garbage collection can be made extremely cheap. Then creating (and garbage collecting) a heap-allocated object takes only four or five instructions, making the functional `printTable` almost as fast as the imperative one (see Section 13.7).

15.7   LAZY EVALUATION

Equational reasoning aids in understanding functional programs. One important principle of equational reasoning is β-*substitution:* If $f(x) = B$ with some function body B, then any application $f(E)$ to an expression E is equivalent to B with every occurrence of x replaced with E:

$$f(x) = B \quad \text{implies that} \quad f(E) \equiv B[x \mapsto E]$$

But consider the PureFunJava program fragments,

```
{int loop (int z) {              {int loop (int z) {
    return if (z>0) z                 return if (z>0) z
           else loop(z);                     else loop(z);
 }                               }
 int f (int x) {                 int f (int x) {
    return if (y>8) x                 return if (y>8) x
           else -y;                          else -y;
 }                               }
 return                          return if (y>8) loop(y)
   f(loop(y));                          else -y;
}                               }
```

If the expression B is `if (y>8) x else -y`, and expression E is `loop(y)`, then clearly the program on the left contains $f(E)$ and the program on the right contains $B[x \mapsto E]$. So these programs are equivalent, using equational reasoning.

However, *the programs do not always behave the same!* If $y = 0$, then the program on the right will return 0, but the program on the left will first get stuck in a call to *loop*(0), which infinite-loops.

Clearly, if we want to claim that two programs are equivalent, then they must behave the same. In PureFunJava, if we obtain program A by doing substition on program B, then A and B will never give different results *if they both halt*; but A or B might not halt on the same set of inputs.

To remedy this (partial) failure of equational reasoning, we can introduce *lazy evaluation* into the programming language. Haskell is the most widely used lazy language. A program compiled with lazy evaluation will not evaluate any expression unless its value is demanded by some other part of the computation. In contrast, *strict* languages such as MiniJava, PureFunJava, ML, C, and Java evaluate each expression as the control flow of the program reaches it.

To explore the compilation of lazy functional languages, we will use the LazyJava language. Its syntax is identical to PureFunJava, and its semantics are almost identical, except that lazy evaluation is used in compiling it.

CALL-BY-NAME EVALUATION

Most programming languages (Pascal, C, ML, Java, MiniJava, PureFunJava) use *call-by-value* to pass function arguments: To compute $f(g(x))$, first $g(x)$ is computed, and this value is passed to f. But if f did not actually need to use its argument, then computing $g(x)$ will have been unnecessary.

To avoid computing expressions before their results are needed, we can use *call-by-name* evaluation. Essentially, each variable is not a simple value, but is a *thunk:* a function that computes the value on demand. The compiler replaces each expression of type `int` with a function value of type `()->int`, and similarly for all other types.

At each place where a variable is created, the compiler creates a function value; and everywhere a variable is used, the compiler puts a function application.

Thus the LazyJava program

```
{int a = 5+7; return a + 10; }
```

is automatically transformed to

```
{int a() {return 5+7;} return a() + 10; }
```

Where are variables created? At variable declarations and at function-parameter bindings. Thus, each variable turns into a function, and at each function-call site, we need a little function declaration for each actual-parameter expression.

```
type c_void_int = () -> int;
type c_void_tree = () -> tree;

class tree {
    c_void_String  key;
    c_void_int  binding;
    c_void_tree left;
    c_void_tree right;
}

public c_void_int look(c_void_tree t, c_void_String k) {
        c_void_int c = t().key().compareTo(k);
        if (c() < 0)  return look(t().left, k);
        else if (c() > 0) return look(t().right, k);
        else return t().binding;
}
```

PROGRAM 15.14. Call-by-name transformation applied to Program 15.3a.

Program 15.14 illustrates this transformation applied to the `look` function of Program 15.3a.

The problem with call-by-name is that each thunk may be executed many times, each time (redundantly) yielding the same value. For example, suppose there is a tree represented by a thunk `t1`. Each time `look(t1,k)` is called, `t1()` is evaluated, which rebuilds the (identical) tree every time!

CALL-BY-NEED

Lazy evaluation, also called *call-by-need*, is a modification of call-by-name that never evaluates the same thunk twice. Each thunk is equipped with a *memo* slot to store the value. When the thunk is first created, the memo slot is empty. Each evaluation of the thunk checks the memo slot: If full, it returns the *memo-ized* value; if empty, it calls the thunk function.

To streamline this process, we will represent a lazy thunk as an object with a *thunk function*, a *memo slot*, and (as with any closure object) instance variables to represent free variables as necessary for use by the thunk function. An *unevaluated* thunk has an empty memo slot, and the thunk function, when called, computes a value and puts it in the memo slot. An *evaluated* thunk has the previously computed value in its memo slot, and its thunk function just returns the memo-slot value.

For example, the LazyJava declaration int twenty = addFive(15) (in Program 15.1) is compiled in a context where the environment pointer EP will point to a record containing the `addFive` function. The representation of `addFive(15)` is not a function call that will go and compute the answer *now*, but a thunk that will remember how to compute it on demand, *later*. We might translate this fragment of the LazyJava program into FunJava as follows:

```
/* this already points to a record containing addFive */
c_void_int twenty = new intThunk(this);
```

which is supported by the auxiliary declarations

```
class intThunk {public int eval(); int memo; boolean done; }

class c_int_int {public int exec(int x);}
class intFuncThunk {public c_int_int eval();
                         c_int_int memo; boolean done; }

class twentyThunk extends intThunk {
    intFuncThunk addFive;
    public int exec() {
        if (!done) {
            memo = addFive.eval().exec(15);
            done = true;
        }
        return memo;
    }
    twentyThunk(addFive) {this.addFive=addFive;}
}

twentyThunk twenty = new twentyThunk(...);
```

To create a thunk such as `twenty`, it must be given values for its free variables (in this case, `addFive`) so that when it later evaluates, it has all the information it needs; this is just the same as closure conversion. To *touch* a lazy thunk `t`, we just compute `t.eval()`. The first time `t.eval()` is executed, it will see that `done` is false, and it will calculate the result and put it in `memo`. Any subsequent time that `t` is touched, `t.eval()` will simply return the `memo` field.

EVALUATION OF A LAZY PROGRAM

Here is a program that uses the `enter` function of Program 15.3b to build a tree mapping {three $\mapsto$ 3!, $-$one $\mapsto$ $(-1)!$}:

Invariant hoisting. i) {
```
      return if (i==0) 1 else i * fact(i-1)
  }.
  tree t0 = new tree("",0,null,null);
  tree t1 = t0.enter("-one", if i=0 then 1 else i * fact(i-1));
  tree t2 = t1.enter("three", fact(3));
  return putInt(t2.look("three", exit));
}
```

A curious thing about this program is that `fact(-1)` is undefined. Thus, if this program is compiled by a (strict) PureFunJava compiler, it will infinite-loop (or will eventually overflow the machine's arithmetic as it keeps subtracting 1 from a negative number).

But if compiled by a LazyJava compiler, the program will succeed, printing three factorial! First, variable `t1` is defined; but this does not actually call `enter` – it merely makes a thunk which will do so on demand. Then, `t2` is defined, which also does nothing but make a thunk. Then a thunk is created for `look(t2,"three")` (but `look` is not actually called).

Finally, a thunk for the expression `putInt(...,exit)` is created. This is the result of the program. But the runtime system then "demands" an `answer` from this program, which can be computed only by calling the outermost thunk. So the body of `putInt` executes, which immediately demands the integer value of its first argument; this causes the `look(t2,"three")` thunk to evaluate.

The body of `look` needs to compare `k` with `t.key`. Since `k` and `t` are each thunks, we can compute an integer by evaluating `k.eval()` and a tree by evaluating `t.eval()`. From the tree we can extract the `key` field; but each field is a thunk, so we must actually do `(t.eval().key)()` to get the integer.

The `t.key` value will turn out to be -1, so `look(t().right,k)` is called. *The program never evaluates the* `binding` *thunk in the* -one *node,* so `fact(-1)` is never given a chance to infinite-loop.

OPTIMIZATION OF LAZY FUNCTIONAL PROGRAMS

Lazy functional programs are subject to many of the same kinds of optimizations as strict functional programs, or even imperative programs. Loops can be identified (these are simply tail-recursive functions), induction variables can be identified, common subexpressions can be eliminated, and so on.

In addition, lazy compilers can do some kinds of optimizations that strict functional or imperative compilers cannot, using equational reasoning.

For example, given a loop

```
type intfun = int->int;

intfun f (int i) {
    public int g(int j) {return h(i) * j;}
    return g;
}
```

an optimizer might like to hoist the invariant computation h(i) out of the function g. After all, g may be called thousands of times, and it would be better not to recompute h(i) each time. Thus we obtain

```
type intfun = int->int;

intfun f (int i) {
    int hi = h(i)
    public int g(int j) {return hi * j;}
    return g;
}
```

and now each time g is called, it runs faster.

This is valid in a lazy language. But in a strict language, this transformation is invalid! Suppose after intfun a = f(8) the function a is never called at all; and suppose h(8) infinite-loops; before the "optimization" the program would have terminated successfully, but afterward we get a nonterminating program. Of course, the transformation is also invalid in an impure functional language, because h(8) might have side effects, and we are changing the number of times h(8) is executed.

Dead-code removal. Another subtle problem with strict programming languages is the removal of *dead code*. Suppose we have

```
int f(int i) {
 int d = g(x);
 return i+2;
}
```

The variable d is never used; it is *dead* at its definition. Therefore, the call to g(x) should be removed. In a conventional programming language, such as MiniJava or FunJava, we cannot remove g(x) because it might have side effects that are necessary to the operation of the program.

```
class intList  {int head; intList tail; intList(head,tail){...}}
type intfun = int->int;
type int2fun = (int,int) -> int;

public int sumSq(intfun inc,int2fun  mul, int2fun add) {
  public intList range(int i, int j) {
    return if (i>j) then null else intList(i, range(inc(i),j));
  }
  public intList squares(intList l) {
    return if (l==null) null
           else intList(mul(l.head,l.head), squares(l.tail));
  }
  int sum(int accum, intList l) {
    return if (l==null) accum else sum(add(accum,l.head), l.tail);
  }
  return sum(0,squares(range(1,100)));
}
```

PROGRAM 15.15. Summing the squares.

In a strict, purely functional language such as PureFunJava, removing the computation g(x) could optimize a nonterminating computation into a terminating one! Though this seems benign, it can be very confusing to the programmer. We do not want programs to change their input/output behavior when compiled with different levels of optimization.

In a lazy language, it is perfectly safe to remove dead computations such as g(x).

Deforestation. In any language, it is common to break a program into one module that produces a data structure and another module that consumes it. Program 15.15 is a simple example; range(i,j) generates a list of the integers from i to j, squares(l) returns the square of each number, and sum(l) adds up all the numbers.

First range builds a list of 100 integers; then squares builds another list of 100 integers; finally, sum traverses this list.

It is wasteful to build these lists. A transformation called *deforestation* removes intermediate lists and trees (hence the name) and does everything in one pass. The deforested sumSq program looks like this:

```
public int sumSq(intfun inc,int2fun  mul, int2fun add) {
 public int f(int accum, int i, int j) {
   return if (i>j) accum else f(add(accum,mul(i,i)),inc(i));
 }
 return f(0,1,100);
}
```

In impure functional languages (where functions can have side effects) deforestation is not usually valid. Suppose, for example, that the functions inc, mul, and add alter global variables, or print on an output file. The deforestation transformation has rearranged the order of calling these functions; instead of

inc(1),   inc(2),   ... inc(100),
mul(1, 1), mul(2, 2), ... mul(100, 100),
add(0, 1), add(1, 4), ... add(328350, 10000)

the functions are called in the order

mul(1, 1),	add(0, 1),	inc(1),
mul(2, 2),	add(1, 4),	inc(2),

$$\vdots$$

mul(100, 100), add(328350, 10000), inc(100)

Only in a pure functional language is this transformation always legal.

STRICTNESS ANALYSIS

Although laziness allows certain new optimizations, the overhead of thunk creation and thunk evaluation is very high. If no attention is paid to this problem, then the lazy program will run slowly no matter what other optimizations are enabled.

The solution is to put thunks only where they are needed. If a function $f(x)$ is certain to evaluate its argument x, then there is no need to pass a thunk for x; we can just pass an evaluated x instead. We are trading an evaluation now for a certain eventual evaluation.

Definition of strictness. We say a function $f(x)$ is *strict in x* if, whenever some actual parameter a would fail to terminate, then $f(a)$ would also fail to terminate. A multi-argument function $f(x_1, \ldots, x_n)$ is strict in x_i if, whenever a would fail to terminate, then $f(b_1, \ldots, b_{i-1}, a, b_{i+1}, \ldots, b_n)$ also fails to terminate, regardless of whether the b_j terminate. Let us take an example:

```
bindingThunk look(tree t, key k) {
   return if (k < t.key.eval()) look(t.left.eval(), k)
          else if (k > t.key.eval()) look(t.right.eval(), k)
          else t.binding;
}
```

PROGRAM 15.16. Partial call-by-name using the results of strictness analysis; compare with Program 15.14.

```
int f(int x, int y) { return x + x + y; }

int g(int x, int y) { return if (x>0) y else x; }

tree h(String x, int y) { return new tree(x,y,null,null); }

int j(int x) { return j(0); }
```

The function f is *strict* in its argument x, since if the result f(x,y) is demanded then f will certainly touch (demand the value of) x. Similarly, f is strict in argument y, and g is strict in x. But g is not strict in its second argument, because g can sometimes compute its result without touching y.

The function h is not strict in either argument. Even though it appears to "use" both x and y, it does not demand (string or integer) values from them; instead it just puts them into a data structure, and it could be that no other part of the program will ever demand values from the key or binding fields of that particular tree.

Curiously, by our definition of strictness, the function j is strict in x even though it never uses x. But the purpose of strictness analysis is to determine whether it is safe to evaluate x before passing it to the function j: Will this cause a terminating program to become nonterminating? In this case, if j is going to be called, it will infinite-loop anyway, so it doesn't matter if we perform a (possibly nonterminating) evaluation of x beforehand.

Using the result of strictness analysis. Program 15.16 shows the result of transforming the look function (of Program 15.3a) using strictness information. A call-by-name transformation has been applied here, as in Program 15.14, but the result would be similar using call-by-need. Function look is strict in both its arguments t and key. Thus, when comparing k<t.key, it does not have to *touch* k and t. However, the t.key field still points to a thunk, so it must be touched.

Since look is strict, callers of look are expected to pass evaluated values,

Function M:

$$M(7, \sigma) = 1$$

$$M(\text{x}, \sigma) = \text{x} \in \sigma$$

$$M(E_1 + E_2, \sigma) = M(E_1, \sigma) \wedge M(E_2, \sigma)$$

$$M(\text{newobject}(E_1, \ldots, E_n), \sigma) = 1$$

$$M(\text{if } (E_1) \ E_2 \text{ else } E_3, \sigma) = M(E_1, \sigma) \wedge (M(E_2, \sigma) \vee M(E_3, \sigma))$$

$$M(\text{f}(E_1, \ldots, E_n), \sigma) = (\text{f}, (M(E_1, \sigma), \ldots, M(E_n, \sigma))) \in H$$

Calculation of H:

$H \leftarrow \{\}$

repeat

    done $\leftarrow$ true

    for each function $\text{f}(\text{x}_1, \ldots, \text{x}_n) = B$

        for each sequence $(b_1, \ldots, b_n)$ of booleans (all 2^n of them)

            if $(\text{f}, (b_1, \ldots, b_n)) \notin H$

                $\sigma \leftarrow \{\text{x}_i | \ b_i = 1\}$ *(σ is the set of x's corresponding*

                if $M(B, \sigma)$ *to 1's in the b vector)*

                    done $\leftarrow$ false

                    $H \leftarrow H \cup \{(\text{f}, (b_1, \ldots, b_n))\}$

until *done*

Strictness (after the calculation of H terminates):

f is strict in its ith argument if

$$(\text{f}, (\underbrace{1, 1, \ldots, 1}_{i-1}, 0, \underbrace{1, 1, \ldots, 1}_{n-i})) \notin H$$

ALGORITHM 15.17. First-order strictness analysis.

---

not thunks. This is illustrated by the recursive calls, which must explicitly *touch* t.left and t.right to turn them from thunks to values.

Approximate strictness analysis. In some cases, such as the functions f, g, and h above, the strictness or nonstrictness of a function is obvious – and easily determined by an optimizing compiler. But in general, exact strictness analysis is not computable – like exact dynamic liveness analysis (see page 210) and many other dataflow problems.

Thus, compilers must use a conservative approximation; where the exact strictness of a function argument cannot be determined, the argument must be assumed nonstrict. Then a thunk will be created for it; this slows down the program a bit, but at least the optimizer will not have turned a terminating program into an infinite-looping program.

Algorithm 15.17 shows an algorithm for computing strictness. It maintains a set H of tuples of the form $(f, (b_1, \ldots, b_n))$, where n is the number of arguments of f and the b_i are booleans. The meaning of a tuple $(f, (1, 1, 0))$ is this: If f is called with three arguments (thunks), and the first two may halt but the third never halts, then f may halt.

If $(f, (1, 1, 0))$ is in the set H, then f might not be strict in its third argument. If $(f, (1, 1, 0))$ is never put into H, then f must be strict in its third argument.

We also need an auxiliary function to calculate whether an *expression* may terminate. Given an expression E and a set of variables σ, we say that $M(E, \sigma)$ means "E may terminate if all the variables in σ may terminate." If E_1 is i+j, and there is some possibility that the thunks i and j may halt, then it is also possible that E_1 will halt too: $M(i + j, \{i, j\})$ is true. But if E_2 is if (kJ) i else j, where i and j could conceivably halt but k never does, then certainly E_2 will not halt, so $M(E_2, \{i, j\})$ is false.

Algorithm 15.17 will not work on the full LazyJava language, because it does not handle functions passed as arguments or returned as results. But for *first-order* programs (without higher-order functions), it does a good job of computing (static) strictness. More powerful algorithms for strictness analysis handle higher-order functions.

FURTHER READING

Church [1941] developed the λ-calculus, a "programming language" of nested functions that can be passed as arguments and returned as results. He was hampered by having no machines to compile for.

Closures. Landin [1964] showed how to interpret λ-calculus on an abstract machine, using closures allocated on a heap. Steele [1978] used closure representations specialized to different patterns of function usage, so that in many cases nonlocal variables are passed as extra arguments to an inner function to avoid heap-allocating a record. Cousineau et al. [1985] showed how closure conversion can be expressed as a transformation back into the source language, so that closure analysis can be cleanly separated from other phases of code generation.

Static links are actually not the best basis for doing closure conversion; for many reasons it is better to consider each nonlocal variable separately, instead of always grouping together all the variables at the same nesting level. Kranz et al. [1986] performed *escape analysis* to determine which closures can be stack-allocated because they do not outlive their creating function and also integrated closure analysis with register allocation to make a high-performance optimizing compiler. Shao and Appel [1994] integrate closures with the use of callee-save registers to minimize the load/store traffic caused by accessing local and nonlocal variables. Appel [1992, Chapters 10 and 12] has a good overview of closure conversion.

Continuations. Tail calls are particularly efficient and easy to analyze. Strachey and Wadsworth [1974] showed that the control flow of any program (even an imperative one) can be expressed as function calls, using the notion of *continuations*. Steele [1978] transformed programs into *continuation-passing style* early in compilation, turning all function calls into tail calls, to simplify all the analysis and optimization phases of the compiler. Kranz et al. [1986] built an optimizing compiler for Scheme using continuation-passing style; Appel [1992] describes a continuation-based optimizing compiler for ML.

Inline expansion. Cocke and Schwartz [1970] describe inline expansion of function bodies; Scheifler [1977] shows that it is particularly useful for languages supporting data abstraction, where there tend to be many tiny functions implementing operations on an abstract data type. Appel [1992] describes practical heuristics for controlling code explosion.

Continuation-based I/O. Wadler [1995] describes the use of monads to generalize the notion of continuation-based interaction.

Lazy evaluation. Algol-60 [Naur et al. 1963] used call-by-name evaluation for function arguments, implemented using thunks – but also permitted side effects, so programmers needed to know what they were doing! Most of its successors use call-by-value. Henderson and Morris [1976] and Friedman and Wise [1976] independently invented lazy evaluation (call-by-need). Hughes [1989] argues that lazy functional languages permit clearer and more modular programming than imperative languages.

Several lazy pure functional languages were developed in the 1980s; the community of researchers in this area designed and adopted the language Haskell [Hudak et al. 1992] as a standard. Peyton Jones [1987; 1992] describes many implementation and optimization techniques for lazy functional languages; Peyton Jones and Partain [1993] describe a practical algorithm for higher-order strictness analysis. Wadler [1990] describes deforestation.

PROGRAM COMPILING FUNCTIONAL LANGUAGES

a. Implement FunJava. A function value should be implemented as an object with an `exec` method.

b. Implement PureFunJava. This is just like FunJava, except that several "impure" features are removed and the predefined functions have different interfaces.

c. Implement optimizations on PureFunJava. This requires changing the `Tree` intermediate language so that it can represent an entire program, including function entry and exit, in a machine-independent way. After inline expansion (and other) optimizations, the program can be converted into the standard `Tree` intermediate representation of Chapter 7.

d. Implement LazyJava.

EXERCISES

15.1 Draw a picture of the closure data structures representing `add24` and `a` in Program 15.1 just at the point where `add24(a)` is about to be called. Label all the components.

*15.2 Figure 15.13 summarizes the instructions necessary to implement `printTable` in a functional or an imperative style. But it leaves out the MOVE instructions that pass parameters to the calls. Flesh out both the functional and imperative versions with all omitted instructions, writing pseudo-assembly language in the style of the program accompanying Graph 11.1 on page 221. Show which MOVE instructions you expect to be deleted by copy propagation.

*15.3 Explain why there are no cycles in the graph of closures and records of a PureFunJava program. Comment on the applicability of reference-count garbage collection to such a program. **Hint:** Under what circumstances are records or closures updated after they are initialized?

15.4 a. Perform Algorithm 15.9 (loop-preheader transformation) on the `look` function of Program 15.3a.

b. Perform Algorithm 15.10 (loop-invariant hoisting) on the result.

c. Perform Algorithm 15.8 (inline expansion) on the following call to `look` (assuming the previous two transformations have already been applied):

```
look(mytree, a+1)
```

15.5 Perform Algorithm 15.17 (strictness analysis) on the following program, showing the set H on each pass through the **repeat** loop.

```
function f(w: int, x: int, y: int, z: int) =
  if z=0 then w+y else f(x,0,0,z-1) + f(y,y,0,z-1)
```

In which arguments is `f` strict?

16

Polymorphic Types

poly-mor-phic: able to assume different forms

Webster's Dictionary

Some functions execute in a way that's independent of the data type on which they operate. Some data structures are structured in the same way regardless of the types of their elements.

As an example, consider a function to concatenate linked lists in Java. We define a `List` class, subclasses for empty and nonempty lists, and a (nondestructive) `append` method:

```
abstract class IntList {
  IntList append(IntList more);
}
class IntCons extends IntList {
  Integer head; IntList tail;
  IntCons (Integer head, IntList tail) {
     this.head=head;  this.tail=tail;
  }
  IntList append(IntList more) {
     return new IntCons(head, tail.append(more));
  }
}
class IntNull extends IntList {
  IntNull () {}
  IntList append(IntList more) {
    return more;
  }
}
```

There's nothing about the code for the `IntList` data type or the `append` method that would be any different if the element type were `String` or `Tree` instead of `Integer`. We might like `append` to be able to work on any kind of list. We could, of course, use the word `Object` instead of `Integer` to declare `head`, but then if we unintentionally mixed Integers and Strings as elements of the same List, the compiler's type-checker wouldn't be able to give us useful feedback: we'd get a runtime exception at a downcast somewhere.

A function is *polymorphic* (from the Greek *many+shape*) if it can operate on arguments of different types. There are two main kinds of polymorphism

Parametric polymorphism. A function is *parametrically polymorphic* if it follows the same algorithm regardless of the type of its argument. The Ada or Modula-3 *generic* mechanism, C++ *templates*, or ML *type schemes* are examples of parametric polymorphism.

Overloading. A function identifier is *overloaded* if it stands for different algorithms depending on the type of its argument. For example, in most languages + is overloaded, meaning integer addition on integer arguments and floating-point addition (which is quite a different algorithm) on floating-point arguments. In many languages, including Ada, C++, and Java, programmers can make overloaded functions of their own.

These two kinds of polymorphism are quite different – almost unrelated – and require different implementation techniques.

16.1   PARAMETRIC POLYMORPHISM

A polymorphic function $f(t\ x)$ takes some parameter x of type t, where t can be *instantiated* at different actual types. In an *explicit* style of parametric polymorphism, we pass the type as an argument to the function, so we write something like f<t>$(t\ x)$, and a function call might look like f<int>(3) or f<string>("three"). In a language with *implicit* parametric polymorphism, we simply write the definition as $f(x)$, and the call as $f(3)$ or f("three") – the type parameter t is unstated. Reasonable programming languages can be designed either way.

In this chapter we will present *Generic Java* (GJ for short), a polymorphic extension of Java (polymorphic functions have also been called *generic* functions in the literature of programming languages). In GJ, classes and methods are polymorphic: Each class and method can take type parameters in triangle brackets:

$$
\begin{aligned}
\mathit{ClassDecl} &\rightarrow \textbf{class } \mathit{id}\ \mathit{TyParams}\ \mathit{Ext}\ \{\ \mathit{VarDecl}^*\ \mathit{MethodDecl}^*\ \} \\
\mathit{Ext} &\rightarrow \textbf{extends } \mathit{Type} \\
&\rightarrow \\
\mathit{MethodDecl} &\rightarrow \textbf{public } \mathit{TyParams}\ \mathit{Type}\ \mathit{id}\ (\ \mathit{FormalList}\ ) \\
&\qquad\quad \{\ \mathit{VarDecl}^*\ \mathit{Statement}^*\ \textbf{return } \mathit{Exp}\ ;\ \} \\
\mathit{TyParams} &\rightarrow\ <\ \mathit{id}\ \mathit{Ext}\ \mathit{TyParRest}^*\ > \\
&\rightarrow \\
\mathit{TyParRest} &\rightarrow\ ,\ \mathit{id}\ \mathit{Ext}
\end{aligned}
$$

In addition to the `int` and `boolean` types (and so on), a *Type* used in declaring variables can now take arguments that are themselves types:

$$
\begin{aligned}
\mathit{Type} &\rightarrow\ \mathit{id} <\ \mathit{Type}\ \mathit{TypeRest}^*\ > \\
\mathit{TypeRest} &\rightarrow\ ,\ \mathit{Type}
\end{aligned}
$$

Finally, class constructors can also take type arguments:

$$
\mathit{Exp}\ \rightarrow\ \textbf{new } \mathit{id} <\ \mathit{Type}\ \mathit{TypeRest}^*\ > (\ )
$$

GJ uses a combination of explicit and implicit polymorphism: The programmer must always write the formal type parameters (at class declarations), but actual type parameters (when calling a class constructor) can often be omitted. In this chapter we'll present only a fully explicit GJ.

Using polymorphism, we can make a generic `List` class with which we can make a list of integers, or a list of strings, but which prevents the unintended mistaking of one for the other:

```
abstract class List<X> {
  List<X> append(List<X> more);
}

class Cons<X> extends List<X> {
 X head; List<X> tail;
 Cons (X head, List<X> tail) {this.head=head; this.tail=tail;}
 List<X> append(List<X> more) {
    return new Cons<X>(head, tail.append(more));
  }
}

class Null<X> extends List<X> {
  Null () {}
  List<X> append(List<X> more) {
    return more;
  }
}
```

Using this class declaration, we could create a list of the integers (3,4) with the expression,

```
List<Integer> list34 =
  new Cons<Integer>(new Integer(3),
    new Cons<Integer>(new Integer(4),
      new Null<Integer>));
```

We can even build a list of int-lists:

```
List<List<Integer>> lislis =
  new Cons<List<Integer>>(list34,
    new Null<List<Integer>>());
```

In GJ we can also *bound* a formal type parameter by specifying that it must be a subclass of a particular base class. Suppose, for example, that we have a class `Printable`:

```
abstract class Printable { void print_me(); }
```

with some subclasses, some of which are declared here and some of which are yet to be declared:

```
class PrintableInt extends Printable {
    int x;
    void print_me() {... print x ...}
}
class PrintableBool extends Printable {
    boolean b;
    void print_me() {... print b ...}
}
```

In ordinary Java we could make a pair-of-printables, as follows:

```
class Pair {
  Printable a;
  Printable b;
  void print_me() { a.print_me(); b.print_me(); }
}
```

and this will work well, as long as we don't mind that in any particular Pair, the a and b components might belong to different subclasses of `Printable`. But if we want to make "coherent" pairs-of-printables, where both components must belong to the same subclass, we can use bounded polymorphism in GJ, as follows:

```
class GPair<X extends Printable> {
  X a;
  X b;
  void print_me() { a.print_me(); b.print_me(); }
}
```

Now every object of type `GPair<PrintableInt>` has `a` and `b` components that are both instances of `PrintableInt`, and correspondingly for `GPair<PrintableBool>`, and for other subclasses of `Printable` that may be declared in the future. We say that `Printable` is the *bound* of type parameter `X`.

Subtyping in GJ. In Java, if we make `class Triple extends Pair`, then `Triple` is a subtype of `Pair`, and any `Triple` object can be passed as a parameter to any method that expects a `Pair`. In GJ, we can make `class GTriple<X extends Printable> extends GPair<X>`, and then `GTriple<PrintableInt>` is a subtype of `GPair<PrintableInt>`. But if `class MyInt extends PrintableInt`, then it's not the case that `GTriple<MyInt>` is a subtype of `GPair<PrintableInt>`. And it's especially not the case that `GTriple` is a subtype of `GPair`, because these are not types, they're type *constructors*, which become types only when applied to arguments.

16.2   POLYMORPHIC TYPE-CHECKING

Type-checking for a polymorphic language is not as straightforward as for a monomorphic language. Before embarking on an implementation, we must be clear about what the typing rules are.

The types used in the basic MiniJava compiler could all be represented as atomic strings: `int`, `boolean`, `int[]`, and class identifiers such as `IntList`. In GJ we have three kinds of type expressions:

Primitive types such as `int` and `boolean`;
Type applications of the form $c \langle t_1, t_2, \ldots t_n \rangle$, where c is a *type constructor* – a polymorphic class such as `List` in our example – and t_1 through t_n are type expressions; and
Type variables such as the `X` in the type expression `ListX`.

All class identifiers will be considered polymorphic, but those with no type arguments can be considered as types of the form `C<>`. In this chapter we will

checkType(T) =
    if T is primitive (int, boolean, etc.) then OK
    else if T is Object then OK
    else if ($T \mapsto \ldots$) is in the type table then OK
    else if T is $C \langle T_1, \ldots, T_n \rangle$
        look up C in the class table, yielding class $C \langle X_1 \vartriangleleft N_1, \ldots, X_n \vartriangleleft N_n \rangle \vartriangleleft N\{\ldots\}$
        for each T_i do checkType(T_i)
        for each T_i do checkSubtype($T_i, [T_1, \ldots, T_n / X_1, \ldots, X_n]N_i$)

checkSubtype(T, U) =
    if $T = U$ then OK
    else if ($T \mapsto T'$) is in the type table then subtype(T', U)
    else if T is $C \langle T_1, \ldots, T_n \rangle$
        look up C in the class table, yielding class $C \langle X_1 \vartriangleleft N_1, \ldots, X_n \vartriangleleft N_n \rangle \vartriangleleft N\{\ldots\}$
        subtype($[T_1, \ldots, T_n / X_1, \ldots, X_n]N, U$)
    else *error*

ALGORITHM 16.1. Checking wellformedness of types and subtyping.

---

omit discussion of array types, though in a "MiniGJ" compiler int[] could be treated as a primitive type.

Syntactic conventions. The type-checking algorithm will have several kinds of variables:

T, T_i, U, V stand for type expressions;
N, N_i, P, Q stand for nonvariable type expressions (that do not contain type variables);
X, X_i, Y, Z stand for type variables;
C stands for class names;
m stands for method names;
f stands for field names;
e stands for program expressions; and
x stands for program variables (local variables of methods).

We will often abbreviate the keyword extends with the symbol $\vartriangleleft$. In discussing the type-checking algorithm we will require that every *TyParams* have an explicit bound, so instead of writing class List<X> we would write class List<X$\vartriangleleft$Object>.

Method types. It's convenient to separate the type of a method from the name of the method. For example, consider the declaration

```
<X extends Printable> GPair<X> firstTwo(List<X> x) { ... }
```

For any type X that's a subclass of `Printable`, the `firstTwo` method takes a list of X's, and returns a pair of X's. The type of the `firstTwo` method is $\langle X \lhd \text{Printable} \rangle \text{List} \langle X \rangle \rightarrow \text{GPair} \langle X \rangle$. (Notice that the *binding* occurrence of X requires a bounding clause $\langle X \lhd \text{Printable} \rangle$, but the applied occurrences of X do not use the $\lhd$ symbol.) In general, the form of a method type is

$$MethodTy \quad \rightarrow \quad TyParams\ TyList \rightarrow Ty$$

meaning that, with type parameters *TyParams* and value parameters whose types are *TyList*, the method returns a value of type *Ty*.

Substitution. Suppose we want to know the type of the `firstTwo` method when it's applied to a list of `PrintableInt`. We take $\text{List} \langle X \rangle \rightarrow \text{GPair} \langle X \rangle$ and substitute `PrintableInt` for X, yielding the method type

$$\text{List} \langle \text{PrintableInt} \rangle \rightarrow \text{GPair} \langle \text{PrintableInt} \rangle$$

We can write a substitution function in the compiler's type-checker to do this; in this chapter we'll write $[V_1, \ldots, V_k / X_1, \ldots, X_k]U$ to mean the substitution of type V_i for every occurrence of type variable X_i in type expression (or function prototype) U. Because class parameterization is not nested in GJ – that is, U cannot contain class declarations – we don't need to worry about internal redeclarations of the type variables X_i; the problem of *avoiding variable capture* (described in Section 15.4) does not occur.

Class table, type table, and var table. Section 5.2 explained that, because classes can mutually refer to each other, type-checking must proceed in two phases: First, build a symbol table (the *class table*) mapping class names to class declarations; second, type-check the interior of the class declarations. The same approach works for GJ. The first phase is quite straightforward; the rest of this section explains the algorithm for the second phase. This phase will use the class table, and maintain a *type table* mapping formal type parameters to their bounds, and a *var table* mapping ordinary (value) variables to their types. For example, in processing the `firstTwo` method (described above), the type table would map X to `Printable`, and the var table would map x to `List<X>`.

getBound(T) =
    if T is a type variable X
    then if $(X \mapsto N)$ is in the type table then N else *error*
    else if T is a nonvariable type N then N
    else *error*

fieldType$(f,)$ =
    if T is $C \langle T_1, \ldots, T_n \rangle$
        look in the class table for `class` $C \langle X_1 \lhd N_1, \ldots, X_n \lhd N_n \rangle \lhd N\{\textit{fields}, \ldots\}$
        if field f with type S is in *fields*
            return $[T_1, \ldots, T_n / X_1, \ldots, X_n]S$
        else return fieldType$(f, [T_1, \ldots, T_n / X_1, \ldots, X_n]N)$
    else *error*

methodType(m, T) =
    if T is $C \langle T_1, \ldots, T_n \rangle$
        look in the class table for `class` $C \langle X_1 \lhd N_1, \ldots, X_n \lhd N_n \rangle \lhd N\{\ldots, \textit{methods}\}$
        if method m is in *methods*, with the declaration
            $\langle Y_1 \lhd P_1, \ldots, Y_k \lhd P_k \rangle\ U\ m(U_1\ x_1\ \ldots\ U_l\ x_l)\{\texttt{return}\ e;\}$
        then return $[T_1, \ldots, T_n / X_1, \ldots, X_n](\langle Y_1 \lhd P_1, \ldots, Y_k \lhd P_k \rangle\ (U_1\ x_1, \ldots, U_l\ x_l) \to U)$
        else return methodType$(m, [T_1, \ldots, T_n / X_1, \ldots, X_n]N)$

ALGORITHM 16.2. Field and method search.

Well-formed types. A type is well formed if every type variable has a bound in the appropriate type table. Thus, the type `List<X>` is well formed when processing the declaration of `firstTwo` because $X \lhd$ `Printable` is in the type table. In general, we must also account for substitutions. Algorithm 16.1 shows the procedure *checktype* for checking wellformedness of types.

Subtyping. In type-checking Java (and GJ) it is often necessary to test whether one type is a subtype of another: A is a subtype of B if, whenever a value of type B is required, a value of type A will suffice. A subtype is not exactly the same as a subclass, but still, in class-based languages like Java, if class A extends B, then there is also a subtype relationship. Checking subtyping in GJ is made more complex by the need to perform type substitution and the need to look up type variables in the type table; Algorithm 16.1 shows how to do it.

checkExp(e) =
   if e is a variable x
     look up ($x \mapsto T$) in the var table; return T
   else if e is a field-selection $e_0.f$
     return fieldType(f, getBound(checkExp(e_0)))
   else if e is a method-call $e_0.m \langle V_1, \ldots, V_n \rangle (e_1, \ldots, e_l)$
     call methodType(m, getBound(checkExp(e_0))), yielding
$$\langle Y_1 \lhd P_1, \ldots, Y_k \lhd P_k \rangle (U_1 \, x_1, \ldots, U_l \, x_l) \to U$$
     for each V_i do checkType(V_i)
     for each V_i do checkSubtype(V_i, $[V_1, \ldots, V_k/Y_1, \ldots, Y_k]P_i$)
     for $i \in 1 \ldots l$ do checkSubtype(checkExp(e_i), $[V_1, \ldots, V_k/Y_1, \ldots, Y_k]U_i$)
     return $[V_1, \ldots, V_k/Y_1, \ldots, Y_k]U$
   else if e is new $N()$
     checktype(N)
     return N

ALGORITHM 16.3. Type-checking expressions. Expressions with integer type are omitted, because they are checked just as in MiniJava

---

Finding the bound of a type. The formal type parameters of a polymorphic class or method are of the form $\langle X \lhd N \rangle$. Inside that class or method, suppose there's a local variable declaration $X \, x$, where X is the type and x is the variable. When type-checking expressions such as the field access $x.f$, we need to know what class x is an instance of. We don't know exactly what class x belongs to – it belongs to some unknown class X – but we do know that X is a subclass of N. Therefore, we take the type X and look up its bound, N, in the type table. The function getBound(T) looks up type bounds.

Looking up field and method types. When type-checking a field access $e.f$ or a method call $e.m \langle T \rangle ()$, one must look up the field f or method m in e's class. This may involve a search through superclasses, and in the process, types must be substituted for type variables. These searches are handled by fieldType and methodType in Algorithm 16.2. Algorithm 16.3 shows how to type-check expressions using all the auxiliary procedures defined thus far.

    Algorithm 16.4 shows how to check class and method declarations. The formal type parameters of the class are added to the type table, then all the methods are checked. For each method, the formal type parameters and the (ordinary) value parameters of the method are added to the type table and

checkClass($cdecl$) =
   suppose $cdecl$ is class $C \langle X_1 \lhd N_1, \ldots, X_n \lhd N_n \rangle \lhd N \{fields, \, methods\}$
   add $(X_1 \mapsto N_1, \ldots X_k \mapsto N_k)$ to the type table
   checkType(N)
   for each N_i do checkType(N_i)
   for each $mdecl$ in $methods$
      suppose $mdecl$ is $\langle Y_1 \lhd P_1, \ldots, Y_j \lhd P_j \rangle \, T \, m(T_1 \, x_1 \, \ldots \, T_l \, x_l)\{\text{return } e; \}$
      add $(Y_1 \mapsto P_1, \ldots Y_j \mapsto P_j)$ to the type table
      checkType(T)
      for each T_i do checkType(T_i)
      for each P_i do checkType(P_i)
      add $(\text{this} \mapsto C \langle X_1, \ldots, X_n \rangle)$ to the var table
      add $(x_1 \mapsto T_1, \ldots x_l \mapsto T_l)$ to the var table
      checkSubtype(checkType(e), T)
      suppose methodType(m, N) is $\langle Z_1 \lhd Q_1, \ldots, Z_j \lhd Q_j \rangle (U_1 \, x_1, \ldots, U_l \, x_l) \to U$
      for each T_i check that $T_i = ([Y_1, \ldots, Y_j / Z_1, \ldots, Z_j] U_i)$
      for each P_i check that $P_i = ([Y_1, \ldots, Y_j / Z_1, \ldots, Z_j] Q_i)$
      checkSubtype(T, $[Y_1, \ldots, Y_j / Z_1, \ldots, Z_j] U$)
      pop j most recent bindings from the type table
      pop $l + 1$ most recent bindings from the var table
   pop k most recent bindings from the type table

ALGORITHM 16.4. Type-checking class declarations.

value table, then the body of the method is type-checked. The four lines ending at the last call to checkSubtype are to make sure that the method overriding is valid; in GJ as in Java, one can only override a method at the same argument and result type as in the superclass, but for GJ there are more substitutions to perform in order to check this.

16.3   TRANSLATION OF POLYMORPHIC PROGRAMS

After a polymorphic program is type-checked, it must be translated into machine code. There are several ways this can be done, four of which we will discuss:

Expansion: Don't generate code for a generic class such as Cons<X>; instead, create a new Cons class for each different class at which <X> is instantiated.

Casting: Generate only a single Cons class, and use Java-style checked runtime casts to operate upon it.

Erasure: Generate only a single Cons class, and operate on it directly.

Type-passing: Generate code for a Cons template class, and pass type parameters at run time.

Expansion and casting have the advantage that they are compatible with standard Java Virtual Machines; erasure is more efficient but incompatible; and type-passing has interesting advantages and disadvantages of its own.

Expansion. It's entirely possible to expand out all the polymorphic class instantiations into ordinary Java classes. This is called the *heterogenous* translation of GJ into Java, because the Cons_Int class will be entirely different and essentially unrelated to the Cons_Bool class, and so on. Templates in C++ work this way as well: They are expanded out into ordinary classes. Expansion is much like inline expansion of ordinary functions; but inline expansion of functions usally can't be done so completely as to eliminate all function definitions, because recursive functions or function calls within loops would expand the program infinitely. In contrast, instantiation of generic classes never depends on program variables and is not recursive.

The advantages of expansion are that the resulting classes are generally compatible with ordinary Java (so that GJ can run in an ordinary Java Virtual Machine), and that the compiled code is fairly efficient (similar to ordinary Java). The disadvantages are that it makes many copies of the same code – at worst, it can cause exponential blowup of the program, but in practice this exponential behavior is rarely seen (expansion of C++ templates is tolerably efficient). Also, expansion interacts badly with the package mechanism of Java (see Exercise 16.3).

Casting. In the *homogenous* translation of GJ into Java, all the type parameters are simply erased. When a type variable is used in the declaration of a local variable or parameter, it is replaced by its bound. Thus, the translation of GPair (from page 339) would be

```
class GPair {
  Printable a;
  Printable b;
  void print_me() { a.print_me(); b.print_me(); }
}
```

which is well-typed Java code. However, a use of GPair such as

```
int sum(GPair<PrintableInt> p) {
  return p.a.x + p.b.x;
}
```

must be translated with casts in order to be legal Java:

```
int sum(GPair p) {
  return ((PrintableInt)(p.a)).x + ((PrintableInt)(p.b)).x;
}
```

Unfortunately, these casts from a superclass to a subclass require a run-time check in ordinary Java, even though (if the Java program results from the translation of a well-typed GJ program) the cast will always succeed. Another (minor) disadvantage of the homogenous translation is that class construction cannot be applied to type variables; i.e., `new X()`, where `X` is a type variable, cannot really be replaced by `new C()`, where `C` is the bound of `X`, because the wrong class will be constructed.

Erasure. If the GJ program is translated directly into machine code, the homogenous translation can safely be done without inserting casts: Just erase the type parameters from the program. The advantage is that there's no duplication of code *and* there's no extra run-time casting. Unfortunately, bypassing Java also means that the Java Virtual Machine Language (JVML, or "Java byte codes") must also be bypassed, since the Java bytecode verifier uses the Java type system, not the GJ type system. This translation technique is therefore incompatible with existing Java Virtual Machines that accept programs in JVML.

Type-passing. Instead of erasing the type parameters, they can be turned into value parameters. A polymorphic method

```
<X1 extends C1> int m (X1 x, int y)
```

can be translated (approximately) as

```
int m (Class X1, X1 x, int y)
```

where a class descriptor is really passed as a run-time argument. One advantage of this translation is that class construction can now be applied to type variables.

An even more significant advantage is that, in principle, it may be possible to divorce class descriptors from the objects that belong to the classes. That is, instead of an object of class `PrintableInt` (see page 338) requiring two words to represent it – the class descriptor and the x field – now only one word would be required. Any place in the program that manipulates a `PrintableInt` would also have an explicit class parameter passed to it in an associated local variable; from this parameter, the virtual method table can be accessed as needed, and the garbage collecter can learn what it needs to know about the layout of objects.

The disadvantage of type-passing is that there is a (small) run-time cost to passing the types, and that it is incompatible with Java and with standard JVMs.

POINTERS, INTEGERS, AND BOXING

Polymorphism in GJ works for object types, but not for `int` and `boolean`. Even in ordinary Java, the class extension mechanism works for objects but not integers. The solution in Java and GJ for programmers who wish to get the benefits of subclassing or polymorphism for `int`s is to make a wrapper class `Integer` that contains an instance variable of type `int`. This is called a *boxed* integer, compared to the raw `int`, which is an *unboxed* value. Boxed values – implemented by pointers to objects containing raw values – are much easier than unboxed values to compile polymorphically:

- They are all the same size (the size of a pointer) so that the same machine code can obliviously manipulate boxed values of different types.
- They can contain type or class descriptors (in the pointed-to object) so that the garbage collector can understand how to traverse them.

Some programming languages (such as ML and C#) automatically box values as necessary to support polymorphism. That is, the programmer never needs to distinguish between `int` and `Integer` because the compiler inserts the coercions automatically. There is still a cost at run time to box and unbox, but it is the same cost that would be paid if the programmer explicitly wrapped the integers in boxes.

16.4   RESOLUTION OF STATIC OVERLOADING

Some languages permit *overloading:* different functions of the same name but different argument types. The compiler must choose between function bodies based on the types of the actual parameters. This is sometimes known as *ad hoc polymorphism,* as opposed to the *parametric polymorphism* described in the previous sections.

Static overloading is not difficult to implement. When processing the declaration of an overloaded function f, the new binding b_n must not hide the old definitions $b_1, \ldots, b_{n-1}$. Instead, the new binding maps f to a list of different implementations, $f \mapsto [b_1, \ldots, b_n]$. Depending on the language semantics, it may be necessary to give an error message if b_n has identical parameter types to one of the b_i.

Then, when looking up f in a place where it is called with actual parameters, the types of the actual parameters will determine which of the bindings b_i should be used.

Some languages allow functions of identical argument types (but different result type) to be overloaded; some languages allow forms of dynamic overloading; see the Further Reading section.

FURTHER READING

One of the first "polymorphic" languages was Lisp [McCarthy 1960], which has no static (i.e., compile-time checkable) type system at all. Consequently, the fully boxed implementation of data was used, so that the data could describe itself to the run-time type-checker as well as to the garbage collector.

The first programming language to use statically type-checked parametric polymorphism was ML, which was originally the *MetaL*anguage of the Edinburgh theorem prover [Gordon et al. 1978] but was later developed into a general-purpose programming language [Milner et al. 1990]. Cardelli [1984] describes a fully boxed implementation of ML.

In the Ada programming language [Ada 1980], the *generic* mechanism allows a function (in fact, an entire package) to be parameterized over types; but full type-checking is done at each call site after the generic is applied to actual parameters, and the *expansion* technique of implementation must be used. In contrast, Algorithm 16.4 can check a generic class independent of how its formal type parameters will eventually be instantiated.

Pierce [2002] provides a comprehensive survey of type systems, including polymorphic types, in the modern notation. Bracha et al. [1998] describe Generic Java (GJ) and its implementation. The type-checking algorithm in Section 16.1 of this chapter is adapted from "Featherweight Generic Java" [Igarashi et al. 2001], which should be read by anyone planning to implement such a type-checker.

Overloading. Ada allows different functions *with the same parameter types* to be overloaded, as long as the result types are different. When the output of such a function is an argument to another overloaded identifier, then there may be zero, one, or many possible interpretations of the expression; the Ada semantics say that the expression is legal only if there is exactly one interpretation. Aho et al. [1986, Section 6.5] discuss this issue and give a resolution algorithm. But Ada-style overloading has not been widely imitated in recent language designs, perhaps because it can confuse the programmer.

Dynamic overloading allows different implementations of a function to be chosen based on the *run-time* type of an actual parameter; it is a form of *dynamic dispatch*. Dynamic dispatch is also used to implement method overriding, a fundamental concept of object-oriented programming (see Chapter 14) – overriding is a form of dynamic dispatch on the `this` parameter, while general dynamic overloading can depend on any or all parameters to a function. *Type classes* in the Haskell language allow overloading and parametric polymorphism to interact in a useful and expressive way [Hall et al. 1996].

EXERCISES

16.1 Show the steps in type-checking the declaration of `append` on page 337 using Algorithm 16.4.

*16.2 Read Section 3.2 of Igarashi et al. [2001] and show how to extend Algorithms 16.3 and 16.4 to handle show type-checking of cast expressions and of class constructors.

16.3 Use the heterogenous translation (that is, expansion) to translate the following GJ program to ordinary Java.

```
package p;
  public class C <X extends Object> { X a; B b; }
  class B { }
package q;
  class D { }
  class E { p.C<D> y; p.C<Object> z; }
```

a. First do the translation ignoring the `package` declarations, the `public` keyword, and the `p.` qualifiers within class `E`. **Hint:** The translation will not have a class `C`, but will have classes `C_D` and `C_Object`.

b. Now, try the translation preserving the package structure. Show that it's impossible for `B` to be package-scope within `p` at the same time that `D` is package-scope within `q`.

17

Dataflow Analysis

anal-y-sis: an examination of a complex, its elements, and their relations

Webster's Dictionary

An optimizing compiler transforms programs to improve their efficiency without changing their output. There are many transformations that improve efficiency:

Register allocation: Keep two nonoverlapping temporaries in the same register.

Common-subexpression elimination: If an expression is computed more than once, eliminate one of the computations.

Dead-code elimination: Delete a computation whose result will never be used.

Constant folding: If the operands of an expression are constants, do the computation at compile time.

This is not a complete list of optimizations. In fact, there can never be a complete list.

NO MAGIC BULLET

Computability theory shows that it will always be possible to invent new optimizing transformations.

Let us say that a *fully optimizing compiler* is one that transforms each program P to a program $\mathbf{Opt}(P)$ that is the *smallest* program with the same input/output behavior as P. We could also imagine optimizing for speed instead of program size, but let us choose size to simplify the discussion.

For any program Q that produces no output and never halts, $\mathbf{Opt}(Q)$ is short and easily recognizable:

$$L_1: \quad \mathbf{goto} \ L_1$$

Therefore, if we had a fully optimizing compiler, we could use it to solve the halting problem; to see if there exists an input on which P halts, just see if **Opt**(P) is the one-line infinite loop. But we know that no computable algorithm can always tell whether programs halt, so a fully optimizing compiler cannot be written either.

Since we can't make a *fully* optimizing compiler, we must build *optimizing compilers* instead. An optimizing compiler transforms P into a program P' that always has the same input/output behavior as P, and might be smaller or faster. We hope that P' runs faster than the optimized programs produced by our competitors' compilers.

No matter what optimizing compiler we consider, there must always exist another (usually bigger) optimizing compiler that does a better job. For example, suppose we have an optimizing compiler A. There must be some program P_x which does not halt, such that $A(P_x) \neq$ **Opt**(P_x). If this were not the case, then A would be a fully optimizing compiler, which we could not possibly have. Therefore, there exists a better compiler B:

$$B(P) = \textbf{if } P = P_x \textbf{ then } [\texttt{L}: \texttt{goto L}] \textbf{ else } A(P)$$

Although we don't know what P_x is, it is certainly just a string of source code, and given that string we could trivially construct B.

The optimizing compiler B isn't very useful – it's not worth handling special cases like P_x one at a time. In real life, we improve A by finding some reasonably general program transformation (such as the ones listed at the beginning of the chapter) that improves the performance of many programs. We add this transformation to the optimizer's "bag of tricks" and we get a more competent compiler. When our compiler knows enough tricks, we deem it *mature*.

This theorem, that for any optimizing compiler there exists a better one, is known as the *full employment theorem for compiler writers*.

17.1   INTERMEDIATE REPRESENTATION FOR FLOW ANALYSIS

In this chapter we will consider *intraprocedural global optimization*. *Intraprocedural* means the analysis stays within a single procedure or function (of a language like MiniJava); *global* means that the analysis spans all the statements or basic blocks within that procedure. *Interprocedural* optimization is more global, operating on several procedures and functions at once.

Each of the optimizing transformations listed at the beginning of the chapter can be applied using the following generic recipe:

Dataflow analysis: Traverse the flow graph, gathering information about what may happen at run time (this will necessarily be a conservative approximation).

Transformation: Modify the program to make it faster in some way; the information gathered by analysis will guarantee that the program's result is unchanged.

There are many dataflow analyses that can provide useful information for optimizing transformations. Like the *liveness analysis* described in Chapter 10, most can be described by *dataflow equations*, a set of simultaneous equations derived from nodes in the flow graph.

QUADRUPLES

Chapter 10's liveness analysis operates on `Assem` instructions, which clearly indicate *uses* and *defs* but whose actual operations are machine-dependent assembly-language strings. Liveness analysis, and register allocation based on it, do not need to know what operations the instructions are performing, just their uses and definitions. But for the analyses and optimizations in this chapter, we need to understand the *operations* as well. Therefore, instead of `Assem` instructions we will use `Tree`-language terms (Section 7.2), simplified even further by ensuring that each Exp has only a single MEM or BINOP node.

We can easily turn ordinary `Tree` expressions into simplified ones. Wherever there is a nested expression of one BINOP or MEM inside another, or a BINOP or MEM inside a JUMP or CJUMP, we introduce a new temporary using ESEQ:

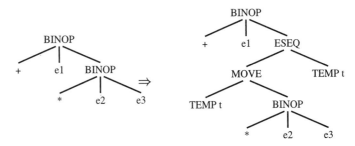

and then apply the `Canon` module to remove all the ESEQ nodes.

We also introduce new temporaries to ensure that any *store* statement (that

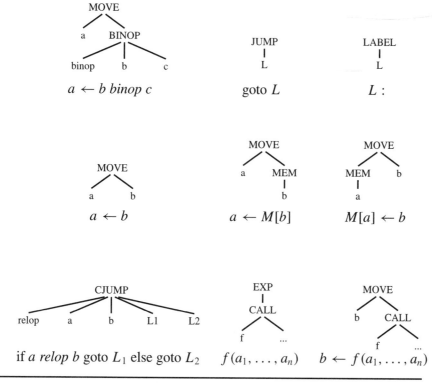

| TABLE 17.1. | Quadruples expressed in the `Tree` language. Occurrences of a, b, c, f, L denote TEMP, CONST, or LABEL nodes only. |

is, a MOVE whose left-hand side is a MEM node) has only a TEMP or a CONST on its right-hand side, and only a TEMP or CONST under the MEM.

The statements that remain are all quite simple; they take one of the forms shown in Table 17.1.

Because the "typical" statement is $a \leftarrow b \oplus c$ with four components $(a, b, c, \oplus)$, these simple statements are often called *quadruples*. We use $\oplus$ to stand for an arbitrary *binop*.

A more efficient compiler would represent quadruples with their own data type (instead of using `Tree` data structures), and would translate from trees to quadruples all in one pass.

Intraprocedural optimizations take these quadruples that come out of the `Canon` phase of the compiler, and transform them into a new set of quadruples. The optimizer may move, insert, delete, and modify the quadruples. The resulting procedure body must then be fed into the instruction-selection phase of the compiler. However, the tree matching will not be very effective on the "atomized" trees where each expression contains only one BINOP or MOVE. After the optimizations are completed, there will be many MOVE statements that define temporaries that are used only once. It will be necessary to find these and turn them back into nested expressions.

We make a control flow graph of the quadruples, with a directed edge from each node (statement) n to its successors – that is, the nodes that can execute immediately after n.

17.2 VARIOUS DATAFLOW ANALYSES

A dataflow analysis of a control flow graph of quadruples collects information about the execution of the program. One dataflow analysis determines how definitions and uses are related to each other, another estimates what values a variable might have at a given point, and so on. The results of these analyses can be used to make optimizing transformations of the program.

REACHING DEFINITIONS

For many optimizations we need to see if a particular assignment to a temporary t can directly affect the value of t at another point in the program. We say that an *unambiguous definition* of t is a particular statement (quadruple) in the program of the form $t \leftarrow a \oplus b$ or $t \leftarrow M[a]$. Given such a definition d, we say that d *reaches* a statement u in the program if there is some path of control-flow edges from d to u that does not contain any unambiguous definition of t.

An *ambiguous* definition is a statement that might or might not assign a value to t. For example, if t is a global variable, and the statement s is a CALL to a function that sometimes modifies t but sometimes does not, then s is an ambiguous definition. But our MiniJava compiler treats escaping variables as memory locations, not as temporaries subject to dataflow analysis. This means that we never have ambiguous definitions; unfortunately, we also lose the opportunity to perform optimizations on escaping variables. For the remainder of this chapter, we will assume all definitions are unambiguous.

We can express the calculation of reaching definitions as the solution of dataflow equations. We label every MOVE statement with a definition ID, and we manipulate sets of definition IDs. We say that the statement $d_1 : t \leftarrow x \oplus y$ *generates* the definition d_1, because no matter what other definitions reach the

Statement s	$gen[s]$	$kill[s]$
$d: t \leftarrow b \oplus c$	$\{d\}$	$defs(t) - \{d\}$
$d: t \leftarrow M[b]$	$\{d\}$	$defs(t) - \{d\}$
$M[a] \leftarrow b$	$\{\}$	$\{\}$
if a relop b goto L_1 else goto L_2	$\{\}$	$\{\}$
goto L	$\{\}$	$\{\}$
$L:$	$\{\}$	$\{\}$
$f(a_1, \ldots, a_n)$	$\{\}$	$\{\}$
$d: t \leftarrow f(a_1, \ldots, a_n)$	$\{d\}$	$defs(t) - \{d\}$

TABLE 17.2.   *Gen* and *kill* for reaching definitions.

beginning of this statement, we know that d_1 reaches the end of it. And we say that this statement *kills* any other definition of t, because no matter what other definitions of t reach the beginning of the statement, they do not reach the end (they cannot directly affect the value of t after this statement).

Let us define $defs(t)$ as the set of all definitions (or definition IDs) of the temporary t. Table 17.2 summarizes the *generate* and *kill* effects of the different kinds of quadruples.

Using *gen* and *kill*, we can compute $in[n]$ (and $out[n]$) the set of definitions that reach the beginning (and end) of each node n:

$$in[n] = \bigcup_{p \in pred[n]} out[p]$$
$$out[n] = gen[n] \cup (in[n] - kill[n])$$

These equations can be solved by iteration: First $in[n]$ and $out[n]$ are initialized to the empty set, for all n; then the equations are treated as assignment statements and repeatedly executed until there are no changes.

We will take Program 17.3 as an example; it is annotated with statement numbers that will also serve as definition IDs. In each iteration, we recalculate *in* and *out* for each statement in turn:

1 : $a \leftarrow 5$
2 : $c \leftarrow 1$
3 : L_1 : if $c > a$ goto L_2
4 : $c \leftarrow c + c$
5 :   goto L_1
6 : L_2 : $a \leftarrow c - a$
7 : $c \leftarrow 0$

PROGRAM 17.3.

---

n	$gen[n]$	$kill[n]$	Iter. 1		Iter. 2		Iter. 3	
			$in[n]$	$out[n]$	$in[n]$	$out[n]$	$in[n]$	$out[n]$
1	1	6		1		1		1
2	2	4,7	1	1,2	1	1,2	1	1,2
3			1,2	1,2	1,2,4	1,2,4	1,2,4	1,2,4
4	4	2,7	1,2	1,4	1,2,4	1,4	1,2,4	1,4
5			1,4	1,4	1,4	1,4	1,4	1,4
6	6	1	1,2	2,6	1,2,4	2,4,6	1,2,4	2,4,6
7	7	2,4	2,6	6,7	2,4,6	6,7	2,4,6	6,7

Iteration 3 serves merely to discover that nothing changed since iteration 2.

Having computed reaching definitions, what can we do with the information? The analysis is useful in several kinds of optimization. As a simple example, we can do *constant propagation:* Only one definition of a reaches statement 3, so we can replace the test $c > a$ with $c > 5$.

AVAILABLE EXPRESSIONS

Suppose we want to do *common-subexpression elimination*; that is, given a program that computes $x \oplus y$ more than once, can we eliminate one of the duplicate computations? To find places where such optimizations are possible, the notion of *available expressions* is helpful.

An expression $x \oplus y$ is *available* at a node n in the flow graph if, on every path from the entry node of the graph to node n, $x \oplus y$ is computed at least once *and* there are no definitions of x or y since the most recent occurrence of $x \oplus y$ on that path.

We can express this in dataflow equations using *gen* and *kill* sets, where the sets are now sets of expressions.

Statement s	$gen[s]$	$kill[s]$
$t \leftarrow b \oplus c$	$\{b \oplus c\} - kill[s]$	*expressions containing t*
$t \leftarrow M[b]$	$\{M[b]\} - kill[s]$	*expressions containing t*
$M[a] \leftarrow b$	$\{\}$	*expressions of the form M[x]*
if $a > b$ goto L_1 else goto L_2	$\{\}$	$\{\}$
goto L	$\{\}$	$\{\}$
$L :$	$\{\}$	$\{\}$
$f(a_1, \ldots, a_n)$	$\{\}$	*expressions of the form M[x]*
$t \leftarrow f(a_1, \ldots, a_n)$	$\{\}$	*expressions containing t, and expressions of the form M[x]*

TABLE 17.4.   *Gen* and *kill* for available expressions.

Any node that computes $x \oplus y$ *generates* $\{x \oplus y\}$, and any definition of x or y *kills* $\{x \oplus y\}$; see Table 17.4.

Basically, $t \leftarrow b + c$ generates the expression $b + c$. But $b \leftarrow b + c$ does not generate $b + c$, because after $b + c$ there is a subsequent definition of b. The statement $gen[s] = \{b \oplus c\} - kill[s]$ takes care of this subtlety.

A *store* instruction ($M[a] \leftarrow b$) might modify any memory location, so it kills any *fetch* expression ($M[x]$). If we were sure that $a \neq x$, we could be less conservative, and say that $M[a] \leftarrow b$ does not kill $M[x]$. This is called *alias analysis*; see Section 17.5.

Given *gen* and *kill*, we compute *in* and *out* almost as for reaching definitions, except that we compute the *intersection* of the *out* sets of the predecessors instead of a union. This reflects the fact that an expression is available only if it is computed on *every* path into the node.

$$in[n] = \bigcap_{p \in pred[n]} out[p] \qquad \text{if } n \text{ is not the start node}$$
$$out[n] = gen[n] \cup (in[n] - kill[n])$$

To compute this by iteration, we define the *in* set of the start node as empty, and initialize all other sets to *full* (the set of all expressions), not empty. This is because the intersection operator makes sets *smaller*, not bigger as the union operator does in the computation of reaching definitions. This algorithm then finds the *greatest* fixed point of the equations.

REACHING EXPRESSIONS

We say that an expression $t \leftarrow x \oplus y$ (in node s of the flow graph) reaches node n if there is a path from s to n that does not go through any assignment to x or y, or through any computation of $x \oplus y$. As usual, we can express *gen* and *kill*; see Exercise 17.1.

In practice, the *reaching expressions* analysis is needed by the *common-subexpression elimination* optimization only for a small subset of all the expressions in a program. Thus, reaching expressions are usually computed ad hoc, by searching backward from node n and stopping whenever a computation $x \oplus y$ is found. Or reaching expressions can be computed during the calculation of available expressions; see Exercise 17.4.

LIVENESS ANALYSIS

Chapter 10 has already covered liveness analysis, but it is useful to note that liveness can also be expressed in terms of *gen* and *kill*. Any use of a variable generates liveness, and any definition kills liveness:

Statement s	$gen[s]$	$kill[s]$
$t \leftarrow b \oplus c$	$\{b, c\}$	$\{t\}$
$t \leftarrow M[b]$	$\{b\}$	$\{t\}$
$M[a] \leftarrow b$	$\{a, b\}$	$\{\}$
if $a > b$ goto L_1 else goto L_2	$\{a, b\}$	$\{\}$
goto L	$\{\}$	$\{\}$
$L:$	$\{\}$	$\{\}$
$f(a_1, \ldots, a_n)$	$\{a_1, \ldots, a_n\}$	$\{\}$
$t \leftarrow f(a_1, \ldots, a_n)$	$\{a_1, \ldots, a_n\}$	$\{t\}$

The equations for *in* and *out* are similar to the ones for reaching definitions and available expressions, but *backward* because liveness is a *backward* dataflow analysis:

$$in[n] = gen[n] \cup (out[n] - kill[n])$$
$$out[n] = \bigcup_{s \in succ[n]} in[s]$$

TRANSFORMATIONS USING DATAFLOW ANALYSIS

Using the results of dataflow analysis, the optimizing compiler can improve the program in several ways.

COMMON-SUBEXPRESSION ELIMINATION

Given a flow-graph statement $s : t \leftarrow x \oplus y$, where the expression $x \oplus y$ is *available* at s, the computation within s can be eliminated.

Algorithm. Compute *reaching expressions*, that is, find statements of the form $n : v \leftarrow x \oplus y$, such that the path from n to s does not compute $x \oplus y$ or define x or y.

Choose a new temporary w, and for such n, rewrite as

$$n : w \leftarrow x \oplus y$$
$$n' : v \leftarrow w$$

Finally, modify statement s to be

$$s : t \leftarrow w$$

We will rely on copy propagation to remove some or all of the extra assignment quadruples.

CONSTANT PROPAGATION

Suppose we have a statement $d : t \leftarrow c$, where c is a constant, and another statement n that uses t, such as $n : y \leftarrow t \oplus x$.

We know that t is constant in n if d reaches n, and no other definitions of t reach n.

In this case, we can rewrite n as $y \leftarrow c \oplus x$.

COPY PROPAGATION

This is like constant propagation, but instead of a constant c we have a variable z.

Suppose we have a statement $d : t \leftarrow z$. and another statement n that uses t, such as $n : y \leftarrow t \oplus x$.

If d reaches n, and no other definition of t reaches n, and there is no definition of z on any path from d to n (including a path that goes through n one or more times), then we can rewrite n as $n : y \leftarrow z \oplus x$.

A good graph-coloring register allocator will do *coalescing* (see Chapter 11), which is a form of copy propagation. It detects any intervening definitions of z in constructing the interference graph – an assignment to z while d is live makes an interference edge (z, d), rendering d and z uncoalesceable.

If we do copy propagation before register allocation, then we may increase the number of spills. Thus, if our only reason to do copy propagation were to delete redundant MOVE instructions, we should wait until register allocation. However, copy propagation at the quadruple stage may enable the recognition of other optimizations such as common-subexpression elimination. For example, in the program

$$a \leftarrow y + z$$
$$u \leftarrow y$$
$$c \leftarrow u + z$$

the two $+$-expressions are not recognized as common subexpressions until after the copy propagation of $u \leftarrow y$ is performed.

DEAD-CODE ELIMINATION

If there is a quadruple $s : a \leftarrow b \oplus c$ or $s : a \leftarrow M[x]$, such that a is not *live-out* of s, then the quadruple can be deleted.

Some instructions have implicit side effects. For example, if the computer is configured to raise an exception on an arithmetic overflow or divide by zero, then deletion of an exception-causing instruction will change the result of the computation.

The optimizer should never make a change that changes program behavior, even if the change seems benign (such as the removal of a run-time "error"). The problem with such optimizations is that the programmer cannot predict the behavior of the program – and a program debugged with the optimizer enabled may fail with the optimizer disabled.

17.4   SPEEDING UP DATAFLOW ANALYSIS

Many dataflow analyses – including the ones described in this chapter – can be expressed using simultaneous equations on finite sets. So also can many of the algorithms used in constructing finite automata (Chapter 2) and parsers (Chapter 3). The equations can usually be set up so that they can be solved by *iteration*: by treating the equations as assignment statements and repeatedly executing all the assignments until none of the sets changes any more.

There are several ways to speed up the evaluation of dataflow equations.

BIT VECTORS

A set S over a finite domain (that is, where the elements are integers in the range $1 - N$ or can be put in an array indexed by $1 - N$) can be represented by a *bit vector*. The ith bit in the vector is a 1 if the element i is in the set S.

In the bit-vector representation, unioning two sets S and T is done by a bitwise-*or* of the bit vectors. If the word size of the computer is W, and the vectors are N bits long, then a sequence of N/W *or* instructions can union two sets. Of course, $2N/W$ fetches and N/W stores will also be necessary, as well as indexing and loop overhead.

Intersection can be done by bitwise-*and*, set complement can be done by bitwise complement, and so on.

Thus, the bit-vector representation is commonly used for dataflow analysis. It would be inadvisable to use bit vectors for dataflow problems where the sets are expected to be very sparse (so the bit vectors would be almost all zeros), in which case a different implementation of sets would be faster.

BASIC BLOCKS

Suppose we have a node n in the flow graph that has only one predecessor, p, and p has only one successor, n. Then we can combine the *gen* and *kill* effects of p and n and replace nodes n and p with a single node. We will take *reaching definitions* as an example, but almost any dataflow analysis permits a similar kind of combining.

Consider what definitions reach *out* of the node n:

$$out[n] = gen[n] \cup (in[n] - kill[n]).$$

We know $in[n]$ is just $out[p]$; therefore

$$out[n] = gen[n] \cup ((gen[p] \cup (in[p] - kill[p])) - kill[n]).$$

By using the identity $(A \cup B) - C = (A - C) \cup (B - C)$ and then $(A - B) - C = A - (B \cup C)$, we have

$$out[n] = gen[n] \cup (gen[p] - kill[n]) \cup (in[p] - (kill[p] \cup kill[n])).$$

If we want to say that node pn combines the effects of p and n, then this last equation says that the appropriate *gen* and *kill* sets for *pn* are

$$gen[pn] = gen[n] \cup (gen[p] - kill[n])$$
$$kill[pn] = kill[p] \cup kill[n].$$

We can combine all the statements of a basic block in this way, and agglomerate the *gen* and *kill* effects of the whole block. The control-flow graph of basic blocks is much smaller than the graph of individual statements, so the multipass iterative dataflow analysis works much faster on basic blocks.

Once the iterative dataflow analysis algorithm is completed, we may recover the dataflow information of an individual statement (such as *n*) within a block (such as *pn* in our example) by starting with the *in* set computed for the entire block and – in one pass – applying the *gen* and *kill* sets of the statements that precede *n* in the block.

ORDERING THE NODES

In a *forward* dataflow problem (such as reaching definitions or available expressions), the information coming *out* of a node goes *in* to the successors. If we could arrange that every node was calculated before its successors, the dataflow analysis would terminate in one pass through the nodes.

This would be possible if the control-flow graph had no cycles. We would *topologically sort* the flow graph – this just gives an ordering where each node comes before its successors – and then compute the dataflow equations in sorted order. But often the graph will have cycles, so this simple idea won't work. Even so, quasi-topologically sorting a cyclic graph by depth-first search helps to reduce the number of iterations required on cyclic graphs; in quasi-sorted order, most nodes come before their successors, so information flows forward quite far through the equations on each iteration.

Depth-first search (Algorithm 17.5) topologically sorts an acyclic graph graph, or quasi-topologically sorts a cyclic graph, quite efficiently. Using *sorted*, the order computed by depth-first search, the iterative solution of dataflow equations should be computed as

> **repeat**
>   **for** $i \leftarrow 1$ **to** N
> $n \leftarrow sorted[i]$
> $in \leftarrow \bigcup_{p \in pred[n]} out[p]$
> $out[n] \leftarrow gen[n] \cup (in - kill[n])$
> **until** no *out* set changed in this iteration

Topological-sort:
$N \leftarrow$ *number of nodes*
for all nodes i
    $mark[i] \leftarrow false$
DFS(*start-node*)

function DFS(i)
    if $mark[i] = false$
        $mark[i] \leftarrow true$
        for each successor s of node i
            DFS(s)
        $sorted[N] \leftarrow i$
        $N \leftarrow N - 1$

ALGORITHM 17.5.   Topological sort by depth-first search.

There is no need to make *in* a global array, since it is used only locally in computing *out*.

For *backward* dataflow problems such as liveness analysis, we use a version of Algorithm 17.5, starting from *exit-node* instead of *start-node*, and traversing *predecessor* instead of *successor* edges.

USE-DEF AND DEF-USE CHAINS

Information about reaching definitions can be kept as *use-def chains*, that is, for each use of a variable x, a list of the definitions of x reaching that use. Use-def chains do not allow faster dataflow analysis per se, but allow efficient implementation of the optimization algorithms that use the results of the analysis.

A generalization of use-def chains is *static single-assignment form*, described in Chapter 19. SSA form not only provides more information than use-def chains, but the dataflow analysis that computes it is very efficient.

One way to represent the results of liveness analysis is via *def-use chains*: a list, for each definition, of all possible uses of that definition. SSA form also contains def-use information.

WORK-LIST ALGORITHMS

If any *out* set changes during an iteration of the **repeat-until** loop of an iterative solver, then all the equations are recalculated. This seems a pity, since most of the equations may not be affected by the change.

A *work-list* algorithm keeps track of just which *out* sets must be recalculated. Whenever node n is recalculated *and its out set is found to change*, all the successors of n are put onto the work list (if they're not on it already). This is illustrated in Algorithm 17.6.

$W \leftarrow$ the set of all nodes
while W is not empty
  remove a node n from W
  $old \leftarrow out[n]$
  $in \leftarrow \bigcup_{p \in pred[n]} out[p]$
  $out[n] \leftarrow gen[n] \cup (in - kill[n])$
  if $old \neq out[n]$
    for each successor s of n
      if $s \notin W$
        put s into W

ALGORITHM 17.6. A work-list algorithm for reaching definitions.

The algorithm will converge faster if, whenever a node is removed from W for processing, we choose the node in W that occurs earliest in the *sorted* array produced by Algorithm 17.5.

The coalescing, graph-coloring register allocator described in Chapter 11 is an example of a work-list algorithm with many different work lists. Section 19.3 describes a work-list algorithm for constant propagation.

INCREMENTAL DATAFLOW ANALYSIS

Using the results of dataflow analysis, the optimizer can perform program transformations: moving, modifying, or deleting instructions. But optimizations can cascade:

- Removal of the dead code $a \leftarrow b \oplus c$ might cause b to become dead in a previous instruction $b \leftarrow x \oplus y$.
- One common-subexpression elimination begets another. In the program

$$x \leftarrow b + c$$
$$y \leftarrow a + x$$
$$u \leftarrow b + c$$
$$v \leftarrow a + u$$

after $u \leftarrow b + c$ is replaced by $u \leftarrow x$, copy propagation changes $a + u$ to $a + x$, which is a common subexpression and can be eliminated.

A simple way to organize a dataflow-based optimizer is to perform a global flow analysis, then make all possible dataflow-based optimizations, then repeat the global flow analysis, then perform optimizations, and so on until no more optimizations can be found. At best this iterates two or three times, so that on the third round there are no more transformations to perform.

But the worst case is very bad indeed. Consider a program in which the statement $z \leftarrow a_1 + a_2 + a_3 + \cdots + a_n$ occurs where z is dead. This translates into the quadruples

$$
\begin{aligned}
x_1 &\leftarrow a_1 + a_2 \\
x_2 &\leftarrow x_1 + a_3 \\
&\vdots \\
x_{n-2} &\leftarrow x_{n-3} + a_{n-1} \\
z &\leftarrow x_{n-2} + a_n
\end{aligned}
$$

Liveness analysis determines that z is dead; then dead-code elimination removes the definition of z. Then another round of liveness analysis determines that x_{n-2} is dead, and then dead-code elimination removes x_{n-2}, and so on. It takes n rounds of analysis and optimization to remove x_1 and then determine that there is no more work to do.

A similar situation occurs with common-subexpression elimination, when there are two occurrences of an expression such as $a_1 + a_2 + a_3 + \cdots + a_n$ in the program.

To avoid the need for repeated, global calculations of dataflow information, there are several strategies:

Cutoff: Perform no more than k rounds of analysis and optimization, for $k = 3$ or so. Later rounds of optimization may not be finding many transformations to do anyway. This is a rather unsophisticated approach, but at least the compilation will terminate in a reasonable time.

Cascading analysis: Design new dataflow analyses that can predict the cascade effects of the optimizations that will be done.

Incremental dataflow analysis: When the optimizer makes a program transformation – which renders the dataflow information invalid – instead of discarding the dataflow information, the optimizer should "patch" it.

Value numbering. The *value-numbering* analysis is an example of a cascading analysis that, in one pass, finds all the (cascaded) common subexpressions within a basic block.

The algorithm maintains a table T, mapping *variables* to *value numbers*, and also mapping triples of the form (*value number, operator, value number*) to value numbers. For efficiency, T should be represented as a hash table. There is also a global number N counting how many distinct values have been seen so far.

$T \leftarrow empty$
$N \leftarrow 0$
for each quadruple $a \leftarrow b \oplus c$ in the block
   if $(b \mapsto k) \in T$ for some k
     $n_b \leftarrow k$
   else
     $N \leftarrow N + 1$
     $n_b \leftarrow N$
     put $b \mapsto n_b$ into T
   if $(c \mapsto k) \in T$ for some k
     $n_c \leftarrow k$
   else
     $N \leftarrow N + 1$
     $n_c \leftarrow N$
     put $c \mapsto n_c$ into T
   if $((n_b, \oplus, n_c) \mapsto m) \in T$ for some m
     put $a \mapsto m$ into T
     mark this quadruple $a \leftarrow b \oplus c$ as a common subexpression
   else
     $N \leftarrow N + 1$
     put $(n_b, \oplus, n_c) \mapsto N$ into T
     put $a \mapsto N$ into T

ALGORITHM 17.7.   Value numbering.

Using T and N, the value-numbering algorithm (Algorithm 17.7) scans the quadruples of a block from beginning to end. Whenever it sees an expression $b + c$, it looks up the value number of b and the value number of c. It then looks up hash($n_b, n_c, +$) in T; if found, it means that $b + c$ repeats the work of an earlier computation; we mark $b + c$ for deletion, and use the previously computed result. If not found, we leave $b + c$ in the program and also enter it in the hash table.

Figure 17.8 illustrates value numbering on a basic block: (a) is the list of quadruples, and (b) is the table (after the algorithm is finished). We can view the table as a directed acyclic graph (DAG), if we view an entry $(m, \oplus, n) \mapsto q$ as a node q with edges to nodes m and n, as shown in Figure 17.8c.

Value numbering is an example of a single dataflow analysis that calculates the effect of cascaded optimizations: in this case, cascaded common-

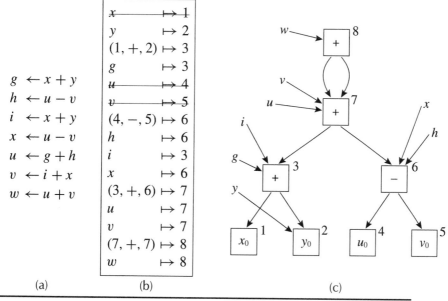

$$g \leftarrow x + y$$
$$h \leftarrow u - v$$
$$i \leftarrow x + y$$
$$x \leftarrow u - v$$
$$u \leftarrow g + h$$
$$v \leftarrow i + x$$
$$w \leftarrow u + v$$

x	$\mapsto 1$
y	$\mapsto 2$
$(1, +, 2)$	$\mapsto 3$
g	$\mapsto 3$
u	$\mapsto 4$
v	$\mapsto 5$
$(4, -, 5)$	$\mapsto 6$
h	$\mapsto 6$
i	$\mapsto 3$
x	$\mapsto 6$
$(3, +, 6)$	$\mapsto 7$
u	$\mapsto 7$
v	$\mapsto 7$
$(7, +, 7)$	$\mapsto 8$
w	$\mapsto 8$

(a) (b) (c)

FIGURE 17.8. An illustration of value numbering. (a) A basic block; (b) the table created by the value-numbering algorithm, with hidden bindings shown crossed out; (c) a view of the table as a DAG.

subexpression elimination. But the optimizer would like to perform a wide variety of transformations – especially when the loop optimizations described in the next chapter are included. It is very hard to design a single dataflow analysis capable of predicting the results of many different optimizations in combination.

Instead, we use a general-purpose dataflow analyzer and a general-purpose optimizer; but when the optimizer changes the program, it must tell the analyzer what information is no longer valid.

Incremental liveness analysis. For example, an incremental algorithm for liveness analysis must keep enough information so that if a statement is inserted or deleted, the liveness information can be efficiently updated.

Suppose we delete this statement $s : a \leftarrow b \oplus c$ from a flow graph on which we have *live-in* and *live-out* information for every node. The changes to the dataflow information are as follows:

1. a is no longer defined here. Therefore, if a is *live-out* of this node, it will now be *live-in* where it was not before.

2. b is no longer used here. Therefore, if b is not *live-out* of this node, it will no longer be *live-in*. We must propagate this change backwards, and do the same for c.

A work-list algorithm will be useful here, since we can just add the predecessor of s to the work list and run until the work list is empty; this will often terminate quickly.

Propagating change (1) does the same kind of thing that the original (nonincremental) work-list algorithm for liveness does: It makes the live-sets bigger. Thus, our proof (Exercise 10.2) that the algorithm finds a least fixed point of the liveness equations also applies to the propagation of additional liveness caused by the deletion of the definition of a. Even the proof that the liveness analysis terminates was based on the idea that any change makes things bigger, and there was an a priori limit to how big the sets could get.

But change (2) makes live-sets smaller, not bigger, so naively running our original algorithm starting from the previously computed *in* and *out* sets may find a fixed point that is not a least fixed point. For example, suppose we have the following program:

0	$d \leftarrow 4$
1	$a \leftarrow 0$
2	$L_1 : b \leftarrow a + 1$
3	$c \leftarrow c + b$
3a	$a \leftarrow d$
4	$a \leftarrow b \cdot 2$
5	if $a < N$ goto L_1
6	return c

Liveness analysis shows that d is *live-in* at statements 1, 2, 3, 3a, 4, 5. But a is not *live-out* of statement 3a, so this statement is dead code, and we can delete it. If we then start with the previously computed dataflow information and use Algorithm 10.4 (page 206) until it reaches a fixed point, we will end up with the column Y of Table 10.7, which is not the best possible approximation of the actual liveness information.

A more refined liveness analysis. Therefore, we must use a better algorithm. The solution is that at each point where a variable d is defined, we must keep track of exactly what uses it might have. Our liveness calculation will be very much like Algorithm 10.4, but it will operate on sets of *uses* instead of sets of *variables*. In fact, it is just like the reaching definitions algorithm in reverse. Let $uses(v)$ be the set of all uses of variable v in the program. Given a statement $s : a \leftarrow b \oplus c$, the set

$$live\text{-}out[s] \cap uses(a)$$

contains all the uses of *a* that could possibly be reached by this definition.

Now, when we delete a quadruple that uses some variable *b*, we can delete that use of *b* from all the *live-in* and *live-out* sets. This gives the least fixed point, as we desire.

Cascades of dead code After deleting statement 3a from the program above, the incremental liveness analysis will find that statement 0 is dead code and can be deleted. Thus, incremental liveness analysis cooperates well with dead-code elimination. Other kinds of dataflow analysis can similarly be made incremental; sometimes, as in the case of liveness analysis, we must first refine the analysis.

17.5   ALIAS ANALYSIS

The analyses we have described in this chapter consider only the values of Tree-language temporaries. Variables that *escape* are represented (by the front end of the compiler) in memory locations with explicit fetches and stores, and we have not tried to analyze the definitions, uses, and liveness of these variables. The problem is that a variable or memory location may have several different names, or *aliases*, so that it is hard to tell which statements affect which variables.

Variables that can be aliases include:

- variables passed as call-by-reference parameters (in Pascal, C++, Fortran);
- variables whose address is taken (in C, C++);
- *l*-value expressions that dereference pointers, such as p.x in MiniJava or *p in C;
- *l*-value expressions that explicitly subscript arrays, such as a[i];
- and variables used in inner-nested procedures (in Pascal, MiniJava, ML).

A good optimizer should optimize these variables. For example, in the program fragment

```
p.x := 5; q.x := 7; a := p.x
```

we might want our *reaching definitions* analysis to show that only one definition of p.x (namely, 5) reaches the definition of a. But the problem is that we cannot tell if one name is an alias for another. Could q point to the same record as p? If so, there are two definitions (5 and 7) that could reach a.

Similarly, with call-by-reference parameters, in the program

```
function f( ref i: int,  ref j: int) =
   (i := 5; j := 7; return i)
```

a naive computation of reaching definitions would miss the fact that i might be the same variable as j, if f is called with f(x,x).

The may-alias relation We use *alias analysis*, a kind of dataflow analysis, to learn about different names that may point to the same memory locations. The result of alias analysis is a *may-alias* relation: p may-alias q if, in some run of the program, p and q might point to the same data. As with most dataflow analyses, static (compile-time) information cannot be completely accurate, so the may-alias relation is conservative: We say that p may-alias q if we cannot prove that p is never an alias for q.

ALIAS ANALYSIS BASED ON TYPES

For languages with *strong typing* (such as Pascal, Java, ML, MiniJava) where if two variables have incompatible types they cannot possibly be names for the same memory location, we can use the type information to provide a useful may-alias relation. Also in these languages the programmer cannot explicitly make a pointer point to a local variable, and we will use that fact as well.

We divide all the memory locations used by the program into disjoint sets, called *alias classes*. For MiniJava, here are the classes we will use:

- For every frame location created by Frame.allocLocal(true), we have a new class;
- For every record field of every record type, a new class;
- For every array type a, a new class.

The semantic analysis phase of the compiler must compute these classes, as they involve the concept of *type*, of which the later phases are ignorant. Each class can be represented by a different integer.

The Translate functions must label every fetch and store (that is, every MEM node in the Tree language) with its class. We will need to modify the Tree data structure, putting an aliasClass field into the MEM node.

Given two MEM nodes $M_i[x]$ and $M_j[y]$, where i and j are the alias classes of the MEM nodes, we can say that $M_i[x]$ may-alias $M_j[y]$ if $i = j$.

This works for MiniJava and Java. But it fails in the presence of call-by-reference or type casting.

```
type list = {head: int,        {int *p, *q;
             tail: list}         int h,i;
var p : list := nil             p = &h;
var q : list := nil             q = &i;
q := list{head=0, tail=nil};    *p = 0;
p := list{head=0, tail=q};      *q = 5;
q.head := 5;                    a = *p;
a := p.head                    }
```

(a) MiniJava program   (b) C program

PROGRAM 17.9.   p and q are not aliases.

ALIAS ANALYSIS BASED ON FLOW

Instead of, or in addition to, alias classes based on types, we can also make alias classes based on *point of creation.*

In Program 17.9a, even though p and q are the same type, we know they point to different records. Therefore we know that a must be assigned 0; the definition q.head:=5 cannot affect a. Similarly, in Program 17.9b we know p and q cannot be aliases, so a must be 0.

To catch these distinctions automatically, we will make an alias class for each point of creation. That is, for every different statement where a record is allocated (that is, for each call to `malloc` in C or `new` in Pascal or Java) we make a new alias class. Also, each different local or global variable whose address is taken is an alias class.

A pointer (or call-by-reference parameter) can point to variables of more than one alias class. In the program

```
1  p := list {head=0, tail=nil};
2  q := list {head=6, tail=p};
3  if a=0
4        then p:=q;
5  p.head := 4;
```

at line 5, q can point only to alias class 2, but p might point to alias class 1 or 2, depending on the value of a.

So we must associate with each MEM node a set of alias classes, not just a single class. After line 2 we have the information $p \mapsto \{1\}, q \mapsto \{2\}$; out of line 4 we have $p \mapsto \{2\}, q \mapsto \{2\}$. But when two branches of control flow merge (in the example, we have the control edges $3 \rightarrow 5$ and $4 \rightarrow 5$) we must merge the alias class information; at line 5 we have $p \mapsto \{1, 2\}, q \mapsto \{2\}$.

Statement s	$trans_s(A)$
$t \leftarrow b$	$(A - \Sigma_t) \cup \{(t, d, k) \mid (b, d, k) \in A\}$
$t \leftarrow b + k$ (k is a constant)	$(A - \Sigma_t) \cup \{(t, d, i) \mid (b, d, i - k) \in A\}$
$t \leftarrow b \oplus c$	$(A - \Sigma_t) \cup \{(t, d, i) \mid (b, d, j) \in A \vee (c, d, k) \in A\}$
$t \leftarrow M[b]$	$A \cup \Sigma_t$
$M[a] \leftarrow b$	A
if $a > b$ goto L_1 else L_2	A
goto L	A
$L:$	A
$f(a_1, \ldots, a_n)$	A
$d : t \leftarrow \texttt{allocRecord}(a)$	$(A - \Sigma_t) \cup \{(t, d, 0)\}$
$t \leftarrow f(a_1, \ldots, a_n)$	$A \cup \Sigma_t$

TABLE 17.10.   Transfer function for alias flow analysis.

Algorithm. The dataflow algorithm manipulates sets of tuples of the form (t, d, k) where t is a variable and d, k is the alias class of all instances of the kth field of a record allocated at location d. The set $in[s]$ contains (t, d, k) if $t - k$ might point to a record of alias class d at the beginning of statement s. This is an example of a dataflow problem where bit vectors will not work as well as a tree or hash-table representation better suited to sparse problems.

Instead of using *gen* and *kill* sets, we use a transfer function: We say that if A is the alias information (set of tuples) on entry to a statement s, then $trans_s(A)$ is the alias information on exit. The transfer function is defined by Table 17.10 for the different kinds of quadruples.

The initial set A_0 includes the binding (FP, *frame*,0), where *frame* is the special alias class of all frame-allocated variables of the current function.

We use the abbreviation Σ_t to mean the set of all tuples (t, d, k), where d, k is the alias class of any record field whose type is compatible with variable t. Cooperation from the front end in providing a "small" Σ_t for each t makes the analysis more accurate. Of course, in a typeless language, or one with type-casts, Σ_t might have to be the set of all alias classes.

The set equations for alias flow analysis are

$$in[s_0] = A_0 \quad \text{where } s_0 \text{ is the start node}$$
$$in[n] = \bigcup_{p \in pred[n]} out[p]$$
$$out[n] = trans_n(in[n])$$

and we can compute a solution by iteration in the usual way.

Producing may-alias information. Finally, we say that

p may-alias q at statement s

if there exists d, k such that $(p, d, k) \in in[s]$ and $(q, d, k) \in in[s]$.

USING MAY-ALIAS INFORMATION

Given the may-alias relation, we can treat each alias class as a "variable" in dataflow analyses such as reaching definitions and available expressions.

To take available expressions as an example, we modify one line of Table 17.4, the *gen* and *kill* sets:

Statement s	$gen[s]$	$kill[s]$
$M[a] \leftarrow b$	{}	$\{M[x] \mid a$ may alias x at $s\}$

Now we can analyze the following program fragment:

$$
\begin{array}{lll}
1: & u & \leftarrow M[t] \\
2: & M[x] & \leftarrow r \\
3: & w & \leftarrow M[t] \\
4: & b & \leftarrow u + w
\end{array}
$$

Without alias analysis, the store instruction in line 2 would *kill* the availability of $M[t]$, since we would not know whether t and x were related. But suppose alias analysis has determined that t may-alias x at 2 is *false*; then $M[t]$ is still available at line 3, and we can eliminate the common subexpression; after copy propagation, we obtain:

$$
\begin{array}{lll}
1: & z & \leftarrow M[t] \\
2: & M[x] & \leftarrow r \\
4: & b & \leftarrow z + z
\end{array}
$$

What we have shown here is intraprocedural alias analysis. But an interprocedural analysis would help to analyze the effect of CALL instructions. For example, in the program

$$
\begin{array}{lll}
1: & t & \leftarrow fp + 12 \\
2: & u & \leftarrow M[t] \\
3: & f(t) \\
4: & w & \leftarrow M[t] \\
5: & b & \leftarrow u + w
\end{array}
$$

does the function f modify $M[t]$? If so, then $M[t]$ is not available at line 4.

However, interprocedural alias analysis is beyond the scope of this book.

ALIAS ANALYSIS IN STRICT PURE-FUNCTIONAL LANGUAGES

Some languages have *immutable* variables that cannot change after their initialization. For example, **const** variables in the C language, most variables in the ML language, and all variables in PureFun-MiniJava (see Chapter 15) are immutable.

Alias analysis is not needed for these variables. The purpose of alias analysis is to determine whether different statements in the program interfere, or whether one definition *kills* another. Though it is true that there could be many pointers to the same value, none of the pointers can cause the value to change, i.e., no immutable variable can be killed.

This is a good thing for the optimizer, and also for the the programmer. The optimizer can do constant propagation and loop-invariant detection (see Chapter 18) without being bothered by aliases; and the programmer can also understand what a segment of the program is doing without the confusion and complexity introduced by stores through aliased pointers.

FURTHER READING

Gödel [1931] proved the *full employment theorem for mathematicians*. Turing [1937] proved that the halting problem is undecidable, and Rice [1953] proved the *full employment theorem for compiler writers*, even before there were any compiler writers.

Ershov [1958] developed value numbering. Allen [1969] codified many program optimizations; Allen [1970] and Cocke [1970] designed the first global dataflow analysis algorithms. Kildall [1973] first presented the fixed-point iteration method for dataflow analysis.

Landi and Ryder [1992] give an algorithm for interprocedural alias analysis.

EXERCISES

17.1 Show the dataflow equations for *reaching expressions* (page 358). Be specific about what happens in the case of quadruples such as $t \leftarrow t \oplus b$ or $t \leftarrow M[t]$, where the defined temporary also appears on the right-hand side. The elements of the *gen* and *kill* sets will be definition IDs, as in *reaching definitions*. **Hint:** If the definition on page 358 is not clear enough to formulate a precise definition, be guided by the role that reaching expressions must play in common-subexpression elimination (page 359).

17.2 Write down the control-flow graph of basic blocks (not just statements) for Program 17.3, and show the *gen* and *kill* sets (for reaching definitions) of each block.

*17.3 Show how to combine the *gen* and *kill* effects of two adjacent statements in the same basic block for each of:

a. Available expressions.

b. Liveness analysis.

17.4 Modify the algorithm for computing *available expressions* to simultaneously compute *reaching expressions*. To make the algorithm more efficient, you may take advantage of the fact that if an expression is not available at statement s, then we do not need to know if it reaches s or not (for purposes of common-subexpression elimination). **Hint: For each available expression $a + b$ that is propagated through statement s, also propagate a set representing all the statements that define $a + b$ and reach s.

17.5 Consider the calculation of *reaching definitions* on the following program:

```
x := 1;
y := 1;
if z <> 0
   then x := 2
   else y := 2;
w := x+y
```

a. Draw a control-flow graph for this program.

b. Show the *sorted* array that results from running Algorithm 17.5 on the program.

c. Calculate reaching definitions, showing the result of each iteration in tabular format as on page 356. How many iterations are required?

*d. Prove that when *reaching definitions* is computed by iteration on an acyclic graph, taking the nodes in the order given by Algorithm 17.5, only one iteration is necessary (the second iteration merely verifies that nothing has changed). **Hint:** Prove, and make use of, the lemma that each node is visited after all of its predecessors.

e. Suppose we order the nodes according to the order they are *first visited* by depth-first search. Calculate reaching definitions using that order, showing the results in tabular format; how many iterations are required?

*17.6 Write down a work-list algorithm for liveness analysis, in a form similar to that of Algorithm 17.6.

18

Loop Optimizations

loop: a series of instructions that is repeated until a terminating condition is reached

Webster's Dictionary

Loops are pervasive in computer programs, and a great proportion of the execution time of a typical program is spent in one loop or another. Hence it is worthwhile devising optimizations to make loops go faster. Intuitively, a loop is a sequence of instructions that ends by jumping back to the beginning. But to be able to optimize loops effectively we will use a more precise definition.

A *loop* in a control-flow graph is a set of nodes S including a *header* node h with the following properties:

- From any node in S there is a path of directed edges leading to h.
- There is a path of directed edges from h to any node in S.
- There is no edge from any node outside S to any node in S other than h.

Thus, the dictionary definition (from *Webster's*) is not the same as the technical definition.

Figure 18.1 shows some loops. A *loop entry* node is one with some predecessor outside the loop; a *loop exit* node is one with a successor outside the loop. Figures 18.1c, 18.1d, and 18.1f illustrate that a loop may have multiple exits, but may have only one entry. Figures 18.1e and 18.1f contain nested loops.

REDUCIBLE FLOW GRAPHS

A *reducible flow graph* is one in which the dictionary definition of *loop* corresponds more closely to the technical definition; but let us develop a more precise definition.

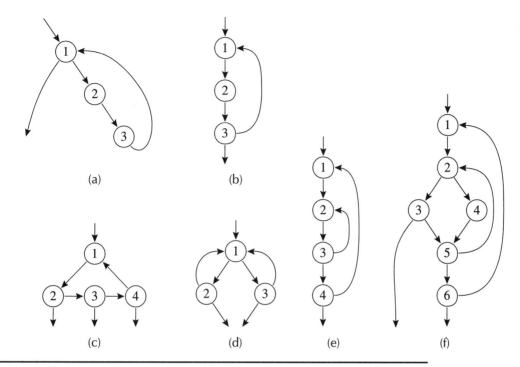

FIGURE 18.1. Some loops; in each case, 1 is the header node.

Figure 18.2a does not contain a loop; either node in the strongly connected component (2, 3) can be reached without going through the other.

Figure 18.2c contains the same pattern of nodes 1, 2, 3; this becomes more clear if we repeatedly delete edges and collapse together pairs of nodes (x, y), where x is the only predecessor of y. That is: Delete $6 \to 9$, $5 \to 4$, collapse $(7, 9)$, $(3, 7)$, $(7, 8)$, $(5, 6)$, $(1, 5)$, $(1, 4)$; and we obtain Figure 18.2a.

An *irreducible flow graph* is one in which – after collapsing nodes and deleting edges – we can find a subgraph like Figure 18.2a. A *reducible flow graph* is one that cannot be collapsed to contain such a subgraph. Without such subgraphs, then any cycle of nodes does have a unique header node.

Common control-flow constructs such as **if-then**, **if-then-else**, **while-do**, **repeat-until**, **for**, and **break** (even multilevel **break**) can only generate reducible flow graphs. Thus, the control-flow graph for a MiniJava or Java function, or a C function without **goto**, will always be reducible.

The following program corresponds to the flow graph in Figure 18.1e, assuming MiniJava were augmented with **repeat-until** loops:

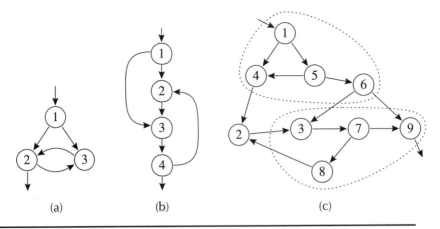

FIGURE 18.2.   None of these contains a loop. Dotted lines indicate reduction of graph (c) by deleting edges and collapsing nodes.

```
function isPrime(n: int) : int =
  (i := 2;
   repeat j := 2;
          repeat if i*j=n
                    then return 0
                    else j := j+1
          until j=n;
          i := i+1
   until i=n;
   return 1)
```

In a functional language, loops are generally expressed using tail-recursive function calls. The isPrime program might be written as:

```
    function isPrime(n: int) : int =
0       tryI(n,2)

    function tryI(n: int, i: int) : int =
1       tryJ(n,i,2)

    function tryJ(n: int, i: int, j: int) : int =
2       if i*j=n
3           then 0
4           else nextJ(n,i,j+1)

    function nextJ(n: int, i: int, j: int) : int =
5       if j=n
            then nextI(n,i+1)
            else tryJ(n,i,j)

    function nextI(n: int, i: int) : int =
6       if i=n
            then 1
            else tryI(n,i)
```

where the numbers 1–6 show the correspondence with the flow-graph nodes of Figure 18.1f.

Because the programmer can arrange these functions in arbitrary ways, flow graphs produced by the tail-call structure of functional programs are sometimes irreducible.

Advantages of reducible flow graphs. Many dataflow analyses (presented in Chapter 17) can be done very efficiently on reducible flow graphs. Instead of using fixed-point iteration ("keep executing assignments until there are no changes"), we can determine an order for computing the assignments, and calculate in advance how many assignments will be necessary – that is, there will never be a need to check to see if anything changed.

However, for the remainder of this chapter we will assume that our control-flow graphs may be reducible or irreducible.

18.1   DOMINATORS

Before we optimize the loops, we must find them in the flow graph. The notion of *dominators* is useful for that purpose.

Each control-flow graph must have a start node s_0 with no predecessors, where program (or procedure) execution is assumed to begin.

A node d *dominates* a node n if every path of directed edges from s_0 to n must go through d. Every node dominates itself.

ALGORITHM FOR FINDING DOMINATORS

Consider a node n with predecessors $p_1, \ldots, p_k$, and a node d (with $d \neq n$). If d dominates each one of the p_i, then it must dominate n, because every path from s_0 to n must go through one of the p_i, but every path from s_0 to a p_i must go through d. Conversely, if d dominates n, it must dominate all the p_i; otherwise there would be a path from s_0 to n going through the predecessor not dominated by d.

Let $D[n]$ be the set of nodes that dominate n. Then

$$D[s_0] = \{s_0\} \qquad D[n] = \{n\} \cup \left(\bigcap_{p \in \text{pred}[n]} D[p] \right) \qquad \text{for } n \neq s_0.$$

The simultaneous equations can be solved, as usual, by iteration, treating each equation as an assignment statement. However, in this case each set $D[n]$ (for

$n \neq s_0$) must be initialized to hold all the nodes in the graph, because each assignment $D[n] \leftarrow \{n\} \cup \ldots$ makes $D[n]$ smaller (or unchanged), not larger.

This algorithm can be made more efficient by ordering the set assignments in quasi-topological order, that is, according to a depth-first search of the graph (Algorithm 17.5). Section 19.2 describes a faster algorithm for computing dominators.

Technically, an unreachable node is dominated by every node in the graph; we will avoid the pathologies this can cause by deleting unreachable nodes from the graph before calculating dominators and doing loop optimizations. See also Exercise 18.4.

IMMEDIATE DOMINATORS

Theorem: In a connected graph, suppose d dominates n, and e dominates n. Then it must be that either d dominates e, or e dominates d.

Proof: (By contradiction.) Suppose neither d nor e dominates the other. Then there is some path from s_0 to e that does not go through d. Therefore any path from e to n must go through d; otherwise d would not dominate n.

Conversely, any path from d to n must go through e. But this means that to get from e to n the path must infinitely loop from d to e to d ... and never get to n.

This theorem tells us that every node n has no more than one *immediate dominator*, $idom(n)$, such that

1. $idom(n)$ is not the same node as n,
2. $idom(n)$ dominates n, and
3. $idom(n)$ does not dominate any other dominator of n.

Every node except s_0 is dominated by at least one node other than itself (since s_0 dominates every node), so every node except s_0 has exactly one immediate dominator.

Dominator tree. Let us draw a graph containing every node of the flow graph, and for every node n an edge from $idom(n)$ to n. The resulting graph will be a tree, because each node has exactly one immediate dominator. This is called the *dominator tree*.

Figure 18.3 shows a flow graph and its dominator tree. Some edges in the dominator tree correspond to single flow-graph edges (such as $4 \rightarrow 6$), but others do not (such as $4 \rightarrow 7$). That is, the immediate dominator of a node is not necessarily its predecessor in the flow graph.

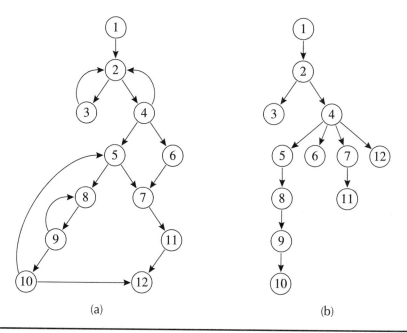

FIGURE 18.3. (a) A flow graph; (b) its dominator tree.

A flow-graph edge from a node n to a node h that dominates n is called a *back edge*. For every back edge there is a corresponding subgraph of the flow graph that is a loop. The back edges in Figure 18.3a are $3 \rightarrow 2$, $4 \rightarrow 2$, $10 \rightarrow 5$, $9 \rightarrow 8$.

LOOPS

The *natural loop* of a back edge $n \rightarrow h$, where h dominates n, is the set of nodes x such that h dominates x and there is a path from x to n not containing h. The *header* of this loop will be h.

The natural loop of the back edge $10 \rightarrow 5$ from Figure 18.3a includes nodes 5, 8, 9, 10 and has the loop 8, 9 nested within it.

A node h can be the header of more than one natural loop, if there is more than one back edge into h. In Figure 18.3a, the natural loop of $3 \rightarrow 2$ consists of the nodes 3, 2 and the natural loop of $4 \rightarrow 2$ consists of 4, 2.

The loop optimizations described in this chapter can cope with any loop, whether it is a natural loop or not, and whether or not that loop shares its header with some other loop. However, we usually want to optimize an *inner* loop first, because most of the program's execution time is expected to be in the inner loop. If two loops share a header, then it is hard to determine which should be considered the inner loop. A common way of solving this problem is to merge all the natural loops with the same header. The result will not necessarily be a natural loop.

If we merge all the loops with header 2 in Figure 18.3a, we obtain the loop 2, 3, 4 – which is not a natural loop.

Nested loops If A and B are loops with headers a and b, respectively, such that $a \neq b$ and b is in A, then the nodes of B are a proper subset of the nodes of A. We say that loop B is nested within A, or that B is the *inner loop*.

We can construct a *loop-nest tree* of loops in a program. The procedure is, for a flow graph G:

1. Compute dominators of G.
2. Construct the dominator tree.
3. Find all the natural loops, and thus all the loop-header nodes.
4. For each loop header h, merge all the natural loops of h into a single loop, *loop*[h].
5. Construct the tree of loop headers (and implicitly loops), such that h_1 is above h_2 in the tree if h_2 is in *loop*[h_1].

The leaves of the loop-nest tree are the *innermost loops*.

Just to have a place to put nodes not in any loop, we could say that the entire procedure body is a pseudo-loop that sits at the root of the loop-nest tree. The loop-nest tree of Figure 18.3 is shown in Figure 18.4.

LOOP PREHEADER

Many loop optimizations will insert statements immediately before the loop executes. For example, *loop-invariant hoisting* moves a statement from inside the loop to immediately before the loop. Where should such statements be put? Figure 18.5a illustrates a problem: If we want to insert statement s into a basic block immediately before the loop, we need to put s at the end of blocks 2 and 3. In order to have one place to put such statements, we insert a new, initially empty, *preheader* node p outside the loop, with an edge $p \rightarrow h$. All edges $x \rightarrow h$ from nodes x inside the loop are left unchanged, but all existing edges $y \rightarrow h$ from nodes y outside the loop are redirected to point to p.

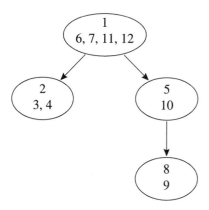

FIGURE 18.4. The loop-nest tree for Figure 18.3a. Each loop header is shown in the top half of each oval (nodes 1, 2, 5, 8); a loop comprises a header node (e.g., node 5), all the other nodes shown in the same oval (e.g., node 10), and all the nodes shown in subtrees of the loop-nest-tree node (e.g., 8, 9).

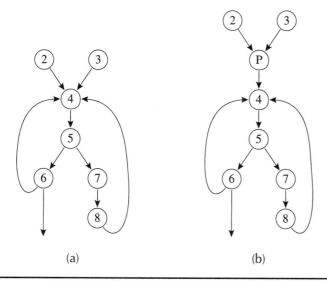

FIGURE 18.5. (a) A loop; (b) the same loop with a preheader.

18.2   LOOP-INVARIANT COMPUTATIONS

If a loop contains a statement $t \leftarrow a \oplus b$ such that a has the same value each time around the loop, and b has the same value each time, then t will also have the same value each time. We would like to *hoist* the computation out of the loop, so it is computed just once instead of every time.

We cannot always tell if a will have the same value every time, so as usual we will conservatively approximate. The definition $d : t \leftarrow a_1 \oplus a_2$ is loop-invariant within loop L if, for each operand a_i,

1. a_i is a constant,
2. *or* all the definitions of a_i that reach d are outside the loop,
3. *or* only one definition of a_i reaches d, and that definition is loop-invariant.

This leads naturally to an iterative algorithm for finding loop-invariant definitions: First find all the definitions whose operands are constant or from outside the loop, then repeatedly find definitions whose operands are loop-invariant.

HOISTING

Suppose $t \leftarrow a \oplus b$ is loop-invariant. Can we hoist it out of the loop? In Figure 18.6a, hoisting makes the program compute the same result faster. But in Figure 18.6b, hoisting makes the program faster but incorrect – the original program does not *always* execute $t \leftarrow a \oplus b$, but the transformed program does, producing an incorrect value for x if $i \geq N$ initially. Hoisting in Figure 18.6c is also incorrect, because the original loop had more than one definition of t, and the transformed program interleaves the assignments to t in a different way. And hoisting in Figure 18.6d is wrong because there is a use of t before the loop-invariant definition, so after hoisting, this use will have the wrong value on the first iteration of the loop.

With these pitfalls in mind, we can set the criteria for hoisting $d : t \leftarrow a \oplus b$ to the end of the loop preheader:

1. d dominates all loop exits at which t is *live-out*,
2. *and* there is only one definition of t in the loop,
3. *and* t is not *live-out* of the loop preheader.

Implicit side effects. These rules need modification if $t \leftarrow a \oplus b$ could raise some sort of arithmetic exception or have other side effects; see Exercise 18.7.

(a) Hoist	(b) Don't	(c) Don't	(d) Don't
L_0 $\quad t \leftarrow 0$ L_1 $\quad i \leftarrow i+1$ $\quad t \leftarrow a \oplus b$ $\quad M[i] \leftarrow t$ $\quad$ if $i < N$ goto L_1 L_2 $\quad x \leftarrow t$	L_0 $\quad t \leftarrow 0$ L_1 $\quad$ if $i \geq N$ goto L_2 $\quad i \leftarrow i+1$ $\quad t \leftarrow a \oplus b$ $\quad M[i] \leftarrow t$ $\quad$ goto L_1 L_2 $\quad x \leftarrow t$	L_0 $\quad t \leftarrow 0$ L_1 $\quad i \leftarrow i+1$ $\quad t \leftarrow a \oplus b$ $\quad M[i] \leftarrow t$ $\quad t \leftarrow 0$ $\quad M[j] \leftarrow t$ $\quad$ if $i < N$ goto L_1 L_2	L_0 $\quad t \leftarrow 0$ L_1 $\quad M[j] \leftarrow t$ $\quad i \leftarrow i+1$ $\quad t \leftarrow a \oplus b$ $\quad M[i] \leftarrow t$ $\quad$ if $i < N$ goto L_1 L_2 $\quad x \leftarrow t$

FIGURE 18.6. Some good and bad candidates for hoisting $t \leftarrow a \oplus b$.

Turning while loops into repeat-until loops. Condition (1) tends to prevent many computations from being hoisted from **while** loops; from Figure 18.7a it is clear that none of the statements in the loop body dominates the loop exit node (which is the same as the header node). To solve this problem, we can transform the **while** loop into a **repeat** loop preceded by an **if** statement. This requires duplication of the statements in the header node, as shown in Figure 18.7b. Statements in the body of a **repeat** loop dominate the loop exit (unless they are in an inner **if**, or if there is a **break** statement), so condition (1) will be satisfied.

18.3   INDUCTION VARIABLES

Some loops have a variable i that is incremented or decremented, and a variable j that is set (in the loop) to $i \cdot c + d$, where c and d are loop-invariant. Then we can calculate j's value without reference to i; whenever i is incremented by a we can increment j by $c \cdot a$.

Consider, for example, Program 18.8a, which sums the elements of an array. Using *induction-variable analysis* to find that i and j are related induction variables, *strength reduction* to replace a multiplication by 4 with an addition, then *induction-variable elimination* to replace $i \geq n$ by $k \geq 4n + a$, followed by miscellaneous copy propagation, we get Program 18.8b. The transformed loop has fewer quadruples; it might even run faster. Let us now

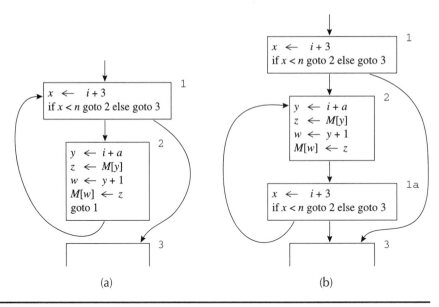

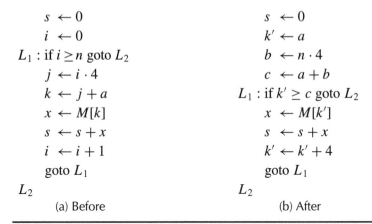

FIGURE 18.7. A **while** loop (a), transformed into a **repeat** loop (b).

$$s \leftarrow 0$$
$$i \leftarrow 0$$
$$L_1 : \text{if } i \geq n \text{ goto } L_2$$
$$j \leftarrow i \cdot 4$$
$$k \leftarrow j + a$$
$$x \leftarrow M[k]$$
$$s \leftarrow s + x$$
$$i \leftarrow i + 1$$
$$\text{goto } L_1$$
$$L_2$$

(a) Before

$$s \leftarrow 0$$
$$k' \leftarrow a$$
$$b \leftarrow n \cdot 4$$
$$c \leftarrow a + b$$
$$L_1 : \text{if } k' \geq c \text{ goto } L_2$$
$$x \leftarrow M[k']$$
$$s \leftarrow s + x$$
$$k' \leftarrow k' + 4$$
$$\text{goto } L_1$$
$$L_2$$

(b) After

PROGRAM 18.8. A loop before and after induction-variable optimizations.

take the series of transformations one step at a time.

We say that a variable such as i is a *basic induction variable*, and j and k are *derived induction variables in the family of* i. Right after j is defined (in the original loop), we have $j = a_j + i \cdot b_j$, where $a_j = 0$ and $b_j = 4$. We can completely characterize the value of j at its definition by (i, a, b), where i is a basic induction variable and a and b are loop-invariant expressions.

$$s \leftarrow 0$$
$$j' \leftarrow i \cdot 4$$
$$b' \leftarrow b \cdot 4$$

$$s \leftarrow 0 \qquad\qquad n' \leftarrow n \cdot 4$$
$$L_1 : \text{if } s > 0 \text{ goto } L_2 \qquad L_1 : \text{if } s > 0 \text{ goto } L_2$$
$$i \leftarrow i + b \qquad\qquad j' \leftarrow j' + b'$$
$$j \leftarrow i \cdot 4 \qquad\qquad j \leftarrow j'$$
$$x \leftarrow M[j] \qquad\qquad x \leftarrow M[j]$$
$$s \leftarrow s - x \qquad\qquad s \leftarrow s - x$$
$$\text{goto } L_1 \qquad\qquad \text{goto } L_1$$
$$L_2 : i \leftarrow i + 1 \qquad\qquad L_2 : j' \leftarrow j' + 4$$
$$s \leftarrow s + j \qquad\qquad s \leftarrow s + j$$
$$\text{if } i < n \text{ goto } L_1 \qquad\qquad \text{if } j' < n' \text{ goto } L_1$$

(a) Before   (b) After

FIGURE 18.9. The basic induction variable i is incremented by different amounts in different iterations; the derived induction variable j is not changed in every iteration.

If there is another derived induction variable with definition $k \leftarrow j + c_k$ (where c_k is loop-invariant), then k is also in the family of i. We can characterize k by the triple $(i, a_j + c_k, b_j)$, that is, $k = a_j + c_k + i \cdot b_j$.

We can characterize the basic induction variable i by a triple in the same way, that is $(i, 0, 1)$, meaning that $i = 0 + i \cdot 1$. Thus every induction variable can be characterized by such a triple.

If an induction variable changes by the same (constant or loop-invariant) amount in every iteration of the loop, we say it is a *linear induction variable*. In Figure 18.9a, the induction variable i is not linear: It is incremented by b in some iterations and by 1 in other iterations. Furthermore, in some iterations $j = i \cdot 4$ and in other iterations the derived induction variable j gets (temporarily) left behind as i is incremented.

DETECTION OF INDUCTION VARIABLES

Basic induction variables. The variable i is a basic induction variable in a loop L with header node h if the only definitions of i within L are of the form $i \leftarrow i + c$ or $i \leftarrow i - c$, where c is loop-invariant.

Derived induction variables. The variable k is a *derived induction variable* in loop L if:

1. There is only one definition of k within L, of the form $k \leftarrow j \cdot c$ or $k \leftarrow j + d$, where j is an induction variable and c, d are loop-invariant;
2. *and* if j is a derived induction variable in the family of i, then:
   (a) the only definition of j that reaches k is the one in the loop,
   (b) *and* there is no definition of i on any path between the definition of j and the definition of k.

Assuming j is characterized by (i, a, b), then k is described by $(i, a \cdot c, b \cdot c)$ or $(i, a + d, b)$, depending on whether k's definition was $j \cdot c$ or $j + d$.

Statements of the form $k \leftarrow j - c$ can be treated as $k \leftarrow j + (-c)$ for purposes of induction-variable analysis (unless $-c$ is not representable, which can sometimes happen with 2's complement arithmetic).

Division. Statements of the form $k \leftarrow j/c$ can be rewritten as $k \leftarrow j \cdot (\frac{1}{c})$, so that k could be considered an induction variable. This fact is useful for floating-point calculations – though we must beware of introducing subtle numerical errors if $1/c$ cannot be represented exactly. If this is an integer division, we cannot represent $1/c$ at all.

STRENGTH REDUCTION

On many machines, multiplication is more expensive than addition. So we would like to take a derived induction variable whose definition is of the form $j \leftarrow i \cdot c$ and replace it with an addition.

For each derived induction variable j whose triple is (i, a, b), make a new variable j' (although different derived induction variables with the same triple can share the same j' variable). After each assignment $i \leftarrow i + c$, make an assignment $j' \leftarrow j' + c \cdot b$, where $c \cdot b$ is a loop-invariant expression that may be computed in the loop preheader. If c and b are both constant, then the multiplication may be done at compile time. Replace the (unique) assigment to j with $j \leftarrow j'$. Finally, it is necessary to initialize j' at the end of the loop preheader, with $j' \leftarrow a + i \cdot b$.

We say two induction variables x, y in the family of i are *coordinated* if $(x - a_x)/b_x = (y - a_y)/b_y$ at every time during the execution of the loop, except during a sequence of statements $z_i \leftarrow z_i + c_i$, where c_i is loop-invariant. Clearly, all the new variables in the family of i introduced by strength reduction are coordinated with each other, and with i.

When the definition of an induction variable $j \leftarrow \cdots$ is replaced by $j \leftarrow j'$, we know that j' is coordinated but j might not be. However, the standard *copy propagation* algorithm can help here, replacing uses of j by uses of j' where there is no intervening definition of j'.

Thus, instead of using flow analysis to learn whether j is coordinated, we just use j' instead, where copy propagation says it is legal to do so.

After strength reduction there is still a multiplication, but it is outside the loop. If the loop executes more than one iteration, then the program should run faster with additions instead of multiplication, on many machines. The results of strength reduction may be disappointing on processors that can schedule multiplications to hide their latency.

Example. Let us perform strength reduction on Program 18.8a. We find that j is a derived induction variable with triple $(i, 0, 4)$, and k has triple $(i, a, 4)$. After strength reduction on both j and k, we have

$$
\begin{aligned}
&s \;\leftarrow 0\\
&i \;\leftarrow 0\\
&j' \leftarrow 0\\
&k' \leftarrow a\\
L_1 : &\text{if } i \geq n \text{ goto } L_2\\
&j \;\leftarrow j'\\
&k \;\leftarrow k'\\
&x \;\leftarrow M[k]\\
&s \;\leftarrow s + x\\
&i \;\leftarrow i + 1\\
&j' \leftarrow j' + 4\\
&k' \leftarrow k' + 4\\
&\text{goto } L_1\\
L_2
\end{aligned}
$$

We can perform *dead-code elimination* to remove the statement $j \leftarrow j'$. We would also like to remove all the definitions of the *useless variable* j', but technically it is not dead, since it is used in every iteration of the loop.

ELIMINATION

After strength reduction, some of the induction variables are not used at all in the loop, and others are used only in comparisons with loop-invariant variables. These induction variables can be deleted.

A variable is *useless* in a loop L if it is dead at all exits from L, and its only use is in a definition of itself. All definitions of a useless variable may be deleted.

In our example, after the removal of j, the variable j' is useless. We can delete $j' \leftarrow j' + 4$. This leaves a definition of j' in the preheader that can now be removed by dead-code elimination.

REWRITING COMPARISONS

A variable k is *almost useless* if it is used only in comparisons against loop-invariant values and in definitions of itself, and there is some other induction variable in the same family that is not useless. An almost-useless variable may be made useless by modifying the comparison to use the related induction variable.

If we have $k < n$, where j and k are coordinated induction variables in the family of i, and n is loop-invariant, then we know that $(j - a_j)/b_j = (k - a_k)/b_k$, so therefore the comparison $k < n$ can be written as

$$a_k + \frac{b_k}{b_j}(j - a_j) \; < \; n.$$

Now, we can subtract a_k from both sides and multiply both sides by b_j/b_k. If b_j/b_k is positive, the resulting comparison is

$$j - a_j \; < \; \frac{b_j}{b_k}(n - a_k),$$

but if b_j/b_k is negative, then the comparison becomes

$$j - a_j \; > \; \frac{b_j}{b_k}(n - a_k)$$

instead. Finally, we add a_j to both sides (here we show the positive case):

$$j \; < \; \frac{b_j}{b_k}(n - a_k) + a_j.$$

The entire right-hand side of this comparison is loop-invariant, so it can be computed just once in the loop preheader.

Restrictions:

1. If $b_j(n - a_k)$ is not evenly divisible by b_k, then this transformation cannot be used, because we cannot hold a fractional value in an integer variable.

2. If b_j or b_k is not constant, but is a loop-invariant value whose sign is not known, then the transformation cannot be used since we won't know which comparison (less-than or greater-than) to use.

Example. In our example, the comparison $i < n$ can be replaced by $k' < a + 4 \cdot n$. Of course, $a + 4 \cdot n$ is loop-invariant and should be hoisted. Then i will be useless and may be deleted. The transformed program is

$$
\begin{aligned}
&s \leftarrow 0 \\
&k' \leftarrow a \\
&b \leftarrow n \cdot 4 \\
&c \leftarrow a + b \\
L_1 : &\text{if } k' < c \text{ goto } L_2 \\
&k \leftarrow k' \\
&x \leftarrow M[k] \\
&s \leftarrow s + x \\
&k' \leftarrow k' + 4 \\
&\text{goto } L_1 \\
L_2
\end{aligned}
$$

Finally, copy propagation can eliminate $k \leftarrow k'$, and we obtain Program 18.8b.

18.4   ARRAY-BOUNDS CHECKS

Safe programming languages automatically insert array-bounds checks on every subscript operation (see the sermon on page 147). Of course, in well-written programs all of these checks are redundant, since well-written programs don't access arrays out of bounds. We would like safe languages to achieve the fast performance of unsafe languages. Instead of turning off the bounds checks (which would not be safe) we ask the compiler to remove any checks that it can prove are redundant.

We cannot hope to remove all the redundant bounds checks, because this problem is not computable (it is as hard as the halting problem). But many array subscripts are of the form $a[i]$, where i is an induction variable. These the compiler can often understand well enough to optimize.

The bounds for an array are generally of the form $0 \le i \wedge i < N$. When N is nonnegative, as it always is for array sizes, this can be implemented as $i \le_u N$, where $\le_u$ is the unsigned comparison operator.

Conditions for eliminating array-bounds checking. Although it seems natural and intuitive that an induction variable must stay within a certain range, and we should be able to tell whether that range does not exceed the bounds of the array, the criteria for eliminating a bounds check from a loop L are actually quite complicated:

1. There is an induction variable j and a loop-invariant u used in a statement s_1, taking one of the following forms:

$$\text{if } j < u \text{ goto } L_1 \text{ else goto } L_2$$
$$\text{if } j \geq u \text{ goto } L_2 \text{ else goto } L_1$$
$$\text{if } u > j \text{ goto } L_1 \text{ else goto } L_2$$
$$\text{if } u \leq j \text{ goto } L_2 \text{ else goto } L_1$$

where L_2 is out of the loop.
2. There is a statement s_2 of the form,   if $k <_u n$ goto L_3 else goto L_4, where k is an induction variable coordinated with j, n is loop-invariant, and s_1 dominates s_2.
3. There is no loop nested within L containing a definition of k.
4. k increases when j does, that is, $b_j/b_k > 0$.

Often, n will be an array length. In a language with static arrays an array length n is a constant. In many languages with dynamic arrays, array lengths are loop-invariant. In MiniJava, Java, and ML the length of an array cannot be dynamically modified once the array has been allocated. The array length n will typically be calculated by fetching the *length* field of some array pointer v. For the sake of illustration, assume the length field is at offset 0 in the array object. To avoid the need for complicated alias analysis, the semantic analysis phase of the compiler should mark the expression $M[v]$ as *immutable*, meaning that no other store instruction can possibly update the contents of the *length* field of the array v. If v is loop-invariant, then n will also be loop-invariant. Even if n is not an array length but is some other loop invariant, we can still optimize the comparison $k <_u n$.

We want to put a test in the loop preheader that expresses the idea that in every iteration, $k \geq 0 \land k < n$. Let k_0 be the value of k at the end of the preheader, and let $\Delta k_1, \Delta k_2, \ldots, \Delta k_m$ be all the loop-invariant values that are added to k inside the loop. Then we can ensure $k \geq 0$ by testing

$$k \geq 0 \land \Delta k_1 \geq 0 \land \cdots \land \Delta k_m \geq 0$$

at the end of the preheader.

Let $\Delta k_1, \Delta k_2, \ldots, \Delta k_p$ be the set of loop-invariant values that are added to k on any path between s_1 and s_2 that does not go through s_1 (again). Then, to ensure $k < n$ at s_2, it is sufficient to ensure that $k < n - (\Delta k_1 + \cdots + \Delta k_p)$ at s_1. Since we know $(k - a_k)/b_k = (j - a_j)/b_j$, this test becomes

$$j < \frac{b_j}{b_k}(n - (\Delta k_1 + \cdots + \Delta k_p) - a_k) + a_j.$$

This will always be true if

$$u < \frac{b_j}{b_k}(n - (\Delta k_1 + \cdots + \Delta k_p) - a_k) + a_j$$

since the test $j < u$ dominates the test $k < n$.

Since everything in this comparison is loop-invariant, we can move it to the preheader as follows. First, ensure that definitions of loop-invariants are hoisted out of the loop. Then, rewrite the loop L as follows: Copy all the statements of L to make a new loop L' with header L'_h. Inside L', replace the statement

if $k < n$ goto L'_3 else goto L'_4

by **goto** L'_3. At the end of the preheader of L, put statements equivalent to

if $k \geq 0 \land k_1 \geq 0 \land \cdots \land k_m \geq 0$
$\quad \land\; u < \frac{b_j}{b_k}(n - (\Delta k_1 + \cdots + \Delta k_p) - a_k) + a_j$
$\quad\quad$ goto L'_h
$\quad$ else goto L_h

The conditional **goto** tests whether k will always be between 0 and n.

Sometimes we will have enough information to evaluate this complicated condition at compile time. This will be true in at least two situations:

1. all the loop-invariants mentioned in it are constants; or
2. n and u are the same temporary variable, $a_k = a_j$, $b_k = b_j$, and there are no Δk's added to k between s_1 and s_2. In a language like MiniJava or Java or ML, this could happen if the programmer writes,

```
let var u := length(A)
    var i := 0
in while i<u
    do (sum := sum + A[i];
        i := i+1)
end
```

The quadruples for `length(A)` will include $u \leftarrow M[A]$, assuming that the length of an array is fetched from offset zero from the array pointer; and the quadruples for A[i] will include $n \leftarrow M[A]$, to fetch n for doing the bounds check. Now the expressions defining u and n are common subexpressions, assuming the expression $M[A]$ is marked so that we know that no other STORE instruction is modifying the contents of memory location $M[A]$.

If we can evaluate the big comparison at compile time, then we can unconditionally use loop L or loop L', and delete the loop that we are not using.

Cleaning up. After this optimization, the program may have several loose ends. Statements after the label L_4' may be unreachable; there may be several useless computations of n and k within L'. The former can be cleaned up by *unreachable-code elimination*, and the latter by *dead-code elimination*.

Generalizations. To be practically useful, the algorithm needs to be generalized in several ways:

1. The loop-exit comparison might take one of the forms

> if $j \leq u'$ goto L_1 else goto L_2
> if $j > u'$ goto L_2 else goto L_1
> if $u' \geq j$ goto L_1 else goto L_2
> if $u' < j$ goto L_2 else goto L_1

which compares $j \leq u'$ instead of $j < u$.

2. The loop-exit test might occur at the bottom of the loop body, instead of before the array-bounds test. We can describe this situation as follows: There is a test

> s_2 : if $j < u$ goto L_1 else goto L_2

where L_2 is out of the loop and s_2 dominates all the loop back edges. Then the Δk_i of interest are the ones between s_2 and any back edge, and between the loop header and s_1.

3. We should handle the case where $b_j/b_k < 0$.

4. We should handle the case where j counts downward instead of up, and the loop-exit test is something like $j \geq l$, for l a loop-invariant lower bound.

5. The induction-variable increments might be "undisciplined"; for example,

```
while i<n-1
  do (if sum<0
        then (i:=i+1; sum:= sum+i; i:=i+1)
        else i := i+2;
      sum := sum + a[i])
```

Here there are three Δi, (of 1, 1, and 2, respectively). Our analysis will assume that any, all, or none of these increments may be applied; but clearly the effect is $i \leftarrow i+2$ on either path. In such cases, an analysis that hoists (and merges) the increments above the **if** will be useful.

$$L_1 : x \leftarrow M[i]$$
$$s \leftarrow s + x$$
$$i \leftarrow i + 4$$
$$\text{if } i < n \text{ goto } L_1' \text{ else } L_2$$

$$L_1 : x \leftarrow M[i] \qquad\qquad L_1' : x \leftarrow M[i]$$
$$s \leftarrow s + x \qquad\qquad\quad s \leftarrow s + x$$
$$i \leftarrow i + 4 \qquad\qquad\quad i \leftarrow i + 4$$
$$\text{if } i < n \text{ goto } L_1 \text{ else } L_2 \qquad \text{if } i < n \text{ goto } L_1 \text{ else } L_2$$
$$L_2 \qquad\qquad\qquad\qquad\qquad\quad L_2$$

             (a) Before   (b) After

PROGRAM 18.10. Useless loop unrolling.

18.5   LOOP UNROLLING

Some loops have such a small body that most of the time is spent incrementing the loop-counter variable and testing the loop-exit condition. We can make these loops more efficient by *unrolling* them, putting two or more copies of the loop body in a row.

Given a loop L with header node h and back edges $s_i \rightarrow h$, we can unroll the loop as follows:

1. Copy the nodes to make a loop L' with header h' and back edges $s_i' \rightarrow h'$.
2. Change all the back edges in L from $s_i \rightarrow h$ to $s_i \rightarrow h'$.
3. Change all the back edges in L' from $s_i' \rightarrow h'$ to $s_i' \rightarrow h$.

For example, Program 18.10a unrolls into Program 18.10b. But nothing useful has been accomplished; each "original" iteration still has an increment and a conditional branch.

By using information about induction variables, we can do better. We need an induction variable i such that every increment $i \leftarrow i + \Delta$ dominates every back edge of the loop. Then we know that each iteration increments i by exactly the sum of all the Δ's, so we can agglomerate the increments and loop-exit tests to get Program 18.11a. But this unrolled loop works correctly only if the original loop iterated an even number of times. We execute "odd" iterations in an *epilogue*, as shown in Program 18.11b.

Here we have shown only the case of unrolling by a factor of two. When a loop is unrolled by a factor of K, then the epilogue is a loop (much like the original one) that iterates up to $K - 1$ times.

$$\text{if } i < n - 8 \text{ goto } L_1 \text{ else } L_2$$
$$L_1 : x \leftarrow M[i]$$
$$s \leftarrow s + x$$
$$x \leftarrow M[i + 4]$$
$$s \leftarrow s + x$$
$$i \leftarrow i + 8$$
$$\text{if } i < n - 8 \text{ goto } L_1 \text{ else } L_2$$

$$L_1 : x \leftarrow M[i]$$
$$s \leftarrow s + x$$
$$x \leftarrow M[i + 4]$$
$$s \leftarrow s + x$$
$$i \leftarrow i + 8$$
$$\text{if } i < n \text{ goto } L_1 \text{ else } L_2$$
$$L_2$$

$$L_2 \quad x \leftarrow M[i]$$
$$s \leftarrow s + x$$
$$i \leftarrow i + 4$$
$$\text{if } i < n \text{ goto } L_2 \text{ else } L_3$$
$$L_3$$

(a) Fragile

(b) Robust

PROGRAM 18.11. Useful loop unrolling; (a) works correctly only for an even number of iterations of the original loop; (b) works for any number of iterations of the original loop.

FURTHER READING

Lowry and Medlock [1969] characterized loops using dominators and performed induction-variable optimizations. Allen [1970] introduced the notion of reducible flow graphs. Aho et al. [1986] describe many optimizations, analyses, and transformations on loops.

Splitting control-flow nodes or edges gives a place into which statements can be moved. The *loop-preheader* transformation described on page 382 is an example of such splitting. Other examples are *landing pads* [Cytron et al. 1986] – nodes inserted in each loop-exit edge; *postbody nodes* [Wolfe 1996] – nodes inserted at the end of a loop body (see Exercise 18.6); and edge splitting to ensure a *unique successor or predecessor* property [Rosen et al. 1988] (see Section 19.1).

Chapter 19 describes other loop optimizations and a faster algorithm for computing dominators.

EXERCISES

18.1 a. Calculate the dominators of each node of this flowgraph:

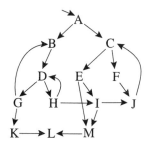

   b. Show the immediate-dominator tree.

   c. Identify the set of nodes in each natural loop.

18.2 Calculate the immediate-dominator tree of each of the following graphs:

   a. The graph of Figure 2.8.

   b. The graph of Exercise 2.3a.

   c. The graph of Exercise 2.5a.

   d. The graph of Figure 3.27.

*18.3 Let G be a control-flow graph, h be a node in G, A be the set of nodes in a loop with header h, and B be the set of nodes in a different loop with header h. Prove that the subgraph whose nodes are $A \cup B$ is also a loop.

*18.4 The immediate-dominator theorem (page 380) is false for graphs that contain unreachable nodes.

   a. Show a graph with nodes d, e, and n such that d dominates n, e dominates n, but neither d dominates e nor e dominates d.

   b. Identify which step of the proof is invalid for graphs containing unreachable nodes.

   c. In approximately three words, name an algorithm useful in finding unreachable nodes.

*18.5 Show that in a connected flowgraph (one without unreachable nodes), a natural loop as defined on page 381 satisfies the definition of loop given on page 376.

18.6 For some purposes it is desirable that each loop-header node should have exactly two predecessors, one outside the loop and one inside. We can ensure that there is only one outside predecessor by inserting a *preheader* node, as described in Section 18.1. Explain how to insert a *postbody* node to ensure that the loop header has only one predecessor inside the loop.

*18.7 Suppose any arithmetic overflow or divide-by-zero will raise an exception at run time. If we hoist $t \leftarrow a \oplus b$ out of a loop, and the loop might not have executed the statement at all, then the transformed program may raise the exception where the original program did not. Revise the criteria for *loop-invariant hoisting* to take account of this. Instead of writing something informal like "might not execute the statement," use the terminology of dataflow analysis and dominators.

18.8 On pages 385–385 the transformation of a **while** loop to a **repeat** loop is described. Show how a **while** loop may be characterized in the control-flow graph of basic blocks (using dominators) so that the optimizer can recognize it. The body of the loop may have explicit **break** statements that exit the loop.

*18.9 For bounds-check elimination, we required (on page 392) that the loop-exit test dominate the bounds-check comparison. If it is the other way around, then (effectively) we have one extra array subscript at the end of the loop, so the criterion

$$a_k + i \cdot b_k \geq 0 \ \wedge \ (n - a_k) \cdot b_j < (u - a_j) \cdot b_k$$

is "off by one." Rewrite this criterion for the case where the bounds-check comparison occurs before the loop-exit test.

*18.10 Write down the rules for unrolling a loop, such that the induction-variable increments are agglomerated and the unrolled loop has only one loop-exit test per iteration, as was shown informally for Program 18.10.

19

Static Single-Assignment Form

dom-i-nate: to exert the supreme determining or guiding influence on

Webster's Dictionary

Many dataflow analyses need to find the use sites of each defined variable or the definition sites of each variable used in an expression. The *def-use chain* is a data structure that makes this efficient: For each statement in the flow graph, the compiler can keep a list of pointers to all the *use* sites of variables defined there, and a list of pointers to all *definition* sites of the variables used there. In this way the compiler can hop quickly from use to definition to use to definition.

An improvement on the idea of def-use chains is *static single-assignment form*, or *SSA form*, an intermediate representation in which each variable has only one definition in the program text. The one (static) definition site may be in a loop that is executed many (dynamic) times, thus the name *static* single-assignment form instead of single-assignment form (in which variables are never redefined at all).

The SSA form is useful for several reasons:

1. Dataflow analysis and optimization algorithms can be made simpler when each variable has only one definition.
2. If a variable has N uses and M definitions (which occupy about $N + M$ instructions in a program), it takes space (and time) proportional to $N \cdot M$ to represent def-use chains – a quadratic blowup (see Exercise 19.8). For almost all realistic programs, the size of the SSA form is linear in the size of the original program (but see Exercise 19.9).
3. Uses and defs of variables in SSA form relate in a useful way to the dominator structure of the control-flow graph, which simplifies algorithms such as interference-graph construction.

$$a \leftarrow x + y \qquad\qquad a_1 \leftarrow x + y$$
$$b \leftarrow a - 1 \qquad\qquad b_1 \leftarrow a_1 - 1$$
$$a \leftarrow y + b \qquad\qquad a_2 \leftarrow y + b_1$$
$$b \leftarrow x \cdot 4 \qquad\qquad b_2 \leftarrow x \cdot 4$$
$$a \leftarrow a + b \qquad\qquad a_3 \leftarrow a_2 + b_2$$

(a)   (b)

FIGURE 19.1. (a) A straight-line program. (b) The program in single-assignment form.

4. Unrelated uses of the same variable in the source program become different variables in SSA form, eliminating needless relationships. An example is the program,

> **for** $i \leftarrow 1$ **to** N **do** $A[i] \leftarrow 0$
> **for** $i \leftarrow 1$ **to** M **do** $s \leftarrow s + B[i]$

where there is no reason that both loops need to use the same machine register or intermediate-code temporary variable to hold their respective loop counters, even though both are named i.

In straight-line code, such as within a basic block, it is easy to see that each instruction can define a fresh new variable instead of redefining an old one, as shown in Figure 19.1. Each new definition of a variable (such as a) is modified to define a fresh new variable ($a_1, a_2, \ldots$), and each use of the variable is modified to use the most recently defined version. This is a form of *value numbering* (see page 365).

But when two control-flow paths merge together, it is not obvious how to have only one assignment for each variable. In Figure 19.2a, if we were to define a new version of a in block 1 and in block 3, which version should be used in block 4? Where a statement has more than one predecessor, there is no notion of "most recent."

To solve this problem we introduce a notational fiction, called a ϕ-function. Figure 19.2b shows that we can combine a_1 (defined in block 1) and a_2 (defined in block 3) using the function $a_3 \leftarrow \phi(a_1, a_2)$. But unlike ordinary mathematical functions, $\phi(a_1, a_2)$ yields a_1 if control reaches block 4 along the edge $2 \rightarrow 4$, and yields a_2 if control comes in on edge $3 \rightarrow 4$.

How does the ϕ-function know which edge was taken? That question has two answers:

- If we must execute the program, or translate it to executable form, we can

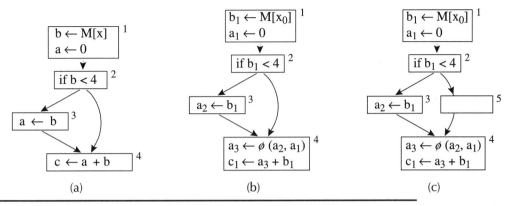

FIGURE 19.2.   (a) A program with a control-flow join; (b) the program transformed to single-assignment form; (c) edge-split SSA form.

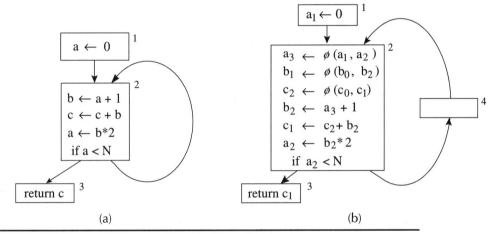

FIGURE 19.3.   (a) A program with a loop; (b) the program transformed to edge-split single-assignment form. a_0, b_0, c_0 are initial values of the variables before block 1.

"implement" the ϕ-function using a MOVE instruction on each incoming edge, as shown in Section 19.6.

- In many cases, we simply need the connection of uses to definitions, and don't need to "execute" the ϕ-functions during optimization. In these cases, we can ignore the question of which value to produce.

Consider Figure 19.3a, which contains a loop. We can convert this to static single-assignment form as shown in Figure 19.3b. Note that variables a and c each need a ϕ-function to merge their values that arrive on edges $1 \rightarrow 2$ and

$2 \rightarrow 2$. The ϕ-function for b_1 can later be deleted by dead-code elimination, since b_1 is a dead variable. The variable c is live on entry (after conversion to SSA, the implicit definition c_0 is live); this might be an uninitialized variable, or perhaps c is a formal parameter of the function whose body this is.

The assignment $c_1 \leftarrow c_2 + b_2$ will be executed many times; thus the variable c_1 is updated many times. This illustrates that we do not have a program with *dynamic* single-assignment (like a pure functional program), but a program in which each variable has only one *static* site of definition.

<table>
<tr><td>19.1</td></tr>
</table>

CONVERTING TO SSA FORM

The algorithm for converting a program to SSA form first adds ϕ-functions for the variables, then renames all the definitions and uses of variables using subscripts. The sequence of steps is illustrated in Figure 19.4.

CRITERIA FOR INSERTING ϕ-FUNCTIONS

We could add a ϕ-function for every variable at each *join* point (that is, each node in the control-flow graph with more than one predecessor). But this is wasteful and unnecessary. For example, block 4 in Figure 19.2b is reached by the same definition of b along each incoming edge, so it does not need a ϕ-function for b. The following criterion characterizes the nodes where a variable's dataflow paths merge:

Path-convergence criterion. There should be a ϕ-function for variable a at node z of the flow graph exactly when *all* of the following are true:

1. There is a block x containing a definition of a,
2. There is a block y (with $y \neq x$) containing a definition of a,
3. There is a nonempty path P_{xz} of edges from x to z,
4. There is a nonempty path P_{yz} of edges from y to z,
5. Paths P_{xz} and P_{yz} do not have any node in common other than z, *and*
6. The node z does not appear within *both* P_{xz} and P_{yz} prior to the end, though it may appear in one or the other.

We consider the start node to contain an implicit definition of *every* variable, either because the variable may be a formal parameter or to represent the notion of $a \leftarrow$ *uninitialized* without special cases.

Note, however, that a ϕ-function itself counts as a definition of a, so the *path-convergence criterion* must be considered as a set of equations to be

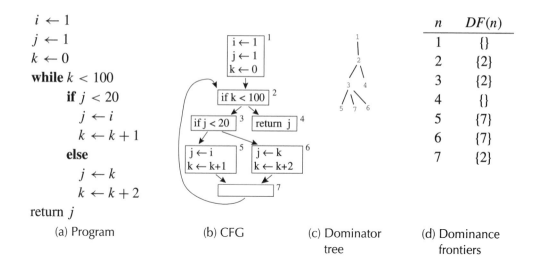

$i \leftarrow 1$
$j \leftarrow 1$
$k \leftarrow 0$
while $k < 100$
    if $j < 20$
        $j \leftarrow i$
        $k \leftarrow k + 1$
    else
        $j \leftarrow k$
        $k \leftarrow k + 2$
return j

(a) Program   (b) CFG   (c) Dominator tree   (d) Dominance frontiers

n	$DF(n)$
1	{}
2	{2}
3	{2}
4	{}
5	{7}
6	{7}
7	{2}

Variable j defined in node 1, but $DF(1)$ is empty. Variable j defined in node 5, $DF(5)$ contains 7, so node 7 needs $\phi(j, j)$. Now j is defined in 7 (by a ϕ-function), $DF(7)$ contains 2, so node 2 needs $\phi(j, j)$. $DF(6)$ contains 7, so node 7 needs $\phi(j, j)$ (but already has it). $DF(2)$ contains 2, so node 2 needs $\phi(j, j)$ (but already has it). Similar calculation for k. Variable i defined in node 1, $DF(1)$ is empty, so no ϕ-functions necessary for i.

(e) Insertion criteria for ϕ-functions

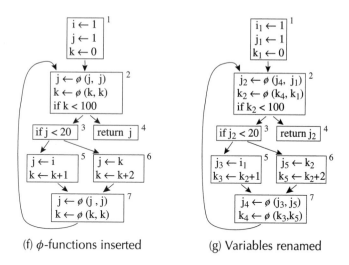

(f) ϕ-functions inserted   (g) Variables renamed

FIGURE 19.4.   Conversion of a program to static single-assignment form. Node 7 is a *postbody* node, inserted to make sure there is only one loop edge (see Exercise 18.6); such nodes are not strictly necessary but are sometimes helpful.

satisfied. As usual, we can solve them by iteration.

Iterated path-convergence criterion:

> **while** there are nodes x, y, z satisfying conditions 1–5
>   **and** z does not contain a ϕ-function for a
> **do** insert $a \leftarrow \phi(a, a, \ldots, a)$ at node Z

where the ϕ-function has as many a arguments as there are predecessors of node z.

Dominance property of SSA form. An essential property of static single-assignment form is that definitions dominate uses; more specifically,

1. If x is the ith argument of a ϕ-function in block n, then the definition of x dominates the ith predecessor of n.
2. If x is used in a non-ϕ statement in block n, then the definition of x dominates node n.

Section 18.1 defines the dominance relation: d dominates n if every path from the start node to n goes through d.

THE DOMINANCE FRONTIER

The iterated path-convergence algorithm for placing ϕ-functions is not practical, since it would be very costly to examine every triple of nodes x, y, z and every path leading from x and y. A much more efficient algorithm uses the dominator tree of the flow graph.

Definitions. x *strictly dominates* w if x dominates w and $x \neq w$. In this chapter we use *successor* and *predecessor* to refer to *graph* edges, and *parent* and *child* to refer to *tree* edges. Node x is an *ancestor* of y if there is a path $x \rightarrow y$ of tree edges, and is a *proper ancestor* if that path is nonempty.

The *dominance frontier* of a node x is the set of all nodes w such that x dominates a predecessor of w, but does not strictly dominate w.

Figure 19.5a illustrates the dominance frontier of a node; in essence, it is the "border" between dominated and undominated nodes.

Dominance frontier criterion. Whenever node x contains a definition of some variable a, then any node z in the dominance frontier of x needs a ϕ-function for a.

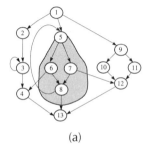
(a)

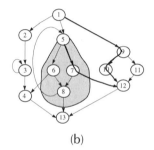
(b)

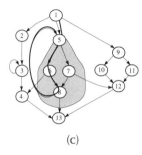
(c)

FIGURE 19.5.   Node 5 dominates all the nodes in the grey area. (a) Dominance frontier of node 5 includes the nodes (4, 5, 12, 13) that are targets of edges crossing from the region dominated by 5 (grey area including node 5) to the region not strictly dominated by 5 (white area including node 5). (b) Any node in the dominance frontier of n is also a point of convergence of nonintersecting paths, one from n and one from the root node. (c) Another example of converging paths $P_{1,5}$ and $P_{5,5}$.

Iterated dominance frontier. Since a ϕ-function itself is a kind of definition, we must iterate the dominance-frontier criterion until there are no nodes that need ϕ-functions.

Theorem. The *iterated dominance frontier criterion* and the *iterated path-convergence criterion* specify exactly the same set of nodes at which to put ϕ-functions.

The end-of-chapter bibliographic notes refer to a proof of this theorem. We will sketch one half of the proof, showing that if w is in the dominance frontier of a definition, then it must be a point of convergence. Suppose there is a definition of variable a at some node n (such as node 5 in Figure 19.5b), and node w (such as node 12 in Figure 19.5b) is in the dominance frontier of n. The root node implicitly contains a definition of every variable, including a. There is a path P_{rw} from the root node (node 1 in Figure 19.5) to w that does not go through n or through any node that n dominates; and there is a path P_{nw} from n to w that goes only through dominated nodes. These paths have w as their first point of convergence.

Computing the dominance frontier. To insert all the necessary ϕ-functions, for every node n in the flowgraph we need $DF[n]$, its dominance frontier. Given the dominator tree, we can efficiently compute the dominance frontiers of all the nodes of the flowgraph in one pass. We define two auxiliary sets

$DF_{\text{local}}[n]$: The successors of n that are not strictly dominated by n;

$DF_{\text{up}}[n]$: Nodes in the dominance frontier of n that are not strictly dominated by n's immediate dominator.

The dominance frontier of n can be computed from DF_{local} and DF_{up}:

$$DF[n] = DF_{\text{local}}[n] \;\cup\; \bigcup_{c \in children[n]} DF_{\text{up}}[c],$$

where $children[n]$ are the nodes whose immediate dominator ($idom$) is n.

To compute $DF_{\text{local}}[n]$ more easily (using immediate dominators instead of dominators), we use the following theorem: $DF_{\text{local}}[n] = $ the set of those successors of n whose immediate dominator is not n.

The following computeDF function should be called on the root of the dominator tree (the start node of the flowgraph). It walks the tree computing $DF[n]$ for every node n: It computes $DF_{\text{local}}[n]$ by examining the successors of n, then combines $DF_{\text{local}}[n]$ and (for each child c) $DF_{\text{up}}[c]$.

```
computeDF[n]  =
    S ← {}
    for each node y in succ[n]              This loop computes DF_local[n]
        if idom(y) ≠ n
            S ← S ∪ {y}
    for each child c of n in the dominator tree
        computeDF[c]
        for each element w of DF[c]         This loop computes DF_up[c]
            if n does not dominate w, or if n = w
                S ← S ∪ {w}
    DF[n] ← S
```

This algorithm is quite efficient. It does work proportional to the size (number of edges) of the original graph, plus the size of the dominance frontiers it computes. Although there are pathological graphs in which most of the nodes have very large dominance frontiers, in most cases the total size of all the DFs is approximately linear in the size of the graph, so this algorithm runs in "practically" linear time.

INSERTING ϕ-FUNCTIONS

Starting with a program not in SSA form, we need to insert just enough ϕ-functions to satisfy the iterated dominance frontier criterion. To avoid re-

Place-ϕ-Functions =
    for each node n
        for each variable a in $A_{\text{orig}}[n]$
            $defsites[a] \leftarrow defsites[a] \cup \{n\}$
    for each variable a
       $W \leftarrow defsites[a]$
       while W not empty
            remove some node n from W
            for each y in $DF[n]$
                if $a \notin A_{\phi}[y]$
                    insert the statement $a \leftarrow \phi(a, a, \ldots, a)$ at the top
                       of block y, where the ϕ-function has as many
                       arguments as y has predecessors
                    $A_{\phi}[Y] \leftarrow A_{\phi}[Y] \cup \{a\}$
                    if $a \notin A_{\text{orig}}[y]$
                       $W \leftarrow W \cup \{y\}$

ALGORITHM 19.6. Inserting ϕ-functions.

---

examining nodes where no ϕ-function has been inserted, we use a work-list algorithm.

Algorithm 19.6 starts with a set V of variables, a graph G of control-flow nodes – each node is a basic block of statements – and for each node n a set $A_{\text{orig}}[n]$ of variables defined in node n. The algorithm computes $A_{\phi}[a]$, the set of nodes that must have ϕ-functions for variable a. Sometimes a node may contain both an ordinary definition and a ϕ-function for the same variable; for example, in Figure 19.3b, $a \in A_{\text{orig}}[2]$ and $2 \in A_{\phi}[a]$.

The outer loop is performed once for each variable a. There is a work list W of nodes that might violate the dominance-frontier criterion.

The representation for W must allow quick testing of membership and quick extraction of an element. Work-list algorithms (in general) do not care *which* element of the list they remove, so an array or linked list of nodes suffices. To quickly test membership in W, we can use a mark bit in the representation of every node n which is set to **true** when n is put into the list, and **false** when n is removed. If it is undesirable to modify the node representation, a list plus a hash table will also work efficiently.

This algorithm does a constant amount of work (a) for each node and edge in the control-flow graph, (*b*) for each statement in the program, (*c*) for each element of every dominance frontier, and (*d*) for each inserted ϕ-function. For a program of size N, the amounts a and b are proportional to N, c is usually approximately linear in N. The number of inserted ϕ-functions (*d*) could be N^2 in the worst case, but empirical measurement has shown that it is usually proportional to N. So in practice, Algorithm 19.6 runs in approximately linear time.

RENAMING THE VARIABLES

After the ϕ-functions are placed, we can walk the dominator tree, renaming the different definitions (including ϕ-functions) of variable a to a_1, a_2, a_3, and so on.

In a straight-line program, we would rename all the definitions of a, and then each use of a is renamed to use the most recent definition of a. For a program with control-flow branches and joins whose graph satisfies the dominance-frontier criterion, we rename each use of a to use the closest definition d of a that is above a in the dominator tree.

Algorithm 19.7 renames all uses and definitions of variables, after the ϕ-functions have been inserted by Algorithm 19.6. In traversing the dominator tree, the algorithm "remembers" for each variable the most recently defined version of each variable, on a separate stack for each variable.

Although the algorithm follows the structure of the dominator tree – not the flowgraph – at each node in the tree it examines all outgoing flow edges, to see if there are any ϕ-functions whose operands need to be properly numbered.

This algorithm takes time proportional to the size of the program (after ϕ-functions are inserted), so in practice it should be approximately linear in the size of the original program.

EDGE SPLITTING

Some analyses and transformations are simpler if there is never a control-flow edge that leads from a node with multiple successors to a node with multiple predecessors. To give the graph this *unique successor or predecessor* property, we perform the following transformation: For each control-flow edge $a \rightarrow b$ such that a has more than one successor and b has more than one predecessor, we create a new, empty control-flow node z, and replace the $a \rightarrow b$ edge with an $a \rightarrow z$ edge and a $z \rightarrow b$ edge.

Initialization:
    for each variable a
        $Count[a] \leftarrow 0$
        $Stack[a] \leftarrow$ empty
        push 0 onto $Stack[a]$

$Rename(n) \; =$
    for each statement S in block n
        if S is not a ϕ-function
            for each use of some variable x in S
                $i \leftarrow top(Stack[x])$
                replace the use of x with x_i in S
            for each definition of some variable a in S
                $Count[a] \leftarrow Count[a] + 1$
                $i \leftarrow Count[a]$
                push i onto $Stack[a]$
                replace definition of a with definition of a_i in S
    for each successor Y of block n,
        Suppose n is the jth predecessor of Y
        for each ϕ-function in Y
            suppose the jth operand of the ϕ-function is a
            $i \leftarrow top(Stack[a])$
            replace the jth operand with a_i
    for each child X of n
        $Rename(X)$
    for each statement S in block n
        for each definition of some variable a in S
            pop $Stack[a]$

ALGORITHM 19.7. Renaming variables.

An SSA graph with this property is in *edge-split SSA form*. Figure 19.2 illustrates edge splitting. Edge splitting may be done before or after insertion of ϕ-functions.

EFFICIENT COMPUTATION OF THE DOMINATOR TREE

A major reason for using SSA form is that it makes the optimizing compiler faster. Instead of using costly iterative bit-vector algorithms to link uses to definitions (to compute reaching definitions, for example), the compiler can just look up the (unique) definition, or the list of uses, of each variable.

For SSA to help make a compiler faster, we must be able to compute the SSA form quickly. The algorithms for computing SSA from the dominator tree are quite efficient. But the iterative set-based algorithm for computing dominators, given in Section 18.1, may be slow in the worst case. An industrial-strength compiler that uses dominators should use a more efficient algorithm for computing the dominator tree.

The near-linear-time algorithm of Lengauer and Tarjan relies on properties of the *depth-first spanning tree* of the control-flow graph. This is just the recursion tree implicitly traversed by the *depth-first search* (DFS) algorithm, which numbers each node of the graph with a *depth-first number (dfnum)* as it is first encountered.

The algorithm is rather technical; those readers who feel content just knowing that the dominator tree can be calculated quickly can skip to Section 19.3.

DEPTH-FIRST SPANNING TREES

We can use depth-first search to calculate a depth-first spanning tree of the control-flow graph. Figure 19.8 shows a CFG and a depth-first spanning tree, along with the *dfnum* of each node.

A given CFG may have many different depth-first spanning trees. From now on we will assume that we have arbitrarily picked one of them – by depth-first search. When we say "*a* is an *ancestor* of *b*" we mean that there is some path from *a* to *b* following only spanning-tree edges, or that $a = b$; "*a* is a *proper ancestor* of *b*" means that *a* is an ancestor of *b* and $a \neq b$.

Properties of depth-first spanning trees. The start node *r* of the CFG is the root of the depth-first spanning tree.

If *a* is a proper ancestor of *b*, then $dfnum(a) < dfnum(b)$.

Suppose there is a CFG path from *a* to *b* but *a* is not an ancestor of *b*. This means that some edge on the path is not a spanning-tree edge, so *b* must have been reached in the depth-first search before *a* was (otherwise, after visiting *a* the search would continue along tree edges to *b*). Thus, $dfnum(a) > dfnum(b)$.

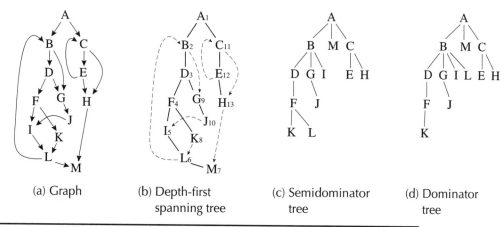

(a) Graph

(b) Depth-first
spanning tree

(c) Semidominator
tree

(d) Dominator
tree

FIGURE 19.8. A control-flow graph and trees derived from it. The numeric labels in part (b) are the *dfnum*s of the nodes.

Therefore, if we know that there is a path from a to b, we can test whether a is an ancestor of b just by comparing the *dfnum*'s of a and b.

When drawing depth-first spanning trees, we order the children of a node in the order that they are visited by the depth-first search, so that nodes to the right have a higher *dfnum*. This means that if a is an ancestor of b, and there is a CFG path from a to b that departs from the spanning tree, it must branch off to the right of the tree path, never to the left.

Dominators and spanning-tree paths. Consider a nonroot node n in the CFG, and its immediate dominator d. The node d must be an ancestor of n in the spanning tree – because any path (including the spanning-tree path) from r to n must include d. Therefore $dfnum(d) < dfnum(n)$.

Now we know that n's immediate dominator must be on the spanning-tree path between r and n; all that's left is to see how high up it is.

If some ancestor x does not dominate n, then there must be a path that departs from the spanning-tree path above x and rejoins it below x. The nodes on the by-passing path are not ancestors of n, so their *dfnum*'s are higher than n's. The path might rejoin the spanning-tree path to n either at n or above n.

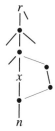

SEMIDOMINATORS

Paths that bypass ancestors of n are useful for proving that those ancestors do not dominate n. Let us consider, for now, only those bypassing paths that rejoin the spanning tree at n (not above n). Let's find the path that departs from the tree at the highest possible ancestor s, and rejoins the tree at n. We will call s the *semidominator* of n.

Another way of saying this is that s is the node of smallest *dfnum* having a path to n whose nodes (not counting s and n) are not ancestors of n. This description of semidominators does not explicitly say that s must be an ancestor of n, but of course any nonancestor with a path to n would have a higher *dfnum* than n's own parent in the spanning tree, which itself has a path to n with no nonancestor internal nodes (actually, no internal nodes at all).

Very often, a node's semidominator is also its immediate dominator. But as the figure at right shows, to find the dominator of n it's not enough just to consider bypassing paths that rejoin the tree at n. Here, a path from r to n bypasses n's semidominator s, but rejoins the tree at node y, above n. However, finding the semidominator s is still a useful step toward finding the dominator d.

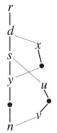

Semidominator Theorem. To find the semidominator of a node n, consider all predecessors v of n in the CFG.

- If v is a proper ancestor of n in the spanning tree (so *dfnum*(v) < *dfnum*(n)), then v is a candidate for *semi*(n).
- If v is a nonancestor of n (so *dfnum*(v) > *dfnum*(n)), then for each u that is an ancestor of v (or $u = v$), let *semi*(u) be a candidate for *semi*(n).

Of all these candidates, the one with lowest *dfnum* is the semidominator of n.

Proof. See the Further Reading section.

Calculating dominators from semidominators. Let s be the semidominator of n. If there is a path that departs from the spanning tree above s, bypasses s, and rejoins the spanning tree at some node between s and n, then s does not dominate n.

However, if we find the node y between s and n with the smallest-numbered semidominator, and *semi*(y) is a proper ancestor of s, then y's immediate dominator also immediately dominates n.

Dominator Theorem. On the spanning-tree path below *semi(n)* and above or including *n*, let *y* be the node with the smallest-numbered semidominator (minimum *dfnum(semi(y))*). Then,

$$idom(n) = \begin{cases} semi(n) & \text{if } semi(y) = semi(n) \\ idom(y) & \text{if } semi(y) \neq semi(n). \end{cases}$$

Proof. See the Further Reading section.

THE LENGAUER-TARJAN ALGORITHM

Using these two theorems, Algorithm 19.9 uses depth-first search (DFS) to compute *dfnum*'s for every node.

Then it visits the nodes in order, from highest *dfnum* to lowest, computing semidominators and dominators. As it visits each node, it puts the node into a spanning forest for the graph. It's called a *forest* because there may be multiple disconnected fragments; only at the very end will it be a single spanning *tree* of all the CFG nodes.

Calculating semidominators requires that, given some edge $v \rightarrow n$, we look at all ancestors of *v* in the spanning tree that have a higher *dfnum* than *n*. When Algorithm 19.9 processes node *n*, only nodes with a higher *dfnum* than *n* will be in the forest. Thus, the algorithm can simply examine all ancestors of *v* that are already in the forest.

We use the Dominator Theorem to compute the immediate dominator of *n*, by finding node *y* with the lowest semidominator on the path from *semi[n]* to *n*. When *s* = *semi[n]* is being computed, it's not yet possible to determine *y*; but we will be able to do so later, when *s* is being added to the spanning forest. Therefore with each semidominator *s* we keep a *bucket* of all the nodes that *s* semidominates; when *s* is linked into the spanning forest, we can then calculate the *idom* of each node in [*s*].

The forest is represented by an *ancestor* array: For each node *v*, *ancestor[v]* points to *v*'s parent. This makes searching upward from *v* easy.

Algorithm 19.10a shows a too-slow version of the AncestorWithLowest-Semi and Link functions that manage the spanning forest. Link sets the *ancestor* relation, and AncestorWithLowestSemi searches upward for the ancestor whose semidominator has the smallest *dfnum*.

But each call to AncestorWithLowestSemi could take linear time (in *N*, the number of nodes in the graph) if the spanning tree is very deep; and AncestorWithLowestSemi is called once for each node and edge. Thus Algorithm 19.9+19.10a has quadratic worst-case time complexity.

DFS(node p, node n) =
   if $dfnum[n] = 0$
      $dfnum[n] \leftarrow N; \quad vertex[N] \leftarrow n; \quad parent[n] \leftarrow p$
      $N \leftarrow N + 1$
      for each successor w of n
         DFS(n, w)

Link(node p, node n) = *add edge $p \rightarrow n$ to spanning forest implied by* ancestor *array*
AncestorWithLowestSemi(node n) = *in the forest, find the nonroot ancestor of n that*
                                      has the lowest-numbered semidominator

Dominators() =
   $N \leftarrow 0; \quad \forall n.\, bucket[n] \leftarrow \{\}$
   $\forall n.\, dfnum[n] \leftarrow 0, \ semi[n] \leftarrow ancestor[n] \leftarrow idom[n] \leftarrow samedom[n] \leftarrow none$
   DFS(none, r)
   for $i \leftarrow N - 1$ **downto** 1   Skip over node 0, the root node.
      $n \leftarrow vertex[i]; \quad p \leftarrow parent[n]; \quad s \leftarrow p$
      for each predecessor v of n These lines calcu-
         if $dfnum[v] \leq dfnum[n]$ late the semidom-
            $s' \leftarrow v$ inator of n, based
         else $s' \leftarrow semi[\text{AncestorWithLowestSemi}(v)]$ on the **Semidom-**
         if $dfnum[s'] < dfnum[s]$ **inator Theorem**.
            $s \leftarrow s'$
      $semi[n] \leftarrow s$ Calculation of n's dominator is deferred
      $bucket[s] \leftarrow bucket[s] \cup \{n\}$ until the path from s to n has been linked
      Link(p, n) into the forest.
      for each v in $bucket[p]$ Now that the path from p to v has been linked into
         $y \leftarrow \text{AncestorWithLowestSemi}(v)$ the spanning forest, these lines calculate the dom-
         if $semi[y] = semi[v]$ inator of v, based on the first clause of the **Domi-**
            $idom[v] \leftarrow p$ **nator Theorem**, or else defer the calculation until
         else $samedom[v] \leftarrow y$ y's dominator is known.
      $bucket[p] \leftarrow \{\}$
   for $i \leftarrow 1$ **to** $N - 1$
      $n \leftarrow vertex[i]$
      if $samedom[n] \neq none$ Now all the deferred dominator calcula-
         $idom[n] \leftarrow idom[samedom[n]]$ tions, based on the second clause of the
                                   Dominator Theorem, are performed.

ALGORITHM 19.9. Lengauer-Tarjan algorithm for computing dominators.

AncestorWithLowestSemi(node v) =
   $u \leftarrow v$
   while $ancestor[v] \neq$ none
      if $dfnum[semi[v]] < dfnum[semi[u]]$
         $u \leftarrow v$
      $v \leftarrow ancestor[v]$
   return u

Link(node p, node n) =
   $ancestor[n] \leftarrow p$

(a) Naive version,
$O(N)$ per operation.

AncestorWithLowestSemi(node v) =
   $a \leftarrow ancestor[v]$
   if $ancestor[a] \neq$ none
      $b \leftarrow$ AncestorWithLowestSemi(a)
      $ancestor[v] \leftarrow ancestor[a]$
      if $dfnum[semi[b]] <$
            $dfnum[semi[best[v]]]$
         $best[v] \leftarrow b$
   return $best[v]$

Link(node p, node n) =
   $ancestor[n] \leftarrow p$; $best[n] \leftarrow n$

(b) With path-compression,
$O(\log N)$ per operation.

ALGORITHM 19.10. Two versions of AncestorWithLowestSemi and Link functions for operations on spanning forest. The naive version (a) takes $O(N)$ per operation (so the algorithm runs in time $O(N^2)$) and the efficient version (b) takes $O(\log N)$ amortized time per operation, for an $O(N \log N)$ algorithm.

Path compression. The algorithm may call AncestorWithLowestSemi(v) several times for the same node v. The first time, AncestorWithLowestSemi traverses the nodes from v to a_1, some ancestor of v, as shown in Figure 19.11a. Then perhaps some new links $a_3 \rightarrow a_2 \rightarrow a_1$ are added to the forest above a_1, so the second AncestorWithLowestSemi(v) searches up to a_3. But we would like to avoid the duplicate traversal of the path from v to a_1. Furthermore, suppose we later call AncestorWithLowestSemi(w) on some child of v. During that search we would like to be able to skip from v to a_1.

The technique of *path compression* makes AncestorWithLowestSemi faster. For each node v in the spanning forest, we allow $ancestor[v]$ to point to some ancestor of v that may be far above v's parent. But we must remember – in $best[v]$ – the best node in the skipped-over path between $ancestor[v]$ and v.

$ancestor[v] =$ Any node above v in the spanning forest.
$best[v] =$ The node whose semidominator has the lowest *dfnum*, in the skipped-over path from $ancestor[v]$ down to v (including v but not $ancestor[v]$).

Now, when AncestorWithLowestSemi searches upwards, it can compress paths by setting $ancestor[v] \leftarrow ancestor[ancestor[v]]$, as long as it updates

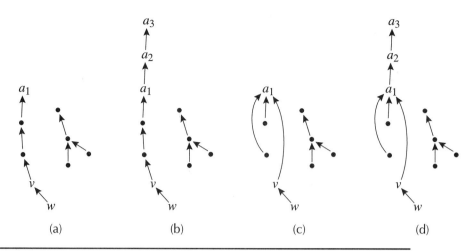

FIGURE 19.11. Path compression. (a) *Ancestor* links in a spanning tree; AncestorWithLowestSemi(v) traverses three links. (b) New nodes a_2, a_3 are linked into the tree. Now AncestorWithLowestSemi(w) would traverse 6 links. (c) AncestorWithLowestSemi(v) with path compression redirects ancestor links, but *best*[v] remembers the best intervening node on the compressed path between v and a_1. (d) Now, after a_2 and a_3 are linked, AncestorWithLowestSemi(w) traverses only 4 links.

best[v] at the same time. This is shown in Algorithm 19.10b.

In a graph of K nodes and E edges, there will be $K-1$ calls to Link and $E+K-1$ calls to AncestorWithLowestSemi. With path compression it can be shown that this takes $O(E \log K)$ time. In terms of the "size" $N = E + K$ of the control-flow graph, Algorithm 19.9+19.10b takes $O(N \log N)$ time.

Balanced path compression. The most sophisticated version of the Lengauer-Tarjan algorithm is Algorithm 19.9 with Link and AncestorWithLowestSemi functions that rebalance the spanning trees, so that the work of path compression is undertaken only when it will do the most good. This algorithm has time complexity $O(N \cdot \alpha(N))$, where $\alpha(N)$ is the slowly growing inverse-Ackermann function that is for all practical purposes constant. In practice it appears that this sophisticated algorithm is about 35% faster than the $N \log N$ algorithm (when measured on graphs of up to 1000 nodes). See also the Further Reading section of this chapter.

19.3   OPTIMIZATION ALGORITHMS USING SSA

Since we are primarily interested in SSA form because it provides quick access to important dataflow information, we should pay some attention to data-structure representations of the SSA graph.

The objects of interest are *statements, basic blocks, and variables*:

Statement Fields of interest are *containing block, previous statement in block, next statement in block, variables defined, variables used.* Each statement may be an *ordinary assignment, φ-function, fetch, store,* or *branch.*

Variable Has a *definition site (statement)* and a list of *use sites.*

Block Has a *list of statements, an ordered list of predecessors, a successor (for blocks ending with a conditional branch, more than one successor).* The order of predecessors is important for determining the meaning $\phi(v_1, v_2, v_3)$ inside the block.

DEAD-CODE ELIMINATION

The SSA data structure makes dead-code analysis particularly quick and easy. A variable is live at its site of definition if and only if its list of uses is not empty. This is true because there can be no other definition of the same variable (it's single-assignment form!) and the definition of a variable dominates every use – so there must be a path from definition to use.[1]

This leads to the following iterative algorithm for deleting dead code:

while there is some variable v with no uses

    and the statement that defines v has no other side effects

      do delete the statement that defines v

In deleting a statement $v \leftarrow x \oplus y$ or the statement $v \leftarrow \phi(x, y)$, we take care to remove the statement from the list of uses of x and of y. This may cause x or y to become dead, if it was the last use. To keep track of this efficiently, Algorithm 19.12 uses a work list W of variables that need to be reconsidered. This takes time proportional to the size of the program plus the number of variables deleted (which itself cannot be larger than the size of the program) – or linear time overall. The only question is how long it takes to delete S from a (potentially long) list of uses of x_i. By keeping x_i's list of uses as a doubly linked list, and having each use of x_i point back *to its own entry in this list*, the deletion can be done in constant time.

---

[1] As usual, we are considering only connected graphs.

$W \leftarrow$ a list of all variables in the SSA program
while W is not empty
    remove some variable v from W
    if v's list of uses is empty
      let S be v's statement of definition
      if S has no side effects other than the assignment to v
        delete S from the program
        for each variable x_i used by S
          delete S from the list of uses of x_i
          $W \leftarrow W \cup \{x_i\}$

ALGORITHM 19.12. Dead-code elimination in SSA form.

If run on the program of Figure 19.3b, this algorithm would delete the statement $b_1 \leftarrow \phi(b_0, b_2)$.

A more aggressive dead-code-elimation algorithm, which uses a different definition of *dead*, is shown on page 426.

SIMPLE CONSTANT PROPAGATION

Whenever there is a statement of the form $v \leftarrow c$ for some constant c, then any use of v can be replaced by a use of c.

Any ϕ-function of the form $v \leftarrow \phi(c_1, c_2, \ldots, c_n)$, where all the c_i are equal, can be replaced by $v \leftarrow c$.

Each of these conditions is easy to detect and implement using the SSA data structure, and we can use a simple work-list algorithm to propagate constants:

$W \leftarrow$ a list of all statements in the SSA program
while W is not empty
    remove some statement S from W
    if S is $v \leftarrow \phi(c, c, \ldots, c)$ for some constant c
      replace S by $v \leftarrow c$
    if S is $v \leftarrow c$ for some constant c
      delete S from the program
      for each statement T that uses v
        substitute c for v in T
        $W \leftarrow W \cup \{T\}$

If we run this algorithm on the SSA program of Figure 19.4g, then the assignment $j_3 \leftarrow i_1$ will be replaced with $j_3 \leftarrow 1$, and the assignment $i_1 \leftarrow 1$ will be deleted. Uses of variables j_1 and k_1 will also be replaced by constants.

The following transformations can all be incorporated into this work-list algorithm, so that in linear time all these optimizations can be done at once:

Copy propagation A single-argument ϕ-function $x \leftarrow \phi(y)$ or a copy assignment $x \leftarrow y$ can be deleted, and y substituted for every use of x.

Constant folding If we have a statement $x \leftarrow a \oplus b$, where a and b are constant, we can evaluate $c \leftarrow a \oplus b$ at compile time and replace the statement with $x \leftarrow c$.

Constant conditions In block L, a conditional branch **if** $a < b$ **goto** L_1 **else** L_2, where a and b are constant, can be replaced by either **goto** L_1 or **goto** L_2, depending on the (compile-time) value of $a < b$. The control-flow edge from L to L_2 (or L_1, respectively) must be deleted; this reduces the number of predecessors of L_2 (or L_1), and the ϕ-functions in that block must be adjusted accordingly (by removing an argument).

Unreachable code Deleting a predecessor may cause block L_2 to become unreachable. In this case, all the statements in L_2 can be deleted; use lists of all the variables that are used in these statements must be adjusted accordingly. Then the block itself should be deleted, reducing the number of predecessors of *its* successor blocks.

CONDITIONAL CONSTANT PROPAGATION

In the program of Figure 19.4b, is j always equal to 1?

- If $j = 1$ always, then block 6 will never execute, so the only assigment to j is $j \leftarrow i$, so $j = 1$ always.
- If sometimes $j > 20$, then block 6 will eventually execute, which assigns $j \leftarrow k$, so that eventually $j > 20$.

Each of these statements is self-consistent; but which is true in practice? In fact, when this program executes, j is never set to any value other than 1. This is a kind of *least fixed point* (analogous to what is described in Section 10.1 on page 209).

The "simple" constant-propagation algorithm has the problem of assuming the block 6 might be executed, and therefore that j might not be constant, and therefore that perhaps $j \geq 20$, and therefore that block 6 might be executed. Simple constant propagation finds a fixed point that is not the least fixed point.

Why would programmers put never-executed statements in their programs? Many programs have statements of the form `if debug then` ... where debug is a constant *false* value; we would not like to let the statements in the debug clauses get in the way of useful optimizations.

The *SSA conditional constant propagation* finds the least fixed point: It *does not assume a block can be executed until there is evidence that it can be*, and it *does not assume a variable is nonconstant until there is evidence*, and so on.

The algorithm tracks the run-time value of each variable as follows:

$\mathcal{V}[v] = \bot$ We have seen no evidence that any assignment to v is ever executed.

$\mathcal{V}[v] = 4$ We have seen evidence that an assignment $v \leftarrow 4$ is executed, but no evidence that v is ever assigned any other value.

$\mathcal{V}[v] = \top$ We have seen evidence that v will have, at various times, at least two different values, or some value (perhaps read from an input file or from memory) that is not predictable at compile time.

Thus we have a lattice of values, with $\bot$ meaning *never defined*, 4 meaning *defined as 4,* and $\top$ meaning *overdefined:*

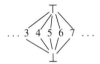

New information can only move a variable up in the lattice.[2]

We also track the executability of each block, as follows:

$\mathcal{E}[B] = false$ We have seen no evidence that block B can ever be executed.

$\mathcal{E}[B] = true$ We have seen evidence that block B can be executed.

Initially we start with $\mathcal{V}[\ ] = \bot$ for all variables, and $\mathcal{E}[\ ] = false$ for all blocks. Then we observe the following:

1. Any variable v with no definition, which is therefore an input to the program, a formal parameter to the procedure, or (horrors!) an uninitialized variable, must have $\mathcal{V}[v] \leftarrow \top$.
2. The start block B_1 is executable: $\mathcal{E}[B_1] \leftarrow true$.
3. For any executable block B with only one successor C, set $\mathcal{E}[C] \leftarrow true$.
4. For any executable assignment $v \leftarrow x \oplus y$, where $\mathcal{V}[x] = c_1$ and $\mathcal{V}[y] = c_2$, set $\mathcal{V}[v] \leftarrow c_1 \oplus c_2$.
5. For any executable assignment $v \leftarrow x \oplus y$, where $\mathcal{V}[x] = \top$ or $\mathcal{V}[y] = \top$, set $\mathcal{V}[v] \leftarrow \top$.

---

[2] Authors in the subfield of dataflow analysis use $\bot$ to mean overdefined and $\top$ to mean never defined; authors in semantics and abstract interpretation use $\bot$ for undefined and $\top$ for overdefined; we are following the latter practice.

6. For any executable assignment $v \leftarrow \phi(x_1, \ldots, x_n)$, where $\mathcal{V}[x_i] = c_1$, $\mathcal{V}[x_j] = c_2$, $c_1 \neq c_2$, the ith predecessor is executable, and the jth predecessor is executable, set $\mathcal{V}[v] \leftarrow \top$.

7. For any executable assignment $v \leftarrow \text{MEM}()$ or $v \leftarrow \text{CALL}()$, set $\mathcal{V}[v] \leftarrow \top$.

8. For any executable assignment $v \leftarrow \phi(x_1, \ldots, x_n)$, where $\mathcal{V}[x_i] = \top$ and the ith predecessor is executable, set $\mathcal{V}[v] \leftarrow \top$.

9. For any assignment $v \leftarrow \phi(x_1, \ldots, x_n)$ whose ith predecessor is executable and $\mathcal{V}[x_i] = c_1$; and for every j either the jth predecessor is not executable, or $\mathcal{V}[x_j] = \bot$, or $\mathcal{V}[x_j] = c_1$, set $\mathcal{V}[v] \leftarrow c_1$.

10. For any executable branch **if** $x < y$ **goto** L_1 **else** L_2, where $\mathcal{V}[x] = \top$ or $\mathcal{V}[y] = \top$, set $\mathcal{E}[L_1] \leftarrow true$ and $\mathcal{E}[L_2] \leftarrow true$.

11. For any executable branch **if** $x < y$ **goto** L_1 **else** L_2, where $\mathcal{V}[x] = c_1$ and $\mathcal{V}[y] = c_2$, set $\mathcal{E}[L_1] \leftarrow true$ or $\mathcal{E}[L_2] \leftarrow true$ depending on $c_1 < c_2$.

An *executable assignment* is an assignment statement in a block B with $\mathcal{E}[B] = true$. These conditions "ignore" any expression or statement in an unexecutable block, and the ϕ-functions "ignore" any operand that comes from an unexecutable predecessor.

The algorithm can be made quite efficient using work lists: There will be one work list W_v for variables and and another work list W_b for blocks. The algorithm proceeds by picking x from W_v and considering conditions 4–9 for any statement in x's list of uses; or by picking a block B from W_b and considering condition 3, and conditions 4–9 for any statement within B. Whenever a block is newly marked executable, it *and its executable successors* are added to W_e. Whenever $\mathcal{V}[x]$ is "raised" from $\bot$ to c or from c to $\top$, then x is added to W_v. When both W_v and W_b are empty, the algorithm is finished. The algorithm runs quickly, because for any x it raises $\mathcal{V}[x]$ at most twice, and for any B it changes $\mathcal{E}[B]$ at most once.

We use this information to optimize the program as follows. After the analysis terminates, wherever $\mathcal{E}[B] = false$, delete block B. Wherever $\mathcal{V}[x] = c$, substitute c for x and delete the assignment to x.

Figure 19.13 shows the conditional constant propagation algorithm executed on the program of Figure 19.4. The algorithm finds that all the j variables are constant (with value 1), k_1 is constant (with value 0), and block 6 is not executed. Deleting unreachable blocks, and replacing uses of constant variables with the constant value – deleting their definitions – leads to some empty blocks and a ϕ-function that has only one argument; these can be simplified, leaving the program of Figure 19.13d.

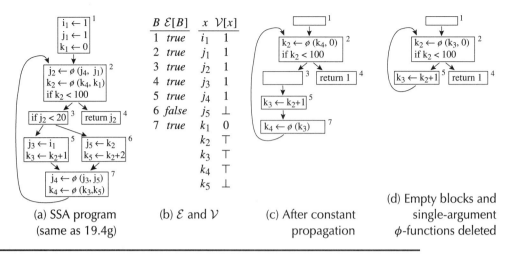

(a) SSA program (same as 19.4g)	(b) $\mathcal{E}$ and $\mathcal{V}$	(c) After constant propagation	(d) Empty blocks and single-argument ϕ-functions deleted

FIGURE 19.13. Conditional constant propagation.

The *unique successor or predecessor* property is important for the proper operation of this algorithm. Suppose we were to do conditional constant propagation on the graph of Figure 19.2b, in a case where $M[x]$ is known to be 1. Then blocks 1, 2, 3, and 4 will be marked executable, but it will not be clear that edge $2 \to 4$ cannot be taken. In Figure 19.2c, block 5 would not be executable, making the situation clear. By using the *edge-split SSA form*, we avoid the need to mark *edges* (not just blocks) executable.

PRESERVING THE DOMINANCE PROPERTY

Almost every reasonable optimizing transformation – including the ones described above – preserves the *dominance property* of the SSA program: The definition of a variable dominates each use (or, when the use is in a ϕ-function, the predecessor of the use).

It is important to preserve this property, since some optimization algorithms (such as Algorithm 19.17) depend on it. Also, the very definition of SSA form – that there is a ϕ-function at the convergence point of any two dataflow paths – implicitly requires it.

But there is one kind of optimization that does not preserve the dominance property. In the program of Figure 19.14a, we can prove that – because the condition $z < 0$ evaluates the same way in blocks 1 and 4 – the use of x_2 in block 5 always gets the value x_1, never x_0. Thus it is tempting to substitute x_1 for x_2 in block 5. But the resulting graph does not have the dominance

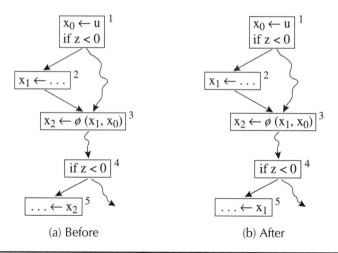

FIGURE 19.14.   This transformation does not preserve the dominance property of SSA form, and should be avoided.

property: Block 5 is not dominated by the definition of x_1 in block 2.

Therefore this kind of transformation – based on the knowledge that two conditional branches test the same condition – is not valid for SSA form.

19.4   ARRAYS, POINTERS, AND MEMORY

For many purposes in optimization, parallelization, and scheduling, the compiler needs to know, "how does statement B depend on statement A?" The transformations of constant propagation and dead-code removal have relied on this dependence information.

There are several kinds of dependence relations:

Read-after-write A defines variable v, then B uses v.
Write-after-write A defines v, then B defines v.
Write-after-read A uses v, then B defines v.
Control A controls whether B executes.

Read-after-write dependences are evident in the SSA graph: A defines v, v's list of uses points to B; or B's *use* list contains v, and v's def-site is A.

Control dependences will be discussed in Section 19.5.

In SSA form, there are no write-after-write or write-after-read dependences. Statements A and B can never write to the same variable, and any use must be "after" (that is, dominated by) the variable's definition.

MEMORY DEPENDENCE

The discussion thus far of assigments and ϕ-function has been only for scalar nonescaping variables. Real programs must also load and store memory words.

One way to get a single-assignment property for memory is to ensure that each memory word is written only once. Although this seems severe, it is just what a pure functional programming language does (see Chapter 15) – with a garbage collector behind the scenes to allow actual reuse of physical memory locations.

However, in an imperative language we must do something else. Consider a sequence of stores and fetches such as this one:

$$
\begin{array}{ll}
1 & M[i] \leftarrow 4 \\
2 & x \;\;\leftarrow M[j] \\
3 & M[k] \leftarrow j
\end{array}
$$

We cannot treat each individual memory location as a separate variable for static-single-assigment purposes, because we don't know whether i, j, and k are the same address.

We could perhaps treat memory as a "variable," where the *store* instruction creates a new value (of the entire memory):

$$
\begin{array}{ll}
1 & M_1 \leftarrow store(M_0, i, 4) \\
2 & x \;\;\leftarrow load(M_1, j) \\
3 & M_2 \leftarrow store(M_1, k, j)
\end{array}
$$

This creates the def-use edges $1 \xrightarrow{M_1} 2$ and $1 \xrightarrow{M_1} 3$. These def-use edges are like any SSA def-use relationship, and we make ϕ-functions for them at join points in the same way.

But there is no edge from $2 \rightarrow 3$, so what prevents the compiler from reordering the statements as follows?

$$
\begin{array}{ll}
1 & M_1 \leftarrow store(M_0, i, 4) \\
3 & M_2 \leftarrow store(M_1, k, j) \\
4 & x \;\;\leftarrow load(M_1, j)
\end{array}
$$

The functional dependences are still correct – if M_1 is viewed as a snapshot of memory after statement 1, then statement 4 is still correct in loading from address j in that snapshot. But it is inefficient – to say the least! – for the computer to keep more than one copy of the machine's memory.

We would like to say that there is a *write-after-read* dependence $2 \rightarrow 3$ to prevent the compiler from creating M_2 before all uses of M_1 have been computed. But calculation of accurate dependence information for memory locations is beyond the scope of this chapter.

A naive but practical solution. In the absence of write-after-read and write-after-write dependence information, we will just say that a store instruction is always presumed live – we will not do dead-code elimination on stores – and we will not transform the program in such a way as to interchange a load and a store, or two stores. Store instructions can be unreachable, however, and unreachable stores can be deleted.

The optimization algorithms presented in this chapter do not reorder instructions, and they do not attempt to propagate dataflow information through memory, so they implicitly use this naive model of loads and stores.

19.5 THE CONTROL-DEPENDENCE GRAPH

Can node x directly control whether node y is executed? The answer to this question can help us with program transformations and optimizations.

Any flowgraph must have an *exit* node. If a control-flow graph represents a single function, then this is the **return** statement of the function; if there are several **return** statements, we assume that each one of them is really a control-flow edge to some unique canonical *exit* node of the CFG.

We say that a node y is *control-dependent* on x if from x we can branch to u or v; from u there is a path to *exit* that avoids y, and from v every path to *exit* hits y:

The *control-dependence graph* (CDG) has an edge from x to y whenever y is control-dependent on x.

We say that y *postdominates* v when y is on every path from v to *exit* – that is, y dominates v in the *reverse* control-flow graph.

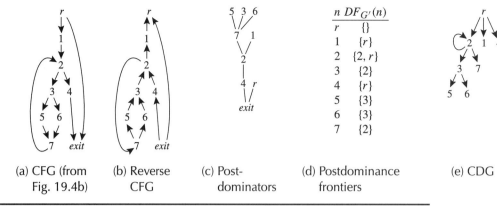

| | | | (a) CFG (from Fig. 19.4b) | (b) Reverse CFG | (c) Post- dominators | (d) Postdominance frontiers | (e) CDG |

FIGURE 19.15. Construction of the control-dependence graph.

Construction of the control-dependence graph. To construct the CDG of a control-flow graph G,

1. Add a new *entry*-node r to G, with an edge $r \rightarrow s$ to the start node s of G (indicating that the surrounding program might enter G) and an edge $r \rightarrow$ *exit* to the exit node of G (indicating that the surrounding program might not execute G at all).
2. Let G' be the *reverse control-flow graph* that has an edge $y \rightarrow x$ whenever G has an edge $x \rightarrow y$; the *start* node of G' corresponds to the *exit* node of G.
3. Construct the dominator tree of G' (its root corresponds to the *exit* node of G).
4. Calculate the dominance frontiers $DF_{G'}$ of the nodes of G'.
5. The CDG has edge $x \rightarrow y$ whenever $x \in DF_{G'}[y]$.

That is, x directly controls whether y executes, if and only if x is in the dominance frontier of y in the reverse control-flow graph.

Figure 19.15 shows the CDG for the program of Figure 19.4.

With the SSA graph and the control-dependence graph, we can now answer questions of the form, "must A be executed before B?" If there is any path $A \rightarrow B$ composed of SSA use-def edges and CDG edges, then there is a trail of data- and control-dependence requiring A to be performed before B.

AGGRESSIVE DEAD-CODE ELIMINATION

One interesting use of the control-dependence graph is in dead-code elimination. Suppose we have a situation such as the one in Figure 19.13d, where conventional dead-code analysis (as described in Section 17.3 or Algorithm 19.12) determines:

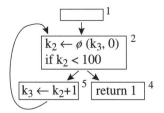

(a) SSA program

(b) Postdominators

n	$DF_{G'}(n)$
r	{}
1	{r}
2	{2,r}
4	{r}
5	{2}

(c) Postdominance frontiers

(d) Control-dependence graph

Block 4 returns, so it is live; no live block is control-dependent on 2, and no live assignment is data-dependent on k_2 or k_3, so nothing else is live.

(e) Finding live statements

return 1	4

(f) After deletion of dead statements

FIGURE 19.16. Aggressive dead-code elimination

- k_2 is live because it's used in the definition of k_3,
- k_3 is live because it's used in the definition of k_2,

but neither variable contributes anything toward the eventual result of the calculation.

Just as conditional constant propagation assumes a block is unreachable unless there is evidence that execution can reach it, *aggressive dead-code elimination* assumes a statement is dead unless it has evidence that it contributes to the eventual result of the program.

Algorithm. Mark *live* any statement that:

1. Performs input/output, stores into memory, returns from the function, or calls another function that might have side effects;
2. Defines some variable v that is used by another live statement; or
3. Is a conditional branch, upon which some other live statement is control-dependent.

Then delete all unmarked statements.

This can be solved by iteration (or by a work-list algorithm). Figure 19.16 shows the amusing result of running this algorithm on the program of Figure 19.13d: The entire loop is deleted, leaving a very efficient program!

Caveat. The aggressive dead-code elimination algorithm will remove output-free infinite loops, which does change the meaning of the program. Instead of producing nothing, the program will execute the statements after the loop, which may produce output. In many environments this is regarded as unacceptable.

But on the other hand, the control-dependence graph is often used in parallelizing compilers: Any two statements that are not control-dependent or data-dependent can be executed in parallel. Even if such a compiler did not delete a useless infinite loop, it might choose to execute the loop in parallel with successor statements (that are not control-dependent on it); this would have approximately the same effect as deleting the infinite loop.

19.6   CONVERTING BACK FROM SSA FORM

After program transformations and optimization, a program in static single-assignment form must be translated into some executable representation without ϕ-functions. The definition $y \leftarrow \phi(x_1, x_2, x_3)$ can be translated as "move $y \leftarrow x_1$ if arriving along predecessor edge 1, move $y \leftarrow x_2$ if arriving along predecessor edge 2, and move $y \leftarrow x_3$ if arriving along predecessor edge 3." To "implement" this definition in an edge-split SSA form, for each i we insert the move $y \leftarrow x_i$ at the end of the ith predecessor of the block containing the ϕ-function.

The *unique successor or predecessor* property prevents redundant moves from being inserted; in Figure 19.2b (without the property), block 2 would need a move $a_3 \leftarrow a_1$ that is redundant if the *then* branch is taken; but in Figure 19.2c, the move $a_3 \leftarrow a_1$ would be in block 5, and never executed redundantly.

Now we can do register allocation on this program, as described in Chapter 11. Although it is tempting simply to assign x_1 and x_2 the same register if they were derived from the same variable x in the original program, it could be that program transformations on the SSA form have made their live ranges interfere (see Exercise 19.11). Thus, we ignore the original derivation of the different SSA variables, and we rely on coalescing (copy propagation) in the register allocator to eliminate almost all of the move instructions.

LivenessAnalysis() =
   for each variable v
      $M \leftarrow \{\}$
      for each site-of-use s of v
         if s is a ϕ-function with
            v as its ith argument
            let p be the ith predecessor of
               the block containing s
            LiveOutAtBlock(p, v)
         else LiveInAtStatement(s, v)

LiveOutAtBlock(n, v) =
   v *is live-out at* n
   if $n \notin M$
      $M \leftarrow M \cup \{n\}$
      let s be the last statement in n
      LiveOutAtStatement(s, v)

LiveInAtStatement(s, v) =
   v *is live-in at* s
   if s is the first statement of some block n
      v *is live-in at* n
      for each predecessor p of n
         LiveOutAtBlock(p, v)
   else
      let s' be the statement preceding s
      LiveOutAtStatement(s', v)

LiveOutAtStatement(s, v) =
   v *is live-out at* s
   let W be the set of variables that s defines
   for each variable $w \in (W - \{v\})$
      add (v, w) to interference graph
   if $v \notin W$
      LiveInAtStatement(s, v)

ALGORITHM 19.17. Calculation of live ranges in SSA form, and building the interference graph. The graph-walking algorithm is expressed as a mutual recursion between *LiveOutAtBlock, LiveInAtStatement,* and *LiveOutAtStatement.* The recursion is bounded whenever *LiveOutAtBlock* finds an already walked block, or whenever *LiveOutAtStatement* reaches the definition of v.

LIVENESS ANALYSIS FOR SSA

We can efficiently construct the interference graph of an SSA program, just prior to converting the ϕ-functions to move instructions. For each variable v, Algorithm 19.17 walks backward from each use, stopping when it reaches v's definition.

The *dominance property of SSA form* ensures that the algorithm will always stay in the region dominated by the definition of v. For many variables this region is small; contrast this with the situation in Figure 19.14 (a non-SSA program), where the algorithm applied to variable x_1 would walk upwards through the $1 \to 3$ edge and traverse the entire program. Because this algorithm processes only the blocks where v is live, its running time is proportional to the size of the interference graph that it constructs (see Exercise 19.12).

Algorithm 19.17 as shown uses recursion (when *LiveInAtStatement* calls

LiveOutAtBlock), and also *tail recursion* (when *LiveInAtStatement* calls *Live-OutAtStatement*, when *LiveOutAtStatement* calls *LiveInAtStatement*, and when *LiveOutAtBlock* calls *LiveOutAtStatement*). Some programming languages or compilers can compile tail recursion very efficiently as a *goto* – see Section 15.6. But when implementing this algorithm in compilers that do not support efficient tail calls, then instead of tail recursion it might be best to use explicit goto's, or use work lists for *LiveOutAtStatement* and *LiveInAtStatement*.

19.7 A FUNCTIONAL INTERMEDIATE FORM

A *functional* programming language is one in which (as discussed in Chapter 15) execution proceeds by binding variables to values, and never modifying a variable once it is initialized. This permits equational reasoning, which is useful to the programmer.

But equational reasoning is even *more* useful to the compiler – many compiler optimizations involve the rewriting of a slow program into an equivalent faster program. When the compiler doesn't have to worry about x's value *now* versus x's value *later*, then these transformations are easier to express.

This single-assignment property is at the heart of both functional programming and SSA form. There is a close relationship between the functional intermediate representations used by functional-language compilers and the SSA form used by imperative-language compilers.

Figure 19.18 shows the abstract syntax of the kind of intermediate representation used in modern functional-language compilers. It aspires to the best qualities of quadruples, SSA form, and lambda-calculus. As in quadruple notation, expressions are broken down into primitive operations whose order of evaluation is specified, every intermediate result is an explicitly named temporary, and every argument of an operator or function is an *atom* (variable or constant). As in SSA form and lambda-calculus, every variable has a single assignment (or *binding*), and every use of the variable is within the *scope* of the binding. As in lambda-calculus, scope is a simple syntactic notion, not requiring calculation of dominators.

Scope. No variable name can be used in more than one binding. Every binding of a variable has a scope within which all the uses of that variable must occur. For a variable bound by **let** $v = \ldots$ **in** *exp*, the scope of v is just the

atom	$\rightarrow c$	Constant integer
atom	$\rightarrow s$	Constant string pointer
atom	$\rightarrow v$	Variable
exp	$\rightarrow$ **let** *fundefs* **in** *exp*	Function declaration
exp	$\rightarrow$ **let** $\underline{v} = atom$ **in** *exp*	Copy
exp	$\rightarrow$ **let** $\underline{v} = binop(atom, atom)$ **in** *exp*	Arithmetic operator
exp	$\rightarrow$ **let** $\underline{v} = M[atom]$ **in** *exp*	Fetch from memory
exp	$\rightarrow M[atom]:=atom;\ exp$	Store to memory
exp	$\rightarrow$ **if** *atom relop atom* **then** *exp* **else** *exp*	Conditional branch
exp	$\rightarrow atom(args)$	Tail call
exp	$\rightarrow$ **let** $\underline{v} = atom(args)$ **in** *exp*	Non-tail call
exp	$\rightarrow$ **return** *atom*	Return
args	$\rightarrow$	
args	$\rightarrow atom\ \ args$	
fundefs	$\rightarrow$	
fundefs	$\rightarrow$ *fundefs* **function** $\underline{v}(formals) = exp$	
formals	$\rightarrow$	
formals	$\rightarrow \underline{v}\ \ formals$	
binop	$\rightarrow$ **plus** | **minus** | **mul** | $\ldots$	
relop	$\rightarrow$ **eq** | **ne** | **lt** | $\ldots$	

FIGURE 19.18. Functional intermediate representation. Binding occurrences of variables are underlined.

---

exp. The scope of a function variable f_i bound in

$$\textbf{let function } f_1(\ldots) = exp_1$$
$$\vdots$$
$$\textbf{function } f_k(\ldots) = exp_k$$
$$\textbf{in } exp$$

includes *all* the exp_j (to allow for mutually recursive functions) as well as the *exp*. For a variable bound as the formal parameter of a function, the scope is the body of that function.

These scope rules make many optimizations easy to reason about; we will take *inline expansion of functions* as an example. As discussed in Section 15.4, when we have a definition $f(x) = E$ and a use $f(z)$ we can replace

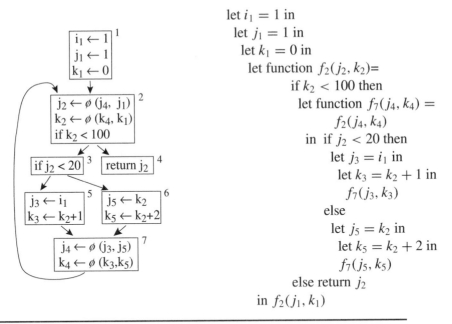

let $i_1 = 1$ in
  let $j_1 = 1$ in
    let $k_1 = 0$ in
      let function $f_2(j_2, k_2) =$
        if $k_2 < 100$ then
          let function $f_7(j_4, k_4) =$
            $f_2(j_4, k_4)$
          in if $j_2 < 20$ then
            let $j_3 = i_1$ in
             let $k_3 = k_2 + 1$ in
              $f_7(j_3, k_3)$
          else
            let $j_5 = k_2$ in
             let $k_5 = k_2 + 2$ in
              $f_7(j_5, k_5)$
        else return j_2
      in $f_2(j_1, k_1)$

PROGRAM 19.19. SSA program of Figure 19.4g converted to functional intermediate form.

the use by a copy of E but with all the x's replaced by z's. In the `Tree` language of Chapter 7 this is difficult to express because there are no functions;
in the functional notation of Chapter 15 the substitution can get complicated
if z is a nonatomic expression (as shown in Algorithm 15.8b). But in the
functional intermediate form of Figure 19.18, where all actual parameters are
atomic, inline expansion becomes very simple, as shown in Algorithm 15.8a.

Translating SSA into functional form. Any SSA program can be translated
into this functional form, as shown in Algorithm 19.20. Each control-flow
node with more than one predecessor becomes a function. The arguments
of that function are precisely the variables for which there are ϕ-functions
at the node. If node f dominates node g, then the function for g will be
nested inside the body of the function for f. Instead of jumping to a node, a
control-flow edge into a ϕ-containing node is represented by a function call.
Program 19.19 shows how a translated program looks.

Translating functional programs into functional intermediate form. A functional program in a language such as PureFun-MiniJava starts in a form that

Translate(*node*) =
    let C be the children of *node* in the dominator tree
    let $p_1, \ldots, p_n$ be the nodes of C that have more than one predecessor
    for $i \leftarrow 1$ to n
        let $a_1, \ldots, a_k$ be the targets of ϕ functions in p_i (possibly $k = 0$)
        let $S_i = $ Translate(p_i)
        let $F_i = $ "`function` $f_{p_i}(a_1, \ldots, a_k) = S_i$"
    let $F = F_1 F_2 \cdots F_n$
    return Statements$(node, 1, F)$

Statements(*node*, *j*, *F*) =
if there are $< j$ statements in *node*
    then let s be the successor of *node*
        if s has only one predecessor
        then return Statements$(s, 1, F)$
        else s has m predecessors
            suppose *node* is the ith predecessor of s
            suppose the ϕ-functions in s are $a_1 \leftarrow \phi(a_{11}, \ldots, a_{1m})$, $\ldots$
$$a_k \leftarrow \phi(a_{k1}, \ldots, a_{km})$$
        return "`let` F `in` $f_s(a_{1i}, \ldots, a_{ki})$"
else if the jth statement of *node* is a ϕ-function
    then return Statements$(node, j + 1, F)$
else if the jth statement of *node* is "return a"
    then return "`let` F `in return` a"
else if the jth statement of *node* is $a \leftarrow b \oplus c$
    then let $S = $ Statements$(node, j + 1, F)$
        return "`let` $a = b \oplus c$ `in` S"
else if the jth statement of *node* is "if $a < b$ goto s_1 else s_2"
    then (in edge-split SSA form) s_1 has only one predecessor, as does s_2
        let $S_1 = $ Translate(s_1)
        let $S_2 = $ Translate(s_2)
        return "`let` F `in if` $a < b$ `then` S_1 `else` S_2"

The cases for $a \leftarrow b$, $a \leftarrow M[b]$, and $M[a] \leftarrow b$ are similar.

ALGORITHM 19.20. Translating SSA to functional intermediate form.

obeys all the scope rules, but arguments are not atomic and variables are not unique. It is a simple matter to introduce well-scoped intermediate temporaries by a recursive walk of expression trees; dominator and SSA calculations are unnecessary.

All of the SSA-based optimization algorithms work equally well on a functional intermediate form; so will the optimizations and transformations on functional programs described in Chapter 15. Functional intermediate forms can also be made explicitly typed, type-checkable, and polymorphic as described in Chapter 16. All in all, this kind of intermediate representation has much to recommend it.

FURTHER READING

The IBM *Fortran H* compiler used dominators to identify loops in control-flow graphs of basic blocks of machine instructions [Lowry and Medlock 1969]. Lengauer and Tarjan [1979] developed the near-linear-time algorithm for finding dominators in a directed graph, and proved the related theorems mentioned in this chapter. It is common to use this algorithm while mentioning the existence [Harel 1985] of a more complicated linear-time algorithm. Finding the "best" node above a given spanning-forest node is an example of a *union-find* problem; analyses of balanced path-compression algorithms for union-find (such as the "sophisticated" version of the Lengauer-Tarjan algorithm) can be found in many algorithms textbooks (e.g., Sections 22.3–22.4 of Cormen et al. [1990]).

Static single-assignment form was developed by Wegman, Zadeck, Alpern, and Rosen [Alpern et al. 1988; Rosen et al. 1988] for efficient computation of dataflow problems such as global value numbering, congruence of variables, aggressive dead-code removal, and constant propagation with conditional branches [Wegman and Zadeck 1991]. Control-dependence was formalized by Ferrante et al. [1987] for use in an optimizing compiler for vector parallel machines. Cytron et al. [1991] describe the efficient computation of SSA and control-dependence graphs using dominance frontiers and prove several of the theorems mentioned in this chapter.

Wolfe [1996] describes several optimization algorithms on SSA (which he calls *factored use-def chains*), including induction-variable analysis.

It is useful to perform several transformations on the flowgraph *before* conversion to SSA form. These include the conversion of while-loops to repeat-loops (Section 18.2); and the insertion of loop *preheader* nodes (see page 382), *postbody* nodes [Wolfe 1996] (Exercise 18.6), and *landing pads* for loop-exit edges [Rosen et al. 1988] (edge-splitting effectively accomplishes the insertion of landing pads). Such transformations provide locations into which statements (such as loop-invariant computations or common subexpressions) may be placed.

Varieties of functional intermediate representations. Functional intermediate forms are all based on lambda-calculus, more or less, but they differ in three important respects:

1. Some are *strict* and some are *lazy* (see Chapter 15).
2. Some have arbitrary nesting of subexpressions; some have *atomic arguments*; and some have *atomic arguments* $+\lambda$, meaning that all arguments except anonymous functions are atomic.
3. Some permit nontail calls *(direct style)* and some support only tail calls *(continuation-passing style)*.

Distinction (1) ceases to matter in continuation-passing style.

The design space of these options has been well explored, as this table shows:

| | Direct style | | Continuation- |
	Strict	Lazy	passing
Arbitrarily nested sub-expressions	Cardelli [1984], Cousineau et al. [1985]	Augustsson [1984]	
Atomic arguments $+\lambda$	Flanagan et al. [1993]		Steele [1978], Kranz et al. [1986]
Atomic arguments	Tarditi [1997]	Peyton Jones [1992]	Appel [1992]

The *functional intermediate form* shown in Figure 19.18 fits in the lower left-hand corner, along with Tarditi [1997]. Kelsey [1995] shows how to convert between SSA and continuation-passing style.

EXERCISES

19.1 Write an algorithm, using depth-first search, to number the nodes of a tree in depth-first order *and* to annotate each node with the number of its highest-numbered descendent. Show how these annotations can be used – once your preprocessing algorithm has been run on a dominator tree – to answer a query of the form "does node i dominate node j?" in constant time.

19.2 Use Algorithm 19.9 to calculate the dominators of the flowgraph of Exercise 18.1, showing the semidominators and spanning forest at various stages.

19.3 For each of the graphs of Figure 18.1 and Figure 18.2, calculate the immediate dominator tree (using either Algorithm 19.9 or the algorithm in Section 18.1), and for each node n calculate $DF_{local}[n]$, $DF_{up}[n]$, and DF.

*19.4 Prove that, for any node v, Algorithm 19.9+19.10b always initializes $best[v] \leftarrow v$ (in the Link function) before calling AncestorWithLowestSemi(v).

19.5 Calculate the dominance frontier of each node in each of these graphs:

a. The graph of Figure 2.8.

b. The graph of Exercise 2.3a.

c. The graph of Exercise 2.5a.

d. The graph of Figure 3.27.

**19.6 Prove that

$$DF[n] = DF_{local}[n] \ \cup \ \bigcup_{Z \in children[n]} DF_{up}[Z]$$

as follows:

a. Show that $DF_{local}[n] \subseteq DF[n]$;

b. Show that for each child Z of n, $DF_{up}[Z] \subseteq DF[n]$;

c. If there is a node Y in $DF[n]$, then therefore there is an edge $U \rightarrow Y$ such that n dominates U but does not strictly dominate Y. Show that if $Y = n$, then $Y \in DF_{local}[n]$, and if $Y \neq n$, then $Y \in DF_{up}[Z]$ for some child Z of N.

d. Combine these lemmas into a proof of the theorem.

19.7 Convert this program to SSA form:

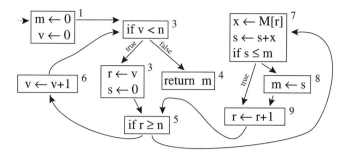

Show your work after each stage:

a. Add a start node containing initializations of all variables.

b. Draw the dominator tree.

c. Calculate dominance frontiers.

d. Insert ϕ-functions.

e. Add subscripts to variables.

f. Use Algorithm 19.17 to build the interference graph.

g. Convert back from SSA form by inserting *move* instructions in place of ϕ-functions.

19.8 This C (or Java) program illustrates an important difference between def-use chains and SSA form:

```
int f(int i, int j) {
  int x,y;
  switch(i) {
    case 0:   x=3;
    case 1:   x=1;
    case 2:   x=4;
    case 3:   x=1;
    case 4:   x=5;
    default: x=9;
  }
  switch(j) {
    case 0:   y=x+2;
    case 1:   y=x+7;
    case 2:   y=x+1;
    case 3:   y=x+8;
    case 4:   y=x+2;
    default: y=x+8;
  }
  return y;
}
```

a. Draw the control-flow graph of this program.

b. Draw the use-def and def-use data structures of the program: For each definition site, draw a linked-list data structure pointing to each use site, and vice versa.

c. Starting from the CFG of part (a), convert the program to SSA form. Draw data structures representing the uses, defs, and ϕ-functions, as described at the beginning of Section 19.3.

d. Count the total number of data-structure nodes in the use-def data, and the total number in the SSA data structure. Compare.

e. Approximate the total sizes of the use-def data structures, and the SSA data structures, if there were N cases in each switch instead of 6.

*19.9 Suppose the graph of Exercise 2.3a is the control-flow graph of a program, and in block 1 there is an assigment to a variable v.

a. Convert the graph to SSA form (insert ϕ-functions for v).

b. Show that for any N, there is a "ladder" CFG with $O(N)$ blocks, $O(N)$ edges, and $O(N)$ assignment statements (all in the first block!), such that the number of ϕ-functions in the SSA form is N^2.

c. Write a program whose CFG looks like this.

d. Show that a program containing deeply nested **repeat-until** loops can have the same N^2 blowup of ϕ-functions.

*19.10 Algorithm 19.7 uses a stack for each variable, to remember the current active definition of the variable. This is equivalent to using environments to process nested scopes, as Chapter 5 explained for type-checking.

a. Rewrite Algorithm 19.7, calling upon the imperative environments of package Symbol (whose interface is given in Program 5.5) instead of using explicit stacks.

b. Rewrite Algorithm 19.7, using the functional-style symbol tables whose Table class is described on page 110.

19.11 Show that optimization on an SSA program can cause two SSA variables a_1 and a_2, derived from the same variable a in the original program, to have overlapping live ranges as described on page 428. **Hint:** Convert this program to SSA, and then do exactly one constant-propagation optimization.

```
while  c<0   do (b := a;  a := M[x]; c := a+b);
return a;
```

*19.12 Let V_c and E_c be the nodes and edges of the CFG, and V_i and E_i be the nodes and edges of the interference graph produced by Algorithm 19.17. Let $N = |V_c| + |E_c| + |V_i| + |E_i|$.

a. Show that the run time of Algorithm 19.17 on the following (weird) program is asymptotically proportional to $N^{1.5}$:

$$v_1 \leftarrow 0$$
$$v_2 \leftarrow 0$$
$$\vdots$$
$$v_m \leftarrow 0$$
$$\text{goto } L_1$$
$$L_1: \quad \text{goto } L_2$$
$$L_2: \quad \text{goto } L_3$$
$$\vdots$$
$$L_{m^2}:$$
$$w_1 \leftarrow v_1$$
$$w_2 \leftarrow v_2$$
$$\vdots$$
$$w_m \leftarrow v_m$$

*b. Show that if every block defines at least one variable, and has no more than c statements and no more than c out-edges (for some constant c), then the time complexity of Algorithm 19.17 is $O(N)$. **Hint:** Whenever LiveOutAtBlock is called, there will be at most c calls to LiveOutAtStatement, and at least one will add an edge to the interference graph.

20

Pipelining and Scheduling

sched·ule: a procedural plan that indicates the time and sequence of each operation

Webster's Dictionary

A simple computer can process one instruction at a time. First it fetches the instruction, then decodes it into opcode and operand specifiers, then reads the operands from the register bank (or memory), then performs the arithmetic denoted by the opcode, then writes the result back to the register back (or memory), and then fetches the next instruction.

Modern computers can execute parts of many different instructions at the same time. At the same time the processor is writing results of two instructions back to registers, it may be doing arithmetic for three other instructions, reading operands for two more instructions, decoding four others, and fetching yet another four. Meanwhile, there may be five instructions delayed, awaiting the results of memory-fetches.

Such a processor usually fetches instructions from a single flow of control; it's not that several programs are running in parallel, but the adjacent instructions of a single program are decoded and executed simultaneously. This is called *instruction-level parallelism* (ILP), and is the basis for much of the astounding advance in processor speed in the last decade of the twentieth century.

A *pipelined* machine performs the write-back of one instruction in the same cycle as the arithmetic "execute" of the next instruction and the operand-read of the previous one, and so on. A *very-long-instruction-word* (VLIW) issues several instructions in the same processor cycle; the compiler must ensure that they are not data-dependent on each other. A *superscalar* machine issues two or more instructions in parallel *if they are not related by data dependence* (which it can check quickly in the instruction-decode hardware); otherwise it issues the instructions sequentially – thus, the program will still operate correctly if data-dependent instructions are adjacent, but it will run faster if the compiler has not scheduled non-data-dependent instructions adjacent to each other. A *dynamic-scheduling* machine reorders the instructions as they are being executed, so that it can issue several non-data-dependent instructions simultaneously, and may need less help from the compiler. Any of these techniques produces instruction-level parallism.

The more instructions can be executed simultaneously, the faster the program will run. But why can't all the instructions of the program be executed in parallel? After all, that would be the fastest possible execution.

There are several kinds of *constraints* on instruction execution; we can optimize the program for instruction-level parallelism by finding the best *schedule* that obeys these constraints:

Data dependence: If instruction A calculates a result that's used as an operand of instruction B, then B cannot execute before A is finished.

Functional unit: If there are k_{fu} multipliers (adders, etc.) on the chip, then at most k_{fu} multiplication (addition, etc.) instructions can execute at once.

Instruction issue: The instruction-issue unit can issue at most k_{ii} instructions at a time.

Register: At most k_r registers can be in use at a time; more specifically, any schedule must have some valid register allocation.

The functional-unit, instruction-issue, and register constraints are often lumped together as *resource constraints* or *resource hazards*.

On a pipelined machine, even if "B cannot *execute* before A," there may be some parts of B's execution (such as instruction-fetch) that can proceed concurrently with A; Figures 20.2 and 20.3 give details.

There are also pseudo-constraints that can often be made to disappear by renaming variables:

Write-after-write: If instruction A writes to a register or memory location, and B writes to the same location, then the order of A and B must not be changed. But often it is possible to modify the program so that A and B write to different locations.

Write-after-read: If A must read from a location before B writes to it, then A and B's order of execution must not be swapped, unless renaming can be done so that they use different locations.

	Cycle 0	Cycle 1	Cycle 2	Cycle 3	Cycle 4	Cycle 5	Cycle 6	Cycle 7	Cycle 8	Cycle 9
ADD	I-Fetch	Read	Unpack	Shift Add	Round Add	Round Shift	Write			
MULT	I-Fetch	Read	Unpack	MultA	MultA	MultA	MultB	MultB Add	Round	Write
CONV	I-Fetch	Read	Unpack	Add	Round	Shift	Shift	Add	Round	Write

FIGURE 20.1. Functional unit requirements of instructions (on the MIPS R4000 processor). This machine's floating-point ADD instruction uses the instruction-fetch unit for one cycle; reads registers for one cycle; unpacks exponent and mantissa; then for the next cycle uses a shifter and an adder; then uses both the adder and a rounding unit; then the rounding unit and a shifter; then writes a result back to the register file. The MULT and CONV instructions use functional units in a different order.

Resource usage of an instruction. We might describe an instruction in terms of the number of cycles it takes to execute, and the resources it uses at different stages of execution. Figure 20.1 shows such a description for three instructions of a hypothetical machine.

If the ith cycle of instruction A uses a particular resource, and the jth cycle of instruction B uses the same resource, then B cannot be scheduled exactly $i - j$ cycles after A, as illustrated in Figure 20.2.

However, some machines have several functional units of each kind (e.g., more than one adder); on such a machine it does not suffice to consider instructions pairwise, but we must consider all the instructions scheduled for a given time.

Data-dependence of an instruction. The same considerations apply to data-dependence constraints. The result of some instruction A is written back to the register file during the **Write** stage of its execution (see Figure 20.1); if instruction B uses this register, then the **Read** stage of B must be after the **Write** stage of A. Some machines have bypass circuitry that may allow the arithmetic stage of B to follow immediately after the arithmetic stage of A; for example, the **Shift/Add** stage of an ADD instruction might be able to immediately follow the **Round** stage of a MULT. These situations are shown in Figure 20.3.

	C1	C2	C3	C4	C5	C6	C7	C8	C9	C10	
ADD	**I-Fetch**	**Read**	**Unpack**	Shift Add	Round Add	Round Shift	Write				
MULT	**I-Fetch**	**Read**	**Unpack**	MultA	MultA	MultA	MultB	MultB Add	Round	Write	X

	C1	C2	C3	C4	C5	C6	C7	C8	C9	C10	
ADD		I-Fetch	Read	Unpack	Shift Add	Round Add	Round Shift	Write			
MULT	I-Fetch	Read	Unpack	MultA	MultA	MultA	MultB	MultB Add	Round	Write	OK

	C1	C2	C3	C4	C5	C6	C7	C8	C9	C10	
ADD			I-Fetch	Read	Unpack	Shift Add	Round Add	Round Shift	Write		
MULT	I-Fetch	Read	Unpack	MultA	MultA	MultA	MultB	MultB Add	Round	Write	OK

	C1	C2	C3	C4	C5	C6	C7	C8	C9	C10	
ADD				I-Fetch	Read	Unpack	Shift Add	**Round Add**	**Round Shift**	**Write**	
MULT	I-Fetch	Read	Unpack	MultA	MultA	MultA	MultB	**MultB Add**	**Round**	**Write**	X

	C1	C2	C3	C4	C5	C6	C7	C8	C9	C10	
ADD				I-Fetch	Read	Unpack	**Shift Add**	**Round Add**	Round Shift	Write	
MULT	Read	Unpack	MultA	MultA	MultA	MultB	**MultB Add**	**Round**	Write		X

	C1	C2	C3	C4	C5	C6	C7	C8	C9	C10	
ADD				I-Fetch	Read	Unpack	Shift Add	Round Add	Round Shift	Write	
MULT	Unpack	MultA	MultA	MultA	MultB	MultB Add	Round	Write			OK

FIGURE 20.2.   If there is only one functional unit of each kind, then an ADD cannot be started at the same time as a MULT (because of numerous resource hazards shown in boldface); nor three cycles after the MULT (because of **Add**, **Round**, and **Write** hazards); nor four cycles later (because of **Add** and **Round** hazards). But if there were two adders and two rounding units, then an ADD *could* be started four cycles after a MULT. Or with dual fetch units, multiple-access register file, and dual unpackers, the MULT and ADD could be started simultaneously.

MultA	MultA	MultA	MultB	MultB Add	Round	Write↓						
						I-Fetch	↑Read	Unpack	Shift Add	Round Add	Round Shift	Write

MultA	MultA	MultA	MultB	MultB Add	Round↓	Write					
			I-Fetch	Read	Unpack	↑Shift Add	Round Add	Round Shift	Write

FIGURE 20.3.   Data dependence. (Above) If the MULT produces a result that is an operand to ADD, the MULT must write its result to the register file before the ADD can read it. (Below) Special bypassing circuitry can route the result of MULT directly to the Shift and Add units, skipping the Write, Read, and Unpack stages.

20.1   LOOP SCHEDULING WITHOUT RESOURCE BOUNDS

Choosing an optimal schedule subject to data-dependence constraints and resource hazards is difficult – it is NP-complete, for example. Although NP-completeness should never scare the compiler writer (graph coloring is NP-complete, but the approximation algorithm for graph coloring described in Chapter 11 is very successful), it remains the case that resource-bounded loop scheduling is hard to do in practice.

We will first describe an algorithm that ignores the resource constraints and finds an optimal schedule subject only to the data-dependence constraints. This algorithm is not useful in practice, but it illustrates the kind of opportunities there are in instruction-level parallelism.

The *Aiken-Nicolau loop pipelining* algorithm has several steps:

1. Unroll the loop;
2. Schedule each instruction from each iteration at the earliest possible time;
3. Plot the instructions in a tableau of iteration-number versus time;
4. Find separated groups of instructions at given slopes;
5. Coalesce the slopes;
6. Reroll the loop.

We use Program 20.4a as an example to explain the notions of *tableau*, *slope*, and *coalesce*. Let us assume that every instruction can be completed in one cycle, and that arbitrarily many instructions can be issued in the same cycle, subject only to data-dependence constraints.

$$
\begin{array}{llll}
\textbf{for } i \leftarrow 1 \textbf{ to } N & & \textbf{for } i \leftarrow 1 \textbf{ to } N & \\
\quad a & \leftarrow j \oplus V[i-1] & \quad a_i & \leftarrow j_{i-1} \oplus b_{i-1} \\
\quad b & \leftarrow a \oplus f & \quad b_i & \leftarrow a_i \oplus f_{i-1} \\
\quad c & \leftarrow e \oplus j & \quad c_i & \leftarrow e_{i-1} \oplus j_{i-1} \\
\quad d & \leftarrow f \oplus c & \quad d_i & \leftarrow f_{i-1} \oplus c_i \\
\quad e & \leftarrow b \oplus d & \quad e_i & \leftarrow b_i \oplus d_i \\
\quad f & \leftarrow U[i] & \quad f_i & \leftarrow U[i] \\
g: V[i] & \leftarrow b & g: V[i] & \leftarrow b_i \\
h: W[i] & \leftarrow d & h: W[i] & \leftarrow d_i \\
\quad j & \leftarrow X[i] & \quad j_i & \leftarrow X[i] \\
\end{array}
$$

(a)   (b)

PROGRAM 20.4.   (a) A **for**-loop to be software-pipelined. (b) After a *scalar-replacement* optimization (in the definition of *a*); and scalar variables labeled with their iteration-number.

Data dependence through memory. For optimal scheduling of stores and fetches, we need to trace data dependence as each value is stored into memory and then fetched back. As discussed on page 424, dependence analysis of memory references is not trivial! In order to illustrate loop scheduling for Program 20.4a without full-fledged dependence analysis, we can use *scalar replacement* to replace the reference to $V[i-1]$ with the (equivalent) b; now we can see that in the resulting Program 20.4b all memory references are independent of each other, assuming that the arrays U, V, W, X do not overlap.

Next we mark each variable in the loop body to indicate whether *this* iteration's value is used, or the *previous* iteration's value, as shown in Program 20.4b. We can construct a *data-dependence* graph as a visual aid in scheduling; solid edges are data dependences within an iteration, and dotted edges are *loop-carried* dependences, as shown in Graph 20.5a.

Now suppose we unroll the loop; the data-dependence graph is a DAG, as shown in Graph 20.5b. Scheduling DAGs is easy if there are no resource constraints; starting from operations with no predecessors, each operation goes as soon as its predecessors have all completed:

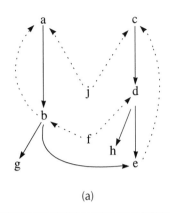
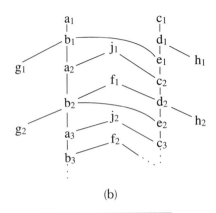

(a)   (b)

GRAPH 20.5.   Data-dependence graph for Program 20.4b: (a) original graph, in which solid edges are same-iteration dependences and dotted edges are loop-carried dependences; (b) acyclic dependences of the unrolled loop.

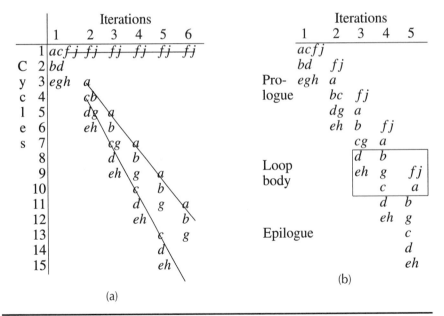

(a)

(b)

TABLE 20.6.   (a) Tableau of software-pipelined loop schedule; there is a group of instructions fj with slope 0, another group abg with slope 2, and a third group $cdeh$ with slope 3. (b) The smaller-slope groups are pushed down to slope 3, and a pattern is found (boxed) that constitutes the pipelined loop.

Cycle	Instructions
1	$a_1 c_1 f_1 j_1 f_2 j_2 f_3 j_3 \cdots$
2	$b_1 d_1$
3	$e_1 g_1 h_1 a_2$
4	$b_2 c_2$
5	$d_2 g_2 a_3$
$\vdots$	$\vdots$

It is convenient to write this schedule in a *tableau* where the rows are successive cycles and the columns are successive iterations of the original loop, as shown in Table 20.6a.

After a few iterations are scheduled, we notice a pattern in the tableau: There is a group of instructions *cdeh* racing down to the lower-right corner with a slope of three cycles per iteration, another group *abg* with a more moderate slope of two cycles per iteration, and a third group *fj* with zero slope. The key observation is that there are *gaps* in the schedule, separating identical groups, that grow larger at a constant rate. In this case the groups of instructions at iteration $i \geq 4$ are identical to the groups at iteration $i + 1$. In general the groups at iteration i will be identical to the groups at $i + c$, where sometimes $c > 1$; see Exercise 20.1.

Theorems:

- If there are K instructions in the loop, the pattern of identical groups separated by gaps will always appear within K^2 iterations (and usually much sooner).
- We can increase the slopes of the less steeply sloped groups, thereby either closing the gaps or at least making them small and nonincreasing, without violating data-dependence constraints.
- The resulting tableau has a repeating set of m identical cycles, which can constitute the body of a pipelined loop.
- The resulting loop is optimally scheduled (it runs in the least possible time).

See the Further Reading section for reference to proofs. But to see why the loop is optimal, consider that the data-dependence DAG of the unrolled loop has some path of length P to the last instruction to execute, and the scheduled loop executes that instruction at time P.

The result, for our example, is shown in Table 20.6b. Now we can find a repeating pattern of three cycles (since three is the slope of the steepest group). In this case, the pattern does not begin until cycle 8; it is shown in a box. This will constitute the *body* of the scheduled loop. Irregularly scheduled instructions before the loop body constitute a *prologue*, and instructions after it constitute the *epilogue*.

Now we can generate the multiple-instruction-issue program for this loop, as shown in Figure 20.7. However, the variables still have subscripts in this "program": The variable j_{i+1} is live at the same time as j_i. To encode this program in instructions, we need to put in MOVE instructions between the different variables, as shown in Figure 20.8.

This loop is optimally scheduled – assuming the machine can execute eight instructions at a time, including four simultaneous loads and stores.

Multicycle instructions. Although we have illustrated an example where each instruction takes exactly one cycle, the algorithm is easily extensible to the situation where some instructions take multiple cycles.

20.2   RESOURCE-BOUNDED LOOP PIPELINING

A real machine can issue only a limited number of instructions at a time, and has only a limited number of load/store units, adders, and multipliers. To be practically useful, a scheduling algorithm must take account of resource constraints.

The input to the scheduling algorithm must be in three parts:

1. A program to be scheduled;
2. A description of what resources each instruction uses in each of its pipeline stages (similar to Figure 20.1);
3. A description of the resources available on the machine (how many of each kind of functional unit, how many instructions may be issued at once, restrictions on what kinds of instructions may be issued simultaneously, and so on).

Resource-bounded scheduling is NP-complete, meaning that there is unlikely to be an efficient optimal algorithm. As usual in this situation, we use an approximation algorithm that does reasonably well in "typical" cases.

MODULO SCHEDULING
Iterative modulo scheduling is a practical, though not optimal, algorithm for resource-bounded loop scheduling. The idea is to use iterative backtracking to find a good schedule that obeys the functional-unit and data-dependence constraints, and then perform register allocation.

$a_1 \leftarrow j_0 \oplus b_0$	$c_1 \leftarrow e_0 \oplus j_0$	$f_1 \leftarrow U[1]$	$j_1 \leftarrow X[1]$	
$b_1 \leftarrow a_1 \oplus f_0$	$d_1 \leftarrow f_0 \oplus c_1$	$f_2 \leftarrow U[2]$	$j_2 \leftarrow X[2]$	
$e_1 \leftarrow b_1 \oplus d_1$	$V[1] \leftarrow b_1$	$W[1] \leftarrow d_1$	$a_2 \leftarrow j_1 \oplus b_1$	
$b_2 \leftarrow a_2 \oplus f_1$	$c_2 \leftarrow e_1 \oplus j_1$	$f_3 \leftarrow U[3]$	$j_3 \leftarrow X[3]$	
$d_2 \leftarrow f_1 \oplus c_2$	$V[2] \leftarrow b_2$	$a_3 \leftarrow j_2 \oplus b_2$		
$e_2 \leftarrow b_2 \oplus d_2$	$W[2] \leftarrow d_2$	$b_3 \leftarrow a_3 \oplus f_2$	$f_4 \leftarrow U[4]$	$j_4 \leftarrow X[4]$
$c_3 \leftarrow e_2 \oplus j_2$	$V[3] \leftarrow b_3$	$a_4 \leftarrow j_3 \oplus b_3$		$i \leftarrow 3$
$L: d_i \leftarrow f_{i-1} \oplus c_i$	$b_{i+1} \leftarrow a_i \oplus f_i$			
$e_i \leftarrow b_i \oplus d_i$	$W[i] \leftarrow d_i$	$V[i+1] \leftarrow b_{i+1}$	$f_{i+2} \leftarrow U[i+2]$	$j_{i+2} \leftarrow X[i+2]$
$c_{i+1} \leftarrow e_i \oplus j_i$	$a_{i+2} \leftarrow j_{i+1} \oplus b_{i+1}$	$i \leftarrow i+1$	if $i < N-2$ goto L	
$d_{N-1} \leftarrow f_{N-2} \oplus c_{N-1}$	$b_N \leftarrow a_N \oplus f_{N-1}$			
$e_{N-1} \leftarrow b_{N-1} \oplus d_{N-1}$	$W[N-1] \leftarrow d_{N-1}$	$V[N] \leftarrow b_N$		
$c_N \leftarrow e_{N-1} \oplus j_{N-1}$				
$d_N \leftarrow f_{N-1} \oplus c_N$				
$e_N \leftarrow b_N \oplus d_N$	$W[N] \leftarrow d_N$			

FIGURE 20.7. Pipelined schedule. Assignments in each row happen simultaneously; each right-hand side refers to the value *before* the assignment. The loop exit test $i < N+1$ has been "moved past" three increments of i, so appears as $i < N-2$.

$a_1 \leftarrow j_0 \oplus b_0$	$c_1 \leftarrow e_0 \oplus j_0$	$f_1 \leftarrow U[1]$	$j_1 \leftarrow X[1]$	
$b_1 \leftarrow a_1 \oplus f_0$	$d_1 \leftarrow f_0 \oplus c_1$	$f'' \leftarrow U[2]$	$j_2 \leftarrow X[2]$	
$e_1 \leftarrow b_1 \oplus d_1$	$V[1] \leftarrow b_1$	$W[1] \leftarrow d_1$	$a_2 \leftarrow j_1 \oplus b_1$	
$b_2 \leftarrow a_2 \oplus f_1$	$c_2 \leftarrow e_1 \oplus j_1$	$f' \leftarrow U[3]$	$j' \leftarrow X[3]$	
$d \leftarrow f_1 \oplus c_2$	$V[2] \leftarrow b_2$	$a \leftarrow j_2 \oplus b_2$		
$e_2 \leftarrow b_2 \oplus d_2$	$W[2] \leftarrow d_2$	$b \leftarrow a \oplus f''$	$f \leftarrow U[4]$	$j \leftarrow X[4]$
$c \leftarrow e_2 \oplus j_2$	$V[3] \leftarrow b$	$a \leftarrow j' \oplus b$		$i \leftarrow 3$
$L: d \leftarrow f'' \oplus c$	$b \leftarrow a' \oplus f'$	$b' \leftarrow b;\ a' \leftarrow a;\ f'' \leftarrow f';\ f' \leftarrow f;\ j'' \leftarrow j';\ j' \leftarrow j$		
$e \leftarrow b' \oplus d$	$W[i] \leftarrow d$	$V[i+1] \leftarrow b$	$f \leftarrow U[i+2]$	$j \leftarrow X[i+2]$
$c \leftarrow e \oplus j''$	$a \leftarrow j' \oplus b$	$i \leftarrow i+1$	if $i < N-2$ goto L	
$d \leftarrow f'' \oplus c$	$b \leftarrow a \oplus f'$	$b' \leftarrow b$		
$e \leftarrow b' \oplus d$	$W[N-1] \leftarrow d$	$V[N] \leftarrow b$		
$c \leftarrow e \oplus j'$				
$d \leftarrow f' \oplus c$				
$e \leftarrow b \oplus d$	$W[N] \leftarrow d$			

FIGURE 20.8. Pipelined schedule, with move instructions.

The algorithm tries to place all the instructions of the loop body in a schedule of Δ cycles, assuming that there will also be a prologue and epilogue of the kind used by the Aiken-Nicolau algorithm. The algorithm tries increasing values of Δ until it reaches a value for which it can make a schedule.

A key idea of *modulo scheduling* is that if an instruction violates functional-unit constraints at time t, then it will not fit at time $t + \Delta$, or at any time t' where $t \equiv t'$ modulo Δ.

Suppose, for example, we are trying to schedule Program 20.4b with $\Delta = 3$ on a machine that can perform only one load instruction at a time. The following loop-body schedule is illegal, with two different loads at cycle 1:

0		
1	$f_i \leftarrow U[i]$	$j_i \leftarrow X[i]$
2		

We can move f_i from cycle 1 of the loop to cycle 0, or cycle 2:

0	$f_i \leftarrow U[i]$	
1		$j_i \leftarrow X[i]$
2		

0		
1		$j_i \leftarrow X[i]$
3	$f_i \leftarrow U[i]$	

Either one avoids the resource conflict. We could move f_i even earlier, to cycle -1, where (in effect) we are computing f_{i+1}, or even later, to cycle 3, where we are computing f_{i-1}:

0		
1		$j_i \leftarrow X[i]$
2	$f_{i+1} \leftarrow U[i + 1]$	

0	$f_{i-1} \leftarrow U[i - 1]$	
1		$j_i \leftarrow X[i]$
3		

But with $\Delta = 3$ we can never solve the resource conflict by moving f_i from cycle 1 to cycle 4 (or to cycle -2), because $1 \equiv 4$ modulo 3; the calculation of f would still conflict with the calculation of j:

0		
1	$f_{i-1} \leftarrow U[i - 1]$	$j_i \leftarrow X[i]$
2		

Effects on register allocation. Consider the calculation of $d \leftarrow f \oplus c$, which occurs at cycle 0 of the schedule in Figure 20.7. If we place the calculation of d in a later cycle, then the data-dependence edges from the definitions of f and c to this instruction would lengthen, and the data-dependence edges from this instruction to the use of d in $W[i] \leftarrow d$ would shrink. If a data-dependence edge shrinks to less than zero cycles, then a data-dependence constraint has been violated; this can be solved by also moving the calculations that use d to a later cycle.

Conversely, if a data-dependence edge grows many cycles long, then we must carry several "versions" of a value around the loop (as we carry f, f', f'' around the loop of Figure 20.8), and this means that we are using more temporaries, so that register allocation may fail. In fact, an *optimal* loop-scheduling algorithm should consider register allocation simultaneously with scheduling; but it is not clear whether optimal algorithms are practical, and the *iterated modulo scheduling* algorithm described in this section first schedules, then does register allocation and hopes for the best.

FINDING THE MINIMUM INITIATION INTERVAL

Modulo scheduling begins by finding a lower bound for the number of cycles in the pipelined loop body:

Resource estimator: For any kind of functional unit, such as a multiplier or a memory-fetch unit, we can see how many cycles such units will be used by the corresponding instructions (e.g., multiply or load, respectively) in the loop body. This, divided by the number of that kind of functional unit provided by the hardware, gives a lower bound for Δ. For example, if there are 6 multiply instructions that each use a multiplier for 3 cycles, and there are two multipliers, then $\Delta \geq 6 \cdot 3/2$.

Data-dependence estimator: For any data-dependence cycle in the data-dependence graph, where some value x_i depends on a chain of other calculations that depends on x_{i-1}, the total latency of the chain gives a lower bound for Δ.

Let $\Delta_{\min}$ be the maximum of these estimators.

Let us calculate $\Delta_{\min}$ for Program 20.4b. For simplicity, we assume that one $\oplus$-arithmetic instruction and one load/store can be issued at a time, and every instruction finishes in one cycle; and we will not consider the scheduling of $i \leftarrow i + 1$ or the conditional branch.

Then the *arithmetic resource estimator* is 5 $\oplus$-instructions in the loop body divided by 1 issuable arithmetic instructions per cycle, or $\Delta \geq 5$. The *load/store resource estimator* is 4 load/store instructions in the loop body divided by 1 issuable memory operations per cycle, or $\Delta \geq 4$. The data-dependence estimator comes from the cycle $c_i \rightarrow d_i \rightarrow e_i \rightarrow c_{i+1}$ in Graph 20.5a, whose length gives $\Delta \geq 3$.

Next, we prioritize the instructions of the loop body by some heuristic that decides which instructions to consider first. For example, instructions that are in critical data-dependence cycles, or instructions that use a lot of scarce resources, should be placed in the schedule first, and then other instructions can be filled in around them. Let $H_1, \ldots, H_n$ be the instructions of the loop body, in (heuristic) priority order.

In our example, we could use $H = [c, d, e, a, b, f, j, g, h]$, putting early the instructions that are in the critical recurrence cycle or that use the arithmetic functional unit (since the resource estimators for this loop tell us that arithmetic is in more demand than load/stores).

The scheduling algorithm maintains a set S of scheduled instructions, each scheduled for a particular time t. The value of $SchedTime[h] = none$ if $h \notin S$, otherwise $SchedTime[h]$ is the currently scheduled time for h. The members of S obey all resource and data-dependence constraints.

Each iteration of Algorithm 20.9 places the highest-priority unscheduled instruction h into S, as follows:

1. In the earliest time slot (if there is one) that obeys all dependence constraints with respect to *already-placed predecessors* of h, and respects all resource constraints.
2. But if there is no slot in Δ consecutive cycles that obeys resource constraints, then there can never be such a slot, because the functional units available at time t are the same as those at $t + c \cdot \Delta$. In this case, h is placed without regard to resource constraints, in the earliest time slot that obeys dependence constraints (with respect to already-placed predecessors), and is later than any previous attempt to place h.

Once h is placed, other instructions are removed to make the subset schedule S legal again: any successors of h that now don't obey data-dependence constraints, or any instructions that have resource conflicts with h.

This placement-and-removal could iterate forever, but most of the time either it finds a solution quickly or there is no solution, for a given Δ. To cut the algorithm off if it does not find a quick solution, a *Budget* of $c \cdot n$ schedule placements is allowed (for $c = 3$ or some similar number), after which this value of Δ is abandoned and the next one is tried.

When a def-use edge associated with variable j becomes longer than Δ cycles, it becomes necessary to have more than one copy of j, with MOVE instructions copying the different-iteration versions in bucket-brigade style. This is illustrated in Figure 20.8 for variables a, b, f, j, but we will not show an explicit algorithm for inserting the moves.

Checking for resource conflicts is done with a *resource reservation table*, an array of length Δ. The resources used by an instruction at time t can be entered in the array at position $t \bmod \Delta$; adding and removing resource-usage

for $\Delta \leftarrow \Delta_{\min}$ **to** ∞
    $Budget \leftarrow n \cdot 3$
    for $i \leftarrow 1$ **to** n
        $LastTime[i] \leftarrow 0$
        $SchedTime[i] \leftarrow none$
    while $Budget > 0$ **and** there are any unscheduled instructions
        $Budget \leftarrow Budget - 1$
        let h be the highest-priority unscheduled instruction
        $t_{\min} \leftarrow 0$
        for each predecessor p of h
            if $SchedTime[p] \neq none$
                $t_{\min} \leftarrow \max(t_{\min}, \ SchedTime[p] + Delay(p, h))$
        for $t \leftarrow t_{\min}$ **to** $t_{\min} + \Delta - 1$
            if $SchedTime[h] = none$
                if h can be scheduled without resource conflicts
                    $SchedTime[h] \leftarrow t$
        if $SchedTime[h] = none$
            $SchedTime[h] \leftarrow \max(t_{\min}, \ 1 + LastTime[h])$
        $LastTime[h] \leftarrow SchedTime[h]$
        for each successor s of h
            if $SchedTime[s] \neq none$
                if $SchedTime[h] + Delay(h, s) > SchedTime[s]$
                    $SchedTime[s] \leftarrow none$
        while the current schedule has resource conflicts
            let s be some instruction (other than h) involved in a resource conflict
            $SchedTime[s] \leftarrow none$
    if all instructions are scheduled
        RegisterAllocate()
        if register allocation succeeded without spilling
            return and report a successfully scheduled loop.

Delay$(h, s) =$
    Given a dependence edge $h_i \rightarrow s_{i+k}$, so that h uses the value of s from the kth previous iteration
        (where $k = 0$ means that h uses the current iteration's value of s);
    Given that the latency of the instruction that computes s is l cycles;
    return $l - k\Delta$

ALGORITHM 20.9. Iterative modulo scheduling.

SchedTime	Resource Table
a 3	⊕ M
b
c 0	0 c
d 1	1 d
e 2	2 e
f	3 a
g	4
h
j

Placing c, d, e, a.

SchedTime	Resource Table
a 3	⊕ M
b 4
c 0	0 c
d 1	1 d
e 2̶	2
f	3 a
g	4 b
h
j

Placing b violates
b → e; remove e.

SchedTime	Resource Table
a 3	⊕ M
b 4
c 0̶ 5	0 c
d 1̶	1
e 2̶ 7 1	2 e
f	3 a
g	4 b
h
j

Placing e violates
e → c; remove c;
placing c violates
c → d; remove d.

SchedTime	Resource Table
a 3	⊕ M
b 4
c 0̶ 5	0 c f
d 1̶ 6	1 d j
e 2̶ 7	2 e g
f 0	3 a h
g 7	4 b
h 8
j 1

Placing
d, f, j, g, h.

FIGURE 20.10. Iterative modulo scheduling applied to Program 20.4b. Graph 20.5a is the data-dependence graph; $\Delta_{min} = 5$ (see page 451); $H = [c, d, e, a, b, f, j, g, h]$.

---

from the table, and checking for conflicts, can be done in constant time.

This algorithm is not guaranteed to find an optimal schedule in any sense. There may be an optimal, register-allocable schedule with initiation interval Δ, and the algorithm may fail to find any schedule with time Δ, or it may find a schedule for which register-allocation fails. The only consolation is that it is reported to work very well in practice.

The operation of the algorithm on our example is shown in Figure 20.10.

OTHER CONTROL FLOW

We have shown scheduling algorithms for simple straight-line loop bodies. What if the loop contains internal control flow, such as a tree of if-then-else statements? One approach is to compute both branches of the loop, and then use a *conditional move* instruction (provided on many high-performance machines) to produce the right result.

For example, the loop at left can be rewritten into the loop at right, using a conditional move:

```
for i ← 1 to N                 for i ← 1 to N
    x ← M[i]                       x ← M[i]
    if x > 0                       u' ← z * x
        u ← z * x                  u ← A[i]
    else u ← A[i]                  if x > 0 move u ← u'
    s ← s + u                      s ← s + u
```

The resulting loop body is now straight-line code that can be scheduled easily.

But if the two sides of the **if** differ greatly in size, and the frequently executed branch is the small one, then executing both sides in every iteration will be slower than optimal. Or if one branch of the **if** has a side effect, it must not be executed unless the condition is true.

To solve this problem we use *trace scheduling*: We pick some frequently executed straight-line path through the branches of control flow, schedule this path efficiently, and suffer some amount of ineffiency at those times where we must jump into or out of the trace. See Section 8.2 and also the Further Reading section of this chapter.

SHOULD THE COMPILER SCHEDULE INSTRUCTIONS?

Many machines have hardware that does dynamic instruction rescheduling at run time. These machines do *out-of-order execution*, meaning that there may be several decoded instructions in a buffer, and whichever instruction's operands are available can execute next, even if other instructions that appeared earlier in the program code are still awaiting operands or resources.

Such machines first appeared in 1967 (the IBM 360/91), but did not become common until the mid-1990s. Now it appears that most high-performance processors are being designed with dynamic (run-time) scheduling. These machines have several advantages and disadvantages, and it is not yet clear whether static (compile-time) scheduling or out-of-order execution will become standard.

Advantages of static scheduling. Out-of-order execution uses expensive hardware resources and tends to increase the chip's cycle time and wattage. The static scheduler can schedule earlier the instructions whose future data-dependence path is longest; a real-time scheduler cannot know the length of the data-dependence path leading from an instruction (see Exercise 20.3). The scheduling problem is NP-complete, so compilers – which have no real-time constraint on their scheduling algorithms – should in principle be able to find better schedules.

Advantages of dynamic scheduling. Some aspects of the schedule are unpredictable at compile time, such as cache misses, and can be better scheduled when their actual latency is known (see Figure 21.5). Highly pipelined schedules tend to use many registers; typical machines have only 32 register names in a five-bit instruction field, but out-of-order execution with run-time *regis-*

COMPARE	I-Fetch	Read	Arith ↓	Write				
BRANCH		I-Fetch	Read	↑ Arith ↓				
ADD			*wait*	*wait*	↑ I-Fetch	Read	Arith	Write

FIGURE 20.11.   Dependence of ADD's instruction-fetch on result of BRANCH.

ter renaming can use hundreds of actual registers with a few static names (see the Further Reading section). Optimal static scheduling depends on knowing the precise pipeline state that will be reached by the hardware, which is sometimes difficult to determine in practice. Finally, dynamic scheduling does not require that the program be recompiled (i.e., rescheduled) for each different implementation of the same instruction set.

20.3   BRANCH PREDICTION

In many floating-point programs, such as Program 20.4a, the basic blocks are long, the instructions are long-latency floating-point operations, and the branches are very predictable **for**-loop exit conditions. In such programs the problem, as described in the previous sections, is to schedule the long-latency instructions.

But in many programs – such as compilers, operating systems, window systems, word processors – the basic blocks are short, the instructions are quick integer operations, and the branches are harder to predict. Here the main problem is fetching the instructions fast enough to be able to decode and execute them.

Figure 20.11 illustrates the pipeline stages of a COMPARE, BRANCH, and ADD instruction. Until the BRANCH has executed, the instruction-fetch of the successor instruction cannot be performed because the address to fetch is unknown.

Suppose a superscalar machine can issue four instructions at once. Then, in waiting three cycles after the BRANCH is fetched before the ADD can be fetched, 11 instruction-issue slots are wasted (3×4 minus the slot that the BRANCH occupies).

Some machines solve this problem by fetching the instructions immediately following the branch; then if the branch is not taken, these fetched-and-decoded instructions can be used immediately. Only if the branch is taken are there stalled instruction slots. Other machines assume the branch will be taken, and begin fetching the instructions at the target address; then if the branch falls through, there is a stall. Some machines even fetch from both addresses simultaneously, though this requires a very complex interface between processor and instruction-cache.

Modern machines rely on *branch prediction* to make the right guess about which instructions to fetch. The branch prediction can be *static* – the compiler predicts which way the branch is likely to go and places its prediction in the branch instruction itself; or *dynamic* – the hardware remembers, for each recently executed branch, which way it went last time, and predicts that it will go the same way.

STATIC BRANCH PREDICTION

The compiler can communicate predictions to the hardware by a 1-bit field of the branch instruction that encodes the predicted direction.

To save this bit, or for compatibility with old instruction sets, some machines use a rule such as "backward branches are assumed to be taken, forward branches are assumed to be not-taken." The rationale for the first part of this rule is that backward branches are (often) loop branches, and a loop is more likely to continue than to exit. The rationale for the second part of the rule is that it's often useful to have predicted-not-taken branches for exceptional conditions; if *all* branches are predicted taken, we could reverse the sense of the condition to make the exceptional case "fall through" and the normal case take the branch, but this leads to worse instruction-cache performance, as discussed in Section 21.2. When generating code for machines that use forward/backward branch direction as the prediction mechanism, the compiler can order the basic blocks of the program in so that the predicted-taken branches go to lower addresses.

Several simple heuristics help predict the direction of a branch. Some of these heuristics make intuitive sense, but all have been validated empirically:

Pointer: If a loop performs an equality comparison on pointers (p=null or p=q), then predict the condition as *false*.

Call: A branch is *less* likely to be the successor that dominates a procedure call (many conditional calls are to handle exceptional situations).

Return: A branch is *less* likely to a successor that dominates a return-from-procedure.

Loop: A branch is *more* likely to the successor (if any) that is the header of the loop containing the branch.

Loop: A branch is *more* likely to the successor (if any) that is a loop preheader, if it does not postdominate the branch. This catches the results of the optimization described in Figure 18.7, where the iteration count is more likely to be > 0 than $= 0$. (B postdominates A if any path from A to program-exit must go through B; see Section 19.5.)

Guard: If some value r is used as an operand of the branch (as part of the conditional test), then a branch is *more* likely to a successor in which r is live and which does not postdominate the branch.

There are some branches to which more than one of the heuristics apply. A simple approach in such cases is to give the heuristics a priority order and use the first heuristic in the order that applies (the order in which they are listed above is a reasonable prioritization, based on empirical measurements).

Another approach is to index a table by every possible subset of conditions that might apply, and decide (based on empirical measurements) what to do for each subset.

SHOULD THE COMPILER PREDICT BRANCHES?

Perfect static prediction results in a dynamic mispredict rate of about 9% (for C programs) or 6% (for Fortran programs). The "perfect" mispredict rate is not zero because any given branch does not go in the same direction more than 91% of the time, on average. If a branch did go the same direction 100% of the time, there would be little need for it! Fortran programs tend to have more predictable branches because more of the branches are loop branches, and the loops have longer iteration counts.

Profile-based prediction, in which a program is compiled with extra instructions to count the number of times each branch is taken, executed on sample data, and recompiled with prediction based on the counts, approaches the accuracy of perfect static prediction.

Prediction based on the heuristics described above results in a dynamic mispredict rate of about 20% (for C programs), or about half as good as perfect (or profile-based) static prediction.

A typical hardware-based branch-prediction scheme uses two bits for every branch in the instruction cache, recording how the branch went the last two times it executed. This leads to misprediction rates of about 11% (for C programs), which is about as good as profile-based prediction.

A mispredict rate of 10% can result in very many stalled instructions – if each mispredict stalls 11 instruction slots, as described in the example on page 456, and there is one mispredict every 10 branches, and one-sixth of all instructions are branches, then 18% of the processor's time is spent waiting for mispredicted instruction-fetches. Therefore it will be necessary to do better, using some combination of hardware and software techniques. Relying on heuristics that mispredict 20% of the branches is better than no predictions at all, but will not suffice in the long run.

FURTHER READING

Hennessy and Patterson [1996] explain the design and implementation of high-performance machines, instruction-level parallelism, pipeline structure, functional units, caches, out-of-order execution, register renaming, branch prediction, and many other computer-architecture issues, with comparisons of compiler versus run-time-hardware techniques for optimization. Kane and Heinrich [1992] describe the pipeline constraints of the MIPS R4000 computer, from which Figures 20.1 and 20.2 are adapted.

CISC computers of the 1970s implemented complex instructions sequentially using an internal microcode that could do several operations simultaneously; it was not possible for the compiler to interleave parts of several macroinstructions for increased parallelism. Fisher [1981] developed an automatic scheduling algorithm for microcode, using the idea of trace scheduling to optimize frequently executed paths, and then proposed a very-long-instruction-word (VLIW) architecture [Fisher 1983] that could expose the microoperations directly to user programs, using the compiler to schedule.

Aiken and Nicolau [1988] were among the first to point out that a single loop iteration need not be scheduled in isolation, and presented the algorithm for optimal (ignoring resource constraints) parallelization of loops.

Many variations of the multiprocessor scheduling problem are NP-complete [Garey and Johnson 1979; Ullman 1975]. The *iterative modulo scheduling* algorithm [Rau 1994] gets good results in practice. In the absence of resource constraints, it is equivalent to the Bellman-Ford shortest-path algorithm [Ford and Fulkerson 1962]. Optimal schedules can be obtained (in principle) by expressing the constraints as an integer linear program [Govindarajan et al. 1996], but integer-linear-program solvers can take exponential time (the problem is NP-complete), and the register-allocation constraint is still difficult to express in linear inequalities.

Ball and Larus [1993] describe and measure the static branch-prediction heuristics shown in Section 20.3. Young and Smith [1994] show a profile-based static branch-prediction algorithm that does *better* than optimal static prediction; the apparent contradiction in this statement is explained by the fact that their algorithm replicates some basic blocks, so that a branch that's 80% taken (with a 20% misprediction rate) might become two different branches, one almost-always taken and one almost-always not taken.

EXERCISES

20.1 Schedule the following loop using the Aiken-Nicolau algorithm:

> **for** $i \leftarrow 1$ **to** N
> $\quad a \quad \leftarrow X[i - 2]$
> $\quad b \quad \leftarrow Y[i - 1]$
> $\quad c \quad \leftarrow a \times b$
> $\quad d \quad \leftarrow U[i]$
> $\quad e \quad \leftarrow X[i - 1]$
> $\quad f \quad \leftarrow d + e$
> $\quad g \quad \leftarrow d \times c$
> $\quad h : X[i] \leftarrow g$
> $\quad j : Y[i] \leftarrow f$

a. Label all the scalar variables with subscripts i and $i - 1$. **Hint:** In this loop there are no loop-carried scalar-variable dependences, so none of the subscripts will be $i - 1$.

b. Perform *scalar replacement* on uses of $X[\,]$ and $Y[\,]$. **Hint:** Now you will have subscripts of $i - 1$ and $i - 2$.

c. Perform *copy propagation* to eliminate variables a, b, e.

d. Draw a data-dependence graph of statements c, d, f, g, h, j; label intra-iteration edges with 0 and loop-carried edges with 1 or 2, depending on the number of iterations difference there is in the subscript.

e. Show the Aiken-Nicolau *tableau* (as in Table 20.6a).

f. Find the identical groups separated by increasing gaps. **Hint:** The identical groups will be c cycles apart, where in this case c is greater than one!

g. Show the steepest-slope group. **Hint:** The slope is not an integer.

h. Unroll the loop k times, where k is the denominator of the slope.

i. Draw the data-dependence graph of the unrolled loop.

j. Draw the tableau for the schedule of the unrolled loop.

k. Find the slope of the steepest-slope group. **Hint:** Now it should be an integer.

l. Move the shallow-slope group(s) down to close the gap.

m. Identify the loop body, the prologue, and the epilogue.

n. Write a schedule showing placement of the prologue, loop body, and epilogue in specific cycles, like Figure 20.7.

o. Eliminate the subscripts on variables in the loop body, inserting move instructions where necessary, as in Figure 20.8.

20.2 Do parts a–d of Exercise 20.1. Then use iterated modulo scheduling to schedule the loop for a machine that can issue three instructions at a time, of which at most one can be a memory instruction and at most one can be a multiply instruction. Every instruction completes in one cycle.

e. Explicitly represent the increment instruction $i_{i+1} \leftarrow i_i + 1$ and the loop branch $k :$ *if* $i_{i+1} \leq N$ *goto loop* in the data-dependence graph, with an edge from i to itself (labeled by 1), from i to k (labeled by 0), and from k to every node in the loop body (labeled by 1).

f. Calculate Δ_{min} based on data-dependence cycles, the 2-instruction per cycle limit, the 1-load/store-per-cycle limit, and the 1-multiply-per-cycle limit. Remark: The Δ required for a data-dependence cycle is the length of the cycle divided by the sum of the edge labels (where edge labels show iteration distance, as described in Exercise 20.1d).

g. Run Algorithm 20.9, showing the SchedTime and Resource tables each time a variable has to be removed from the schedule, as in Figure 20.10. Use the priority order $H = [i, k, c, d, g, f, h, j]$.

h. Eliminate the subscripts on variables in the loop body, inserting move instructions where necessary, as in Figure 20.8. If the move instructions don't fit into the 3-instruction-issue limit, then it's time to increase Δ and try again.

20.3 Consider the following program:

$L :$		$L :$
$a : a \leftarrow U[i]$		$a : a \leftarrow U[i]$
$b : b \leftarrow a \times a$		$d : d \leftarrow d \times a$
$c : V[i] \leftarrow b$		$b : b \leftarrow a \times a$
$i : i \leftarrow i + 1$		$c : V[i] \leftarrow b$
$d : d \leftarrow d \times a$		$i : i \leftarrow i + 1$
$e :$ if $d < 1.0$ goto L		$e :$ if $d < 1.0$ goto L
(I) Unscheduled		(II) Scheduled

Suppose these loops are to be run on an out-of-order execution machine with these characteristics: Each instruction takes exactly one cycle, and may be executed as soon as its operands are ready *and* all preceding conditional branches have been executed. Several instructions may be executed at once, except that there is only one multiply unit. If two multiply instructions are ready, the instruction from an earlier iteration, or occurring first in the same iteration, is executed.

The program was originally written as shown in loop (I); the compiler has rescheduled it as loop (II). For each of the two loops:

a. Draw the data-dependence graph, showing loop-carried dependences with a dashed line.

b. Add the control dependence as a loop-carried edge from e to each of the other nodes.

c. To simulate how the machine will execute the loop, show the Aiken-Nicolau *tableau*, with the restriction that b and d must never be put in the same cycle. In a cycle where b and d's predecessors are both ready, prefer the instruction from the earlier iteration, or from earlier in the same iteration.

d. Compute the steepest slope in the tableau; how many cycles per iteration does the loop take?

e. Can compiler scheduling be useful for dynamically rescheduling (out-of-order execution) machines?

20.4 On many machines, instructions after a conditional branch can be executed even before the branch condition is known (the instructions do not *commit* until after the branch condition is verified).

Suppose we have an out-of-order execution machine with these characteristics: An add or branch takes one cycle; a multiply takes 4 cycles; each instruction may be executed as soon as its operands are ready. Several instructions may be executed at once, except that there is only one multiply unit. If two multiply instructions are ready, the instruction from an earlier iteration, or occurring first in the same iteration, is executed.

For a machine with this behavior, do parts a–e of Exercise 20.3 for the following programs:

$L:$	$L:$
$a: a \leftarrow e \times u$	$b: b \leftarrow e \times v$
$b: b \leftarrow e \times v$	$a: a \leftarrow e \times u$
$c: c \leftarrow a + w$	$c: c \leftarrow a + w$
$d: d \leftarrow c + x$	$d: d \leftarrow c + x$
$e: e \leftarrow d + y$	$e: e \leftarrow d + y$
$f: \text{if } e > 0.0 \text{ goto } L$	$f: \text{if } e > 0.0 \text{ goto } L$
(I) Unscheduled	(II) Scheduled

20.5 Write a short program that contains an instance of each of the branch-prediction heuristics *(pointer, call, return, loop header, loop preheader, guard)* described on pages 457–458. Label each instance.

20.6 Use branch-prediction heuristics to predict the direction of each of the conditional branches in the programs of Exercise 8.6 (page 175) and Figure 18.7b (page 386); explain which heuristic applies to each prediction.

21

The Memory Hierarchy

mem-o-ry: a device in which information can be inserted and stored and from which it may be extracted when wanted

hi-er-ar-chy: a graded or ranked series

Webster's Dictionary

An idealized *random access memory* (RAM) has N words indexed by integers such that any word can be fetched or stored – using its integer address – equally quickly. Hardware designers can make a big slow memory, or a small fast memory, but a big fast memory is prohibitively expensive. Also, one thing that speeds up access to memory is its nearness to the processor, and a big memory must have some parts far from the processor no matter how much money might be thrown at the problem.

Almost as good as a big fast memory is the combination of a small fast *cache memory* and a big slow *main memory*; the program keeps its frequently used data in cache and the rarely used data in main memory, and when it enters a phase in which datum x will be frequently used it may move x from the slow memory to the fast memory.

It's inconvenient for the programmer to manage multiple memories, so the hardware does it automatically. Whenever the processor wants the datum at address x, it looks first in the cache, and – we hope – usually finds it there. If there is a *cache miss* – x is not in the cache – then the processor fetches x from main memory and places a copy of x in the cache so that the next reference to x will be a *cache hit*. Placing x in the cache may mean removing some other datum y from the cache to make room for it, so that some future access to y will be a cache miss.

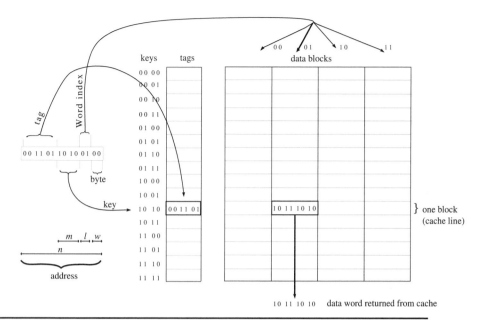

FIGURE 21.1. Organization of a direct-mapped cache. *Key* field of the address is used to index the *tags* array and the *data blocks*; if *tags*[*key*] matches the *tag* field of the address then the data is valid (cache hit). *Word index* is used to select a word from the cache block.

21.1 CACHE ORGANIZATION

A *direct-mapped* cache is organized in the following way to do this quickly. There are 2^m blocks, each holding 2^l words of 2^w bytes; thus, the cache holds 2^{w+l+m} bytes in all, arranged in an array *Data*[*block*][*word*][*byte*]. Each block is a copy of some main-memory data, and there is a *tag* array indicating where in memory the current contents come from. Typically, the word size 2^w might be 4 bytes, the block size 2^{w+l} might be 32 bytes, and the cache size 2^{w+l+m} might be as small as 8 kilobytes or as large as 2 megabytes.

tag	key	word	byte
$(n-(m+l+w))$ bits	m bits	l	w

Given an address x, the cache unit must be able to find whether x is in the cache. The address x is composed of n bits, $x_{n-1}x_{n-2}\ldots x_2x_1x_0$ (see Figure 21.1). In a *direct-mapped* cache organization, we take the middle bits as the *key* $= x_{w+l+m-1}x_{w+l+m-2}\ldots x_{w+l}$, and hold the data for x in *Data*[*key*].

The high bits $x_{n-1}x_{n-2} \ldots x_{w+l+m}$ form the *tag*, and if *Tags*[*key*] $\neq$ *tag*, then there is a *cache miss* – the word we require is not in cache. In this case, contents of *data*[*key*] are sent back to main memory, and the contents of memory at address $x_{n-1} \ldots x_{w+l}$, are fetched into the kth cache block (and also sent to the CPU). Access time for main memory is much longer than the cache access time, so frequent misses are undesirable.

The next time address x is fetched, if no intervening instruction has fetched another address with the same key but different tag, there will be a *cache hit*: *Tags*[*key*] $=$ *tag*, and bits $x_{w+l-1} \ldots x_w$ will address a word within the *key*th block: The contents of *data*[*key*][$x_{w+l-1} \ldots x_w$] are transferred to the processor. This is much faster than going all the way to main memory for the data. If the fetching instruction is a byte-fetch (instead of a word-fetch), then (typically) the processor takes care of selecting the byte $x_{l-1} \ldots x_0$ from the word.

Another common organization is the *set-associative* cache, which is quite similar but can hold more than one block with the same *key* value. The compiler optimization strategies presented in this chapter are valid for both direct-mapped caches and set-associative caches, but they are a bit more straightforward to analyze for direct-mapped caches.

Write-hit policy. The paragraphs above explain what happens on a *read*, when the CPU asks for data at address x. But what happens when the CPU writes data at address x? If x is in the cache, this is a *write hit*, which is easy and efficient to process. On a write hit, main memory may be updated now (write-through), or only when the cache block is about to be flushed from the cache (write-back), but the choice of write-hit policy does not much affect the compilation and optimization of sequential programs.

Write-miss policy. If the CPU writes data at an address not in the cache, this is a *write miss*. Different machines have different write-miss policies:

Fetch-on-write. Word x is written to the cache. But now the other data words in the same cache block belonged to some other address (that had the same *key* as x), so to make a valid cache block the other words are fetched from main memory. Meanwhile, the processor is stalled.

Write-validate. Word x is written to the cache. The other words in the same cache block are marked *invalid*; nothing is fetched from main memory, so the processor is not stalled.

Write-around. Word x is written directly to main memory, and not to the cache. The processor is not stalled, as no response is required from the memory sys-

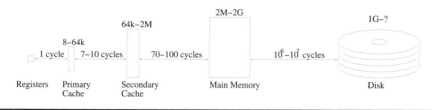

FIGURE 21.2. The memory hierarchy.

tem. Unfortunately, the next time x is fetched there will be a read miss, which will delay the processor.

The write-miss policy can affect how programs should be optimized (see pages 475 and 480).

Several layers of cache. A modern machine has a *memory hierarchy* of several layers, as shown in Figure 21.2: Inside the processor are *registers*, which can typically hold about 200 bytes in all and can be accessed in 1 processor cycle; a bit farther away is the *primary cache*, which can typically hold 8–64 kilobytes and be accessed in about 2–3 cycles; then the *secondary cache* can hold about a megabyte and be accessed in 7–10 cycles; *main memory* can hold 100 megabytes and be accessed in 100 cycles. The primary cache is usually split into an *instruction cache* – from which the processor fetches instructions to execute, and a *data cache*, from which the processor fetches and stores operands of instructions. The secondary cache usually holds both instructions and data.

Many processors can issue several instructions per cycle; the number of *useful* instructions in a cycle varies, depending on data-dependence and resource constraints (see page 441), but let us suppose that two useful instructions can be completed in each cycle, on the average. Then a primary-cache miss is a 15-instruction delay (7–10 cycles, times 2), and a secondary-cache miss is a 200-instruction delay.

This cache organization has several consequences of interest to the programmer (and often to the compiler):

Byte fetch: Fetching a single byte is often more expensive than fetching a whole word, because the memory interface delivers a whole word at a time, so the processor must do extra shifting.

Byte store: Storing a single byte is *usually* more expensive than storing a whole word, because the other bytes of that word must be fetched from the cache and stored back into it.

Temporal locality: Accessing (fetching or storing) a word that has been recently accessed will usually be a cache hit.

Spatial locality: Accessing a word in the same cache block as one that has been accessed recently will usually be a cache hit.

Cache conflict: If address a and address $a + i \cdot 2^{w+b+m}$ are both frequently accessed, there will be many cache misses because accessing one will throw the other out of the cache.

The compiler can do optimizing transformations that do not decrease the number of instructions executed, but that decrease the number of cache misses (or other memory stalls) that the program encounters.

21.2 CACHE-BLOCK ALIGNMENT

The typical cache-block size (B = about 8 words, more or less) is similar to the typical data-object size. We may expect that an algorithm that fetches one field of an object will probably fetch other fields as well.

If x straddles a multiple-of-B boundary, then it occupies portions of two different cache blocks, both of which are likely to be active at the same time. On the other hand, if x does not cross a multiple-of-B boundary, then accessing all the fields of x uses up only one cache block.

To improve performance by using the cache effectively, the compiler should arrange that data objects are not unnecessarily split across blocks.

There are simple ways to accomplish this:

1. Allocate objects sequentially; if the next object does not fit in the remaining portion of the current block, skip to the beginning of the next block.
2. Allocate size-2 objects in one area of memory, all aligned on multiple-of-2 boundaries; size-4 objects in another area, aligned on multiple-of-4 boundaries, and so on. This eliminates block-crossing for many common-sized objects, without wasted space between the objects.

Block alignment can waste some space, leaving unused words at the end of some blocks, as shown in Figure 21.3. However, the execution speed may improve; for a given phase of the program, there is a set S of frequently accessed objects, and alignment may reduce the number of cache blocks occupied by S from a number greater than the cache size to a number that fits in the cache.

Alignment can be applied both to global, static data and to heap-allocated data. For global data, the compiler can use assembly-language alignment directives to instruct the linker. For heap-allocated records and objects, it is not

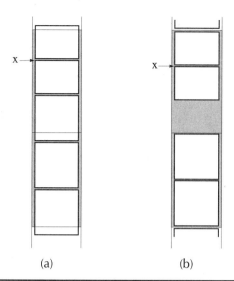

(a)   (b)

FIGURE 21.3.   Alignment of data objects (or basic blocks) to avoid crossing cache-block boundaries is often worthwhile, even at the cost of empty space between objects.

the compiler but the memory allocator within the runtime system that must place objects on cache-block boundaries, or otherwise minimize the number of cache-block crossings.

ALIGNMENT IN THE INSTRUCTION CACHE

Instruction "objects" (basic blocks) occupy cache blocks just as do data records, and the same considerations of block-crossing and alignment apply to instructions. Aligning the beginning of frequently executed basic blocks on multiple-of-B boundaries increases the number of basic blocks that fit simultaneously in the instruction cache.

Infrequently executed instructions should not be placed on the same cache blocks as frequently executed instructions. Consider the program

```
P;
if  x then  Q;
R;
```

where x is rarely true. We could generate code for it in either of the ways shown in Figure 21.4; but placing Q out-of-line means that this series of statements (usually) occupies two cache blocks, but placing Q straddling cache blocks between P and R will mean that even in the common case, where Q

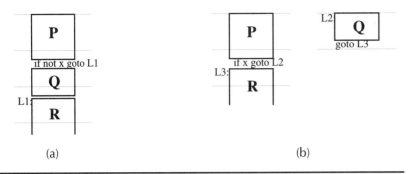

(a)   (b)

FIGURE 21.4.   If *x* is rarely true, basic-block placement (a) will occupy three in-cache blocks, while (b) will usually occupy only two.

---

is not executed, this part of the program will occupy three blocks in the cache.

On some machines it is particularly important to align the target of a branch instruction on a power-of-2 boundary. A modern processor fetches an aligned block of *k* (2 or 4 or more) words. If the program branches to some address that is not on a multiple-of-*k* boundary, then the instruction-fetch is not fetching *k* useful instructions.

An optimizing compiler should have a *basic-block-ordering* phase, after instruction selection and register allocation. *Trace scheduling* (as described in Section 8.2) can then be used to order a frequently executed path through a contiguous set of cache blocks; in constructing a trace through a conditional branch, it is important to follow the most-likely-taken out-edge, as determined by *branch prediction* (as described in Section 20.3).

21.3   PREFETCHING

If a load instruction misses the primary (or secondary) cache, there will be a 7–10 cycle delay (or a 70–100 cycle delay, respectively) while the datum is fetched from the next level of the memory hierarchy. In some cases, the need for that datum is predictable many cycles earlier, and the compiler can insert *prefetch* instructions to start the fetching earlier.

A *prefetch* instruction is a hint to the hardware to start bringing data at address *x* from main memory into the cache. A prefetch never stalls the processor – but on the other hand, if the hardware finds that some exceptional condition (such as a page fault) would occur, the prefetch can be ignored. When *prefetch*(*x*) is successful, it means that the next load from *x* will hit the cache; an unsuccessful prefetch might cause the next load to miss the cache, but the program will still execute correctly. Many machines now have some form of prefetch instruction.

Of course, one reasonable alternative is – instead of starting the fetch earlier – to just delay the instruction that uses the result of the fetch until later, using the software-pipelining techniques described in Chapter 20. In fact, processors that dynamically reorder instructions (to account for operands not ready) achieve this effect without any special work by the compiler.

The problem with using software pipelining or dynamic rescheduling to hide secondary-cache misses is that it increases the number of live temporaries. Consider the following dot-product loop as an example:

$$
\begin{aligned}
L_1 : & x \leftarrow M[i] \\
& y \leftarrow M[j] \\
& z \leftarrow x \times y \\
& s \leftarrow s + z \\
& i \leftarrow i + 4 \\
& j \leftarrow j + 4 \\
& \textbf{if } i < N \textbf{ goto } L_1
\end{aligned}
$$

If the data for the i and j arrays are not in the primary cache, or if N is large (> 8 kilobytes or so) so that the arrays cannot possibly fit in the cache, then each time i or j crosses to a new multiple-of-B boundary (into a new cache block), there will be a cache miss. In effect, the miss rate will be exactly W/B, where W is the word size and B is the block size. Typical values for W/B are $\frac{1}{4}$ or $\frac{1}{8}$, and this is a rather high miss rate.

The penalty for a primary cache miss is perhaps 7 cycles, or (on a dual-instruction-issue-per-cycle machine) 14 instructions. This would stall the processor of an early-'90s machine for 14 instructions, but a good late-'90s machine with out-of-order execution will find some other instruction to execute that is not data-dependent on the load.

The effective order of execution, on a dynamic-instruction-reordering machine, is shown in Figure 21.5a. When $x_1 \leftarrow M[i_0]$ is fetched there is a cache miss, so instructions data-dependent on x_1 cannot be issued for 11 cycles. In the meantime, i_1 and j_1, and even i_2 and j_2 can be computed; and the fetch $x_2 \leftarrow M[i_1]$ can be issued.

As the number of uncompleted loop iterations increases, the number of live or reserved registers increases proportionately. The cache misses for x_2, x_3, x_4 are the *same* miss as for x_1 because they are all in the same cache

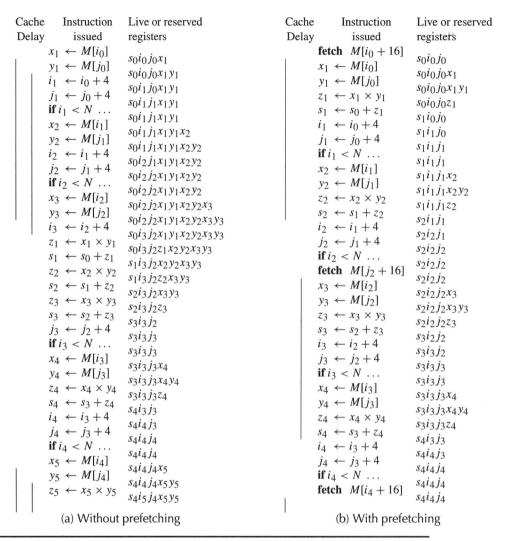

Cache Delay	Instruction issued	Live or reserved registers
	$x_1 \leftarrow M[i_0]$	
	$y_1 \leftarrow M[j_0]$	$s_0 i_0 j_0 x_1$
	$i_1 \leftarrow i_0 + 4$	$s_0 i_0 j_0 x_1 y_1$
	$j_1 \leftarrow j_0 + 4$	$s_0 i_1 j_0 x_1 y_1$
	if $i_1 < N$ ...	$s_0 i_1 j_1 x_1 y_1$
	$x_2 \leftarrow M[i_1]$	$s_0 i_1 j_1 x_1 y_1$
	$y_2 \leftarrow M[j_1]$	$s_0 i_1 j_1 x_1 y_1 x_2$
	$i_2 \leftarrow i_1 + 4$	$s_0 i_1 j_1 x_1 y_1 x_2 y_2$
	$j_2 \leftarrow j_1 + 4$	$s_0 i_2 j_1 x_1 y_1 x_2 y_2$
	if $i_2 < N$ ...	$s_0 i_2 j_2 x_1 y_1 x_2 y_2$
	$x_3 \leftarrow M[i_2]$	$s_0 i_2 j_2 x_1 y_1 x_2 y_2$
	$y_3 \leftarrow M[j_2]$	$s_0 i_2 j_2 x_1 y_1 x_2 y_2 x_3$
	$i_3 \leftarrow i_2 + 4$	$s_0 i_2 j_2 x_1 y_1 x_2 y_2 x_3 y_3$
	$z_1 \leftarrow x_1 \times y_1$	$s_0 i_3 j_2 x_1 y_1 x_2 y_2 x_3 y_3$
	$s_1 \leftarrow s_0 + z_1$	$s_0 i_3 j_2 z_1 x_2 y_2 x_3 y_3$
	$z_2 \leftarrow x_2 \times y_2$	$s_1 i_3 j_2 x_2 y_2 x_3 y_3$
	$s_2 \leftarrow s_1 + z_2$	$s_1 i_3 j_2 z_2 x_3 y_3$
	$z_3 \leftarrow x_3 \times y_3$	$s_2 i_3 j_2 x_3 y_3$
	$s_3 \leftarrow s_2 + z_3$	$s_2 i_3 j_2 z_3$
	$j_3 \leftarrow j_2 + 4$	$s_3 i_3 j_2$
	if $i_3 < N$ ...	$s_3 i_3 j_3$
	$x_4 \leftarrow M[i_3]$	$s_3 i_3 j_3$
	$y_4 \leftarrow M[j_3]$	$s_3 i_3 j_3 x_4$
	$z_4 \leftarrow x_4 \times y_4$	$s_3 i_3 j_3 x_4 y_4$
	$s_4 \leftarrow s_3 + z_4$	$s_3 i_3 j_3 z_4$
	$i_4 \leftarrow i_3 + 4$	$s_4 i_3 j_3$
	$j_4 \leftarrow j_3 + 4$	$s_4 i_4 j_3$
	if $i_4 < N$ ...	$s_4 i_4 j_4$
	$x_5 \leftarrow M[i_4]$	$s_4 i_4 j_4$
	$y_5 \leftarrow M[j_4]$	$s_4 i_4 j_4 x_5$
	$z_5 \leftarrow x_5 \times y_5$	$s_4 i_4 j_4 x_5 y_5$
		$s_4 i_5 j_4 x_5 y_5$

(a) Without prefetching

Cache Delay	Instruction issued	Live or reserved registers
	fetch $M[i_0 + 16]$	
	$x_1 \leftarrow M[i_0]$	$s_0 i_0 j_0$
	$y_1 \leftarrow M[j_0]$	$s_0 i_0 j_0 x_1$
	$z_1 \leftarrow x_1 \times y_1$	$s_0 i_0 j_0 x_1 y_1$
	$s_1 \leftarrow s_0 + z_1$	$s_0 i_0 j_0 z_1$
	$i_1 \leftarrow i_0 + 4$	$s_1 i_0 j_0$
	$j_1 \leftarrow j_0 + 4$	$s_1 i_1 j_0$
	if $i_1 < N$ ...	$s_1 i_1 j_1$
	$x_2 \leftarrow M[i_1]$	$s_1 i_1 j_1$
	$y_2 \leftarrow M[j_1]$	$s_1 i_1 j_1 x_2$
	$z_2 \leftarrow x_2 \times y_2$	$s_1 i_1 j_1 x_2 y_2$
	$s_2 \leftarrow s_1 + z_2$	$s_1 i_1 j_1 z_2$
	$i_2 \leftarrow i_1 + 4$	$s_2 i_1 j_1$
	$j_2 \leftarrow j_1 + 4$	$s_2 i_2 j_1$
	if $i_2 < N$ ...	$s_2 i_2 j_2$
	fetch $M[j_2 + 16]$	$s_2 i_2 j_2$
	$x_3 \leftarrow M[i_2]$	$s_2 i_2 j_2$
	$y_3 \leftarrow M[j_2]$	$s_2 i_2 j_2 x_3$
	$z_3 \leftarrow x_3 \times y_3$	$s_2 i_2 j_2 x_3 y_3$
	$s_3 \leftarrow s_2 + z_3$	$s_2 i_2 j_2 z_3$
	$i_3 \leftarrow i_2 + 4$	$s_3 i_2 j_2$
	$j_3 \leftarrow j_2 + 4$	$s_3 i_3 j_2$
	if $i_3 < N$ ...	$s_3 i_3 j_3$
	$x_4 \leftarrow M[i_3]$	$s_3 i_3 j_3$
	$y_4 \leftarrow M[j_3]$	$s_3 i_3 j_3 x_4$
	$z_4 \leftarrow x_4 \times y_4$	$s_3 i_3 j_3 x_4 y_4$
	$s_4 \leftarrow s_3 + z_4$	$s_3 i_3 j_3 z_4$
	$i_4 \leftarrow i_3 + 4$	$s_4 i_3 j_3$
	$j_4 \leftarrow j_3 + 4$	$s_4 i_4 j_3$
	if $i_4 < N$ ...	$s_4 i_4 j_4$
	fetch $M[i_4 + 16]$	$s_4 i_4 j_4$

(b) With prefetching

FIGURE 21.5. Execution of a dot-product loop, with 4-word cache blocks.

(a) Without prefetching, on a machine with dynamic instruction reordering, the number of outstanding instructions (reserved registers) grows proportionally to the cache-miss latency.

(b) With prefetching, the hardware reservation table never grows large. (Steady-state behavior is shown here, not the initial transient.)

block, so x_1, x_2, x_3, x_4 all become available at about the same time. Iterations 5–8 (which use the next cache block) would be dynamically scheduled like iterations 1–4, and so on.

The primary-cache latency, illustrated here, is usually small enough to handle without prefetching techniques. But with a secondary cache-miss latency of 200 instructions (i.e., 29 loop iterations), there will be about 116 outstanding instructions (computations of x, y, z, s waiting for the cache miss), which may exceed the capacity of the machine's instruction-issue hardware.

Prefetch instructions. Suppose the compiler inserts a *prefetch* instruction for address a, in advance of the time a will be fetched. This is a hint to the computer that it should start transferring a from main memory into the cache. Then, when a is fetched a few cycles later by an ordinary load instruction, it will hit the cache and there will be no delay.

Many machines don't have a prefetch instruction as such, but many machines do have a nonblocking *load* instruction. That is, when $r_3 \leftarrow M[r_7]$ is performed, the processor does not stall even on a cache miss, *until r_3 is used as an operand of some other instruction.* If we want to prefetch address a, we can just do $r_t \leftarrow M[a]$, and then *never use the value of r_t.* This will start the load, bringing the value into cache if necessary, but not delay any other instruction. Later, when we fetch $M[a]$ again, it will hit the cache. Of course, if the computation was already *memory-bound* – fully utilizing the load/store unit while the arithmetic units are often idle – then prefetching using ordinary *load* instructions may not help.

If the computation accesses every word of an array sequentially, it uses several words from each cache block. Then we don't need to prefetch every word – just one word per cache block is enough. Assuming a 4-byte word and 16-byte cache block, the dot-product loop with prefetching looks something like this:

L_1 : **if** $i \bmod 16 = 0$ **then** prefetch $M[i + K]$
    if $j \bmod 16 = 0$ **then** prefetch $M[j + K]$
    $x \leftarrow M[i]$
    $y \leftarrow M[j]$
    $z \leftarrow x \times y$
    $s \leftarrow s + z$
    $i \leftarrow i + 4$
    $j \leftarrow j + 4$
    if $i < N$ **goto** L_1

```
L₁ : prefetch M[i + K]             L₁ : n ← i + 16
      prefetch M[j + K]                  if n + K ≥ N goto L₃
      x ← M[i]                           prefetch M[i + K]
      y ← M[j]                           prefetch M[j + K]
      z ← x × y                    L₂ : x ← M[i]
      s ← s + z                          y ← M[j]
      i ← i + 4                          z ← x × y
      j ← j + 4                          s ← s + z
      if i ≥ N goto L₂                   i ← i + 4
      x ← M[i]                           j ← j + 4
      y ← M[j]                           if i < n goto L₂
      z ← x × y                          goto L₁
      s ← s + z                    L₃ : x ← M[i]
      i ← i + 4                          y ← M[j]
      j ← j + 4                          z ← x × y
      if i ≥ N goto L₂                   s ← s + z
      x ← M[i]                           i ← i + 4
      y ← M[j]                           j ← j + 4
      z ← x × y                          if i < N goto L₃
      s ← s + z
      i ← i + 4
      j ← j + 4
      if i ≥ N goto L₂
      x ← M[i]
      y ← M[j]
      z ← x × y
      s ← s + z
      i ← i + 4
      j ← j + 4
      if i < N goto L₁
L₂ :
```

PROGRAM 21.6. Inserting prefetches using loop unrolling or nested loops.

The value K is chosen to match the expected cache-miss latency. For a secondary-cache-miss latency of 200 instructions, when each loop iteration executes 7 instructions and advances i by 4, we would use $K = 200 \cdot 4/7$ rounded up to the nearest multiple of the block size, that is, about 128. Figure 21.5b uses prefetching to "hide" a cache latency of 11 instructions, so $K = 16$, the block size. An additional improvement that may be helpful on some machines, when K is small, is to avoid overlapping the prefetch latencies so the memory hardware needn't process two misses simultaneously.

In practice, we don't want to test $i \bmod 16 = 0$ in each iteration, so we unroll the loop, or nest a loop within a loop, as shown in Program 21.6. The loop-unrolled version on the left could be further improved – in ways unrelated to prefetching – by removing some of the intermediate **if** statements, as described in Section 18.5.

Prefetching for stores. Sometimes we can predict at compile time that a *store* instruction will miss the cache. Consider the following loop:

for $i \leftarrow 0$ to $N - 1$
  $A[i] \leftarrow i$

If the array A is larger than the cache, or if A has not recently been accessed, then each time i crosses into a new cache block there will be a write miss. If the write-miss policy is *write-validate*, then this is no problem, as the processor will not be stalled and all the marked-invalid words will be quickly overwritten with valid data. If the policy is *fetch-on-write*, then the stalls at each new cache block will significantly slow down the program. But prefetching can be used here:

for $i \leftarrow 0$ to $N - 1$
  if i mod *blocksize* $= 0$ then **prefetch** $A[i + K]$
  $A[i] \leftarrow i$

As usual, unrolling the loop will remove the **if**-test. The $A[i + K]$ value that's prefetched will contain *garbage* – dead data that we know will be overwritten. We perform the prefetch only to avoid the write-miss stall.

If the write-miss policy is *write-around*, then we should prefetch only if we expect the $A[i]$ values to be fetched soon after they are stored.

Summary. Prefetching is applicable when

- The machine has a prefetch instruction, or a nonblocking load instruction that can be used as a prefetch;
- The machine does not dynamically reorder instructions, or the dynamic reorder buffer is smaller than the particular cache latency that we desire to hide; *and*
- The data in question is larger than the cache, or not expected to be already in cache.

We will not describe the algorithm for inserting prefetch instructions in loops, but see the Further Reading section.

<table>
<tr><td>21.4</td><td></td></tr>
</table>

21.4   LOOP INTERCHANGE

The most fundamental way of using the cache effectively is the reuse of cached data. When nested loops access memory, successive iterations of a loop often reuse the same word, or use adjacent words that occupy the same cache block. If it is the *innermost* loop whose iterations reuse the same values, then there will be many cache hits. But if one of the outer loops reuses a cache block, it may be that execution of the inner loop stomps through the cache so heavily that by the time the next outer-loop iteration executes, the cache block will have been flushed.

Consider the following nested loops, for example.

> **for** $i \leftarrow 0$ **to** $N - 1$
>   **for** $j \leftarrow 0$ **to** $M - 1$
>   **for** $k \leftarrow 0$ **to** $P - 1$
> $A[i, j, k] \leftarrow (B[i, j - 1, k] + B[i, j, k] + B[i, j + 1, k])/3$

The value $B[i, j + 1, k]$ is reused in the next iteration of the j loop (where its "name" is $B[i, j, k]$), and then is reused again in the iteration after that. But in the meantime, the k loop brings $3P$ elements of the B array, and P elements of the A array, through the cache. Some of these words may very well conflict with $B[i, j + 1, k]$, causing a cache miss the next time it is fetched.

The solution in this case is to interchange the j and k loops, putting the j loop innermost:

> **for** $i \leftarrow 0$ **to** $N - 1$
>   **for** $k \leftarrow 0$ **to** $P - 1$
>   **for** $j \leftarrow 0$ **to** $M - 1$
> $A[i, j, k] \leftarrow (B[i, j - 1, k] + B[i, j, k] + B[i, j + 1, k])/3$

Now $B[i, j, k]$ will always be a cache hit, and so will $B[i, j - 1, k]$.

To see whether interchange is legal for a given pair of loops, we must examine the data-dependence graph of the calculation. We say that iteration (j, k) depends on iteration (j', k') if (j', k') computes values that are used by (j, k) (read-after-write), or stores values that are overwritten by (j, k) (write-after-write), or reads values that are overwritten (write-after-read). If the interchanged loops execute (j', k') before (j, k), *and* there is a dependence, then the computation may yield a different result, and the interchange is illegal.

In the example shown above, there is *no* dependence between any iterations of the nested loops, so interchange is legal.

See the Further Reading section for a discussion of the analysis of dependence relations for array accesses in nested loops.

21.5 BLOCKING

The technique of *blocking* reorders a computation so that all the computations that use one portion of the data are completed before moving on to the next portion. The following nested loop for matrix multiplication, $C = AB$, illustrates the need for blocking:

for $i \leftarrow 0$ **to** $N - 1$
   for $j \leftarrow 0$ **to** $N - 1$
      for $k \leftarrow 0$ **to** $N - 1$
         $C[i, j] \leftarrow C[i, j] + A[i, k] \cdot B[k, j]$

If both A and B fit into the cache simultaneously, then the k loop will run without cache misses; and there may be only one cache miss for $C[i, j]$ on each iteration of the j loop.

But suppose the cache is large enough to hold only $2 \cdot c \cdot N$ matrix elements (floating-point numbers), where $1 < c < N$. For example, multiplying 50×50 matrices of 8-byte floats on a machine with an 8-kilobyte cache, $c = 10$. Then *every reference to $B[k, j]$ in the inner loop will be a cache miss*, because – since the last time that particular cell of B was accessed – the entire B matrix will have been marched through the cache, dumping out the "old" values. Thus, each iteration of the inner loop will have a cache miss.

Loop interchange cannot help here, because if the j loop is outermost, then A will suffer cache misses, and if the k loop is outermost, then C will suffer misses.

The solution is to reuse rows of the A matrix and columns of the B matrix while they are still in cache. A $c \times c$ block of the matrix C can be calculated from c rows of A and c columns of B, as follows (see also Figure 21.7):

for $i \leftarrow i_0$ **to** $i_0 + c - 1$
   for $j \leftarrow j_0$ **to** $j_0 + c - 1$
      for $k \leftarrow 0$ **to** $N - 1$
         $C[i, j] \leftarrow C[i, j] + A[i, k] \cdot B[k, j]$

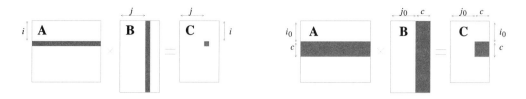

FIGURE 21.7. Matrix multiplication. Each element of C is computed from a row of A and a column of B. With blocking, a $c \times c$ block of the C matrix is computed from a $c \times N$ block of A and a $N \times c$ block of B.

Only $c \cdot N$ elements of A and $c \cdot N$ elements of B are used in this loop, and *each element is used c times*. Thus, at a cost of $2 \cdot c \cdot N$ cache misses to bring this portion of A and B into cache, we are able to compute $c \cdot c \cdot N$ iterations of the inner loop, for a miss rate of $2/c$ misses per iteration.

All that remains is to nest this set of loops inside outer loops that compute each $c \times c$ block of C:

> **for** $i_0 \leftarrow 0$ **to** $N - 1$ **by** c
>   **for** $j_0 \leftarrow 0$ **to** $N - 1$ **by** c
>   **for** $i \leftarrow i_0$ **to** $\min(i_0 + c - 1, N - 1)$
>   **for** $j \leftarrow j_0$ **to** $\min(j_0 + c - 1, N - 1)$
>   **for** $k \leftarrow 0$ **to** $N - 1$
> $C[i, j] \leftarrow C[i, j] + A[i, k] \cdot B[k, j]$

This optimization is called *blocking* because it computes one block of the iteration space at a time. There are many nested-loop programs on which an optimizing compiler can automatically perform the blocking transformation. Crucial to the situation are loops whose iterations are not data-dependent on each other; in matrix multiplication, the calculation of $C[i, j]$ does not depend on $C[i', j']$, for example.

Scalar replacement. Even though the access to $C[i, j]$ in the matrix-multiply program will almost always hit the cache (since the same word is being used repeatedly in the k loop), we can still bring it up one level in the memory hierarchy – from primary cache into registers! – by the *scalar replacement* optimization. That is, when a particular array element is used as a scalar for repeated computations, we can "cache" it in a register:

```
for i ← i₀ to i₀ + c − 1
    for j ← j₀ to j₀ + c − 1
        s ← C[i, j]
        for k ← 0 to N − 1
            s ← s + A[i, k] · B[k, j]
        C[i, j] ← s
```

This reduces the number of fetches and stores in the innermost loop by a factor of 2.

Blocking at every level of the memory hierarchy. To do blocking optimizations, the compiler must know how big the cache is – this determines the best value of c, the block size. If there are several levels of the memory hierarchy, then blocking can be done at each level. Even the machine's registers should be considered as a level of the memory hierarchy.

Taking again the example of matrix multiply, we suppose there are 32 floating-point registers, and we want to use d of them as a kind of cache. We can rewrite the $c \times c$ loop (of the blocked matrix multiply) as follows:

```
for i ← i₀ to i₀ + c − 1
    for k₀ ← 0 to N − 1 by d
        for k ← k₀ to k₀ + d − 1
            T[k − k₀] ← A[i, k]
        for j ← j₀ to j₀ + c − 1
            s ← C[i, j]
            for k ← k₀ to k₀ + d − 1
                s ← s + T[k − k₀] · B[k, j]
            C[i, j] ← s
```

Unroll and jam. *Loop unrolling must be used for register-level blocking, since registers cannot be indexed by subscripts. So we unroll the k-loops d times and keep each $T[k]$ in a separate scalar temporary variable (for illustration, we will use $d = 3$, though $d = 25$ would be more realistic):*

```
for i ← i₀ to i₀ + c − 1
    for k₀ ← 0 to N − 1 by 3
        t₀ ← A[i, k₀];  t₁ ← A[i, k₀ + 1];  t₂ ← A[i, k₀ + 2]
        for j ← j₀ to j₀ + c − 1
            C[i, j] ← C[i, j] + t₀ · B[k₀, j] + t₁ · B[k₀ + 1, j] + t₂ · B[k₀ + 2, j]
```

The register allocator will ensure, of course, that the t_k are kept in registers. Every value of $A[i, k]$ fetched from the cache is used c times; the B values still need to be fetched, so the number of memory accesses in the inner loop goes down by almost a factor of two.

A high-tech compiler would perform – on the same loop! – blocking transformations for the primary cache and for the secondary cache, and scalar replacement and unroll-and-jam for the register level of the memory hierarchy.

21.6   GARBAGE COLLECTION & THE MEMORY HIERARCHY

Garbage-collected systems have had the reputation as cache-thrashers with bad cache locality: After all, it would appear that a garbage collection touches all of memory in random-access fashion.

But a garbage collector is really a kind of memory manager, and we can organize it to manage memory for improved locality of reference.

Generations: When generational copying garbage collection is used, the youngest generation (allocation space) should be made to fit inside the secondary cache. Then each memory allocation will be a cache hit, and each youngest-generation garbage collection will operate almost entirely within the cache as well – only the objects promoted to another generation may cause cache-write misses. (Keeping the youngest generation inside the primary cache is impractical, since that cache is usually so small that too-frequent garbage collections would be required.)

Sequential allocation: With copying collection, new objects are allocated from a large contiguous free space, sequentially in order of address. The sequential pattern of stores to initialize these objects is easy for most modern write-buffers to handle.

Few conflicts: The most frequently referenced objects tend to be the newer ones. With sequential allocation of objects in the youngest generations, the *keys* of these newer objects (in a direct-mapped cache) will be all different. Consequently, garbage-collected programs have significantly lower conflict-miss rates than programs that use explicit freeing.

Prefetching for allocation: The sequential initializing stores cause cache-write misses (in the primary cache, which is much smaller than the allocation space) at the rate of one miss per B/W stores, where B is the cache block size and W is the word size. On most modern machines (those with write-validate cache policies) these misses are not costly, because a *write* miss does not cause the processor to wait for any data. But on some machines (those with fetch-on-write or write-around policies) a write miss is costly. One solution is to prefetch the block well in advance of storing into it. This does not require analysis of any loops in the program (like the technique shown in Section 21.3) – instead, as the allocator creates a new object at address a, it prefetches word $a + K$. The value K is related to the cache-miss latency and also the frequency of allocation versus other computation, but a value of $K = 100$ should work well in almost all circumstances.

Grouping related objects: If object x points to object y, an algorithm that accesses x will likely access y soon, so it is profitable to put the two objects in the same block. A copying collector using *depth-first* search to traverse the live data will automatically tend to put related objects together; a collector using *breadth-first* search will not. Copying in depth-first order improves cache performance – but only if the cache blocks are larger than the objects.

These cache-locality improvement techniques are all applicable to *copying* collection. Mark-and-sweep collectors, which cannot move the live objects, are less amenable to cache management; but see the Further Reading section.

FURTHER READING

Sites [1992] discusses several kinds of instruction- and data-cache alignment optimizations. Efficient approximation algorithms for the traveling salesman problem (TSP) can be applied to basic-block ordering, to minimize the instruction-fetch penalties for branches [Young et al. 1997].

Mowry et al. [1992] describe an algorithm for inserting prefetch instructions in **for**-loops, taking care not to insert prefetches (which do, after all, have an instruction-issue cost) where the data in question is likely to be in cache already.

The Lisp Machine's garbage collector used depth-first search to group related objects on the same page to minimize page faults [Moon 1984]. Koopman et al. [1992] describe prefetching for a garbage-collected system. Diwan et al. [1994], Reinhold [1994], and Gonçalves and Appel [1995] analyze the cache locality of programs that use copying garbage collection. For mark-sweep collectors, Boehm et al. [1991] suggest that (to improve page-level locality) new objects should not be allocated into mostly full pages containing old objects, and that the sweep phase should be done incrementally so that pages and cache blocks are "touched" by the sweep just before they are allocated by the program.

The techniques for optimizing the memory locality of programs with nested loops have much in common with techniques for parallelizing loops. For example, in a parallel implementation of matrix multiplication, having each processor compute one *row* of the C matrix requires that processor to have N^2 elements of A and N elements of B, or $O(N^2)$ words of interprocessor communication. Instead, each processor should compute one *block* of C (where the block size is $\sqrt{N} \times \sqrt{N}$); then each processor requires $N \cdot \sqrt{N}$ words of A and of B, which is only $O(N^{1.5})$ words of communication. Many of the compilers that use blocking and loop-nest optimizations to generate the most memory-efficient code for uniprocessors are parallelizing compilers – with the parallelization turned off!

To generate good parallel code – or to perform many of the loop optimizations described in this chapter, such as blocking and interchange – it's necessary to analyze how array accesses are data-dependent on each other. Array dependence analysis is beyond the scope of this book, but is covered well by Wolfe [1996].

Callahan et al. [1990] show how to do scalar replacement; Carr and Kennedy [1994] show how to calculate the right amount of unroll-and-jam for a loop based on the characteristics of the target machine.

Wolf and Lam [1991] describe a compiler optimization algorithm that uses blocking, tiling (like blocking but where the tiles can be skewed instead of rectangular), and loop interchange to achieve locality improvements on many kinds of nested loops.

The textbook by Wolfe [1996] covers almost all the techniques described in this chapter, with particular emphasis on automatic parallelization but also with some treatment of improving memory locality.

EXERCISES

*21.1 Write a program in C for multiplying 1000×1000 double-precision floating-point matrices. Run it on your machine and measure the time it takes.

    a. Find out the number of floating-point registers on your machine, the size of the primary cache, and the size of the secondary cache.

    b. Write a matrix-multiply program that uses blocking transformations at the *secondary cache* level only. Measure its run time.

c. Modify your program to optimize on both levels of the cache; measure its run time.

d. Modify the program again to optimize over both levels of the cache *and* use registers via unroll-and-jam; view the output of the C compiler to verify that the register allocator is keeping your temporary variables in floating-point registers. Measure the run time.

*21.2 Write a program in C for multiplying 1000 × 1000 double-precision floating-point matrices. Use the C compiler to print out assembly language for your loop. If your machine has a prefetch instruction, or a nonstalling load instruction that can serve as a prefetch, insert prefetch instructions to hide secondary-cache misses. Show what calculations you made to take account of the cache-miss latency. How much faster is your program with prefetching?

APPENDIX ▬▬▬▬▬▬

MiniJava Language Reference Manual

MiniJava is a subset of Java. The meaning of a MiniJava program is given by its meaning as a Java program. Overloading is not allowed in MiniJava. The MiniJava statement System.out.println(...); can only print integers. The MiniJava expression e.length only applies to expressions of type int[].

A.1 LEXICAL ISSUES

Identifiers: An *identifier* is a sequence of letters, digits, and underscores, starting with a letter. Uppercase letters are distinguished from lowercase. In this appendix the symbol *id* stands for an identifier.

Integer literals: A sequence of decimal digits is an *integer constant* that denotes the corresponding integer value. In this appendix the symbol *INTEGER_LITERAL* stands for an integer constant.

Binary operators: A *binary operator* is one of

&& < + - *

In this appendix the symbol *op* stands for a binary operator.

Comments: A comment may appear between any two tokens. There are two forms of comments: One starts with /*, ends with */, and may be nested; another begins with // and goes to the end of the line.

A.2 GRAMMAR

In the MiniJava grammar, we use the notation N^*, where N is a nonterminal, to mean 0, 1, or more repetitions of N.

Program	→	*MainClass ClassDecl**
MainClass	→	**class** *id* { **public static void main** (**String** [ ] *id*)
		{ *Statement* } }
ClassDecl	→	**class** *id* { *VarDecl* MethodDecl** }
	→	**class** *id* **extends** *id* { *VarDecl* MethodDecl** }
VarDecl	→	*Type id* ;
MethodDecl	→	**public** *Type id* (*FormalList*)
		{ *VarDecl* Statement** **return** *Exp* ; }
FormalList	→	*Type id FormalRest**
	→	
FormalRest	→	, *Type id*
Type	→	**int** [ ]
	→	**boolean**
	→	**int**
	→	*id*
Statement	→	{ *Statement** }
	→	**if** (*Exp*) *Statement* **else** *Statement*
	→	**while** (*Exp*) *Statement*
	→	**System.out.println** (*Exp*) ;
	→	*id* = *Exp* ;
	→	*id* [*Exp*] = *Exp* ;
Exp	→	*Exp op Exp*
	→	*Exp* [*Exp*]
	→	*Exp* . **length**
	→	*Exp* . *id* (*ExpList*)
	→	*INTEGER_LITERAL*
	→	**true**
	→	**false**
	→	*id*
	→	**this**
	→	**new int** [*Exp*]
	→	**new** *id* ( )
	→	! *Exp*
	→	(*Exp*)
ExpList	→	*Exp ExpRest**
	→	
ExpRest	→	, *Exp*

485

A.3   SAMPLE PROGRAM

```
class Factorial {
    public static void main(String[] a) {
        System.out.println(new Fac().ComputeFac(10));
    }
}
class Fac {
    public int ComputeFac(int num) {
        int num_aux;
        if (num < 1)
            num_aux = 1;
        else
            num_aux = num * (this.ComputeFac(num-1));
        return num_aux;
    }
}
```

Bibliography

ADA 1980. Military standard: Ada programming language. Tech. Rep. MIL-STD-1815, Department of Defense, Naval Publications and Forms Center, Philadelphia, PA.

AHO, A. V., GANAPATHI, M., AND TJIANG, S. W. K. 1989. Code generation using tree matching and dynamic programming. *ACM Trans. on Programming Languages and Systems* 11(4), 491–516.

AHO, A. V., JOHNSON, S. C., AND ULLMAN, J. D. 1975. Deterministic parsing of ambiguous grammars. *Commun. ACM* 18(8), 441–452.

AHO, A. V., SETHI, R., AND ULLMAN, J. D. 1986. *Compilers: Principles, Techniques, and Tools*. Addison-Wesley, Reading, MA.

AIKEN, A. AND NICOLAU, A. 1988. Optimal loop parallelization. In Proc. SIGPLAN '88 Conf. on Prog. Lang. Design and Implementation. *SIGPLAN Notices* 23(7), 308–17.

ALLEN, F. E. 1969. Program optimization. *Annual Review of Automatic Programming* 5, 239–307.

ALLEN, F. E. 1970. Control flow analysis. *SIGPLAN Notices* 5(7), 1–19.

ALPERN, B., WEGMAN, M. N., AND ZADECK, F. K. 1988. Detecting equality of variables in programs. In *Proc. 15th ACM Symp. on Principles of Programming Languages*. ACM Press, New York, 1–11.

AMIEL, E., GRUBER, O., AND SIMON, E. 1994. Optimizing multi-method dispatch using compressed dispatch tables. In OOPSLA '94: 9th Annual Conference on Object-Oriented Programming Systems, Languages, and Applications. *SIGPLAN Notices* 29(10), 244–258.

APPEL, A. W. 1992. *Compiling with Continuations*. Cambridge University Press, Cambridge, England.

APPEL, A. W., ELLIS, J. R., AND LI, K. 1988. Real-time concurrent collection on stock multiprocessors. In Proc. SIGPLAN '88 Conf. on Prog. Lang. Design and Implementation. *SIGPLAN Notices* 23(7), 11–20.

APPEL, A. W. AND SHAO, Z. 1996. Empirical and analytic study of stack versus heap cost for languages with closures. *J. Functional Programming* 6(1), 47–74.

ARNOLD, K. AND GOSLING, J. 1996. *The Java Programming Language*. Addison Wesley, Reading, MA.

AUGUSTSSON, L. 1984. A compiler for lazy ML. In *Proc. 1984 ACM Conf. on LISP and Functional Programming*. ACM Press, New York, 218–27.

BACKHOUSE, R. C. 1979. *Syntax of Programming Languages: Theory and Practice*. Prentice-Hall International, Englewood Cliffs, NJ.

BAKER, H. G. 1978. List processing in real time on a serial computer. *Commun.*

ACM 21(4), 280–294.

BALL, T. AND LARUS, J. R. 1993. Branch prediction for free. In Proc. ACM SIGPLAN '93 Conf. on Prog. Lang. Design and Implementation. *SIGPLAN Notices* 28(6), 300–313.

BAUER, F. L. AND EICKEL, J. 1975. *Compiler Construction: An Advanced Course.* Springer-Verlag, New York.

BIRTWISTLE, G. M., DAHL, O.-J., MYHRHAUG, B., AND NYGAARD, K. 1973. *Simula Begin.* Petrocelli/Charter, New York.

BOBROW, D. G., DEMICHIEL, L. G., GABRIEL, R. P., KEENE, S. E., KICZALES, G., AND MOON, D. A. 1989. Common Lisp Object System specification. *Lisp and Symbolic Computation* 1(3), 245–293.

BOEHM, H.-J. 1993. Space efficient conservative garbage collection. In Proc. ACM SIGPLAN '93 Conf. on Prog. Lang. Design and Implementation. *SIGPLAN Notices* 28(6), 197–206.

BOEHM, H.-J. 1996. Simple garbage-collector-safety. In Proc. ACM SIGPLAN '96 Conf. on Prog. Lang. Design and Implementation. *SIGPLAN Notices* 31(5), 89–98.

BOEHM, H.-J., DEMERS, A. J., AND SHENKER, S. 1991. Mostly parallel garbage collection. In Proc. ACM SIGPLAN '91 Conf. on Prog. Lang. Design and Implementation. *SIGPLAN Notices* 26(6), 157–164.

BOEHM, H.-J. AND WEISER, M. 1988. Garbage collection in an uncooperative environment. *Software—Practice and Experience* 18(9), 807–820.

BRACHA, G., ODERSKY, M., STOUTAMIRE, D., AND WADLER, P. 1998. Making the future safe for the past: Adding genericity to the Java programming language. In *Object Oriented Programming: Systems, Languages, and Applications (OOPSLA),* C. Chambers, Ed. Vancouver, BC, 183–200.

BRANQUART, P. AND LEWI, J. 1971. A scheme for storage allocation and garbage collection in Algol-68. In *Algol 68 Implementation,* J. E. L. Peck, Ed. North-Holland, Amsterdam.

BRIGGS, P., COOPER, K. D., AND TORCZON, L. 1994. Improvements to graph coloring register allocation. *ACM Trans. on Programming Languages and Systems* 16(3), 428–455.

BROWN, M. R. AND TARJAN, R. E. 1979. A fast merging algorithm. *Journal of the Association for Computing Machinery* 26(2), 211–226.

BUMBULIS, P. AND COWAN, D. D. 1993. RE2C: A more versatile scanner generator. *ACM Letters on Programming Languages and Systems* 2(1–4), 70–84.

BURKE, M. G. AND FISHER, G. A. 1987. A practical method for LR and LL syntactic error diagnosis and recovery. *ACM Trans. on Programming Languages and Systems* 9(2), 164–167.

CALLAHAN, D., CARR, S., AND KENNEDY, K. 1990. Improving register allocation for subscripted variables. In Proc. ACM SIGPLAN '90 Conf. on Prog. Lang. Design and Implementation. *SIGPLAN Notices* 25(6), 53–65.

CARDELLI, L. 1984. Compiling a functional language. In *1984 Symp. on LISP and Functional Programming.* ACM Press, New York, 208–17.

CARR, S. AND KENNEDY, K. 1994. Improving the ratio of memory operations to floating-point operations in loops. *ACM Trans. on Programming Languages and Systems* 16(6), 1768–1810.

CATTELL, R. G. G. 1980. Automatic derivation of code generators from machine descriptions. *ACM Trans. on Programming Languages and Systems* 2(2), 173–190.

CHAITIN, G. J. 1982. Register allocation and spilling via graph coloring. *SIGPLAN Notices* 17(6), 98–105. Proceeding of the ACM SIGPLAN '82 Symposium on Compiler Construction.

CHAMBERS, C. AND LEAVENS, G. T. 1995. Typechecking and modules for multimethods. *ACM Trans. on Programming Languages and Systems* 17(6), 805–843.

CHAMBERS, C., UNGAR, D., AND LEE, E. 1991. An efficient implementation of SELF, a dynamically-typed object-oriented language based on prototypes. *Lisp and Symbolic Computation* 4(3), 243–281.

CHEN, W. AND TURAU, B. 1994. Efficient dynamic look-up strategy for multi-methods. In *European Conference on Object-Oriented Programming (ECOOP '94)*.

CHENEY, C. J. 1970. A nonrecursive list compacting algorithm. *Commun. ACM* 13(11), 677–678.

CHOW, F., HIMELSTEIN, M., KILLIAN, E., AND WEBER, L. 1986. Engineering a RISC compiler system. In *Proc. COMPCON Spring 86*. IEEE, 132–137.

CHURCH, A. 1941. *The Calculi of Lambda Conversion*. Princeton University Press, Princeton, NJ.

COCKE, J. 1970. Global common subexpression elimination. *SIGPLAN Notices* 5(7), 20–24.

COCKE, J. AND SCHWARTZ, J. T. 1970. Programming languages and their compilers: Preliminary notes. Tech. rep., Courant Institute, New York University.

COHEN, J. 1981. Garbage collection of linked data structures. *Computing Surveys* 13(3), 341–367.

COHEN, N. H. 1991. Type-extension type tests can be performed in constant time. *ACM Trans. on Programming Languages and Systems* 13(4), 626–629.

COLLINS, G. E. 1960. A method for overlapping and erasure of lists. *Commun. ACM* 3(12), 655–657.

CONNOR, R. C. H., DEARLE, A., MORRISON, R., AND BROWN, A. L. 1989. An object addressing mechanism for statically typed languages with multiple inheritance. *SIGPLAN Notices* 24(10), 279–285.

CONWAY, M. E. 1963. Design of a separable transition-diagram compiler. *Commun. ACM* 6(7), 396–408.

CORMEN, T. H., LEISERSON, C. E., AND RIVEST, R. L. 1990. *Introduction to Algorithms*. MIT Press, Cambridge, MA.

COUSINEAU, G., CURIEN, P. L., AND MAUNY, M. 1985. The categorical abstract machine. In *Functional Programming Languages and Computer Architecture, LNCS Vol. 201*, J. P. Jouannaud, Ed. Springer-Verlag, New York, 50–64.

CYTRON, R., FERRANTE, J., ROSEN, B. K., WEGMAN, M. N., AND ZADECK, F. K. 1991. Efficiently computing static single assignment form and the control dependence graph. *ACM Trans. on Programming Languages and Systems* 13(4), 451–490.

CYTRON, R., LOWRY, A., AND ZADECK, K. 1986. Code motion of control structures in high-level languages. In *Proc. 13th ACM Symp. on Principles of Programming Languages*. ACM Press, New York, 70–85.

DEREMER, F. L. 1971. Simple LR(*k*) grammars. *Commun. ACM* 14, 453–460.

DERSHOWITZ, N. AND JOUANNAUD, J.-P. 1990. Rewrite systems. In *Handbook of Theoretical Computer Science*, J. van Leeuwen, Ed. Vol. B. Elsevier, Amsterdam, 243–320.

DIJKSTRA, E. W., LAMPORT, L., MARTIN, A. J., SCHOLTEN, C. S., AND STEFFENS, E. F. M. 1978. On-the-fly garbage collection: An exercise in cooperation. *Commun. ACM* 21(11), 966–975.

DIWAN, A., MOSS, E., AND HUDSON, R. 1992. Compiler support for garbage collection in a statically typed language. In Proc. ACM SIGPLAN '92 Conf. on Prog. Lang. Design and Implementation. *SIGPLAN Notices* 27(7), 273–282.

DIWAN, A., MOSS, J. E. B., AND MCKINLEY, K. S. 1996. Simple and effective analysis of statically typed object-oriented programs. In OOPSLA '96: 11th Annual Conference on Object-Oriented Programming Systems, Languages, and Applications. *SIGPLAN Notices* 31, 292–305.

DIWAN, A., TARDITI, D., AND MOSS, E. 1994. Memory subsystem performance of programs using copying garbage collection. In *Proc. 21st Annual ACM SIGPLAN-SIGACT Symp. on Principles of Programming Languages*. ACM Press, New York, 1–14.

DIXON, R., MCKEE, T., SCHWEIZER, P., AND VAUGHAN, M. 1989. A fast method dispatcher for compiled languages with multiple inheritance. In OOPSLA '89: Object-Oriented Programming: Systems, Languages, and Applications. *SIGPLAN Notices* 24(10), 211–214.

ERSHOV, A. P. 1958. On programming of arithmetic operations. *Commun. ACM* 1(8), 3–6.

FELDMAN, J. AND GRIES, D. 1968. Translator writing systems. *Commun. ACM* 11(2), 77–113.

FENICHEL, R. R. AND YOCHELSON, J. C. 1969. A LISP garbage-collector for virtual-memory computer systems. *Commun. ACM* 12(11), 611–612.

FERRANTE, J., OTTENSTEIN, K. J., AND WARREN, J. D. 1987. The program dependence graph and its use in optimization. *ACM Trans. on Programming Languages and Systems* 9(3), 319–349.

FISHER, J. A. 1981. Trace scheduling: A technique for global microcode compaction. *IEEE Transactions on Computers* C-30(7), 478–490.

FISHER, J. A. 1983. Very long instruction word architectures and the ELI-512. In *Proc. 10th Symposium on Computer Architecture*. 140–150.

FLANAGAN, C., SABRY, A., DUBA, B. F., AND FELLEISEN, M. 1993. The essence of compiling with continuations. In *Proceedings of the ACM SIGPLAN '93 Conference on Programming Language Design and Implementation*. ACM Press, New York, 237–247.

FORD, L. R. AND FULKERSON, D. R. 1962. *Flows in Networks*. Princeton University Press, Princeton, NJ.

FRASER, C. W. AND HANSON, D. R. 1995. *A Retargetable C Compiler: Design and Implementation*. Benjamin Cummings, Redwood City, CA.

FRASER, C. W., HENRY, R. R., AND PROEBSTING, T. 1992. BURG—fast optimal instruction selection and tree parsing. *SIGPLAN Notices* 24(4), 68–76.

FRIEDMAN, D. P. AND WISE, D. S. 1976. Cons should not evaluate its arguments. In *Automata, Languages and Programming*, S. Michaelson and R. Milner, Eds. Edinburgh University Press, 257–284.

GAREY, M. R. AND JOHNSON, D. S. 1979. *Computers and Intractability: A Guide to the Theory of NP-completeness*. W. H. Freeman, New York.

GEORGE, L. AND APPEL, A. W. 1996. Iterated register coalescing. *ACM Trans. on Programming Languages and Systems* 18(3), 300–324.

GLANVILLE, R. S. AND GRAHAM, S. L. 1978. A new method for compiler code generation. In *Fifth ACM Symposium on Principles of Programming Languages*. 231–40.

GÖDEL, K. 1931. Über formal unentscheidbare Sätze der Principia Mathematica and verwandter Systeme I. *Monatshefte für Mathematik und Physik* 38, 173–198.

GOLDBERG, A., ROBSON, D., AND INGALLS, D. H. H. 1983. *Smalltalk-80: The Language and Its Implementation*. Addison-Wesley, Reading, MA.

GONÇALVES, M. J. R. AND APPEL, A. W. 1995. Cache performance of fast-allocating programs. In *Proc. Seventh Int'l Conf. on Functional Programming and Computer Architecture*. ACM Press, New York, 293–305.

GORDON, M. J. C., MILNER, A. J. R. G., MORRIS, L., NEWEY, M. C., AND
    WADSWORTH, C. P. 1978. A metalanguage for interactive proof in LCF. In *Fifth ACM
    Symp. on Principles of Programming Languages*. ACM Press, New York.

GOVINDARAJAN, R., ALTMAN, E. R., AND GAO, G. R. 1996. A framework for
    resource-constrained rate-optimal software pipelining. *IEEE Transactions on Parallel
    and Distributed Systems* 7(11), 1133–1149.

GRAY, R. W. 1988. γ-GLA—a generator for lexical analyzers that programmers can use. In
    USENIX Conference Proceedings. USENIX Association, Berkeley, CA, 147–160.

GRIES, D. 1971. *Compiler Construction for Digital Computers*. John Wiley & Sons, New
    York.

HALL, C. V., HAMMOND, K., PEYTON JONES, S. L., AND WADLER, P. L. 1996. Type
    classes in Haskell. *ACM Trans. on Programming Languages and Systems* 18(2),
    109–138.

HAREL, D. 1985. A linear time algorithm for finding dominators in flow graphs and related
    problems. In *Proc. 7th Annual ACM Symp. on Theory of Computing*. ACM Press, New
    York, 185–194.

HEILBRUNNER, S. 1981. A parsing automata approach to LR theory. *Theoretical Computer
    Science* 15, 117–157.

HENDERSON, P. AND MORRIS, J. H. 1976. A lazy evaluator. In *Third ACM Symp. on
    Principles of Prog. Languages*. ACM Press, New York, 123–142.

HENNESSY, J. L. AND PATTERSON, D. A. 1996. *Computer Architecture: A Quantitative
    Approach*, Second ed. Morgan Kaufmann, San Mateo, CA.

HOPCROFT, J. E. AND ULLMAN, J. D. 1979. *Introduction to Automata Theory, Languages,
    and Computation*. Addison-Wesley, Reading, MA.

HOPKINS, M. E. 1986. Compiling for the RT PC ROMP. In *Tutorial, Reduced Instruction
    Set Computers*, W. Stallings, Ed. IEEE Computer Society, Los Angeles, 196–203.

HUDAK, P., PEYTON JONES, S., AND WADLER, P. 1992. Report on the programming
    language Haskell, a non-strict, purely functional language, version 1.2. *SIGPLAN
    Notices* 27(5).

HUGHES, J. 1989. Why functional programming matters. *Computer Journal* 32(2), 98–107.

IGARASHI, A., PIERCE, B. C., AND WADLER, P. 2001. Featherweight Java: A minimal
    core calculus for Java and GJ. *ACM Trans. on Programming Languages and
    Systems* 23(3), 396–450.

JOHNSON, S. C. 1975. Yacc – yet another compiler compiler. Tech. Rep. CSTR-32, AT&T
    Bell Laboratories, Murray Hill, NJ.

JONES, R. AND LINS, R. 1996. *Garbage Collection: Algorithms for Automatic Dynamic
    Memory Management*. John Wiley & Sons, Chichester, England.

KANE, G. AND HEINRICH, J. 1992. *MIPS RISC Architecture*. Prentice-Hall, Englewood
    Cliffs, NJ.

KELSEY, R. A. 1995. A correspondence between continuation passing style and static single
    assignment form. In Proceedings ACM SIGPLAN Workshop on Intermediate
    Representations. *SIGPLAN Notices* 30(3), 13–22.

KEMPE, A. B. 1879. On the geographical problem of the four colors. *American Journal of
    Mathematics* 2, 193–200.

KILDALL, G. A. 1973. A unified approach to global program optimization. In *Proc. ACM
    Symp. on Principles of Programming Languages*. ACM Press, New York, 194–206.

KNUTH, D. E. 1965. On the translation of languages from left to right. *Information and
    Control* 8, 607–639.

KNUTH, D. E. 1967. *The Art of Computer Programming, Vol. I: Fundamental Algorithms*.

Addison Wesley, Reading, MA.

KOOPMAN, P. J., LEE, P., AND SIEWIOREK, D. P. 1992. Cache behavior of combinator graph reduction. *ACM Trans. on Programming Languages and Systems* 14(2), 265–297.

KRANZ, D., KELSEY, R., REES, J., HUDAK, P., PHILBIN, J., AND ADAMS, N. 1986. ORBIT: An optimizing compiler for Scheme. *SIGPLAN Notices (Proc. Sigplan '86 Symp. on Compiler Construction)* 21(7), 219–33.

LANDI, W. AND RYDER, B. G. 1992. A safe approximation algorithm for interprocedural pointer aliasing. In Proc. ACM SIGPLAN '92 Conf. on Prog. Lang. Design and Implementation. *SIGPLAN Notices* 26(6), 235–248.

LANDIN, P. J. 1964. The mechanical evaluation of expressions. *Computer J.* 6(4), 308–320.

LENGAUER, T. AND TARJAN, R. E. 1979. A fast algorithm for finding dominators in a flowgraph. *ACM Trans. on Programming Languages and Systems* 1(1), 121–141.

LEONARD, T. E., Ed. 1987. *VAX Architecture Reference Manual.* Digital Press, Bedford, MA.

LESK, M. E. 1975. Lex—a lexical analyzer generator. Tech. Rep. Computing Science Technical Report 39, Bell Laboratories, Murray Hill, NJ.

LEWIS, P. M. I. AND STEARNS, R. E. 1968. Syntax-directed translation. *Journal of the ACM* 15, 464–488.

LIEBERMAN, H. AND HEWITT, C. 1983. A real-time garbage collector based on the lifetimes of objects. *Commun. ACM* 26(6), 419–429.

LIPPMAN, S. B. 1996. *Inside the C++ Object Model.* Addison Wesley, Reading, MA.

LIPTON, R. J., MARTINO, P. J., AND NEITZKE, A. 1997. On the complexity of a set-union problem. In *Proc. 38th Annual Symposium on Foundations of Computer Science.* IEEE Computer Society Press, Los Alamitos, CA, 110–115.

LOWRY, E. S. AND MEDLOCK, C. W. 1969. Object code optimization. *Commun. ACM* 12(1), 13–22. Corrigendum 12(6), 332.

MCCARTHY, J. 1960. Recursive functions of symbolic expressions and their computation by machine – I. *Commun. ACM* 3(1), 184–195.

MCCARTHY, J. 1963. Towards a mathematical science of computation. In *Information Processing (1962).* North-Holland, Amsterdam, 21–28.

MCCARTHY, J., ABRAHAMS, P. W., EDWARDS, D. J., HART, T. P., AND LEVIN, M. I. 1962. *LISP 1.5 Programmer's Manual.* M.I.T., RLE and MIT Computation Center, Cambridge, MA.

MCNAUGHTON, R. AND YAMADA, H. 1960. Regular expressions and state graphs for automata. *IEEE Trans. on Electronic Computers* 9(1), 39–47.

MILNER, R., TOFTE, M., AND HARPER, R. 1990. *The Definition of Standard ML.* MIT Press, Cambridge, MA.

MOON, D. A. 1984. Garbage collection in a large LISP system. In *ACM Symposium on LISP and Functional Programming.* ACM Press, New York, 235–246.

MOWRY, T. C., LAM, M. S., AND GUPTA, A. 1992. Design and evaluation of a compiler algorithm for prefetching. In Proc. 5rd Int'l Conf. on Architectural Support for Programming Languages and Operating Systems. *SIGPLAN Notices* 27(9), 62–73.

NAUR, P., BACKUS, J. W., BAUER, F. L., GREEN, J., KATZ, C., MCCARTHY, J., PERLIS, A. J., RUTISHAUSER, H., SAMELSON, K., VAUQUOIS, B., WEGSTEIN, J. H., VAN WIJNGAARDEN, A., AND WOODGER, M. 1963. Revised report on the algorithmic language ALGOL 60. *Commun. ACM* 6(1), 1–17.

NELSON, G., Ed. 1991. *Systems Programming with Modula-3.* Prentice-Hall, Englewood Cliffs, NJ.

PATTERSON, D. A. 1985. Reduced instruction set computers. *Commun. ACM* 28(1), 8–21.

PAXSON, V. 1995. Flex—Fast lexical analyzer generator. Lawrence Berkeley Laboratory, Berkeley, CA, ftp://ftp.ee.lbl.gov/flex-2.5.3.tar.gz.

PELEGRI-LLOPART, E. AND GRAHAM, S. L. 1988. Optimal code generation for expression trees: An application of BURS theory. In *15th ACM Symp. on Principles of Programming Languages*. ACM Press, New York, 294–308.

PEYTON JONES, S. AND PARTAIN, W. 1993. Measuring the effectiveness of a simple strictness analyser. In *Functional Programming: Glasgow 1993*, K. Hammond and M. O'Donnell, Eds. Springer Workshops in Computer Science. Springer, New York, 201–220.

PEYTON JONES, S. L. 1987. *The Implementation of Functional Programming Languages*. Prentice-Hall, Englewood Cliffs, NJ.

PEYTON JONES, S. L. 1992. Implementing lazy functional languages on stock hardware: The Spineless Tagless G-machine. *Journal of Functional Programming* 2(2), 127–202.

PIERCE, B. C. 2002. *Types and Programming Languages*. MIT Press, Cambridge, Mass.

RAU, B. R. 1994. Iterative modulo scheduling: An algorithm for software pipelining loops. In *Proc. 27th Annual International Symposium on Microarchitecture*. ACM Press, New York, 63–74.

REINHOLD, M. B. 1994. Cache performance of garbage-collected programs. In Proc. SIGPLAN '94 Symp. on Prog. Language Design and Implementation. *SIGPLAN Notices* 29(6), 206–217.

RICE, H. G. 1953. Classes of recursively enumerable sets and their decision problems. *Transactions of the American Mathematical Society* 89, 25–59.

ROSE, J. R. 1988. Fast dispatch mechanisms for stock hardware. In OOPSLA '88: 3rd Annual Conference on Object-Oriented Programming Systems, Languages, and Applications. *SIGPLAN Notices* 23(11), 27–35.

ROSEN, B. K., WEGMAN, M. N., AND ZADECK, F. K. 1988. Global value numbers and redundant computations. In *Proc. 15th ACM Symp. on Principles of Programming Languages*. ACM Press, New York, 12–27.

SCHEIFLER, R. W. 1977. An analysis of inline substitution for a structured programming language. *Commun. ACM* 20(9), 647–654.

SEDGEWICK, R. 1997. *Algorithms in C*, Third ed. Addison Wesley, Reading, MA.

SETHI, R. AND ULLMAN, J. D. 1970. The generation of optimal code for arithmetic expressions. *J. Assoc. Computing Machinery* 17(4), 715–28.

SHAO, Z. AND APPEL, A. W. 1994. Space-efficient closure representations. In *Proc. 1994 ACM Conf. on Lisp and Functional Programming*. ACM Press, New York, 150–161.

SHAW, R. A. 1988. Empirical analysis of a Lisp system. Ph.D. thesis, Stanford University, Palo Alto, CA.

SITES, R. L., Ed. 1992. *Appendix A: Software Considerations*. Digital Press, Boston.

SOBALVARRO, P. G. 1988. A lifetime-based garbage collector for LISP systems on general-purpose computers. Tech. Rep. 1417, MIT Artificial Intelligence Laboratory.

STEELE, G. L. 1975. Multiprocessing compactifying garbage collection. *Commun. ACM* 18(9), 495–508.

STEELE, G. L. 1978. Rabbit: a compiler for Scheme. Tech. Rep. AI-TR-474, MIT, Cambridge, MA.

STOY, J. E. 1977. *Denotational Semantics: The Scott-Strachey Approach to Programming Language Theory*. MIT Press, Cambridge, MA.

STRACHEY, C. AND WADSWORTH, C. 1974. Continuations: A mathematical semantics which can deal with full jumps. Technical Monograph PRG-11, Programming Research Group, Oxford University.

STROUSTRUP, B. 1997. *The C++ Programming Language*, Third ed. Addison-Wesley, Reading, MA.

TANENBAUM, A. S. 1978. Implications of structured programming for machine architecture. *Commun. ACM* 21(3), 237–246.

TARDITI, D. 1997. Design and implementation of code optimizations for a type-directed compiler for Standard ML. Ph.D. thesis, Carnegie Mellon University, Pittsburgh, PA.

TURING, A. M. 1937. On computable numbers, with an application to the Entscheidungsproblem. *Proceedings of the London Mathematical Society* 42, 230–265.

ULLMAN, J. D. 1975. NP-complete scheduling problems. *Journal of Computer and System Sciences* 10, 384–393.

UNGAR, D. M. 1986. *The Design and Evaluation of a High Performance Smalltalk System.* MIT Press, Cambridge, MA.

WADLER, P. 1990. Deforestation: Transforming programs to eliminate trees. *Theoretical Computer Science* 73, 231–248.

WADLER, P. 1995. How to declare an imperative. In *International Logic Programming Symposium*, J. Lloyd, Ed. MIT Press, Cambridge, MA.

WEGMAN, M. N. AND ZADECK, F. K. 1991. Constant propagation with conditional branches. *ACM Trans. on Programming Languages and Systems* 13(2), 181–210.

WENTWORTH, E. P. 1990. Pitfalls of conservative collection. *Software—Practice and Experience* 20(7), 719–727.

WILSON, P. R. 1997. Uniprocessor garbage collection techniques. *ACM Computing Surveys*, (to appear).

WOLF, M. E. AND LAM, M. S. 1991. A data locality optimizing algorithm. In Proc ACM SIGPLAN '91 Conf. on Prog. Lang. Design and Implementation. *SIGPLAN Notices* 26(6), 30–44.

WOLFE, M. 1996. *High Performance Compilers for Parallel Computing.* Addison Wesley, Redwood City, CA.

YOUNG, C., JOHNSON, D. S., KARGER, D. R., AND SMITH, M. D. 1997. Near-optimal intraprocedural branch alignment. In Proc. ACM SIGPLAN '97 Conf. on Prog. Lang. Design and Implementation. *SIGPLAN Notices* 32(5), 183–193.

YOUNG, C. AND SMITH, M. D. 1994. Improving the accuracy of static branch prediction using branch correlation. In ASPLOS VI: Sixth International Conference on Architectural Support for Programming Languages and Operating Systems. *SIGPLAN Notices* 29(11), 232–241.

Index

abstract data type, 5
abstract syntax, *see* syntax, abstract
access link, *see* static link
activation record, 6, 116–125
Ada, 336, 348, 349
addressing mode, 183, 188
ADT, *see* abstract data type
Aiken-Nicolau algorithm, 444–448, 459
alias
    analysis, 357, 369–374, 392
    in coalescing register allocation, 234
alignment, *see* cache alignment
alloca, 197
allocation
    of activation records, 116, 118, 156
    of arrays and records, 151
    of heap data, 275
    register, *see* register allocation
alphabet, 18
ambiguous grammar, *see* grammar
analysis
    dataflow, *see* dataflow analysis
    liveness, *see* liveness
antidependence, *see* dependence, write-after-
    read
approximation
    dataflow analysis, 209, 212, 352
    in garbage collection, 257
    of spill effect, 220
    of strictness, 331
argument, *see* parameter
array, 144, 146, 151
    bounds check, 148, 391–395
Assem module, 191
associativity, *see* right-associative, left-

associative, nonassociative
attribute grammar, 12
available expressions, 356

Baker's algorithm, 274
basic block, 170, 172, 361, 365, 382
beta reduction, *see* inline expansion
binding, 103–110, *see also* precedence
    in type environment, 111
blacklist, 281
block structure, *see* function, nested
blocking, 477–480, 482
branch prediction, 456–459
buffered input, 33
bypass datapaths, 442, 444

C programming language
    linking to, 153
    writing compiler for, 18, 90, 116, 117,
        122, 130, 139, 144–146, 150, 151,
        197, 322, 369, 371, 374, 377
C++, 291, 336, 369
cache, 464–467
    alignment, 468–470
    and garbage collection, 267, 480–481
cache alignment, 481
CALL, 162, 163, 168
call
    by name, 322
    by need, 323
    by reference, 123, 124
callee-save, *see* register, callee-save
caller-save, *see* register, caller-save
Canon module, 163
canonical tree, *see* intermediate represen-
    tation, canonical

495

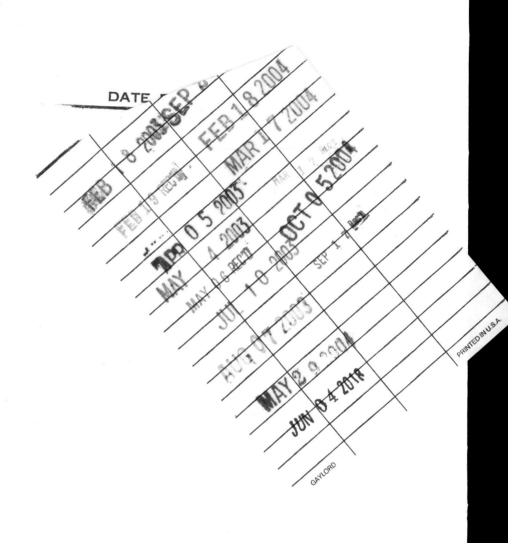

DATE

FEB 8 2003 SEP 8

FEB 18 2004

FEB 19 REC'D

MAR 17 2004

MAR 12 REC'D

DEC 0 5 2003

OCT 0 5 2004

MAY 4 2003

MAY 0 6 REC'D

JUL 1 0 2003

SEP 1 7

AUG 07 2003

MAY 2 9 2004

JUN 0 4 2010

GAYLORD

PRINTED IN U.S.A.